DAVID & W.G. STEEL'S
MAP OF
OREGON, WASHINGTON,
AND
WESTERN IDAHO.

SHERMAN

On the Cattle Ranges of the Oregon Country

On the Cattle Ranges
of the Oregon Country

By J. ORIN OLIPHANT

SEATTLE & LONDON
University of Washington Press

To *FREDERICK MERK*

Preface

THIS study is concerned with the breeding of cattle on open ranges in the Oregon Country. It begins in 1792 with the first appearance of cattle on the Northwest Coast of America, and it ends in 1890, when the Pacific Northwest—a term here used interchangeably with that of Oregon Country—had achieved political maturity and was advancing toward economic maturity. By that year much of the arable land of the Columbia Basin— land once famous for its bunch grass—was being farmed, and on the remaining overstocked and deteriorating ranges in this basin cattlemen with their herds and sheepmen with their flocks were contending angrily and ominously for summer pasturage. Consequently, by 1890 a new era in the history of breeding cattle for beef was emerging in this region—open-range grazing of such cattle in the Columbia Basin, and no doubt in other parts of the Pacific Northwest, was rapidly giving way to the raising of beef cattle as an aspect of general farming operations.

The finding of materials for this study has been as difficult as it has been frustrating. This project began as an effort to make a quantitative study that would open the way to a comparison of the range-cattle industry in the Oregon Country with such industry in other regions of the United States, but this effort was soon abandoned. Adequate statistics are wanting, as are also the records and letters of most of the stockmen—assuming, of course, that such men ever kept records or wrote letters about their business. Consequently, the purpose of this study shifted to that of gathering, from widely scattered sources, data that would permit a description, in broad outline, of the rise, expansion, and decline of the range-cattle industry in most areas of the old Oregon Country that had become American.

Owing to the nature of most of the data acquired, problems of organization and of composition have arisen. Topics treated in one context have occasionally reappeared in other contexts, and more than once I have provided detailed evidence to illustrate a tendency rather than risk a pleasing generalization based upon evidence that could not be thoroughly tested. Moreover, it has been necessary to leave some gaps unclosed because there was no material with which to fill them. Nevertheless, this narrative will give a connected account of an enterprise that is an integral part of the history of the colonization and of the early economic development of the Oregon Country. It should do more than that. It should show that the Pacific Northwest, thanks in part to its rising cattle industry, had from the early days of its settlement interesting economic relations with contiguous areas, and that presently, its isolation having been broken, it came to be nationally recognized, at least for several years, as a significant part of the vast cattle country of the American West.

This book has been long in the making. It was begun in 1929 as a doctoral dissertation, and, despite numerous and prolonged interruptions, the work needed for its completion was continued from that time forward. Some of the material has been obtained by revising, abridging, or expanding articles of mine that appeared in various historical quarterlies. For the privilege of reusing such material I am indebted to the *Pacific Northwest Quarterly* (successor to the *Washington Historical Quarterly*), to the *Oregon Historical Quarterly*, and to *Agricultural History*.

In my quest of materials for this study, I have traveled far and wide, and wherever I have gone I have received courteous treatment and have been given unrestricted access to the holdings of all the libraries that I visited. For all such courtesies I am deeply grateful. To a few persons my debt of gratitude is so great that I cannot pass them by with a generalized statement.

These persons are Dr. Frederick Merk, Emeritus Professor of History in Harvard University; the late Dr. C. S. Kingston, one-time Professor of History in the Eastern Washington College of Education (now Eastern Washington State College); the late Professor Charles W. Smith, one-time librarian of the University of Washington; Mrs. Lewis A. McArthur (Nellie B. Pipes), one-time librarian of the Oregon Historical Society; and Mrs. Robert Helms of Grants Pass, Oregon. My final word of gratitude is to my wife, who has suffered all the hardships endured by every woman whose husband would, in the words of Dr. Samuel Johnson, "turn over half a library to make one book."

J. ORIN OLIPHANT

Salem, Oregon
June, 1968

Contents

ABBREVIATIONS USED IN NOTES

ABCFM	American Board of Commissioners for Foreign Missions
AH	Agricultural History
AHR	American Historical Review
BCHQ	British Columbia Historical Quarterly
MVHR	Mississippi Valley Historical Review
OHQ	Oregon Historical Quarterly
OPA	Oregon Pioneer Association
PNQ	Pacific Northwest Quarterly
WHQ	Washington Historical Quarterly

On the Cattle Ranges of the Oregon Country

CHAPTER I

The Days of Small Things

CATTLE belonging to Spaniards were seen on the Northwest Coast of America by English explorers as early as 1792. In the late summer of that year, Captain George Vancouver, commander of a British exploring expedition and a commissioned agent of the British government, arrived there to meet a commissioned agent of the Spanish government and receive from him (pursuant to the Nootka Convention of 1790) property of which British subjects had been dispossessed at Nootka Sound by a Spanish officer in 1789. In his *Voyage of Discovery*, Captain Vancouver tells us that when two of his ships—the *Discovery* and the *Chatham* —dropped anchor in Friendly Cove on August 28, 1792, he and his men were hospitably received, and through succeeding days were graciously entertained, by the Spanish agent, Don Juan Francisco de la Bodega y Quadra. According to an unidentified member of the crew of the *Chatham*, not only did Señor Bodega y Quadra send "a couple of fine sheep with a large stock of Cabbages &c on board each of the vessels and also a cask of rum to the Ship's Company" on the evening of August 29, but also thereafter, thanks to the "Hospitable and friendly attention" of this man, "the vessels in the Cove were regularly supplied with Hot Rolls, Milk & Vegetables every morning." Our nameless diarist also says that the livestock which he saw at Nootka Sound, consisting of "about ten head of cattle, some sheep & goats,

3

Pigs, and Poultry of all kinds," was augmented on November 2, 1792, when the Spanish frigate *Princessa* arrived from the Spanish settlement on Neah Bay, bringing "no less than 8 head of cattle, besides Poultry in abundance, Hogs, Goats, Sheep &c."[1]

From another diarist, John Boit, a youthful sailor on the famous American ship *Columbia,* who saw the *Princessa* depart from Neah Bay, we learn that the Spaniards had erected there "a Cross upon the beach, and had about 10 Houses and several good Gardens." Finally, both Captain Vancouver and Archibald Menzies (the latter a British naturalist and an assistant surgeon on the *Discovery)* reported that the cattle of the Spaniards, both at Nootka Sound and at Neah Bay, were "black cattle."[2]

Thus, as early as 1792, Spaniards not only had tilled the soil of the western coast of Vancouver Island and of the southern shore of the Strait of Juan de Fuca, but also had cared for cattle and other livestock within the bounds of present-day British Columbia and Washington.

From these small beginnings large things might have come. But that was not to be. Spain was now deep in the twilight of her imperial grandeur. Nearly two decades before 1792, her last effort to push northward her defensive frontier from New Spain into Alta California by means of missions, presidios, and pueblos had bogged down at the bay of San Francisco. In 1790 her long-asserted monopoly of the Northwest Coast was broken by the Nootka Convention.[3] Her attempt to establish an outpost at Neah Bay in 1792 proved to be a gasping effort and a futile gesture, and well before the end of the 1790's Spain had lost both the power and the will to found and maintain settlements on the

[1] George Vancouver, *A Voyage of Discovery to the North Pacific Ocean, and Round the World* ... (London, 1801), II, 336-72; Edmond S. Meany (ed.), *A New Vancouver Journal on the Discovery of Puget Sound* ... (Seattle, Wash., 1915), pp. 17, 32. See also Archibald Menzies, *Menzies' Journal of Vancouver's Voyage, April to October, 1792,* ed. C. F. Newcombe (Archives of British Columbia, Memoir No. 5) (Victoria, B.C., 1923), p. 126.

[2] John Boit, *A New Log of the Columbia,* ed. Edmond S. Meany (Seattle, Wash., 1921), pp. 46-47; Henry R. Wagner, *Spanish Explorations in the Strait of Juan de Fuca* (Santa Ana, Calif., 1933), chap. iv; Vancouver, *Voyage of Discovery,* II, 351; Menzies, *Journal,* p. 127.

[3] William Ray Manning's *Nootka Sound Controversy* (American Historical Association, *Report,* 1904) is still the standard work on the subject with which it deals.

Northwest Coast of America. Pursuant to the Adams-Onís Treaty of 1819, negotiated when her American empire was falling apart, she surrendered to the United States her claim to all the territory lying west of the Rocky Mountains and north of the forty-second parallel, which parallel thus became the southern boundary of the Oregon Country. Six years later, when Russia by treaties with the United States and Great Britain gave up her claim to the territory lying west of the Rocky Mountains and south of 54°40', the northern boundary of the Oregon Country was established at the last-named line. Accordingly, from 1825 until 1846 this vast territory remained at least nominally in dispute between Great Britain and the United States; but from 1818 forward it was legally open to occupancy on equal terms by the subjects or citizens of these two countries.[4] During these years of so-called joint occupation, British and American settlers laid securely the foundations of both agriculture and animal husbandry, in no small part with Spanish cattle from California; and for many years in the valley of the Columbia the breeding of cattle and the raising of crops were closely related enterprises.[5]

Agriculture and stock breeding in the Oregon Country were made practicable by the needs of fur traders, the first white men to occupy the Columbia Valley. These enterprises, however, were a long time in gathering momentum. As early as 1795, the captain of the ship *Ruby* planted a garden on an island in the lower Columbia River and harvested a few beans and a good crop of potatoes. How many other captains of ships during the next few years did likewise we do not know. But we do know that, in 1810, Captain Nathan Winship took into the Columbia River the ship *Albatross,* which carried livestock and other essentials for a settlement that was begun at Oak Point. Here the prospective settlers planted a garden, but high water and hostile Indians caused

[4] Philip Coolidge Brooks, *Diplomacy and the Borderlands: The Adams-Onís Treaty of 1819* (Berkeley, Calif., 1919), *passim*; Samuel Flagg Bemis, *A Short History of American Foreign Policy and Diplomacy* (New York, 1959), pp. 147-49, 151-53.
[5] The first scholarly study of the beginnings of cattle breeding in the Pacific Northwest was C. S. Kingston's "Introduction of Cattle into the Pacific Northwest," *WHQ*, XIV (July, 1923), 163-85.

the abandonment of this project.[6] Accordingly, it remained to the Astorians, partners of John Jacob Astor in the ill-starred Pacific Fur Company, to begin in 1811 what proved to be continuous cultivation of crops and breeding of livestock in the valley of the Columbia. Near the mouth of the Columbia River, these men built an establishment which they called Fort Astoria, and subsequently they erected other posts in the interior. But their stay in this valley was short, for in 1813 the Astorians, acting without Astor's consent, sold to representatives of the British North West Company of Montreal the enterprise which Astor's money had made possible in that far-off country. Meanwhile, however, they had landed from the ship *Tonquin* in 1811 about fifty hogs and had planted a few potatoes and the seeds of other vegetables. The potatoes did well, producing a crop of fifty bushels in 1813. And in 1812 the *Beaver,* the second ship which Astor sent to the Columbia River, had brought sixty more hogs to Astoria; but it appears that the Astorians had no cattle in the valley of the Columbia.[7]

The men of the North West Company, who monopolized the fur trade of the interior of the Pacific Northwest between 1813 and 1821, receive the credit for starting the breeding of cattle in the Oregon Country. Presumably this enterprise began on April 23, 1814, when the ship *Isaac Todd* landed at Astoria (now become Fort George) "two young bulls and two heifers brought from San Francisco." In the years immediately following, other kinds of livestock, and perhaps more cattle, were taken to the Columbia River, for in October, 1817, Peter Corney observed that the traders at Fort George had "about 12 head of cattle, with some pigs and goats, imported here from California; [but, he continued,] their stock does not increase, for want of care, the wolves often carrying off goats and pigs."[8]

    [6] Grace P. Morris, "Development of Astoria, 1811-1850," *OHQ,* XXXVIII (December, 1937), 417-18; F. W. Howay, "Early Followers of Captain Gray," *WHQ,* XVIII (January, 1927), 14-15; Leslie M. Scott, "Soil Repair Lessons in Willamette Valley," *OHQ,* XVIII (March, 1917), 56; Anna Jerzyk, "Winship Settlement in 1810 was Oregon's Jamestown," *OHQ,* XLI (June, 1940), 175-81.
    [7] Gabriel Franchère, *Narrative of a Voyage to the Northwest Coast of America* ... trans. J. V. Huntington (New York, 1854), pp. 81, 98, 231-32; Morris, "Development of Astoria," p. 419.
    [8] Elliott Coues (ed.), *New Light on the Early History of the Greater Northwest;*

During the next few years, some attention was given to gardening at Fort George, and the livestock increased; but, broadly speaking, there, as at other North West Company posts in the Columbia Valley, agricultural pursuits and the breeding of livestock were carried on in an indifferent manner. The traders believed that their business was trading, not farming. Accordingly, instead of making adequate use of the resources of the country to produce food, they squandered money on imported food and on articles of luxury. Such indifference to sound business practices, it appears, became characteristic of all aspects of management in the Columbia Department of the North West Company. Partly for this reason, the Governor and Committee of the Hudson's Bay Company, successor in 1821 to the North West Company, were doubtful, as early as 1822, whether the trade of their company in the Pacific Northwest should be continued.[9]

The task of ascertaining information needed to answer this question was assigned to a young man, George Simpson, who had been appointed governor of the Northern Department of Rupert's Land, "including the Department of the Columbia," in which the enlarged and reorganized Hudson's Bay Company had been granted exclusive British trading rights for twenty-one years. It was a difficult task, but Simpson—intelligent and energetic, possessing an almost incomparable power to drive himself, willing to turn his coat in order to keep in favor with his superiors in London, and capable of harshness as inexorable as the wilderness in which his company operated—gave himself tirelessly to the service of the Hudson's Bay Company. By the summer of 1824 he had set right for the "honorable company" many things in its holdings east of the Rockies. Now he was ready to deal with the problems of this company in the department of the Columbia.

Leaving York Factory, on Hudson Bay, with a small party in a "North Canoe" on August 15, 1824, he succeeded by incessant

---

The Manuscript Journals of Alexander Henry . . . and of David Thompson . . . 1799-1814 (New York, 1897), II, 895; Peter Corney, Voyages in the Northern Pacific . . . (Honolulu, 1896), p. 81A.

[9] Morris, "Development of Astoria," p. 419; John Scouler, "Dr. John Scouler's Journal of a Voyage to N. W. America," OHQ, VI (June, 1905), 166; Frederick Merk (ed.), Fur Trade and Empire: George Simpson's Journal . . . 1824-1825 . . . (Cambridge, Mass., 1931), pp. xxiv-xxv, 175-76.

traveling in reaching Fort George within eighty-four days, despite the fact that en route he had stopped at Spokane House, Fort Okanogan, and Fort Walla Walla. What he had observed during his journey down the Columbia River did not hearten him. For this part of his trip his journal glows with a fiery wrath that lightens the mordant sarcasm informing his comments on much of what he saw. Everywhere on the Columbia, he tells us, too many persons were doing too little; everywhere in this country money was being wasted because food-producing resources at hand were not being used; everywhere along this river wrong persons were doing things in wrong ways; everywhere in the department of the Columbia everything was overexpanded—the fur trade excepted. This being the case, George Simpson would see to it that presently there would be a great shaking up of things in the valley of the Columbia.

A new era was not long in coming. Governor Simpson believed that the department of the Columbia should be reformed, not abandoned; and, as a means of achieving this object, in the spring of 1825 he loosed a chilly wind of austerity which swept through the whole department, blighting the ideas of luxurious living and wasteful practices in the fur trade as effectively as a springtime Chinook wind cleared the Columbia Valley of ice and snow. Henceforth efficiency and economy would replace slovenliness and extravagance. Henceforth both the gentlemen and the lesser servants of the Hudson's Bay Company not only would work to expand the fur trade and make it more efficient, but also would accept as a legitimate activity any pursuit that promised to lessen the cost of such trade. Henceforth there would prevail the notion, until then considered odd, that the resources of both land and water should be so exploited that they would not only meet the needs of the department for food, but also provide a surplus of pork, beef, grain, butter, fish, and other articles for an export trade. Thus in the middle 1820's there was generated, among other things, a pressing concern about agricultural pursuits and the breeding of livestock in the valley of the Columbia.

Action followed hard upon decision. Before Governor Simpson left the lower Columbia Valley on his return to Rupert's Land, Fort George had been abandoned, and—pursuant to a request of

George Canning, the British Foreign Secretary—a new establishment to replace it had been set up on the north bank of the Columbia at a place called Belle Vue Point, opposite the mouth of the Willamette River. This new establishment, named Fort Vancouver, presently became the company's main depot in the Columbia Department. Its site had been chosen in part because of its beauty, but in greater part because of its advantages for agricultural pursuits and for the breeding of cattle and other livestock.[10]

Simpson left the newly christened Fort Vancouver on March 19, 1825, on his return journey up the Columbia, and six days later he was at Fort Walla Walla. Here he delivered to the chief trader, John W. Dease, ten bushels of seed potatoes from Vancouver; and here, characteristically, he gave Mr. Dease "a long lecture" on the advantage of cultivating gardens at this fort.

This was the beginning of more drastic changes at posts in the interior. Continuing his journey up the Columbia, Simpson made arrangements to abandon Spokane House and to establish in lieu of it a new post near the Kettle Falls of the Columbia. Here, at a point three-quarters of a mile above the portage, he "lined out" on April 14, 1825, the site of a new establishment called Fort Colvile. Simpson believed that the advantages of this site for agricultural operations were so great that he easily persuaded himself that Colvile could raise enough grain and potatoes to feed all the Indians on the Columbia River, and enough hogs and cattle to supply the British navy with pork and beef.[11] Although, as the sequel would show, such optimism would not be completely justified, Fort Colvile did soon become the most important agricultural post in the interior of the department of the Columbia.

Responsibility for maintaining the new order in the valley of the Columbia was vested in Dr. John McLoughlin, a chief factor

[10] Merk (ed.), *Fur Trade and Empire,* pp. xiii-xxv, 3-65, 123-24; J. H. Pelly to George Canning, Dec. 9, 1825, *ibid.,* p. 258; George Simpson to H. U. Addington, Jan. 5, 1826, in T. C. Elliott (ed.), "The Northwest Boundaries (Some Hudson's Bay Correspondence)," *OHQ,* XX (December, 1919), 334.

[11] Merk (ed.), *Fur Trade and Empire,* pp. 128-29, 139. The name of a later American military post and of the present-day town in this part of the state of Washington is spelled *Colville.*

of the Hudson's Bay Company, who had proved his worth during
eighteen years in the service of the North West Company. Mc-
Loughlin had come from York Factory to Fort George in 1824,
traveling much of the way in company with Governor Simpson.
Like Simpson, McLoughlin was both able and strong willed; and
he was eight years older than Simpson. The two men did not
always agree. But from the time that Simpson left him in charge
of Fort Vancouver on March 19, 1825, until his retirement from
the service of the company some twenty years later, McLoughlin
made his influence felt increasingly in the department of the
Columbia.[12] His responsibility, however, was to administer basic
policies, not to make them; but the enterprise that he managed
expanded and became increasingly diverse—so much so that Mc-
Loughlin was presently overseeing not only the fur trade, but
also the manufacture of both lumber and flour, the salting of
salmon, and the exportation of these and other commodities. He
also superintended farming operations and the breeding of livestock, and after 1839 both of these enterprises became large at
certain posts in his department.[13] But the breeding of cattle in
the department of the Columbia is our primary concern, and to
this enterprise McLoughlin, without neglecting the agricultural
enterprise, gave careful attention.

Although, as he said, he began at Fort Vancouver in 1825 with
"3 Bulls, 23 Cows, 5 Heifers, and 9 Steers," McLoughlin could
boast, in August, 1829, of having 200 head of cattle. In March of
that year Governor Simpson had expressed his delight at the progress of farming operations at Fort Vancouver; but the goal that
had been set for this "branch" of the company's business would
not be reached until there was an annual production in the de-

[12] One of the more recent biographies of Dr. John McLoughlin is Richard G.
Montgomery's *The White-Headed Eagle: John McLoughlin, Builder of an Empire*
(New York, 1934). But see especially W. Kaye Lamb's "Introductions" to the
three volumes entitled *The Letters of John McLoughlin from Fort Vancouver to
the Governor and Committee, 1825-1846*, ed. E. E. Rich (Hudson's Bay Record
Society, *Publications*, Vols. IV, VI, VII, 1941-44).

[13] Burt Brown Barker (ed.), *Letters of Dr. John McLoughlin Written at Vancouver, 1829-1833* (Portland, Ore., 1948), *passim*; John S. Galbraith, *The Hudson's Bay Company as an Imperial Factor, 1821-1869* (Berkeley and Los Angeles,
1957), pp. 200-202; E. H. Oliver (ed.), *The Canadian Northwest . . .* (Ottawa,
1915), II, 790.

partment of the Columbia of eight thousand bushels of grain, a herd of six hundred head of cattle, and enough pigs to permit the curing annually of ten thousand pounds of pork.[14]

The progress in enlarging the herd of cattle at Fort Vancouver had been achieved, at least in part, by not killing cattle for beef. In enforcing this policy, McLoughlin had the full support of Governor Simpson, who, by 1829, was aware that McLoughlin had been criticized for refusing to supply beef to ships that came from England.[15] Regardless of the consequences, Simpson urged McLoughlin not to deviate from the established policy. Accordingly, this policy was maintained, and on March 10, 1835, Dr. McLoughlin could write that, on the large farm at Fort Vancouver, he not only was raising wheat, peas, oats, and other grains, but also was caring for a herd of cattle which had increased from seventeen to six hundred. The climate was so mild that it was not necessary to make hay for the cattle, because "they feed out all winter." In September, 1836, Mrs. Marcus Whitman, then a guest at Fort Vancouver, wrote in her diary that the estimated number of cattle owned by the Hudson's Bay Company in all its "settlements" west of the Rockies was 1,000 head, and early in October of that year the Reverend Henry H. Spalding wrote that there were 700 head of horned cattle at Fort Vancouver, and from "20 to 100 at several other posts." Moreover, company inventories taken in 1837 show that there were then 685 head of cattle at Fort Vancouver and 170 head at Forts Nisqually and Langley. Accordingly, Dr. Marcus Whitman may have been nearly correct when, on May 5, 1837, he wrote to the American Board of Commissioners for Foreign Missions, saying that the Hudson's Bay

[14] McLoughlin to the Governor and Committee, Aug. 5, 1829, and Oct. 31, 1837, in Rich (ed.), *Letters of McLoughlin, First Series,* pp. 79, 207; Burt Brown Barker, *The McLoughlin Empire and Its Rulers* (Glendale, Calif., 1959), p. 328; George Simpson to McLoughlin, March 15, 1829, in Merk (ed.), *Fur Trade and Empire,* p. 310.

[15] "As to Beef," wrote McLoughlin on Oct. 31, 1837, "from '25 to '36, we never killed more than a Bull Calf or Two annually for the purpose of getting rennet. Last year we killed Forty Head of cattle, and this year I think we will kill about the same Number, which will furnish enough of Beef for our vessels in the Country, however we will only kill Oxen and cows which bear no calves." The reason for not killing cattle sooner, he said, was that one hundred oxen were needed to do the work of the farm and of the sawmill. Rich (ed.), *Letters of McLoughlin, First Series,* pp. 206-7.

Company had at its various posts in the Oregon Country about twelve hundred head of cattle.[16]

At its interior posts in the department of the Columbia, the keeping of cattle was as much a part of the company's policy as was the cultivating of gardens and, where practicable, of farms. As we have seen, Simpson ordered that potatoes be planted at Fort Walla Walla as early as 1825; five years later Indian corn was being raised at this post. Nor was cattle breeding at Walla Walla being neglected. On January 4, 1831, Dr. McLoughlin sent four calves to this post, and in 1832 he sent four more. Thereafter it appears that this establishment was never without cattle. During the years 1834 and 1835, visitors at Walla Walla remarked about the horses, cattle, and other livestock as well as about the abundance of corn, potatoes, and other garden vegetables. On September 1, 1836, Mrs. Marcus Whitman was served butter for breakfast at Walla Walla, and she observed that cows and goats were numerous, and that the cattle and the swine at Walla Walla were the "fattest" that she had ever seen.[17]

Farther eastward, in the Snake River Valley, Hudson's Bay Company employees cultivated gardens and kept cattle at two posts—Fort Boise and Fort Hall—both of which were founded in 1834. The Whitmans and the Spaldings left five of their cattle at Fort Boise in 1836, and two years later Mrs. Cushing Eells and Mrs. Elkanah Walker "feasted" on "plenty of vegetable," butter, and milk from those same cows. It appears that after 1839 this fort was without cattle.[18] Farther eastward in this valley was Fort

[16] Barker, *McLoughlin Empire*, p. 328; Narcissa Whitman, "Journal," OPA, *Transactions* (1891), p. 64; Henry H. Spalding to the Porters, Oct. 2, 1836, *OHQ*, XIII (October, 1912), 374; McLoughlin to the Governor and Committee, Oct. 31, 1837, Rich (ed.), *Letters of McLoughlin . . . First Series*, p. 207; ABCFM, Letters and Papers, CXXXVIII, No. 83 (MSS in the Houghton Library, Harvard University).

[17] McLoughlin to George Barnston, Sept. 25, 1830, in Barker (ed.), *Letters of McLoughlin*, pp. 130, 179, 240; John K. Townsend, *Sporting Excursions in the Rocky Mountains, Including a Journey to the Columbia River . . .* (London, 1840), I, 267; Samuel Parker, *Journal of an Exploring Tour Beyond the Rocky Mountains . . . in the Years 1835, '36, and '37* (Ithaca, N.Y., 1838), p. 123; Narcissa Whitman, "Journal," p. 58.

[18] Clifford M. Drury, *Marcus Whitman, M.D., Pioneer and Martyr* (Caldwell, Ida., 1937), p. 151; Clifford M. Drury (ed.), *First White Women over the Rockies . . .* (Glendale, Calif., 1963), II, 113; Thomas J. Farnham, *Travels in the Great Western Prairies, the Anahuac and Rocky Mountains, and in the Oregon*

Hall, founded near present-day Pocatello by an American trader, Nathaniel J. Wyeth, who sold it to the Hudson's Bay Company in 1837. Wyeth had left three head of cattle at this post in 1834, and in 1838 the missionary party that would reinforce the Whitmans and the Spaldings left some of their cattle, with the understanding that the Hudson's Bay Company would give them a like number of cattle after they had reached their destination. A year later Thomas Farnham was served newly churned butter at Fort Hall. For a few years we hear little about cattle at Fort Hall, but by 1845 this post had a lively trade with emigrants en route to California or Oregon, who exchanged cattle for horses and flour. In that year, as Joel Palmer tells us, only "cattle or money" would be accepted at Fort Hall for goods or provisions.[19]

Northward of Fort Vancouver, above the forty-ninth parallel, the Hudson's Bay Company established Fort Langley on the lower Fraser River in 1827; and about midway between this post and Fort Vancouver it founded Fort Nisqually on Puget Sound in 1833. These establishments engaged in both farming and livestock. As early as March, 1829, Dr. McLoughlin promised to send to Fort Langley grain, garden seeds, and cattle, and Archibald McDonald wrote in February, 1831, saying that this post had twenty pigs, and that the cattle sent from the Columbia River were doing well. In 1832 Dr. McLoughlin promised to send both ploughs and cattle to Fort Langley, and two years later farming had become significant there. In 1839, after the Hudson's Bay Company had agreed to provide grain and other provisions for the Russians at Sitka, Dr. McLoughlin established two dairies at Fort Langley. Meanwhile, at Fort Nisqually some farming and tending of cattle had been carried on from the beginning, and by the early 1840's the newly formed Puget's Sound Agricultural Company

Territory, Vol. XXVIII in R. G. Thwaites (ed.), *Early Western Travels* (Cleveland, 1906), p. 114; Joel Palmer, *Journal of Travels over the Rocky Mountains to the Mouth of the Columbia River . . . During the Years 1845 and 1846*, Vol. XXX in *Early Western Travels* (1906), pp. 86-87.

[19] Hiram Martin Chittenden, *The American Fur Trade of the Far West . . .* (New York, 1902), I, 451; Drury (ed.), *First White Women over the Rockies*, II, 109; Farnham, *Travels in the Great Western Prairies*, p. 89; Palmer, *Journal of Travels*, pp. 86-87.

was grazing large herds of cattle at Nisqually.[20] To this subject we shall presently return.

Two hundred miles south of Fort Vancouver, the Hudson's Bay Company trading post on the Umpqua River had acquired by 1844 forty head of cattle and a farm on which an "abundance of grain" was raised. In subsequent years the number of livestock at Fort Umpqua was somewhat increased.[21]

Meanwhile, on the upper Columbia, near the mouth of the Okanogan River, cattle and other livestock were being kept at Fort Okanogan, an establishment erected by the Astorians in 1811 and rebuilt on a new site by the North West Company in 1816. As early as 1832, Dr. McLoughlin was interested in sending cattle to this post, and by 1836 both horses and cattle were being grazed at Fort Okanogan. Five years later, while on a journey down the Columbia River, Governor Simpson stopped there long enough to "rifle some pans of milk," and in the same year Lieutenant Robert E. Johnson, of the Wilkes Exploring Expedition, reported that some goats and thirty-five head of "very fine cattle" produced an "abundance of milk and butter." As yet, he continued, neither goats nor cattle were permitted to be slaughtered there.[22]

Still farther up the Columbia, near the Kettle Falls, the new Fort Colvile rapidly became important for its production of crops, cattle, and other livestock. As soon as the site of this post had been determined, Governor Simpson ordered that two men be sent there from Spokane House to plant five or six bushels of potatoes; and in April, 1826, the express from Vancouver brought "3 pigs & 3 young cows" to Colvile. Farming began in 1826, and the crops of potatoes and grain were so abundant and the live-

[20] Galbraith, *Hudson's Bay Company as Imperial Factor*, pp. 137, 200; Barker (ed.), *Letters of McLoughlin*, pp. 7, 278; McLoughlin to Governor Simpson, March 20, 1840, in Rich (ed.), *Letters of McLoughlin, Second Series*, pp. 231, 236; Robie L. Reid, "Early Days at Old Fort Langley," *BCHQ*, I (April, 1937), 71-85, and a supplement entitled "Fort Langley Correspondence," *ibid.*, I (July, 1937), 187-94.
[21] H. M. Chittenden and A. T. Richardson (eds.), *Life, Letters and Travels of Father Pierre Jean de Smet, S. J., 1801-1873 . . .* (New York, 1905), IV, 1557; undated letter from "Z," in the Portland *Weekly Oregonian*, March 1, 1851.
[22] Barker (ed.), *Letters of McLoughlin*, pp. 253, 329; Parker, *Exploring Tour*, p. 296; George Simpson, *Narrative of a Journey Round the World . . .* (London, 1847), I, 156; Charles Wilkes, *Narrative of the United States Exploring Expedi-

stock did so well that by March, 1828, John Work presumed that Colvile would within a year cease to be dependent on the Indians for provisions. In September, 1829, an American trader, Joshua Pilcher, observed that this post was well supplied with its own bacon, butter, and milk; and nearly a year later Dr. McLoughlin wrote that Colvile was expected to supply "the Interior of the Columbia" with pork and flour. By 1835, according to the Reverend Samuel Parker, Colvile was the company's only inland post at which farming and the raising of livestock were significant activities. Less than two years later, Archibald McDonald remarked, "Your 3 calves are up to 55 & your 3 Grunters would have swarmed the country if we did not make it a point to keep them down to 150." By this time, moreover, McDonald had acquired some "St. Louis Cows & horses." Somewhat more than four years later the meticulous Governor Simpson, after riding around the farm at Colvile, expressed approval of the "buildings, crops, and cattle"; and in the same year—1841—an officer of the Wilkes Exploring Expedition remarked that there were 196 head of "fine cattle" at Colvile.[23]

Thus we have seen that, within a few years after 1825, gentlemen and other servants of the Hudson's Bay Company were keeping livestock and cultivating gardens or farms at widely dispersed posts in order to promote more economically the fur trade in the department of the Columbia. By 1845, when two British agents—Lieutenant Henry J. Warre and Lieutenant M. Vavasour—examined the Oregon Country, the Hudson's Bay Company and its satellite, the Puget's Sound Agricultural Company, had herds of horses and cattle of varying sizes at posts extending southward from Fort Langley to Fort Umpqua, and eastward from Fort Vancouver to Fort Hall. But their largest herds of cattle, for reasons which presently we shall see, were, respectively, at Nisqually, Vancouver, and Cowlitz.[24]

---

tion . . . (Philadelphia, 1845), IV, 434.

[23] T. C. Elliott (ed.), "Journal of John Work," WHQ, V (October, 1914), 284; "Journals of John McLeod, Sr.," William Kittson to John McLeod, March 8, 1827, and John W. Dease to John McLeod, March 25, 1828 (MSS in the Oregon Historical Society, Portland); Joshua Pilcher to John H. Eaton in 21st Cong., 2nd sess., S. Ex. Doc. 39 (Serial 203), p. 9; Barker (ed.), Letters of McLoughlin, p. 122; Simpson, Narrative, I, 151; Parker, Exploring Tour, p. 172.

[24] See note 13, above.

The fur traders, however, were not the only pioneer agriculturists and breeders of livestock in the old Oregon Country. Beginning in 1834, they were joined in such enterprises by American missionaries to Indians in this country. These missionaries resorted to farming and the breeding of livestock for reasons substantially the same as those of the fur traders—namely, personal comfort and the more effective promotion of their legitimate labors.[25] But the missionaries had an additional reason for engaging in such enterprises: that of showing the Indians how to settle down and support themselves by agriculture and animal husbandry. This seemed a prerequisite to teaching the Indians the white man's way of life and religious faith.

The first Protestant missionaries in Oregon, the Reverend Jason Lee and his associates, were Methodists. Late in 1834, with the encouragement and help of Dr. McLoughlin, they established a mission in the Willamette Valley. Lee and his companions, who crossed the Rocky Mountains with Nathaniel Wyeth, brought with them a few head of cattle; but they left their livestock at Fort Walla Walla in exchange for stock and provisions to be given them at Fort Vancouver.[26] In the spring of 1835 they fenced a tract of thirty acres and planted it with seeds provided by Dr. McLoughlin, who also lent the mission "seven oxen, one bull and eight cows with their calves." As this mission was enlarged by reenforcements in subsequent years, both farming and cattle-raising operations were extended. Its missionary operations also were expanded, and in 1838 cattle from the Willamette Valley were driven to the Methodist missionary station at The Dalles on the Columbia River. Three years later other cattle were driven from the Willamette Valley to the Methodist missionary station at Clatsop.[27] In brief, early Methodist missionaries made a signif-

[25] The Reverend Joseph H. Frost said that he and other persons drove a band of horses and cattle from the Willamette Valley to Clatsop to promote the "prosperity of the missionary station at Clatsop." Nellie B. Pipes (ed.), "Journal of Joseph H. Frost, 1840-43," *OHQ*, XXXV (September and December, 1934), 355.
[26] Cornelius J. Brosnan, *Jason Lee, Prophet of the New Oregon* (New York, 1932), chap. iii; "Diary of Reverend Jason Lee," *OHQ*, XVII (September, 1916), 258. In his entry for Oct. 1, 1834, Jason Lee says that Dr. McLoughlin had "lent us 8 oxen, 8 cows and 8 calves"—*ibid.*, XVII (December, 1916), 400.
[27] Brosnan, *Jason Lee*, p. 75; John McLoughlin, "Copy of a Document Found in the Private Papers of the Late Dr. John McLoughlin," in OPA, *Transactions*

icant contribution to the beginnings of animal husbandry in what would presently become the state of Oregon.

But Methodist missionaries were not the only Protestants sent to minister to Indians in the valley of the Columbia. Two years after the arrival of Jason Lee in this valley, Dr. and Mrs. Marcus Whitman and the Reverend and Mrs. Henry H. Spalding, missionaries of the American Board of Commissioners for Foreign Missions, began the establishment of missionary stations in the "upper country"—one at Waiilatpu, near Fort Walla Walla, to be occupied by the Whitmans, and the other at Lapwai on the Clearwater River, to be occupied by the Spaldings. The two families had brought a small band of cattle, five of which, as we have seen, they had left at Fort Boise, with the expectation of receiving from the Hudson's Bay Company a like number at Fort Walla Walla. Both Spalding and Whitman, at their respective stations, became farmers and breeders of livestock, and, as the years passed, the numbers of their cattle and other livestock increased. In September, 1837, Spalding obtained at Colvile "about 35 bushels of grain for seed, 2 oxen, 3 hogs & 1200 pounds of flour," besides "a supply of seeds, flour & hogs for Doct. Whitman." A year later Spalding had twelve head of cattle, and by 1840 Whitman had twenty head of cattle of various sorts. Like the Hudson's Bay Company, Whitman adhered to the policy of not killing any of his cattle for beef until the summer of 1841. Until then the Whitmans had eaten horseflesh.[28]

Meanwhile, the Oregon Mission of the American Board was considerably enlarged in 1838 by the coming of three other missionaries and their wives: the Reverend and Mrs. Cushing Eells, the Reverend and Mrs. Elkanah Walker, and the Reverend and Mrs. Asa B. Smith. This party began the overland journey with

(1880), p. 51; "Oregon Mission Record Book," *OHQ*, XXIII (September, 1922), 262.

[28] Drury, *Marcus Whitman*, pp. 151-54, 233; Henry H. Spalding to the Reverend David Greene, Sept. 4, 1837, in ABCFM, Letters and Papers, CXXXVIII, No. 22; Clifford M. Drury, *Henry Harmon Spalding, Pioneer of Old Oregon* (Caldwell, Ida., 1936), pp. 161, 185; Marcus Whitman to David Greene, Nov. 11, 1841, in ABCFM, Letters and Papers, CXXXVIII, No. 96. In a letter begun on Oct. 6, 1841, Mrs. Marcus Whitman wrote to her parents, saying, "We do not need to kill any more horses for meat, for we killed a very fat beef a short time ago"—OPA, *Transactions* (1891), p. 153.

thirteen head of cattle. At Fort Laramie they left four of their cattle because of sore feet, and at Fort Hall they left all that remained of their small band with the understanding, as we already have learned, that they would receive from the Hudson's Bay Company a like number of cattle in the valley of the Columbia. The Eellses and the Walkers settled at Tshimakain, in the Spokane country, where, besides their missionary labors, they did some farming and kept a few head of cattle and other livestock. The Smiths, for a short time, occupied a station at Kamiah, about sixty miles east of Lapwai. On February 6, 1840, Smith wrote that he was cultivating enough land to provide provisions for his own use, and that the American cow, on which he had relied for milk, had died three days before from eating a poisonous plant. His only remaining cow, obtained from the Hudson's Bay Company in exchange for one left at Fort Hall, was Spanish in origin and of poor quality. But on September 28, 1840, in a report on the Oregon Mission to the American Board, he said that there were nine head of cattle at Kamiah, of which three were cows. He reported that elsewhere in this mission (those at Waiilatpu not included), there were thirty-eight head of cattle, of which thirteen were at Tshimakain. All told, at Lapwai, Kamiah, and Tshimakain there were forty-seven head of cattle, of which nineteen were cows or heifers.[29]

During the next seven years, the livestock of the Oregon Mission of the American Board increased considerably. After the massacre at Waiilatpu, late in November, 1847, Spalding prepared an inventory of the property of the Oregon Mission, showing that at Waiilatpu there had been 46 horses, 92 sheep, and 290 head of cattle, and that at Lapwai, in December, 1847, there were 31 hogs, 39 horses, and 92 head of cattle. A few months later, when the station at Tshimakain was abandoned, there were 20 head of cattle to be disposed of. Of these, seven were sold, two were exchanged for horses, one was lent to an Indian chief, seven were

[29] Drury, *First White Women over the Rockies*, II, 58, 75, 88, 109, 113, 164, 306, 312-13; Clifford M. Drury (ed.), *The Diaries and Letters of Henry H. Spalding and Asa Bowen Smith Relating to the Nez Percé Mission, 1838-1842* (Glendale, Calif., 1958), pp. 125, 186.

sent to Colvile for safe-keeping, and three were turned over to the soldiers for food.[30]

Despite the rather wide dispersal of agricultural operations and of the raising of livestock at trading posts and missionary stations in the Oregon Country before 1848, the center of such activities through the 1830's and the early 1840's remained at Fort Vancouver. The Hudson's Bay Company, through its chief factor, Dr. McLoughlin, endeavored to control the developing economy of the valley of the Columbia River as completely as it dominated the interior fur trade of this region. Broadly speaking, the company was the market for the produce of this country, and, furthermore, company policy in respect to horses and cattle strengthened its grip on the economic activities of those persons in the Oregon Country who were not subject to its jurisdiction.[31] To retired servants of the company who settled in the Willamette Valley, as well as to Americans who came to reside in the Oregon Country, whether they were missionaries or not, McLoughlin was both hospitable and generously disposed. To those who needed it, he extended credit so that they might acquire from the company clothing, food, farming utensils, and wheat for seed. But the company would sell neither horses nor cattle to prospective settlers.[32] It would, however, lend such animals to them, the conditions of these loans, as explained by William A. Slacum, an American who visited Oregon as an agent of the United States, being that the "*produce* of the neat cattle and horses" belonged to the company and could "be called for at any time." If cattle so held should die, the loss would be the company's. Borrowed horses were to be "returned in kind, or the sum of $8, the current value of the horse," would be charged.

Under such conditions, the early settlers in the Willamette

[30] Drury, *Marcus Whitman*, p. 417; Drury, *Henry Harmon Spalding*, p. 349; Drury (ed.), *First White Women over the Rockies*, II, 346; Clifford M. Drury, *Elkanah and Mary Walker, Pioneers Among the Spokanes* (Caldwell, Ida., 1940), p. 217.

[31] On the policy of the company in respect to its fur trade, see Merk (ed.), *Fur Trade and Empire*, p. 286, and Galbraith, *Hudson's Bay Company as Imperial Factor*, chap. v.

[32] See the letter of Henry H. Spalding to William and Edward Porter and their wives, Oct. 2, 1836, in *OHQ*, XIII (October, 1912), 374.

Valley might live comfortably, but they could hardly hope to acquire for themselves large herds of cattle. During the 1830's, however, some American cattle were driven overland to the valley of the Columbia, and in 1835 Nathaniel Wyeth imported from the Sandwich Islands "some cattle sheep goats & hogs which were placed on Wappatoo Island," where Wyeth had established Fort William. Here he "grazed all the animals [which he had] obtained from the Islands [,] California and from the Indians."[33]

It is possible, although not likely, that Lieutenant Charles Wilkes was right when he affirmed, in 1841, that the Hudson's Bay Company deserved much credit for having introduced into the valley of the Columbia "the best breeds from England." But, whether Wilkes was right or wrong about this matter, most of the cattle then in the Oregon Country were Spanish in origin, and thus, by universal testimony, inferior to American cattle.[34] Nevertheless, such cattle were cheap and could be driven from California into the Willamette Valley. Here was a fact not overlooked by early settlers in the Oregon Country.

The first successful attempt to drive a herd of cattle from California to Oregon owed much to William A. Slacum, who, as a result of his conversations with the Reverend Jason Lee, Ewing Young, and other settlers in the Willamette Valley, concluded "that nothing was wanting to insure comfort, wealth, and every happiness to the people" of the Willamette Valley "but the possession of neat cattle." Accordingly, he offered free passage on the brig Loriot to any settlers who wished to go to California to buy cattle. The offer was accepted, and at a meeting at the Methodist Mission on January 13, 1837, articles of agreement were adopted for "a joint stock concern" to be called the Willamette

[33] Slacum had entered the Columbia River on the brig Loriot late in December, 1836. "Slacum's Report on Oregon, 1836-7," OHQ, XIII (June, 1912), 195, reprinted from 25th Cong., 2nd sess., S. Ex. Doc. 24, Vol. I. On Wyeth's importations see F. G. Young (ed.), Correspondence and Journals of Captain Nathaniel J. Wyeth, 1831-6, Vol. I of Sources of the History of Oregon (Eugene, Ore., 1899), p. 255.

[34] Edmond S. Meany (ed.), Diary of Wilkes in the Northwest (Seattle, Wash., 1926), p. 38. Henry H. Spalding said that a Spanish cow would give about one-fourth as much milk as an American cow. Spalding to David Greene, ABCFM, Letters and Papers, CXXXVIII, No. 35.

Cattle Company. Ewing Young was chosen leader of the party to go to California, and P. L. Edwards was designated its treasurer; and these two men were named joint purchasers of cattle. Slacum, besides investing some money of his own in this venture, advanced to Jason Lee the sum of five hundred dollars. Dr. Mc-Loughlin also invested more than five hundred dollars in this enterprise, and other persons contributed sums in varying amounts. The total contributions were enough to permit the purchase of a large band of cattle. Young and Edwards bought in California more than seven hundred head of cattle, but they lost some of them during the drive to Oregon. An entry in the Record Book of the Oregon Methodist Mission on November 27, 1837, tells us that "the California cattle Co. had arrived safely" in the Willamette Valley with "over six hundred head of neat cattle mostly heifers and some horses."[35]

The successful outcome of this enterprise laid the foundation for the prosperity of the early settlers in the Willamette Valley, and opened the way to the expansion of cattle breeding in the Oregon Country. As early as the summer of 1838, a small company of Americans and Indians left the Willamette Valley to get cattle in California, but gave up the undertaking when they were attacked by Indians at the Rogue River. Later in that year, Captain John A. Sutter, who had come overland to Oregon in 1838, was reported to be planning a drive of cattle from California to the Willamette Valley. But, whatever may have been attempted or accomplished in moving cattle from California to Oregon during the next three or four years,[36] there can be no doubt that a

[35] "Oregon Mission Record Book," pp. 251-52, 258; F. G. Young, "Ewing Young and His Estate," OHQ, XXI (September, 1920), 209; Jason Lee to the Corresponding Secretary of the Missionary Society of the Methodist Episcopal Church, in the New York Christian Advocate and Journal, XI (June 8, 1837), 166; McLoughlin, "Copy of a Document," pp. 51-52; Philip L. Edwards, California in 1837 . . . (Sacramento, 1890), passim. On the disposal of Slacum's interest in this enterprise, see Wilkes, U.S. Exploring Expedition, IV, 359.

[36] James Douglas to the Governor and Committee, Oct. 18, 1838, Rich (ed.), Letters of McLoughlin, First Series, pp. 241-42, 256; Charles H. Carey, A General History of Oregon Prior to 1861 (Portland, Ore., 1935), I, 333, 371. On Aug. 19, 1842, the Reverend Alvin F. Waller wrote that cattle were "annually being driven from California"—Christian Advocate and Journal, XVIII (Nov. 8, 1843), 50. On March 19, 1844, "A Pioneer," writing from New Madrid, Mo., said that he had recently come from Oregon by way of California, and that "several thousand"

large herd of cattle and other livestock was driven from California to the Willamette Valley in 1843. This enterprise had been promoted by a small group of men, headed by Joseph Gale, who built in 1841-42 a small boat called the *Star of Oregon*. In the autumn of 1842, they sailed this boat to California and exchanged it for 350 head of cattle. In the spring of 1843, this party, now enlarged to forty-two men (one of whom was Jacob Lease), spent 75 days en route from California to the Willamette Valley, arriving with most of its 1,250 head of cattle, 600 mares, horses, and mules, and "nearly 3,000 sheep." Subsequently Joseph Gale affirmed that this importation "done away with the stock monopoly and set the people of Oregon in a fair way of getting on in the future."[37]

However that may have been, the Puget's Sound Agricultural Company, formed four years earlier as a satellite of the Hudson's Bay Company, had enlarged its holdings of livestock in 1841 by importing more than six hundred cows and more than three thousand ewes which James Douglas, a chief factor of the Hudson's Bay Company, had purchased in California early in that year. This importation, like the policy Simpson had introduced in 1825, aroused excitement that was felt as far inland as Kettle Falls. Writing from Fort Colvile on March 30, 1842, Archibald McDonald said that the event was more important than the visit of the Wilkes Exploring Expedition or the emigration of colonists from the Red River Settlement to the farms at Nisqually and Cowlitz.[38]

The company which imported this livestock was the institutional expression of an idea nearly ten years old. Its emergence was accelerated by an agreement signed in Hamburg on February 6, 1839, whereby the Hudson's Bay Company leased a coastal

---

head of cattle had been driven from California to Oregon "last spring." Reprinted from the St. Louis, Mo., *New Era* in the *New York Weekly Tribune*, April 13, 1844.

[37] Joseph Gale, "The Schooner Star," OPA, *Transactions* (1891), pp. 190-91; address of Colonel J. W. Nesmith, reported in the Portland *Morning Oregonian*, June 16, 1880; S. A. Clarke, *Pioneer Days of Oregon History* (Portland, Ore., 1905), I, 616-27.

[38] James Douglas to Dr. John McLoughlin, March 23, 1841, Rich (ed.), *Letters of McLoughlin, Second Series*, p. 256; James Douglas, "Trading Expedition, 1840-41" (MS in the Provincial Library, Victoria, B.C.); Archibald McDonald to Edward Ermatinger, March 30, 1842 (MS in the Provincial Library, Victoria).

strip south of Cape Spencer from the Russian American Company. In return for this ten-year lease, the Hudson's Bay Company would, among other things, pay annually two thousand land-otter skins, and for ten years would supply the Russian company with certain quantities of wheat, flour, salted beef, butter, hams, and other provisions. This arrangement permitted the Russian American Company to get rid of Fort Ross, now an unprofitable establishment, which it had founded near Bodega Bay in California in 1812 for the dual purpose of promoting the hunting of sea otters and of producing foodstuffs for its posts on the Northwest Coast; it also gave effect to Governor Simpson's offer of March 21, 1829, to supply the Russian American Company with various grains and salted pork and beef, and thereby opened the way to the enlargement of farming operations and the increased breeding of livestock under the auspices of the Hudson's Bay Company in the valley of the Columbia.[39]

To fulfill part of the above-mentioned contract, the Hudson's Bay Company hastened into being the Puget's Sound Agricultural Company, a subsidiary empowered to raise flocks and herds "with a view to the production of Wool, Hides, and Tallow, and for the cultivation of other produce on the West side of the Rocky Mountains." It was formed because the Hudson's Bay Company could not lawfully engage in such an enterprise. Its stock could be owned only by officers or stockholders of the Hudson's Bay Company, and its operations were entrusted to Dr. McLoughlin as an addition to his other duties in the department of the Columbia.[40]

Ironically, Dr. McLoughlin was now charged with the supervision of an enterprise not to his liking, but one which embodied the substance of one of his cherished ideas. Presumably he was toying with this idea as early as November 24, 1830, when he

[39] Galbraith, *Hudson's Bay Company as Imperial Factor*, p. 154; E. O. Essig, "The Russian Settlement at Ross," *QCHS*, XII (September, 1933), 191-216; Donald C. Davidson, "Relations of the Hudson's Bay Company with the Russian American Company on the Northwest Coast," *BCHQ*, V (January, 1941), 33-51; Oliver (ed.), *Canadian Northwest*, II, 267, 311-12.

[40] Galbraith, *Hudson's Bay Company as Imperial Factor*, pp. 192-217; Lamb, "Introduction," in Rich (ed.), *Letters of McLoughlin, Third Series*, pp. xi-xiii; Leonard A. Wrinch, "The Formation of the Puget's Sound Agricultural Company," *WHQ*, XXIV (January, 1933), 6.

instructed Captain A. Simpson to find out whether cattle, horses, and mules could be taken from California. Perhaps because of what he thus learned, Dr. McLoughlin and some of his associates issued, on March 10, 1832, a prospectus for "The Oregon Beef & Tallow Company." This company, a private venture to be undertaken by officers of the Hudson's Bay Company in their own interest, would be capitalized at three thousand pounds, and would be empowered to open an export trade from the Oregon Country in "tallow, beef, horns," and other commodities. To set this trade in motion, it was proposed that several hundred head of cattle be brought from California to graze in the valley of the Columbia.[41]

McLoughlin revealed one of his reasons for wishing to expand the breeding of cattle in the Oregon Country when he remarked to Dr. W. F. Tolmie on May 12, 1833, that, since the trade in furs was dying out, the servants of the Hudson's Bay Company might profitably engage in the breeding of cattle "for the sake of the hides and tallow." Whether he was then thinking of the future welfare of all Hudson's Bay Company employees in the Oregon Country, or only that of high-ranking officers, there can be little doubt that his interest in importing cattle from California was keen as late as August 17, 1832, when he wrote to John Work, saying that cattle could be obtained in California at six dollars a head, and that, under certain conditions, he would "take a thousand head." But four days later he wrote to Work asking him to forget about this business for the time being. Perhaps he had heard news that gave him pause.[42]

Governor Simpson objected to Dr. McLoughlin's project not because he opposed the enlargement of cattle breeding in the department of the Columbia, but because he thought that such an undertaking should be conducted by the Hudson's Bay Company "as a branch of the Fur Trade." The Governor and Committee agreed with Simpson, and on December 10, 1834, informed

[41] Merk (ed.), *Fur Trade and Empire*, p. 332; Barker (ed.), *Letters of Mc-Loughlin*, p. 161; Lamb, "Introduction," in Rich (ed.), *Letters of McLoughlin, Third Series*, pp. xiv-xvii; Galbraith, *Hudson's Bay Company as Imperial Factor*, pp. 193-95.
[42] "Diary of Dr. W. F. Tolmie," *WHQ*, XXIII (July, 1932), 217; Barker (ed.), *Letters of McLoughlin*, pp. 292-93, 295.

Dr. McLoughlin of this decision, authorized the expenditure of three thousand pounds for the purchase of cattle, and recommended that a farm for cattle breeding be established north of the Columbia River. Despite his disappointment, McLoughlin investigated proposed sites for such a farm, and on September 30, 1836, reported that at Nisqually and at the head of Puget Sound there was "pasturage for an immense number of cattle"; and more than a year later he pointed out objections to forming such an establishment on Whidbey Island. Progress was slow, and ideas about the enterprise changed. In January, 1837, the Governor and Committee informed Dr. McLoughlin that the company desired to acquire a grazing farm with a view to establishing an export trade not only in tallow and hides, but also in wool; and that the cattle to stock such a farm would be obtained from California or from the Sandwich Islands.[43]

Presently, however, Dr. McLoughlin was dragging his heels in respect to this matter while the Governor and Committee in London sought a renewal of the company's license to trade in the country west of Rupert's Land. One of the arguments that the company offered in support of its claim for a renewal was that it intended not only to expand its agricultural operations in the Oregon Country and to enlarge therein its breeding of livestock, but also to encourage the settlement in that country of its retired servants and "other emigrants." On May 30, 1838, the company's license was renewed for twenty-one years.[44]

Meanwhile, some steps had been taken toward realizing the company's desire to enlarge its cattle-breeding and sheep-breeding operations in the Oregon Country, for on October 18, 1838, James Douglas, writing from Fort Vancouver, informed the Governor and Committee that the ship *Nereide* had arrived at Nisqually on July 16 with 434 head of sheep from California. Moreover, he affirmed that any number of wild cattle could be procured from California at seven dollars a head, a price which

[43] Galbraith, *Hudson's Bay Company as Imperial Factor*, pp. 194-95; McLoughlin to the Governor and Committee, Sept. 30, 1835, Rich (ed.), *Letters of McLoughlin, First Series*, pp. 138, 155; Lamb, "Introduction," in *ibid.*, *Third Series*, p. xvi.
[44] Galbraith, *Hudson's Bay Company as Imperial Factor*, pp. 195-96.

he thought was high. He also made known the fact that the "Cowelitz Farm" was being established.[45]

Accordingly, when the Puget's Sound Agricultural Company was formed, the Hudson's Bay Company transferred to it the establishment at Nisqually and the recently opened farm at Cowlitz, the former to be used as a grazing farm and the latter to be used principally for raising wheat. The Council for the Northern Department of Rupert's Land decided, in June, 1839, that the prices for the livestock thus transferred should be twenty shillings a head for horned cattle, five shillings a head for sheep, and forty shillings a head for horses.[46] As superintendent of the newly formed company, Dr. McLoughlin would receive, in addition to his usual salary, a stipend of five hundred pounds a year.

Because it considered its recently completed agreement with the Russian-American Company of great importance, the Hudson's Bay Company was much interested in the well-being of the Puget's Sound Agricultural Company. Accordingly, in 1839 and 1840 the Council for the Northern Department of Rupert's Land directed Chief Factor McLoughlin to give his "particular attention" to promoting the concerns of this company. Dr. McLoughlin was equal to the task. He arrived at Fort Vancouver from his furlough in Europe on October 17, 1839, and for months he concentrated on the new company and the problem of fulfilling the contract with the Russian American Company. His principal concern, as he confessed to Governor Simpson on March 20, 1840, was to provide enough butter. To help meet this need he had "established two dairies at Fort Langley, one at Nisqually, [and] one at Cowelitz." He intended, moreover, to establish five dairies at Fort Vancouver. Nevertheless, he was afraid that he could not produce the quantity of milk required, because the cows were "bad milkers."[47]

Dr. McLoughlin had put his finger on the real cause for worrying; the Spanish cows, as others also had testified, gave little milk. This was no doubt the reason that he "alerted" the em-

[45] Rich (ed.), *Letters of McLoughlin, First Series,* pp. 250-51, 264.

[46] See note 13, above.

[47] Lamb, "Introduction," in Rich (ed.), *Letters of McLoughlin, Third Series,* p. xiii; Galbraith, *Hudson's Bay Company as Imperial Factor,* p. 199; Rich (ed.), *Letters of McLoughlin, Second Series,* pp. 3, 230-36.

ployees of the company at various posts to make a major effort to produce butter. As early as April 2, 1840, Archibald McDonald, writing from Colvile, remarked, somewhat facetiously, that their "dairyman" was "hard at work scouring up his milk tureens in order to meet our share of a very heavy demand in Butter & Cheese that is to be made upon all Cattleholders in the Columbia for the fulfillment of our Contract with the Russians to the tune of 200 firkins in the article [of] Butter alone."[48]

No doubt also for this reason surplus cattle at posts in the interior were transferred to establishments west of the Cascade Mountains. In the summer of 1841, cattle from Forts Colvile, Okanogan, and Walla Walla were driven through Snoqualmie Pass to the farm at Nisqually; and on September 13 of that year Dr. McLoughlin, in a letter to Father Jean de Smet, said that probably the "next year" he would "order down" to Fort Vancouver "the supernumerary cattle" at the establishments of the Hudson's Bay Company in the Snake Country.[49] Finally, it was no doubt partly because Spanish cattle were "poor milkers" that an additional herd of such cattle was brought from California to the farm at Nisqually in 1841. No better cattle were then available.

The part of the agreement pledging the Hudson's Bay Company to supply the Russian American Company with foodstuffs proved to be so unsatisfactory to the Russians that it was dropped when the leasing agreement was renewed in 1849. Nevertheless, the Puget's Sound Agricultural Company, although a political and economic failure, continued in business. But its operations were less extensive than originally planned, perhaps because of its lack of success in bringing in settlers who would continue to work as servants of the company. In any event, Governor Simpson wrote to Dr. McLoughlin on March 1, 1842, say-

[48] "Letters of Archibald McDonald to Edward Ermatinger and Others" (MSS in the Provincial Library, Victoria, B.C.).

[49] Edward Huggins to C. B. Bagley, Nov. 5, 1903, quoting from a paper by A. C. Anderson on the origin of the Puget's Sound Agricultural Company (MS in the University of Washington Library, Seattle); diary of Henry H. Spalding, in Drury (ed.), *Diaries and Letters of Spalding and Smith*, p. 322; Chittenden and Richardson (eds.), *Father Pierre Jean de Smet*, IV, 1556. By the summer of 1855, the Hudson's Bay Company was using an overland route to carry to Puget Sound the furs that it had gathered in the interior. Steilacoom *Puget Sound Courier*, July 5, 1855.

ing that "no further steps should be taken towards procuring any more sheep or cattle from California." The holdings of the company in livestock, as shown in an inventory on March 31, 1845, consisted of 8,833 head of sheep, 2,436 head of horned cattle, 301 horses and mules, and 182 hogs. Seven months later, a report of Lieutenants Warre and Vavasour shows that, at Nisqually and at Cowlitz, there were 301 head of horses, 2,436 head of cattle, and 6,857 head of sheep. This report also shows that, at twenty-three posts of the Hudson's Bay Company and its satellite company west of the Rockies, there were 1,716 head of horses, 4,430 head of cattle, 8,848 head of sheep, and 1,906 hogs. Apart from those at Nisqually and at Cowlitz, the largest such holdings, by far, were at Fort Vancouver, where there were 702 head of horses, 1,377 head of cattle, 1,891 head of sheep, and 1,581 hogs. Fort Langley had 15 head of horses, 195 head of cattle, and 180 hogs; and Fort Colvile had 350 head of horses, 96 head of cattle, and 73 hogs. Of the 3,005 acres under cultivation at various company posts, 240 acres were at Fort Langley, 100 at Fort Nisqually, 1,200 at Fort Vancouver, 118 at Fort Colvile, and 50 at Fort Umpqua.[50] In 1865, in presenting its claims for damages inflicted upon its property by trespassing American citizens, the Puget's Sound Agricultural Company affirmed that, on June 15, 1846, when the treaty determining the boundary between British territory and American territory in the old Oregon Country was concluded, it possessed at Nisqually and at Cowlitz 3,100 head of neat cattle, 356 head of horses, and 5,300 head of sheep, having in all a total value of £25,000.[51]

Although the treaty on the boundary guaranteed to the Hudson's Bay Company and the Puget's Sound Agricultural Company their possessory rights south of the forty-ninth parallel, the United States reserved the right to buy such of these lands as it

[50] Galbraith, Hudson's Bay Company as Imperial Factor, pp. 164, 204-17; "Hudson's Bay Co. Correspondence" in Certain Correspondence of the Foreign Office and of the Hudson's Bay Company Copied From Original Documents, 1898 (Ottawa, 1899), Part II, pp. 76-77; Rich (ed.), Letters of McLoughlin, Second Series, p. 268; WHQ, XVIII (January, 1927), 59; Joseph Schafer (ed.), "Documents Relative to Warre and Vavasour," OHQ, X (March, 1909), 60.

[51] British and American Joint Commission, Memorials to the Commissioners . . . Presented April 17, 1865 (Washington, D.C., 1865), p. 27. See also Robert C. Clark, History of the Willamette Valley, Oregon (Chicago, 1927), I, 199.

considered of "public and political importance." This right, in the
course of time, it exercised. For several years after 1846, however, the Hudson's Bay Company remained in possession of its
establishments south of forty-nine, and the Puget's Sound Agricultural Company continued to operate its farms at Nisqually
and Cowlitz. At Nisqually the company sold cattle, salted beef,
and sheep to the Hudson's Bay Company and to the branch of
the Puget's Sound Agricultural Company on Vancouver Island;
and here also it sold livestock to buyers from California, Oregon,
and parts of Washington. For several years it supplied beef to the
crews of ships, to shops in Olympia, and to American troops at
Fort Steilacoom. Before 1850, however, both the Hudson's Bay
Company and the Puget's Sound Agricultural Company were troubled by the encroachments of Americans upon their respective
properties, and from the early 1850's forward the herds of the
Puget's Sound Agricultural Company were rapidly dispersed and
depleted, some of the cattle being hunted and shot by Americans.
Eventually, this situation was taken in hand by the American and
the British governments, which, pursuant to a treaty they concluded in 1863, appointed a British-American Joint Commission
to determine how much the American government should pay to
the two companies for the extinguishment of their possessory
rights on American soil. After collecting evidence which filled
numerous printed volumes, the Joint Commission, on September
10, 1869, awarded $450,000 to the Hudson's Bay Company and
$200,000 to the Puget's Sound Agricultural Company for the sur-
render of their respective possessory rights. These sums the American government paid in September, 1871.[52]

The Puget's Sound Agricultural Company, by increasing the
number of Spanish cattle in the Oregon Country, had a considerable influence on the early economic development of this region.

[52] 29th Cong., 1st sess., S. Doc. 476, pp. 1-3. Trespassers on land claimed by
the Puget's Sound Agricultural Company were being warned off as early as Novem-
ber, 1849. Victor J. Farrar (ed.), "The Nisqually Journal," *WHQ*, XI (January,
1920), 65. In the matter of the claims of this company, see Galbraith, *Hudson's
Bay Company as Imperial Factor*, pp. 251-82, and, in the published papers of the
British and American Joint Commission, the *Evidence on the Part of the Puget's
Sound Agricultural Company, Claimants* (Montreal, 1868), pp. 104-9, and the
Opinions and Award of the Commissioners . . . Pronounced September 10, 1869
(Montreal, 1869).

But this influence was submerged after 1841, for year after year American settlers brought livestock overland to the Pacific Northwest in increasing numbers. By 1843 this colonizing movement had acquired considerable proportions; presently American influence in the Oregon Country became dominant, and within a few years American cattle had largely replaced the inferior Spanish cattle in this region.

The migration of 1843 consisted of more than a thousand persons, who perhaps brought to the valley of the Columbia as many as two thousand head of cattle and other livestock. This company being large, and some of its members having many head of loose cattle to drive and guard, it is not surprising that presently a division took place that produced a "light column" and a "cow column." Moreover, because this migration was the first significant expression of the "Oregon fever," it attracted nation-wide attention, and letters of advice from some of its members to prospective settlers in Oregon were eagerly laid hold of and published and republished in newspapers in the United States. Their advice seldom if ever tended to allay the "Oregon fever."[53] Here there is space for examining only three such letters. In one Peter H. Burnett, who subsequently became governor of California, advised the use of ox teams for the journey overland, and suggested bringing to Oregon as many loose cattle as possible. "Milch cows on the road," he said, "are exceedingly useful, as they give an abundance of milk all the way, though less toward the close of it." The American cattle, he insisted in another letter, "are greatly superior to the Spanish for milk, as they give more milk, and are more gentle." Similar advice was given in still another letter by S. M. Gilmore, who, besides recommending the use of ox teams for the journey, urged immigrants to bring "a plenty of loose cattle, cows and heifers particularly, as they are but little trouble and are worth a great deal." You "will find," he continued, "stout young cows to answer in place of oxen, in case you should not have sufficient."[54]

[53] Jesse Applegate, "A Day with the Cow Column in 1843," OPA, *Transactions* (1876), pp. 57-65. Contemporaneous accounts of migrations to Oregon appeared in the Baltimore *Niles' National Register*, and numerous journals of such immigrants have been printed in OPA, *Transactions*.

[54] Reprinted from the *New York Herald* of Jan. 6, 1845, in *OHQ*, III (Decem-

This migration, besides attracting much attention to Oregon and giving Americans control of its civil affairs, increased the wealth of this country, as William Strong later wrote, by bringing to the Willamette Valley "a large band of improved horses and cattle to take the place of the Indian pony and the long-horned, light-bodied and half wild Spanish cattle, which had been imported from California by the Willamette Cattle Company in 1837." It did more than that. It helped to improve the cattle in Oregon east of the Cascades. "I have seen," wrote John C. Fremont in October, 1843, "in descending the Walawalah river, a fine drove of several hundred cattle, which they [some immigrants of 1843] had exchanged for California cattle, to be received at Vancouver, and which are considered a very inferior breed."[55]

Also of considerable size were the overland migrations in later years. In 1844 the number of immigrants was large, and in 1845 it was still larger. In those years people came by the hundreds and cattle by the thousands. In 1846 more than 1,500 head of cattle and other livestock passed the toll gate on the Mount Hood road before the end of October, and a year later 1,918 persons, 450 wagons, 500 sheep, and 4,976 horses, cattle, and mules passed that gate.[56]

Little would be gained by studying in detail the overland migrations in subsequent years. It is enough to say that, before 1860, thousands of immigrants came overland and that they brought with them perhaps tens of thousands of livestock. The immigration of 1852 was reported to be very large, and that of 1853 to be even larger. In a statement published on October 22,

---

ber, 1902), 419; letter dated at "Linnton," Oregon, July 25, 1844, and reprinted from the St. Louis *Republican* in *Niles' National Register*, Nov. 2, 1844, p. 130; letter dated at Fort Vancouver on Nov. 11, 1843, and reprinted from the *Weston Journal* (Missouri), in the *OHQ*, IV (September, 1903), 282.

[55] William Strong, "The Annual Address," OPA, *Transactions* (1878), p. 15; John C. Fremont, *Narrative of the Exploring Expedition to the Rocky Mountains in the Year 1842, and to Oregon and North California in the Years 1843-44* (Syracuse, N.Y., 1847), p. 251.

[56] Rich (ed.), *Letters of McLoughlin, Third Series*, pp. 47, 178; Melvin Clay Jacobs, *Winning Oregon: A Study in an Expansionist Movement* (Caldwell, Ida., 1938), pp. 52-65, 211; McLoughlin to Captain John Gordon, Sept. 15, 1845, *OHQ*, XXIX (March, 1928), 59; Charles H. Carey (ed.), "Diary of Reverend George Gary," *OHQ*, XXIV (September, 1923), 291-93; Oregon City *Oregon Spectator*, Oct. 22, 1846, Oct. 28, 1847. For additional information on this subject, consult the *Oregon Spectator Index, 1846-1854* (Portland, 1941), I, 258-63.

1853, the agent for the Indians at "Utilla [Umatilla]" reported that 6,449 persons had passed his agency that year, together with 1,269 wagons, 9,077 oxen, 6,518 cows, 2,009 hogs, 327 mules, and 1,500 sheep. Also in that year, significantly, forty-six of the immigrants, having eleven wagons, sixty-two head of work cattle, and twenty cows, went to Puget Sound by the "emigrant road."[57] Six years later the editor of the *Dalles Journal* ascertained that in the autumn of 1859 "446 men, 115 women, 187 wagons, 206 horses and mules, and 1898 head of cattle" had come overland that year to the valley of the Columbia.[58]

The overland migrations not only revolutionized the incipient enterprise of cattle breeding in the Pacific Northwest; they also confirmed an already widely spread belief that the Pacific Northwest was a choice country for pastoral pursuits—a country abounding in nutritious grasses and having winters so mild that cattle and other livestock could subsist without feeding or shelter.[59] Sustained by this belief, settlers during the 1840's had occupied the Willamette Valley, had pushed southward into the Umpqua Valley and the Rogue River Valley, and, after 1846, had moved into the country north and east of the Columbia River. Before the Whitman massacre in November, 1847, some white settlers and considerable livestock were in the country east of the Cascades. The federal census of 1850 reported 41,729 head of cattle on farms in the Oregon Territory. Of these, 9,427 were milch cows and 8,114 were working oxen.[60]

The spread of settlers with their livestock continued during the 1850's. As early as October, 1850, Colonel Isaac N. Ebey took a claim on Whidbey Island, and by 1852 Indians there were complaining because the settlers' cattle were destroying their potatoes. Also in 1853 there were, significantly, fifty-three trespassers on land claimed by the Puget's Sound Agricultural Company at Fort Nisqually. Much farther south, more settlers were driving their cattle into the Rogue River Valley. Meanwhile, in the early

[57] News from Oregon in the San Francisco *Daily Alta California*, Aug. 13, Sept. 14, 1852; Salem *Oregon Statesman*, Sept. 27, 1853; *Weekly Oregonian*, Oct. 22, 1853; Olympia *Columbian*, Oct. 15, 1853.

[58] Reprinted in the *San Francisco Herald*, Oct. 15, 1859.

[59] See Chapter VIII of this book.

[60] *Compendium of the Seventh Census* (1850), pp. 170, 334.

1850's, a few settlers had moved cattle into the Walla Walla Valley, others had entered the country of the Nez Percé Indians, and George C. Bumford and Lloyd Brooks had occupied the site of the Whitman missionary station. Also at this time, or perhaps a little later, Louis Moragné, in the Tucannon Valley, owned "fifty horses and many cattle."[61] At the outbreak of the Indian war in 1855, the upper valley of the Columbia contained a considerable number of cattle, many of which belonged to Indians.

From the beginning of the overland migrations to this country, the Indians east of the Cascades made considerable progress in acquiring cattle. Previously, thanks to the Hudson's Bay Company's policy against selling cattle, it is unlikely that they obtained many from this company—at least before the late 1830's or the early 1840's. It appears, however, that as early as 1831 Dr. McLoughlin did send a young heifer to a Cayuse chief.[62] On May 5, 1837, Dr. Whitman wrote to the American Board, saying, among other things, that one of the Cayuse chiefs had "3 or four cows & heifers," and that a chief of the Walla Wallas also had a few head of cattle.[63] These exceptions apart, before 1842 the Indians east of the Cascades undoubtedly received most of their cattle from missionaries in that part of the country. It was the desire of the early Protestant missionaries in Oregon, as it later was also the desire of the Catholic missionaries in this country, to turn the Indians from their nomadic habits to a settled way of life sustained by agricultural pursuits.[64] As Dr. Whitman explained to the American Board in May, 1838, the Indians, if they were to be won to the Christian way of life, must be "attracted & retained by the plough & hoe." Before the end of that year both

[61] Edmond S. Meany, *History of the State of Washington* (New York, 1909), p. 227; Victor J. Farrar (ed.), "Diary of Colonel and Mrs. I. N. Ebey," *WHQ*, VIII (April, 1917), 135; "Oregon Bound: Letters of S. H. Taylor to the Watertown [Wisconsin] Chronicle, 1853-54," *OHQ*, XXII (June, 1921), 149; the Reverend T. Dwight Hunt in the New York *Home Missionary*, XXVIII (November, 1855), 265; Isaac I. Stevens, *Narrative and Final Report of Explorations for a Route for a Pacific Railroad . . .* in the U. S. Department of War, *Reports of Explorations and Surveys . . .* (Washington, D.C., 1860), XII, Pt. 1, 152, 198.
[62] Barker (ed.), *Letters of McLoughlin*, p. 188; Rich (ed.), *Letters of McLoughlin, First Series*, p. 244.
[63] ABCFM, Letters and Papers, CXXXVIII, No. 83.
[64] Jason Lee to the Corresponding Secretary of the Missionary Society of the Methodist Episcopal Church, Jan. 18, 1837, in the *Christian Advocate and Journal*, XI (June 9, 1837), 166.

he and Spalding were pleased with the Indians' progress in till-
ing the soil. Such progress continued in subsequent years, and by
1845 Dr. Whitman reported that not only were the Indians near
Waiilatpu doing more farming than ever before, but were making
better fences—"a thing much needed," he affirmed, "for most of
them . . . [were then] getting more or less cows and other
cattle."[65]

Whitman and Spalding had encouraged the Indians to get
cattle as well as to till the soil, but before 1842 the Indians near
Waiilatpu and Lapwai had acquired few cattle.[66] The turning
point came early in that year. In a letter dated February 18,
1842, Spalding said that not only had he distributed "several
heifers" among the Indians of his neighborhood, but also that
several Indians near his station were "expecting to take horses to
the Willamette next spring to exchange for cows."[67] Thus began a
trade between the Indians of the "upper country" and the early
settlers of the Willamette Valley, a trade perhaps as significant
for these Indians as the trade begun when the Willamette Cattle
Company brought cattle from California in 1837 had been for the
settlers in the Willamette Valley. This new trade was watched
with interest by the Protestant missionaries in Oregon. It was
specifically noted by Mrs. W. H. Gray in the upper country in
July, 1842, and by the Reverend Alvin Waller in the lower country a month later.[68] In a significant letter dated in Boston on
April 7, 1843, Dr. Whitman told one of the secretaries of the
American Board that "during the last season a number of cattle"
had been brought by Indians into the upper country, the cattle
having been obtained by exchanging one horse for "one cow of
the California breed." As a result of this importation, he continued, "The Indians have from fifty to seventy horned cattle mostly
cows which they have obtained partly from the H B Company,

[65] Marcus Whitman to David Greene, May 8, 1838, April 7, 1843, ABCFM,
Letters and Papers, CXXXVIII, Nos. 85 and 98; Marcus Whitman to his father,
April 8, 1845, OPA, Transactions (1893), p. 69.

[66] Wilkes, U. S. Exploring Expedition, IV, 460; Simpson, Narrative, I, 164;
Henry H. Spalding to David Greene, July 12, 1841, ABCFM, Letters and Papers,
CXXXVIII, No. 37.

[67] Henry H. Spalding to D. Allen, Feb. 18, 1842, in Eliza Spalding Warren,
Memoirs of the West: The Spaldings (Portland, Ore., 1916), pp. 74-75.

[68] Drury (ed.), First White Women over the Rockies, II, 257; A. F. Waller to

the set[t]lers—Methodist Mission on the Wallamette, the Boards Mission & then the last year from emigrants."[69]

In a few words, Dr. Whitman had said much: Before 1842, Indians in the upper Columbia Valley had obtained cattle from the Hudson's Bay Company, from settlers and Methodist missionaries in the Willamette Valley, and from the nearby missionaries of the American Board. In 1842, these Indians had begun to get cattle from immigrants who had come overland. Thereafter, during the 1840's they rapidly increased their holdings of cattle, partly by trading in the Willamette Valley, but principally, it appears, by trading Indian horses for American cows to the increasing number of overland immigrants. Mrs. Marcus Whitman tells us that in 1844 they were going as far east as Fort Hall to exchange their horses for cattle.[70]

Meanwhile, at Tshimakain, a station of the American Board in the Spokane country, Indians had also been increasing their holdings of cattle. In 1844 the Reverend Elkanah Walker was giving cows to Indians in exchange for horses. During the next two years the Indians near this station presumably acquired a considerable number, for their losses of both horses and cattle during the winter of 1846-47 were very heavy. "The Old Chief," wrote Mrs. Cushing Eells to her mother on April 6, 1847, "[who] says he had over 50 horned cattle, now has two."[71]

Eastward of Tshimakain, in what is now northern Idaho and western Montana, the Indians near missions founded by the Jesuits also acquired small herds of cattle. By 1845 Father de Smet could report that the Jesuit fathers had introduced at their various stations "of the upper Oregon" more than sixty head of cattle, as well as hogs and poultry, and in July of that year he counted thirty head of cattle belonging to the Pend d'Oreilles of

Fuller Atchinson, Aug. 19, 1842, in the *Christian Advocate and Journal*, XVIII (Nov. 8, 1843), 50.

[69] ABCFM, Letters and Papers, CXXXVIII, No. 98.

[70] *Missionary Herald*, XXXIX (1843), 383; Henry H. Spalding to Levi Chamberlain, Oct. 10, 1843, *OHQ*, XXXIII (December, 1932), 354; OPA, *Transactions* (1888), p. 115; *ibid.* (1893), p. 66. See also J. B. Littlejohn to Elijah White, Nov. 1, 1844, in 29th Cong., 1st sess., S. Ex. Doc. 1 (Serial 470), p. 624.

[71] Elkanah Walker to David Greene, March 27, 1844, ABCFM, Letters and Papers, CXXXVIII, No. 82; Drury (ed.), *First White Women over the Rockies*, II, 313, n. 17.

the bay. Here, he was interested to learn, the squaws had learned to milk and to churn butter. In September, 1846, he wrote that the livestock on the farm at the Flathead Mission of St. Mary's included a herd of forty head of cattle.[72]

Thus, even before the end of the 1840's, cattle were rather widely dispersed among the Indians of middle Oregon. Some of them had thrived so well that during the Cayuse War volunteers from western Oregon, while spending the winter of 1847-48 in the "middle country," reported that they "never saw fat cattle until they saw them at Waiilatpu" in February, 1848. These cattle, the editor of the *Oregon Spectator* remarked on July 13, 1848, "were Indian cattle, subsisting without shelter, upon the natural grasses of the country alone." Fascinated by the pastoral wealth of a country which he presumed was being opened to colonization, this editor further remarked that in "Middle and Eastern Oregon there is more land covered with a dense growth of rich grass, upon which horses, cattle and sheep will subsist throughout the year, than all the meadow, pasture, and plow land in all New England! Who," he concluded, "can estimate the wealth of such lands?"

Meanwhile, west of Waiilatpu, Indians in the Yakima Valley had also been acquiring cattle, at first probably from Forts Vancouver and Nisqually, but later by trade with immigrants in the Grande Ronde Valley and at The Dalles. By the middle 1850's, many of these Indians were said to be wealthy in horses and cattle.[73]

Elsewhere in the upper country Indians were increasing their holdings of cattle during the 1850's, principally, we may presume, by a continuing brisk trade with immigrants. The evidence of such trade is abundant for the years 1851, 1852, and 1853, and the progress that these Indians had made before the end of 1854 in tending livestock and in raising crops enlivens the reports of members of the party which Governor Isaac I. Stevens led westward in 1853 to ascertain a route for a northern railroad

---

[72] Chittenden and Richardson (eds.), *Father Pierre Jean de Smet*, II, 471, 571, III, 998.

[73] A. J. Splawn, *Ka-mi-akin, Last Hero of the Yakimas* (2nd ed.; Portland, Ore., 1944), pp. 17-18; U. S. War Department, *Reports of Explorations and Surveys* (Washington, D.C., 1855), I, 407-8, 410, 630.

from Lake Superior to Puget Sound. From men of this party we learn that the Flatheads in 1854 not only had a good grazing country, but also possessed about a thousand American cattle, "which were introduced by the worthy and zealous Father de Smet." There were fewer cattle at the Pend d'Oreille and the Coeur d'Alene missions, but farther south the Nez Percé, the Walla Walla, and the Yakima Indians were fairly well supplied with cattle. The chiefs of the Yakimas, as George Gibbs wrote in March, 1854, had made progress in cultivating crops and had acquired a "considerable number of cattle, which, in summer, . . . [found] good bunch-grass on the hills." Another member of this party brightened his report by recording his astonishment at seeing an Indian woman at the Coeur d'Alene Mission use both hands in milking a cow, "something," he said, "rarely seen amongst the Indians."[74]

Some of the cattle and many of the horses belonging to the Indians in the upper country survived the war of 1855-56 and its aftermath of 1858. But the loss was heavy. The Yakimas lost more than a few head of cattle, the Cayuses as a whole were impoverished, and the Walla Wallas were ruined.[75] Moreover, the northern Indians—the Coeur d'Alenes, Spokanes, and Palouses— were reported to have suffered the loss of a thousand horses "and a large number of cattle, . . . all of which were either killed or appropriated to the use of the United States," in 1858, when Colonel George Wright led a punitive expedition against them from Fort Walla Walla. As late as September, 1860, the Cayuse Indians had only three hundred head of cattle, and the Walla Wallas had none. This war carried in its train personal as well as tribal catastrophes, not the least of which was the impoverishment of the formerly powerful Yakima chief, Kamiakin, who

[74] Major Benjamin Alvord, *Report*, 34th Cong., 3rd sess., H. Ex. Doc. 76 (Serial 906), p. 113; OPA, *Transactions* (1904), pp. 322-23; *ibid.* (1914), pp. 181-82; *ibid.* (1920), p. 329; "Overland from Indiana to Oregon: The Dinwiddie Journal," *The Frontier*, VIII (March, 1928), 126; U. S. War Department, *Reports of Explorations and Surveys*, I, 149; *ibid.*, XII, Pt. 2, 133-34, 153, 162, 166.

[75] Robert M. Painter and W. C. Painter, "Journals of the Indian War of 1855-56," *WHQ*, XV (January, 1924), 11-31; *Weekly Oregonian*, Jan. 5, 1856; 34th Cong., 3rd sess., H. Ex. Doc. 76 (Serial 906), pp. 191, 195; Secretary of the Interior, *Report* (Dec. 3, 1857), 35th Cong., 1st sess., H. Ex. Doc. 2 (Serial 942), pp. 641, 662, 667; *ibid.* (1859), p. 782.

once had "possessed thousands of horses and a large number of cattle"; but who now, having lost everything, was reduced "to the most abject poverty."[76]

For prospective settlers in middle Oregon, however, Colonel Wright's campaign of 1858 was the prologue to two important events: first, the revocation on October 31, 1858, of the order of August 20, 1856, closing the Indian country east of the Cascades, and, secondly, the ratification by the Senate of the United States on March 9, 1859, of the treaties that Governor Isaac I. Stevens and General Joel Palmer had negotiated with Indian tribes in eastern Washington and eastern Oregon in 1855. Henceforth these Indians would be confined to reservations, and the vast areas which they had surrendered to the United States would be opened to occupation by white men.[77] As stockmen and settlers from east of the Rockies and west of the Cascades were beginning to enter this intermontane country of rich and wide-spreading grasslands, the economy of the settled parts of the Oregon Country was being nervously stimulated by new and demanding markets in mining communities arising north of the international border.

[76] Secretary of War, Report (1858), 35th Cong., 2nd sess., S. Ex. Doc. 1 (Serial 975), pp. 394, 396, 403; Olympia Pioneer and Democrat, Oct. 5, 1858; Commissioner of Indian Affairs, Report (1860), p. 432; Father Pierre Jean de Smet to Captain A. Pleasanton, May 25, 1859, in Secretary of War, Report (1859), 36th Cong., 1st sess., S. Ex. Doc. 2, II, 101; Splawn, Ka-mi-akin, p. 121. On Colonel Wright's expedition against the "northern Indians," see B. F. Manring, The Conquest of the Coeur d'Alenes, Spokanes, and Palouses (Spokane, Wash., 1912), and, more especially, Robert I. Burns, The Jesuits and the Indian Wars of the Northwest (New Haven and London, 1966), chaps. vii and viii.

[77] Legislature of Washington Territory, Message of the Governor ... [and] ... the Correspondence with the Secretary of War ... (Olympia, 1857), p. 59; Ethel M. Peterson, "Oregon Indians and Indian Policy, 1849-1871" (Master's thesis, University of Oregon, Thesis Series No. 3, 1939), p. 40.

CHAPTER II

Cattle for a Mining Kingdom

By 1858 the excitement of a gold rush had ceased to be novel both to Oregonians and to their neighbors north of the Columbia River. For fully a decade after gold was discovered in California, these people were exposed, at different times and with varying degrees of intensity, to excitement of this sort throughout the vast region extending from the Queen Charlotte Islands in the north to northern California in the south. As early as 1850, when the first governor of Vancouver Island reported to the British Colonial Secretary the discovery of a "very rich specimen of gold ore" in the Queen Charlotte Islands, Oregonians and others were "mining successfully" not only on the Umpqua and Rogue rivers in southern Oregon, but also "on both sides of the Columbia River" above the Cascades.[1] In the autumn of 1853, there were reports of further discoveries of gold in Washington Territory, and in the spring of the next year a responsible person predicted that henceforth the people of Washington Territory could "reasonably count upon gold as one of the staple productions" of their territory.[2] Somewhat more than a year later, a sizable rush was getting under way to "new and rich gold diggings" near old Fort Colvile. "Already," as the Reverend Ezra Fisher wrote from Oregon City

[1] T. A. Rickard, *Historic Backgrounds of British Columbia* (Vancouver, B.C., 1948), p. 292; Ezra Fisher, "Correspondence," *OHQ*, XVII (September, 1916), 300, 316; Oregon City *Oregon Spectator*, March 20, Nov. 11, 1851.
[2] Olympia *Columbian*, Oct. 1, 1853; Olympia *Pioneer and Democrat*, April 8, 1853; letter from A. M. P., dated at Olympia, O.T., Dec. 20, 1851, in the *Oregon Spectator*, Oct. 28, 1851.

on August 2, 1855, "about 1000 of the American population of the Willamette Valley" were on the way to these mines, and others were preparing to set out. "Money," Mr. Fisher added significantly, "is extremely scarce in this valley."[3]

No doubt money at this time was equally hard to come by in the Puget Sound country, for on August 3, 1855, the editor of the Olympia *Pioneer and Democrat* wrote that not only had "one or two additional parties" left Olympia for the mines near Fort Colvile, but also that he had heard that the "people of Steilacoom, and other places, . . . [were] also on the move in that direction."[4] These mines, however, did not acquire the magnetic power of the Fraser River mines; but they no doubt helped to prepare the minds of people on the Pacific Coast for a northward rush in 1858.

Major discoveries of gold in the north could be expected to stimulate the economy of the Oregon Country as such discoveries in California had stimulated it a few years before. Until 1847 most of the produce which left the Columbia River was destined for the Sandwich Islands, and the trade of this river was dominated by the Hudson's Bay Company. So important and of such character was the trade between Oregon and the Sandwich Islands that, by the middle 1840's, Oregonians were thinking of these islands as the "West Indies of Oregon." Although through the years small shipments of butter, cheese, and beef went from the Columbia River to Honolulu, the principal exports, as late as 1847, were lumber, fish, and flour.[5] Honolulu was not an attractive market for cattlemen in Oregon.

By the spring of 1847 California was not only in the process of

<hr/>

[3] *OHQ*, XX (March, 1919), 123.

[4] On this subject see not only the *Pioneer and Democrat*, Aug. 17, Sept. 7, 1855, but also the message which Governor Fayette McMullin sent to the legislature of Washington Territory on Dec. 12, 1857, in the Territory of Washington, *Council Journal* (1857), p. 19.

[5] Testimony of Thomas Lowe in Victoria on Aug. 5, 1865, before examiners of the British and American Joint Commission for the Settlement of the Claims of the Hudson's Bay and Puget's Sound Agricultural Companies, in *Evidence on the Part of the Hudson's Bay Company* (Montreal, 1868), p. 24; "Report of Lieutenant Peel on Oregon in 1845-46," *OHQ*, XXIX (March, 1928), 61-63; Duncan Finlayson to John McLeod, Feb. 25, 1833, *WHQ*, II (January, 1908), 166-67; Honolulu *Sandwich Island Gazette and Journal of Commerce*, March 31, Dec. 15, 1838; Honolulu *Polynesian*, Jan. 25, May 31, 1845, June 5, 1847; Alvin F. Waller to

becoming American, but also was embarrassed by a failure of crops, a heavy immigration, and its involvement in the war between Mexico and the United States. It therefore began to be a promising market for the produce of the Oregon Country. Before the end of that year, the ship which carried J. Quinn Thornton from the Columbia River to San Francisco was "laden with flour, lumber, potatoes, and butter"; and he observed that another vessel, carrying a similar cargo from Oregon, had put into San Francisco Bay. This trade continued, and the rush of miners to California in 1849, which temporarily upset Oregon's economy, soon provided that territory with a varied and thriving trade with its southern neighbor, including a trade in livestock.[6] The produce of Oregon now began to move rapidly into California, and presently the gold of California was making glad the hearts of Oregonians.

As early as April 9, 1849, Governor Joseph Lane reported to the Secretary of State that farms in Oregon were being neglected, and that "a large portion of the horses and oxen" of that territory were being taken to the mines in California.[7] A year later, as Dr. W. F. Tolmie testified in 1865, California was offering for the first time "a steady market" for cattle from Oregon.[8] Moreover, by the end of 1851 new mines in southern Oregon were providing a market which, broadly speaking, was an extension of the California market. Presumably because of this market, prices for beef and other commodities in the Umpqua Valley and the Rogue River Valley, in November, 1852, were said to be from "25 to 100 per cent" higher than prices in Lebanon, a few miles from Salem, where fresh beef was then quoted at fourteen to sixteen cents a pound; and on February 15, 1853, at Jacksonville in the Rogue

---

G. P. Disosway, in the New York *Christian Advocate and Journal*, XV (Feb. 10, 1841), 102; Arthur L. Throckmorton, *Oregon Argonauts: Merchant Adventurers on the Western Frontier* (Portland, Ore., 1961), pp. 54-62, 87-95.

[6] *Oregon Spectator*, Sept. 7, Oct. 12, 1848; J. Quinn Thornton, *Oregon and California in 1848* ... (New York, 1849), I, 379; Throckmorton, *Oregon Argonauts*, pp. 87-98; Portland *Weekly Oregonian*, Sept. 1, 1855; Oregon City *Oregon Argus*, Nov. 20, 1858.

[7] 31st Cong., 1st sess., S. Ex. Doc. 52 (Serial 561), p. 4.

[8] British and American Joint Commission, *Evidence on the Part of the Puget's Sound Agricultural Company, Claimants* (Montreal, 1868), p. 127.

River Valley, the price of "poor beef" ranged from twenty-five to thirty cents a pound.[9]

By 1853 cattle were being driven into California from more than one direction. On June 12 a letter from Fort Laramie said that cattle and other livestock were moving westward by tens of thousands toward California, and in December of the same year a resident of Oregon City said that Oregon had acquired a "large trade in lumber, cattle, pigs, poultry, etc., with California."[10] During the next three years, the record of the movement of cattle into California is not altogether clear. Although we do know that the price of cattle in western Arkansas in the spring of 1854 had risen considerably because more than three thousand head, gathered in three counties of that state, had been driven to California,[11] we do not know whether in those years the trade in cattle from Oregon to California was large or small. But, whatever its extent may have been, it undoubtedly had become large by June, 1857, when herds of considerable size—some from the Umpqua Valley and others from the Willamette Valley—were passing southward through Red Bluff. Moreover, at about the same time, the *Yreka Union* reported that there was a large migration of people and livestock from Oregon to California, and that much of the livestock in this migration had been driven "over the Pitt river road to the lower valleys." Also in 1857 two hundred head of cattle were shipped from Puget Sound to San Francisco.[12]

During the next two years, cattle by the thousands were driven from Oregon to California. In September, 1858, a San Francisco newspaper quoted the Shasta *Courier* as saying that, by June of that year, "some 12,673 cattle, brought from Oregon, had crossed

[9] Jesse Applegate to Thomas Ewbank, Dec. 20, 1851, in the *Report of the Commissioner of Patents* (1851), Pt. 2, p. 470; Ezra Fisher, "Correspondence," *OHQ*, XVII (December, 1916), 476; *Columbian*, April 16, 1853. On the effect of the mines on southern Oregon, see Throckmorton, *Oregon Argonauts*, pp. 162-68, 196-97.

[10] Jefferson City, Mo., *Jefferson Inquirer*, Aug. 6, 1853; *New York Chronicle*, Jan. 28, 1854.

[11] *New York Weekly Tribune*, May 13, 1854, quoting the *Van Buren Intelligencer*.

[12] San Francisco *Weekly Bulletin*, Jan. 27, July 11, 1857; *Pioneer and Democrat*, March 5, 1858.

at that point."[13] Also, at about the same time the *Jacksonville Sentinel* was quoted by the *Oregon Statesman* of June 15, 1858, as saying that cattle "in very large numbers" were being driven from Oregon to California, the total number of which, "during the present season," would perhaps be more than twenty thousand head. On June 25, 1858, a correspondent in Corvallis wrote to a newspaper in San Francisco, saying that cattle "in abundance" were on their way to California." A few weeks later a New York daily newspaper learned from a correspondent in San Francisco that each year there were driven from Oregon to California "from 10,000 to 20,000 head of horned cattle and sheep."[14]

Equally great, it appears, was the overland movement of cattle from Oregon to California in 1859. A newspaper in Marysville, California, on June 25 of that year, quoted the *Yreka Union* as saying that Maurice Baker, who had gone to Oregon the preceding autumn and had returned with 250 head of cattle, believed that there were more than "20,000 head on the road, in droves ranging up to 1,100." But these droves, he thought, were moving in the wrong direction; for, as he pointed out, two- to four-year-old steers worth twenty-two to forty-five dollars a head in Oregon would bring much less in a sagging California market.[15] By the autumn of 1859, the demand in California for nearly all kinds of produce from Oregon had declined so much that on November 30 J. B. Knapp, writing from the Oregon Fruit Depot in San Francisco to the editor of the *Oregon Farmer*, could say that there was then in San Francisco "very little Oregon produce in the market except fruit." Because, as he continued, there was "a large amount of States' meat" in that market, "Oregon meats could not be sold [there] in any quantity" except at ruinous prices. Principally because of this decline of prices, an economic depression had settled upon the Willamette Valley before the end of 1859. Accordingly, the editor of the *Oregon Farmer*, observing that the editor of the Roseburg *Express* had reported on May 15, 1860, that large droves of cattle had "passed through town the past week, en route

[13] San Francisco *National*, Sept. 23, 1858.
[14] *San Francisco Herald*, July 5, 1858; *New York Daily Tribune*, Dec. 29, 1858.
[15] Marysville *Weekly California Express*, June 25, 1859.

for southern Oregon and northern California," was perhaps letting his wish become the father of his thought when he said that farmers "in the upper Willamette, who furnish beef cattle for the southern market will soon feel the burdens of the present hard times lightened from their shoulders."[16]

But before this time settlers in the lower Willamette Valley, as well as in Washington Territory, had decided that their prosperity would come not from California, but from a new country lying northward and eastward of the Columbia River, a new land of Ophir, which presently, they hoped, would yield much gold to stimulate the entire economy of the Pacific Northwest. The rise of mining communities in this northern country, and their effect on the movement of cattle into, and through, the grasslands of what earlier had been called middle and upper Oregon, we shall now endeavor to describe.

The thousands of miners who flocked to the Fraser River country in 1858 were ushering in a new era in the history of both the British and the American Pacific Northwest. Within a few years, miners and prospectors had entered widely separated areas of present-day British Columbia and had penetrated deeply into many districts in American territory immediately south of this province. By 1862 the rush to the rich Cariboo fields was under way. In that year gold was found in the Kootenay district, and in the autumn of 1864 mines were discovered in the Big Bend of the upper Columbia River. Nor was this all. South of the forty-ninth parallel other large mining districts had earlier been opened in what today we call Idaho, eastern Oregon, and western Montana. The discovery of gold in the Clearwater country by Captain E. D. Pierce in 1860 opened the way to these later discoveries. In 1861, while the rush to the Clearwater mines was under way, other placer mines were found north of the Salmon River in northern Idaho and on the John Day and the Powder rivers in eastern Oregon. A year later Warren's Diggings, south of the Salmon River, were discovered, as well as high-yielding mines in the Boise Basin; and in 1863 mines were opened in the country drained by the Owyhee River. Northeastward of these districts, between

[16] Portland *Oregon Farmer*, Dec., 1859, May 21, 1860.

1862 and 1864, rich mines in present-day Montana were opened on Grasshopper Creek, in Alder Gulch, and in Last Chance Gulch.[17]

Here, then, were the far-flung districts of the new northern mining kingdom, a kingdom which sprawled across an international boundary, and which demanded, and could pay for, goods. This demand set in motion activities directly affecting people from California to British Columbia, and from Chicago and St. Louis to the Willamette Valley and Puget Sound. Men who washed the earth for gold needed food, clothing, shelter, and tools; and for these, as well as for other things which they wanted but did not need, they were willing to spend money lavishly.

Because what they had to sell could, to a great extent, provide its own means of transportation, cattlemen in Oregon responded quickly to the needs of the miners on the Fraser River. By the middle of July, 1858, cattle by the hundreds were passing through Oregon City on the way to "the new mines," and before the middle of August of that year the editor of a newspaper in Olympia was complaining about the difficulty of getting vessels to carry cattle down Puget Sound. "For the last few weeks," he wrote,

large bands of beef cattle have been driven here from Oregon, for the supply of the market at Bellingham Bay, Victoria, etc. As we have had no steamer running from the head of the Sound, connecting with those places, for the past few weeks, much disappointment and difficulty has been experienced in getting them to market. Several hundred have been driven down the trail to Seattle and thence lightered to Whidby's [sic] Island and other places north. Beef [he concluded] is *beef* in that direction.

Within a few days, however, the bark *Gold Hunter* was carrying cattle from Olympia to Bellingham Bay.[18]

These shipments were no doubt designed to further an attempt by some Americans, operating from the mushroom town of Whatcom on Bellingham Bay, to compete with Victoria for the trade of

---

[17] F. W. Howay, *British Columbia: The Making of a Province* (Toronto, 1928), chaps. xvii, xix, xxv; Walter N. Sage, *Sir James Douglas and British Columbia* (Toronto, 1930), pp. 203-34; William J. Trimble, *The Mining Advance into the Inland Empire* ... (Madison, Wis., 1914), chaps. i-v. See also Throckmorton, *Oregon Argonauts*, pp. 162-67, and Leslie M. Scott, "The Pioneer Stimulus of Gold," *OHQ*, XVIII (September, 1917), 147-66.

[18] *Oregon Argus*, July 7, 1858; "Beef Cattle from Oregon," *Pioneer and Democrat*, Aug. 13, Sept. 3, 1858.

the Fraser River mines. Although these men spent considerable money to construct two Whatcom trails, their endeavor did not succeed. Their first trail reached the Fraser River below Fort Hope; their second led to the Thompson River. Neither trail was practicable; the Whatcom boom collapsed, and Victoria continued to prosper from her trade with the mines of western British Columbia. Nevertheless, as late as January, 1860, the schooner *General Harney* sailed from Port Townsend for Bellingham Bay with fifty head of cattle which were intended to be driven "by way of the Whatcom trail [presumably the first one] to Fort Hope, and thence by the H. B. Company's trail to the Smilkemeen [*sic*], for the use of the miners."[19]

Thus we have obtained a preliminary glimpse of a route by which stockmen of western Oregon carried on, during the era of placer gold mining in the Pacific Northwest, an important trade in cattle and other livestock. It was one of the two principal routes leading from the Columbia River to the mines in British North America. Cattle destined for these mines came northward from the Rogue River Valley, the Umpqua Valley, and the Willamette Valley as far as the Columbia River. Here the route divided. The cattle taking the eastern route were sent, either by boat or by overland trail, to The Dalles, and then driven northward by way of the Okanogan Valley; those that took the western route were carried by boat to Monticello (now Kalama), and then went northward by the old Cowlitz road to the head of Puget Sound. From here they were sent by boat down Puget Sound to the northern markets, of which the principal one was Victoria. Although Victoria received some shipments of cattle, preserved beef, and dairy products from San Francisco, Portland, and the Sandwich Islands, for many years after 1858 this market, as well as those of western British Columbia, was supplied with fresh meat imported principally by way of Puget Sound.[20]

[19] R. L. Reid, "The Whatcom Trails to the Fraser River Mines in 1858," *WHQ*, XVIII (July and October, 1927), 199-206, 271-76; *National*, Aug. 25, 1858, quoting from the Whatcom *Northern Light* of Aug. 19, 1858; *Port Townsend Register*, Jan. 18, 1860.

[20] For this subject in general, see J. Orin Oliphant, "The Cattle Trade on Puget Sound, 1858-1890," *AH*, VII (July, 1933), 129-49. In 1858 and 1859, some of the steamers carried, among other things, small numbers of cattle, hogs, and sheep

But this era's Puget Sound cattle trade, although largely originating in western Oregon, was not exclusively a trade in cattle from Oregon. Nor was it exclusively a trade to markets on Vancouver Island and in British Columbia. Puget Sound was part of a convenient route to markets for cattle bred both in Washington and in Oregon, and some of the cattle carried on this route were sold in the rising markets south of the border. As early as autumn of 1860, the editor of a newspaper in Port Townsend acknowledged, grudgingly, that, for the 535 head of cattle consumed annually in Port Townsend, "the neat little sum of $16,050 is sent to Oregon, every cent of which should be saved" for the farmers of Washington. Presently, it appears, some Washington farmers were sending cattle northward on Puget Sound; but a man trading in cattle from Oregon to Victoria testified as late as September, 1865, that Vancouver Island and British Columbia were obtaining from Washington Territory only a small part of their fresh meats.[21]

When the foregoing testimony was given, the trade in cattle on Puget Sound had been flourishing for several years. The trade of 1858 had increased in 1859, and had become still larger in 1860. During 1859 the steamers *Constitution, Wilson G. Hunt, Julia,* and *Eliza Anderson* had been employed, more or less regularly, in this trade; and between January and December of that year Victoria had imported from ports on Puget Sound, according to an unofficial report, 2,145 head of cattle, horses, and sheep valued at $73,207. Also in that year, Victoria imported from Portland, San Francisco, and the Sandwich Islands, cattle, sheep, and dairy products. In 1860 Victoria continued to receive similar imports from these places, but in that year most of the cattle that it received came on vessels that cleared at Port Townsend. The *Eliza Anderson,* a vessel that served many years as a cattle boat on Puget Sound, was then regularly employed in carrying cattle from ports on Puget Sound to Victoria, and in that year other vessels carrying cattle occasionally cleared from Port Townsend for

from Portland and Astoria to Victoria. National Archives, Record Group 36 (Astoria, Ore.), folders 18, 33, 121, 138, 139, 140.
[21] Port Townsend *North-West,* Oct. 25, 1860; Robert M. Hutchinson, testifying in Victoria on Sept. 25, 1865, before the British and American Joint Commission. *Evidence on the Part of the Puget's Sound Agricultural Company,* p. 130.

Victoria.[22] In the total exports from the Puget Sound district to Victoria during the first quarter of 1860, valued at $51,835.64, there were included 501 head of cattle worth $23,900, and 56 quarters of beef worth $1,040. During the third quarter of that year, exports worth $57,335.10 from the Puget Sound district to Victoria included 331 head of cattle and calves worth $12,930; and exports of the value of $4,945.88 from the same district to New Westminster included 39 head of cattle worth $1,000. During the last quarter of that year, 310 head of cattle worth $14,059 were cleared from Port Townsend for Victoria.[23]

The growing importance of Victoria's imports from Washington was not overlooked by contemporaneous reporters. After reading in the *Port Townsend Register* of February 6, 1861, a statement of the exports from Puget Sound in 1860, the editor of the Victoria *British Colonist* observed that Victoria was the largest foreign customer of Washington Territory: that more lumber, cattle, and other products had been exported from that territory to Victoria in 1860 than had been shipped from Port Townsend to all other ports put together. Exports from Puget Sound to Victoria, including $300 worth of lumber to Barclay Sound, had amounted to $206,671. Of this sum, $96,435 accounted for 3,624 head of cattle, sheep, hogs, and mules. "Nearly one-half of our imports [from Washington Territory] the last year was cattle," he said. But, he continued, "Oregon doubtless was made tributary to supply them to some extent," and for that reason he thought that credit should not be given "to the Sound for the whole amount of the exports of the Territory."[24]

Between 1861 and 1864, the Victoria market expanded rapidly, but in 1865 it contracted. During this five-year period, Washington Territory's share in this market averaged nearly a quarter million dollars a year; but, from the data at hand, it is not possible to segregate from the annual totals the exact sums representing imports of cattle by the Puget Sound route. The customhouse rec-

[22] "The steamer *Eliza Anderson*, recently built in this city, left on Saturday last for Victoria, under command of Capt. Wells." *Weekly Oregonian*, March 5, 1859.

[23] Oliphant, "Cattle Trade on Puget Sound," pp. 131-33, and the works therein cited.

[24] *Port Townsend Register*, April 18, Nov. 14, 1860, and the Victoria *British Colonist*, Feb. 15, 1861.

ords are not available, and the accounts in the newspapers are incomplete. But the scanty evidence we have indicates that this trade was important. Moreover, Victoria's prosperity during those years suggests that there would be a large demand for the products of such a trade, and the want of evidence showing that cattle in considerable numbers were being sent to that market by other routes argues strongly in favor of a substantial trade in cattle by the route much used in the years just preceding this period.[25]

The shares of Oregon and Washington in the imports of Victoria between 1861 and 1865 become both interesting and meaningful when compared with Victoria's imports from other places during those years. From all countries, the imports of Victoria rose in value from $2,335,089 in 1861 to $5,578,923 in 1864, and then dropped to $2,902,871 in 1865. During the same years, the city's imports from San Francisco rose in value from $1,288,359 in 1861 to $2,345,066 in 1862, and then receded steadily to $1,284,-687 in 1865. Victoria's imports from the Sandwich Islands during those years disclose an erratic tendency, for they rose in value from $54,382 in 1861 to $113,486 in 1862, fell to $19,836 in 1864, and then rose to $93,678 in 1865. Oddly enough, her imports directly from Oregon during those years, which no doubt included a small number of cattle each year, fell in value from $216,203 in 1861 to $75,370 in 1862, and then rose rapidly and steadily to $181,160 in 1865. More consistent than any of the others here mentioned were the imports from Washington Territory. From a value of $228,250 in 1860, these imports fell slightly to a value of $224,793 in 1862, then rose steadily to a value of $277,123 in 1864; but they fell to the value of $222,056 in 1865.

Part of this trade from Washington Territory consisted in the trade in cattle on Puget Sound. From newspaper reports of clearances of vessels from Port Townsend, we know that such a trade was continuous in 1861. At regular and frequent intervals during that year, the *Eliza Anderson* sailed from Port Townsend to Vic-

[25] During these years, vessels plying between Portland and Victoria carried to Victoria small numbers of cattle and small quantities of beef. *Oregon Farmer*, March 16, 1861; *Weekly Oregonian*, March 29, May 24, 1862; *British Colonist*, April 12, May 24, 1862; Portland *Daily Times*, June 30, 1863; *British Colonist*, Oct. 20, 1863; Portland *Morning Oregonian*, Oct. 6, 1863; *Weekly Oregonian*, Dec. 19, 1863; *British Colonist*, Jan. 5, Sept. 6, 1864.

toria with cattle as its principal cargo. Less frequently the
schooner *Flying Mist* and the steamer *Enterprise,* carrying similar
cargoes, were reported in the weekly list of clearances from Puget
Sound to Victoria. During the first quarter of 1861, according to
unofficial compilations, Victoria imported through Port Townsend
410 head of cattle worth $13,760, and during the last quarter 824
head worth $17,475. The ports of Puget Sound, however, had no
monopoly of the Victoria cattle market in that year, for in March,
1861, Victoria received from Honolulu 68 head of cattle worth
$2,420, and from Portland, 85 head worth $3,740. In October of
that year, the Victoria imports of cattle from Astoria and San
Francisco were valued at $3,000.

During the spring of 1862, shipments of cattle from Puget
Sound to Victoria were made regularly, and probably were continued throughout that year; but, owing to incomplete records,
we cannot be certain about this matter. One explanation of the
dearth of records in newspapers on this trade in 1862 is given by
the editor of the Port Townsend *North-West:* "Friday, Jan. 24th—
10 o'clock A. M. Victor Smith, Collector of Customs, special agent,
&c., denied us at this hour access to the books of the Custom
House. We are therefore unable to present any Marine Report.
We are, hereafter, dependent upon facilities entirely outside the
Custom House." An additional explanation for the lack of records
during the last quarter of that year may be that an act of Congress designating Port Angeles as the port of entry for the Puget
Sound district from October 1, 1862, made the records of the customhouse of this district inaccessible to editors in Port Townsend.
But, whatever the reason may be, there is a disconcerting dearth
of reports on the transactions of the customhouse of the Puget
Sound district for most of 1862. From an American consular report from Victoria, however, we learn that, during the first half of
1862, Victoria imported through Port Townsend $115,608 worth
of livestock, provisions, and other goods. For the second half of
the year no such report has been found, but there is some evidence of a continuing trade in livestock from Puget Sound to Victoria. In the autumn of 1862, the *Eliza Anderson* was reported to
be carrying on her trips down the sound "large numbers of cattle
and sheep," and in December of that year the steamer *Emily*

Harris was reported to have sailed from Olympia with cattle for Victoria.

In the summer of 1863 the Puget Sound cattle trade was interrupted temporarily by a government embargo on exports of livestock from the United States. The interruption caused considerable excitement in the Pacific Northwest. On July 1, 1863, the *Morning Oregonian* published a letter from Olympia in which the writer declared that Captain Finch of the *Eliza Anderson* had been told by Victor Smith, collector of customs for the Puget Sound district, that no more livestock could be transported to points north of the international boundary. "There are several hundred head of beef cattle in Thurston and Pierce counties contracted for and awaiting shipment to Victoria," this writer declared. "The English navy and military posts, as well as the people, have all to be supplied with American beef. I hope, for the credit of the Government, that this miserable appointee [meaning Victor Smith] is not doing this out of revenge." But the editor of the *Morning Oregonian,* being better informed than his angry correspondent in Olympia, expressed the belief that this instruction had been issued to the collector of customs pursuant to the provisions of a recent order of the Department of War forbidding the exportation of horses and cattle from the United States on the ground that they might be needed in the United States for military purposes.

Meanwhile, the collector of the Puget Sound district had written to the Department of the Treasury regarding the order, and had been informed by the Acting Secretary of the Treasury, in a letter dated August 4, 1863, that, in view of the "condition of things on the Pacific Coast, it . . . [was] not deemed expedient at present to suspend or modify the order prohibiting such shipments." This letter was published in the *British Colonist* of September 8, accompanied by this enlightening comment:

In connection with the above [letter], we are informed that letters received last mail by the collector of the Puget Sound district are of such a nature, that that officer will not be at liberty to permit even the shipment of dressed meats as heretofore. . . . Of the feeling which this prohibitory order will engender on both sides of the Sound there cannot be two opinions. In our case, although we may suffer temporary inconvenience, there is a remedy within our reach which ultimately will tend to benefit rather than injure these colonies.

With the people of Washington Territory the case is widely different, and we fail ourselves to see "the condition of things on the Pacific coast," which renders it expedient for the United States Government thus to evince an unfriendly spirit towards a neighboring power, and at the same time inflict injury upon its own loyal and unoffending subjects. Let our friends however on the other side represent their own grievances and fight their own battles; we have now a certainty to deal with, and the sooner we bestir ourselves the better.

That rigorous enforcement of the prohibitory order would have given rise to an illicit trade in cattle and beef across the border is altogether probable. Fortunately, a change of policy soon reopened legitimate trade. On September 4, 1863, President Lincoln signed an executive order modifying the order issued by the Department of War on May 13, 1863, so as to permit any state or territory bounded by the Pacific coast to export livestock raised in any part of such state or territory. A notice of the modification was immediately telegraphed by Salmon P. Chase, Secretary of the Treasury, to the collector of customs in San Francisco, together with an instruction to him to notify "all the collectors." Chase's telegram was published in the *Morning Oregonian* of September 12, accompanied by an explanatory remark saying that the prohibition, as originally issued, "was not intended to apply to the Pacific coast, but only to those regions which might be deprived of part of their material which might be useful in war." Whether or not this explanation was true, the modification of the prohibitory order was in accord with reason, for the remoteness of the Pacific coast from the theater of action makes it difficult to understand how the disposal of livestock in the Pacific Northwest could have affected the outcome of the Civil War then in progress in the eastern states.[26]

Nothing illustrates more clearly the importance of the trade in cattle from the American to the British Northwest than its temporary obstruction. Accordingly, the satisfaction occasioned by the lifting of the embargo was as great as had been the resentment caused by its establishment. The true state of feeling about this

[26] Oliphant, "Cattle Trade on Puget Sound," pp. 134-39.

matter, north as well as south of the border in the far Northwest, was no doubt correctly expressed in a letter from Victoria dated September 24, 1863:

... The "beef embargo" caused much complaint here and in Washington Territory. It had the effect of materially advancing the price of beef, mutton, and pork. The butchers were about raising the price of beef to 40 cents a pound, when happily the news arrived that the "embargo" was dispensed with by Government so far as this coast was concerned. This news caused great rejoicing. . . .[27]

Before the end of September, 1863, Victoria once again was receiving by the usual channels both cattle and products of the dairy. Neither the volume nor the value of such imports for 1863, however, can be accurately determined. But the embarrassment caused by the temporary interruption of this part of the trade of the American Northwest with the British Northwest was no doubt considerable, for in January, 1864, the American consul in Victoria wrote that the people on Vancouver Island were "almost wholly dependent on California, Oregon, and Washington Territory" for their supply of "beef, pork, bacon, and provisions generally"; and, as late as February, 1864, a scarcity of meat in Victoria was attributed to the failure of the *Eliza Anderson* to bring over "the usual quantity of live stock."[28]

For 1864, as for preceding years, the available statistics for the trade in cattle from the American Northwest to Victoria are unsatisfactory. For the fiscal year ending on June 30, 1864, the American official statement of exports of cattle from Oregon and Washington shows 2,337 head worth $71,342. For nine months of the calendar year 1864 Victoria's imports of cattle from the Puget Sound district, according to the *British Colonist*, totaled 2,967 head worth $72,682; and, during the same period, Victoria imported directly from Oregon 133 head of cattle worth $1,750. For the full calendar year 1864, however, Washington Territory, according to the American consul in Victoria, shipped to Victoria "beef cattle, hogs, sheep and horses to the value of $166,186.00."

[27] "From a Temporary Sojourner in Victoria, V. I.," *Morning Oregonian*, Oct. 5, 1863.
[28] *British Colonist*, Sept. 8-29, 1863; 38th Cong., 2nd sess., H. Ex. Doc. 60, XI, 156; Olympia *Washington Standard*, Feb. 3, 1864.

But, he continued, it "is but fair to state that at least one-half of this stock was driven overland from Oregon, and shipped here, from ports in Washington Territory." As in earlier years, the *Eliza Anderson* continued to be employed in this trade.

During 1865, this trade appears to have differed little from that of 1864.[29] For the fiscal year ending on June 30, 1865, the American official statement shows that exports from the United States to the British American possessions on the Pacific coast totaled 3,438 head of cattle worth $146,045. Although some of this trade passed to British Columbia by way of trails through eastern Washington, perhaps the greater part of it moved northward by way of Puget Sound. During this fiscal year, there were exported from the Puget Sound district 3,315 head of cattle valued at $143,706, and from Oregon, 53 head worth $1,289.[30] In fact, so important was this trade in the latter part of 1865 that a newspaper in Olympia could say that the "driving of fat cattle and sheep from Oregon to this Territory, to supply the markets on the Sound, Victoria, and British Columbia, is growing into quite a successful business, in which several drovers are exclusively engaged."[31]

One of these drovers was Robert M. Hutchinson, a native-born American. In testimony which he gave in Victoria on September 25, 1865, for the British and American Joint Commission, he corroborated in substance what we have already learned about the cattle trade on Puget Sound. He also affirmed, among other things, that he had "been engaged in bringing cattle to Victoria from Oregon *via* Washington Territory for nearly four years," and that, before removing to Vancouver Island in the spring of 1864, he had "resided constantly in the Umpqua Valley" since 1853. To supply the demand for beef and mutton for the markets of Puget Sound, Vancouver Island, and British Columbia, cattle and sheep from Oregon, he said, were driven "from two to four hundred miles," and during their journey northward passed overland through Washington Territory to Puget Sound. Here it was neces-

[29] Oliphant, "Cattle Trade on Puget Sound," p. 140; *British Colonist*, Feb. 9–Sept. 6, 1864; Olympia *Pacific Tribune*, June 18, 1864; *Washington Standard*, Dec. 5, 1864.

[30] *Report of the Secretary of the Treasury . . . on the Commerce and Navigation of the United States for the Year Ending June 30, 1865*, pp. 3, 57.

[31] *Washington Standard*, Nov. 5, 1865.

sary to pasture them "for from one to twelve months" preparatory
to their being marketed. So great was the need for ground for this
purpose that all the pasture lands "in the vicinity of Puget Sound"
were insufficient to meet the wants of the drovers. Because of the
"superior advantages" afforded by the Nisqually plains for pasturing livestock, the nearby port of Steilacoom became the principal
point for shipping cattle and sheep northward to market.

As to the number of cattle shipped annually from Puget Sound
to Victoria and New Westminster, Hutchinson testified that, for
the year ending July 1, 1865, he had shipped to Victoria from
Steilacoom "about twelve hundred head of cattle, and about four
thousand five hundred head of sheep," and he believed that he
had shipped "from the Sound to this market during that time
about one half of the cattle and sheep that were shipped."[32]

More than a year later, in testimony given for the British and
American Joint Commission in Olympia, W. W. Miller, a broker
and moneylender, corroborated Hutchinson's testimony about
driving cattle from Oregon to Puget Sound for shipment to various markets on the sound. While waiting to ship their cattle to
such markets, the dealers "were necessarily compelled to feed or
graze them." He believed that "some of the large dealers" always
kept stock on hand, ready to be shipped according to the demands of the various markets.[33]

Equally illuminating is the testimony which Jesse Applegate
gave to representatives of the Joint Commission in Oregon City
on August 24, 1866. "At present," he said, "cattle and sheep dealers for the Victoria market purchase stock from me, in the Umpqua Valley, southern Oregon." Proceeding cautiously with his testimony, being careful to say that some of the questions put to him
he answered "from information," Applegate asserted that, since
the discovery of mines in British Columbia in 1858, large numbers

[32] British and American Joint Commission, *Evidence on the Part of the Puget's
Sound Agricultural Company*, pp. 129-31. In testimony given in Victoria on the
same day, Dr. W. F. Tolmie affirmed that, because of the encroachments of
Americans upon the land claimed by the Puget's Sound Agricultural Company at
Nisqually, this company lost considerable money by not being able to lease its
"enclosed fields as pasture to Oregon drovers." *Ibid.*, p. 128.
[33] British and American Joint Commission, *Evidence for the United States in
the Matter of the Puget's Sound Agricultural Company* (Washington, D.C., 1867),
pp. 80-82.

of cattle, horses, sheep, and swine had been purchased annually
in Oregon to supply the markets of Puget Sound, Vancouver Island, and British Columbia. The "stock designed for Victoria markets," he continued, "are taken by way of the Cowlitz to Puget's
Sound, [and] from there shipped; those for British Columbia, by
way of the Columbia river. By the Victoria markets, I mean to include the other markets in British America, most convenient to
that point." Dealers found it profitable, he declared, to take cattle
in large droves from Oregon. Since these cattle could only be
gradually shipped to market, it became necessary to pasture them
adjacent to Puget Sound. Near Steilacoom, Applegate's attention
had been called to two large enclosures in which, he was told,
cattle driven from Oregon were allowed to rest and graze. Steilacoom, he also was told, was the best cattle-shipping point on
Puget Sound.[34]

Although not the exclusive market for cattle and other livestock that were shipped down Puget Sound before 1866, Victoria
had been from the beginning of this trade the most important
market for all such livestock. By 1865, however, Victoria's boom
days were drawing to a close, if we may trust the reports of Allen
Francis, the American consul at that port. According to Francis,
a business depression that started in the summer of 1864 had
caused a serious decline in the imports of Victoria in 1865. Business failures had occurred there, as well as in British Columbia,
and, because of floods, 1865 had been a disastrous year for mining
interests in British Columbia. In 1866 an anticipated rush to the
Big Bend mines by way of Victoria did not take place, and in the
autumn of that year Francis reported that business in Victoria
was prostrated. "No city on the Pacific coast," he wrote, "occupies
a more deplorable position commercially than does Victoria. . . .
A general collapse pervades every branch of business."

During the remaining years of this decade, the American consul at Victoria continued to paint doleful pictures of economic
conditions there and in western British Columbia. As late as 1867,
imports were still declining; a "settled despondency" seemed to
pervade the whole community. Nor, according to him, did busi-

[34] *Ibid.*, pp. 31-33.

ness in Victoria recover in 1868 or 1869. The discovery of new diggings in Kootenay excited little interest in Victoria, for that area was being supplied chiefly from the Walla Walla Valley. The departure of people from Victoria had not ceased in 1869, and, as one indication of the changing times, it was observed in that year that considerable attention was being given to the breeding of livestock on the mainland of British Columbia, which could supply the Cariboo mines at "much lower rates" than the Victoria market could afford.[35]

Nevertheless, through the later 1860's and beyond, the American trade in cattle to Victoria by way of Puget Sound persisted, even though the union of British Columbia and Vancouver Island, in November, 1866, had the effect of depriving Victoria of the privileges of a "free port." Although an American consular report affirms that by 1868 new duties had stimulated agriculture on Vancouver Island and had excluded from the market of Victoria many of the products of California, Oregon, and Washington Territory, in 1869 the island was producing only half of what it was consuming. Much of what this community needed, including cattle, continued to arrive on ships which cleared at Port Townsend.[36]

During the fiscal year ending June 30, 1866, the exportation of American cattle to the British Northwest amounted to 2,008 head worth $93,200. There appears, however, to be no way of determining how many head were shipped from ports on Puget Sound. But that many of them were seems altogether likely, for Allen Francis, in his consular report from Victoria for the first quarter of 1867, wrote that the imports of this city "represented as from Washington Territory [$31,744.31] embrace the cattle, sheep, and

[35] 39th Cong., 1st sess., H. Ex. Doc. 56, X, 113; 39th Cong., 2nd sess., H. Ex. Doc. 81, XIII, 117-18; 40th Cong., 2nd sess., H. Ex. Doc. 160, XIV, 201-6; 40th Cong., 3rd sess., H. Ex. Doc. 87, XIV, 294; 41st Cong., 3rd sess., H. Ex. Doc. 18, VI, 224.

[36] Allen Francis, American consul in Victoria, wrote on Sept. 30, 1862, as follows: "Victoria, in one sense, is a free port; that is, no duties are collected on imports, but all merchandise, produce, etc., before landing, are required to take out 'landing permits,' the cost of which is governed by their value." 37th Cong., 3rd sess., H. Ex. Doc. 63, XII, 145. See also 40th Cong., 2nd sess., H. Ex. Doc. 160, XIV, 202; 40th Cong., 2nd sess., H. Ex. Doc. 87, XIV, 293; 41st Cong., 3rd sess., H. Ex. Doc. 18, VI, 224.

swine driven from Oregon through that Territory to Puget Sound, and shipped on steamers to this port." For the fiscal year ending June 30, 1867, all the American exports of cattle to British possessions on the Pacific coast, consisting of 670 head worth $22,790, were sent from the Puget Sound district; and during 1868 all such exports, consisting of 1,555 head of cattle worth $70,424, were sent from this district (with the exception of 51 head received by sea from Oregon). For the year ending June 30, 1869, the value of all livestock exported from the United States to British North America (Canada excepted) was $123,275, and for the same year the value of all livestock exported from the Puget Sound district was $108,370, and from Oregon, $13,929. The cattle exports for this year are not segregated. Thereafter, during the years covered by this study, British Columbia was a declining market for cattle from the Untied States.[37]

In the meantime, the exploitation of placer mines in British Columbia had stimulated enormously the economic development of both Oregon and Washington east of the Cascades. The Columbia River provided a part of the principal eastern route to these mines, and presently it also became the large part of the principal route to the American mining districts, opened at various places and in different times, south of the forty-ninth parallel. By the spring of 1859 steamboats were operating on the Columbia below the Cascades, between the Cascades and The Dalles, and above Celilo Falls, and thus were providing—with the aid of portages at the Cascades, The Dalles, and Celilo Falls—a means by which miners and other persons by the thousands reached the interior. The river also provided a route by which provisions, tools, and other commodities were transported by thousands of tons to the miners and other persons who presently would be toiling or gambling in remote mountain gulches.

Naturally, at appropriate places along this river, landings were established, and here and there, at economically strategic places like The Dalles, for example, towns arose. Eastward of The Dalles, in the Walla Walla Valley near the site of the abandoned

[37] 40th Cong., 2nd sess., H. Ex. Doc. 160, XIV, 202; *Seattle Intelligencer*, Dec. 2, 1867; *Pacific Tribune*, Sept. 12, 1868, quoting the Portland *Commercial*; Oliphant, "Cattle Trade on Puget Sound," pp. 145-49.

Whitman missionary station at Waiilatpu, and adjacent to an American military post established in 1856, the town of Walla Walla (at first called Steptoeville) arose. Before the end of 1859, this town, situated "half a mile from the garrison," contained "ten stores, two hotels, [and] a dozen gambling and drinking saloons."[38] In the prescient opinion of a former missionary, presumably the Reverend Cushing Eells, the delightful region in which Steptoeville was situated was pictured as one which, because of its "inexhaustible prairies of the finest grass and its mild climate," would soon become a "vast storehouse for untold herds of cattle, sheep and horses," and thus be "the supplying point for the multitudes that . . . [would] flock every year, from the Willamette and Rogue river valleys and from California, to the Northern mines."[39]

Still farther eastward, at the confluence of the Snake and the Clearwater rivers, and not far from the abandoned Spalding missionary station, the townsite of Lewiston was "laid off" on the Nez Percé Reservation in October, 1861. By June, 1862, this town, situated at the head of steamboat navigation on the Snake River, had become a thriving and "progressive" place, with a population of "eight hundred to one thousand." To serve these people, as well as those who now were, or soon would be, living in mining communities, it had three drug stores, two jewelry stores, six hotels, seven attorneys, nine doctors, "twenty-five liquor saloons, about ten gambling establishments, and about twenty places whose names might put the paper to blush." In this new and progressive town of Lewiston, the cost of living was high, for in June, 1862, flour was selling for twenty-five cents a pound, butter for one dollar a pound, fresh beef for eighteen to twenty-five cents a pound, and whiskey for three to five dollars a gallon.

From a letter written in Lewiston in June, 1862, we get a glimpse of the importance of this town. Boats from "below," we are told,

arrive [here] twice a week, and bring about eight hundred tons [of] assorted merchandise per month, and from one hundred and fifty to two hundred tons are brought by wagons and pack animals. All this goes off rapidly, and

[38] "The Walla Walla Region," New York *Home Missionary*, XXXIII (June, 1860), 31.
[39] *Ibid.*

the sales are estimated at from one hundred and fifty to two hundred thousand dollars per week. These figures look large for a place grown up this spring, but it is the principal out-fitting place for a large mining country, and a mining population of fifteen or twenty thousand. The streets are filled with wagons and pack-trains.[40]

From The Dalles,[41] Walla Walla (Steptoeville),[42] and Lewiston, as well as from landings on the Columbia River at Umatilla, Wallula, and White Bluffs, supplies were carried by pack trains to mines in British Columbia; to mines on the Clearwater River, on the Salmon River, on the Powder River, on the Owyhee River, and in Boise Basin; and, presently, to mines in the western part of the present state of Montana. Moreover, wherever it was practicable to do so—as, for example, on the Mullan Road (completed in 1862) which connected Fort Walla Walla and Fort Benton, and on roads from Walla Walla, Lewiston, and landings on the Columbia River to mines in Idaho—both ox teams and mule teams were used to draw freight wagons. From all these places cattle and other livestock were driven to supply fresh meat to various mining districts of the "upper country." Drovers, like packers, were supplying essential wants of all these mining communities.

By 1860 the part of the river that served these various routes to the mining districts was falling into the grasp of a powerful monopoly called the Oregon Steam Navigation Company, which soon used its control of the Cascades and The Dalles–Celilo portages to shut out all competition by steamboats between Portland

[40] Observer, writing from "Lewiston, W. T., June 18, 1862," in the *Weekly Oregonian*, July 28, 1862; Commissioner of Indian Affairs, *Report* (1862), p. 567.

[41] From the booming Dalles City, Veritas, on April 20, 1863, wrote as follows: "Some idea may be formed of the number of men and amount of freight going from here direct to the mines overland, from the fact that an average of 200 pack animals and from ten to twelve freight wagons, carrying from 3,000 [to] 5,000 pounds each, leave town daily, and miners probably average not less than 150 per day, bound in various directions. For some time past John Day river mines appear to have carried the day with most of them, though many are bound for Boise." Salem *Oregon Statesman*, May 4, 1863.

[42] "A large number of persons have left this city [Walla Walla] during the week for Powder River. The majority of them have left on foot, taking only a small amount of provisions with them. They hope to be met there by pack teams from the Dalles." Walla Walla *Washington Statesman*, April 5, 1862. As late as June, 1874, "large droves of cattle" were "weekly passing through La Grande en route to the mines of Union and Baker counties and of Idaho." *Sacramento Daily Union*, June 9, 1874.

and the country east of the Cascades. Nor was this company satisfied with what it had thus far acquired.[43] In 1865, in an effort to get the trade to the Big Bend mines in British Columbia, it launched and operated on the upper Columbia River the steamboat *Forty-Nine,* which plied across the international boundary; it also, in the later 1860's, operated boats on Lake Pend Oreille and on Clark's Fork of the Columbia as links in a chain of communication from the Columbia River to the mines in western Montana; and it even attempted to navigate the tortuous waters of the Snake River above Lewiston.[44] This monopoly persisted, and through the decade of the 1870's, when placer mining in the Pacific Northwest had for the most part been abandoned to Chinese gleaners, the O.S.N. levied a heavy tribute on settlers in eastern Washington. "Like a serpent," as one editor in southeastern Washington wrote in 1878, "the O.S.N. drags its weary length up and down the Columbia and Snake rivers, winding its cold blighting coils around the growing industries of this young and thrifty country. It aims its deadly fangs at each and all who dare to oppose its most heartless and damnable rules and schemes."[45]

Stockmen who sold cattle and other livestock to the miners were not entirely at the mercy of this monopoly. Although large numbers of cattle were sent up the Columbia River on steamboats during the 1860's, perhaps even larger numbers of cattle during that decade, and later, were driven long distances from the valleys of western Oregon through passes in the Cascade Mountains[46] to rich grasslands lying between the Cascades and the

[43] T. C. Elliott, *The Dalles-Celilo Portage: Its History and Influence* (Portland, Ore., 1915), pp. 25-38.

[44] Trimble, *Mining Advance,* p. 127. In a letter from Portland, Ore., July 20, 1867, J. C. Ainsworth wrote to Lieutenant Colonel R. S. Williamson, saying: "There are now three steamboats navigating Clark's fork of the Columbia, from the foot of Pend d'Oreille lake to Thompson falls." 40th Cong., 2nd sess., H. Ex. Doc. 1, II, Part 2, 510.

[45] Dayton *Columbia Chronicle,* May 11, 1878.

[46] Earle K. Stewart, "Transporting Livestock by Boat up the Columbia, 1861-1868," *OHQ,* L (December, 1949), 251-59. On the driving of cattle through passes in the Cascades, see Robert W. Sawyer, "Beginnings of the McKenzie Highway, 1862," *OHQ,* XXXI (September, 1930), 261-68; *Oregon Statesman,* June 10, 1865; Jacksonville *Oregon Sentinel,* June 29, 1867; Silver City, Ida., *Owyhee Avalanche,* Nov. 23, 1867, quoting The Dalles *Mountaineer.* As early as July 1, 1871, the *Morning Oregonian* reported that more than "3,000 cattle have been driven over the Cascade mountains from Linn county this year."

Rockies, there to graze while en route to the mining country; and from time to time herds of these cattle from grazing districts in the Walla Walla, Klickitat, and Yakima valleys and other places beat trails northward to Cariboo and Kootenay and eastward or southeastward to the Salmon River, the Owyhee River, and the Boise Basin. The men who owned these herds, like the stockmen engaged contemporaneously in the Puget Sound cattle trade, needed pasture grounds for their cattle en route to market; but the men who took cattle from western Oregon across the Cascades came upon spacious pastures where their cattle could graze, without cost to their owners, the year through in preparation for their final journey to markets either northward or eastward.

The principal overland route of American packers and drovers to British Columbia was pioneered in 1858 and 1859 by David McLoughlin, Joel Palmer, and Major Mortimer Robinson.[47] Thereafter the trade by this route increased greatly. From The Dalles, from the Walla Walla and Yakima valleys, and perhaps from other places, pack trains and cattle were moved to the Okanogan Valley, and thence northward across the boundary by a route formerly used by the Hudson's Bay Company.[48] By 1862 the need for American meat at British Columbia mines had become so urgent that the provincial governor, Sir James Douglas, specifically directed "the Gold Commissioner of Shimilcomeen [sic] to encourage the importation of sheep and cattle from the Southern frontier. Two or three thousand head of live cattle driven into the mines [he said] would effectually relieve us for the present year and I expect that number of cattle at least."[49] This expectation was no doubt fulfilled, for in a book published a year later a British writer affirmed that "the upper country" of

[47] Stanley S. Spaid, "The Later Life and Activities of General Joel Palmer," OHQ, LV (December, 1954), 313-14; Weekly Oregonian, Sept. 4, 1858; Oregon Statesman, Aug. 2, 1859.

[48] For a description of this route, see the letter of Lieutenant H. Spencer Palmer to Colonel R. C. Moody, Nov. 23, 1859, in Further Papers Relative to the Affairs of British Columbia, III (London, 1860), 83-84. A typescript of George Masiker's diary of a trip by this route with a band of horses from Oregon to the Fraser River in 1862 is in the library of the University of Oregon.

[49] Sir James Douglas to the Lord Bishop, British Columbia, May 19, 1862, in a typed copy of Douglas' Private Official Letter Book, 1859-64 (MSS in the Provincial Library, Victoria, B.C.).

British Columbia was supplied with cattle driven overland from Washington Territory. Droves of cattle, he said, were purchased in Oregon and then driven

by the Dalles, Columbia River, Okanagan River, Osooyos Lake, western shore of Okanagan Lake, Thompson River, Buonaparte River, and thence to the Cariboo country. The profit obtained by persons employed in this business [he said] is very large, as may be seen at once from the fact that beasts purchased in Oregon at $10 per head are sold three or four months afterwards in the north at $50 per head, and cost literally nothing for food by the way.[50]

The Cariboo market came to be greatly prized by cattlemen south of the border. To meet the demand of this market and of another mining market recently opened south of the border in the Nez Percé country, cattle, by the early spring of 1861, were moving rapidly and in considerable numbers from western Oregon, some of them by boat up the Columbia River and others overland through passes in the Cascades. The interest in this movement of livestock toward the "northern mines" is strikingly revealed in an article published in a Portland newspaper and reprinted in Victoria on March 2, 1861:

There are now 1500 head of beeves on the road from the Dalles to the northern mines. C. K. Dawson is here with 6000 dollars from the mines, buying cattle and mules for the upper mining country. There are 150 yoke of cattle on the way from this valley bound for the northern mines. Mr. Thomas has 200 head of beeves on the road for these mines; Murphy & Allen have started from the Clikitat [sic] valley with 300 head of beeves for the mines; Mr. Nott has 180 head of beeves on the Yakima, and 300 head in this valley, destined for the northern mines; John Todd & Grover have 300 head of beeves in Yamhill county, destined for the northern mines; Harry Love is now on the way with 150 head of beeves for the Nez Perce mines.[51]

The movement of cattle to Cariboo was continuous during 1861. On March 5 the Oregon Steam Navigation Company announced "greatly reduced rates" for conveying cattle up the Columbia to the Cascades or to The Dalles, and, perhaps in part because of this announcement, the Morning Oregonian could say on March 22 that, since its last weekly issue, it had been told that

[50] R. C. Lundin-Brown, British Columbia: An Essay (New Westminster, B.C., 1863), p. 21.
[51] British Colonist, March 2, 1861, quoting the Portland Times.

"about 1000 head of cattle . . . [had] passed the Cascades seeking a market in the mines of British Columbia and Washington Territory." In that year young Jack Splawn began his career taking cattle to British Columbia by helping to drive from the Yakima Valley to Cariboo a band of cattle belonging to Major John Thorp. Early in November "Mr. Knott, an Oregon drover, started from Portland with 1300 head of cattle for the Cariboo mines," intending to winter them "in the vicinity of Kamloops, and push forward to the diggings early in the spring." In December, 1861, a correspondent of the Walla Walla *Washington Statesman* wrote from The Dalles, saying that a large number of cattle were "brought up, at advanced prices, for the Cariboo market."[52]

During the next three years, while the Cariboo market was rising to its zenith, great numbers of cattle were moved from western Oregon to the country east of the Cascades. Many of them eventually went to Cariboo, but, because of the vague language used in describing this movement, we cannot tell precisely how many went to any one of the markets then available. But we do know that during 1862 there was a considerable movement of cattle eastward from the valleys of western Oregon, some by the Columbia River and others by overland routes. Occasionally, we learn the precise destination of a given band. We know, for example, that early in May of that year James Heatherly and A. J. Welch left Lane County "with 800 head of sheep and between three and 400 head of cattle for Cariboo." More often, however, we are merely told that bands of cattle were destined for the "northern mines," as was the case when, on May 12, 1862, Henry Fuller of Polk County crossed on the ferry at Portland "three hundred and sixty-five head of fine beef cattle . . . bound for the Northern mines." Whatever may have been the destination of such bands of cattle, a trustworthy newspaper estimated, on October 25, 1862, that 46,000 head of cattle had been taken from western Oregon across the Cascades during the preceding summer.[53] Since the Cariboo mines offered as rewarding a market as

[52] *Morning Oregonian*, March 22, April 3, 1861; A. J. Splawn, *Ka-mi-akin, Last Hero of the Yakimas* (2nd ed., Portland, Ore., 1944), p. 162; *British Colonist*, Nov. 9, 1861; *Washington Statesman*, Feb. 1, 1862.

[53] Portland *Pacific Christian Advocate*, May 10, 1862; Daniel M. Drumheller,

any in the northern mining country, we may presume that the drovers did not disregard Governor Douglas' encouragement to seek that market.

The Cariboo market continued to be an attractive one to American drovers. Some cattle from Oregon went there in 1863, and perhaps even more in 1864. On January 24, 1864, a correspondent of a Victoria newspaper wrote from Richfield to inform "enterprising cattle drivers" that not more than "about forty head of cattle" were available in that market, and that in Richfield beef was selling for sixty-five cents a pound. Less than a month later, however, this correspondent could write that, because "a large herd of cattle [had] arrived on the creek a few days since," the price of beef had fallen to fifty cents a pound. Subsequently, other herds must have arrived at those mines, for in Richfield on June 1, 1864, it was reported that on Williams Creek fresh meat was worth only forty cents a pound.[54] Meanwhile, many persons had gone from the Walla Walla Valley to the Willamette Valley to purchase cattle and horses for the upper country, and early in May, 1864, a Walla Walla newspaper observed that large droves of cattle and sheep were "still crossing the mountains from the Willamette, destined for the various mining regions of the upper country." A few weeks later, Johnson and Calvin had arrived in the Walla Walla Valley with a band of 497 head of cattle which they had driven from the Umpqua Valley. Still earlier in that year, cattle in large numbers were sent by boat from Portland up the Columbia River, and several herds were driven from the Rogue River Valley into eastern Oregon. One of these herds, as the Jacksonville *Oregon Intelligencer* reported on May 7, 1864, would "leave in a few days for the John Day, Boise and Owyhee mines by way of the Rogue River road, across the Cascade Mountains." Nevertheless, despite this heavy eastward movement from western Oregon, cattle ready for slaughter were scarce in the

---

"Uncle Dan" Drumheller Tells Thrills of Western Trails in 1854 (Spokane, Wash., 1925), pp. 66-67; *Weekly Oregonian*, May 17, Oct. 25, 1862.

[54] *British Colonist*, Feb. 16, March 8, June 21, 1864. In its issue for June 28, 1864, the *British Colonist* says: "Mr. Thos. Manifee, of Williams Lake, started about 10 days ago from the Dalles with 300 head of cattle for Cariboo. Beedy (since arrived) had also started with a large drove some days before."

Walla Walla Valley in November, 1864, partly because most of the cattle had been driven into that valley too late to be fattened for the fall market.

One such herd, which came into the Walla Walla Valley in midsummer of 1864, was ready to set out for the Cariboo market in May, 1865. Other herds also left for the Cariboo market in 1865, and in August some drovers, returning to Walla Walla after having driven a band to Thompson River, reported selling their cattle for seventy dollars a head to Cariboo butchers, who had met them at the river. They also reported that at Thompson River as many as two thousand head of cattle were awaiting a market.[55]

By this time the Cariboo market was beginning to decline, and by 1868 it had ceased to exist.[56] But in British Columbia as a whole the market continued strong through 1866, for in 1864 the British Columbia mining market had broadened to include the Kootenay mines. By the summer of 1864, as Judge F. W. Howay has told us, there were probably one thousand men at White Horse Creek, who received most of their supplies, including beef, from Walla Walla, Lewiston, and Wallula; but some of their beef cattle came from places as far away as Salt Lake City. Within two years, however, the yield of these mines had declined so much that the white miners were rapidly selling their claims to Chinese gleaners.[57]

But the mining market in British Columbia was not yet played out for American drovers. As we have seen, gold had been discovered on bars in the northern Big Bend of the Columbia River as early as 1864, and in 1865 there was a considerable movement of miners from Colville to this region. According to the report of the American consul in Victoria, made on January 10, 1866, the discovery of new mines in this region, late in 1865, was expected to make the Big Bend mines the attraction of 1866. He was largely

[55] *Washington Statesman*, Feb. 27, May 6, July 22, 1864; *Weekly Oregonian*, March 19–May 21, 1864; *Walla Walla Statesman* (formerly *Washington Statesman*), Nov. 18, 1864, May 5, Aug. 18, 1865.
[56] Splawn, *Ka-mi-akin*, p. 290.
[57] Howay, *British Columbia*, p. 165; *Washington Statesman*, Nov. 14, 1863, March 5–June 10, 1864; *Walla Walla Statesman*, Sept. 21, 1866; Seattle *Puget Sound Weekly*, Oct. 1, 1866.

right, but the testing of these mines in that year proved to be disheartening.[58]

Yet, despite this discouragement, the American trade in cattle and other commodities to eastern British Columbia seemed to be worth keeping. Between March 1 and December 1, 1866, the deputy collector of customs at the Little Dalles of the Columbia reported shipments to British Columbia of livestock from Oregon and from Washington Territory, via the Yakima Valley and "Soogoos Lake," amounting to 2,754 head of sheep, 2,265 head of cattle, 483 horses, 43 mules, 1,132 pack animals, and 264 saddle horses. These animals were valued at $348,292.[59] But thereafter, it appears, the trade to the northern mines began to dwindle. Nevertheless, in April, 1867, and again in July, 1868, the steamboat *Forty-Nine* was carrying cattle and other things up the Columbia River from the Little Dalles to the Big Bend mines.[60] The American trade to the Kootenay district, moreover, had not entirely disappeared by this time. In 1867 cattle were driven from the Walla Walla Valley to the Kootenay mines, and cattle which had crossed the Cascade Mountains from the Rogue River Valley were grazing on the Klamath Plain, preparatory to being sent to the northern mines.[61] Five years later Joseph Freeman set out from Walla Walla with 250 head of cattle for this country, but sold there only about half of his band. While returning with the remainder, he met and purchased a drove of 500 head of cattle en route from Colville to Montana, which he took to a range on the Snake River. He reported that "large numbers of Texas cattle" had been driven to Kootenay, where they "sell very low." In 1876

[58] The Dalles *Daily Mountaineer*, Dec. 15, 1865; Howay, *British Columbia*, pp. 167-69; 39th Cong., 1st sess., H. Ex. Doc. 56 (Serial 1260), X, 113-16; *Walla Walla Statesman*, March 2, 9, 23, June 1, 1866.

[59] J. Ross Browne, *Report on the Mineral Resources of the States and Territories West of the Rocky Mountains* (Washington, D.C., 1868), p. 559.

[60] *Walla Walla Statesman*, Dec. 8, 1865, May 4, 11, 18, Aug. 10, 1866, July 31, 1868; letter of D. J. Schnebly from "Spokane Bridge, July 3, 1868," in the Helena *Montana Post*, July 31, 1868; J. C. Ainsworth to R. S. Williamson, July 20, 1867, in 40th Cong., 2nd sess., H. Ex. Doc. 1, II, Part 2, 510. The *Forty-Nine* was dismantled in 1878. *Morning Oregonian*, June 21, 1878.

[61] *Sacramento Daily Union*, Oct. 11, 1867, quoting the *Walla Walla Statesman*; *Oregon Sentinel*, June 29, 1867.

Kootenay was receiving cattle from Flat Head Lake and from Bonner's Ferry.[62]

To help meet the needs of the mining markets both north and south of the international boundary, cattle drives from California began relatively early in the history of placer mining in the Pacific Northwest. As Asa S. Mercer wrote in later years, the miners in this region "had to be fed, and a few enterprising ranch men from California hastened thither with large herds of beef steers."[63] The heavy losses of cattle in Oregon and Washington during the winter of 1861-62 no doubt stimulated this movement of cattle from California, for in March, 1862, a newspaper in Walla Walla was quoting The Dalles *Mountaineer* as saying that "large trains of mules and droves of cattle are now on the way from California for Salmon River and the Cariboo country." This movement continued, and, beginning in 1864, when California was still distressed by a heavy drought and when cattlemen of that state were much exasperated by a recently enacted "herd" law, this northern market and the grasslands of eastern Oregon and eastern Washington became attractive "outlets" for their starving herds.[64] We get a further glimpse of this movement when we read of the arrival in the Walla Walla Valley in July, 1865, of some four hundred head of cattle from California; and a letter written in Wallula in August, 1866, provides an interesting, though narrow, perspective of the driving of cattle from California to the northern mines during the preceding six or seven years. Here we are told that 650 head of cattle belonging to Jerome Harper and J. H. Parsons had recently arrived at Wallula from Marysville, California, and had safely swum the Snake River. This herd was en route to Cariboo. Harper and Parsons were said to be "heavy cattle dealers" who, since 1860, had been driving from "600 to 1,000 head every year" from California to British Columbia.[65]

[62] *Mountaineer*, Aug. 17, 1872, quoting the *Walla Walla Union*; *Morning Oregonian*, Nov. 23, 1876.

[63] A. S. Mercer, "The Cattle Industry of California," in U. S. Bureau of Animal Industry, *Third Annual Report* (1886), p. 240.

[64] *Washington Statesman*, March 29, 1862, quoting from the *Mountaineer*; *Sacramento Daily Union*, Feb. 27, March 2, 3, 30, April 11, June 13, 1864; *Red Bluff Semi-Weekly Independent*, June 16, 1864.

[65] *Walla Walla Statesman*, July 28, 1865, Aug. 17, 1866.

In eastern Oregon and eastern Washington some California herds mingled with western Oregon or western Washington herds to form a growing "pool" of cattle, which, after 1861, helped to supply beef to mining communities north and south of the international border. Among the men whose cattle were destined for American communities were J. M. Blossom, of Portland, who crossed the Willamette River at Portland on April 25, 1863, with a large drove of cattle for the Salmon River mines; W. C. Hill, also of Portland, who passed through Walla Walla at the beginning of May in that year with another drove for the Salmon River market; and others who, early in June 1862, drove several large bands through Walla Walla "on their way to the Salmon River and South Fork mines."[66] But most of the cattle which crossed the Cascades during the early and middle years of the 1860's, or which came up from California in those years, were simply headed for the grazing country east of the Cascades—a country which, as many reports said, was blessed with a salubrious climate and widely distributed pasture lands made beautiful by waving grasses. From these luscious pastures, bands of cattle were driven to whichever mining market seemed to be the most attractive at the moment.

The Walla Walla Valley, because of its favorable geographical position, relatively mild climate, and abundant facilities for farming and grazing, played an important part in the provisioning of the northern mining country. Numerous herds of cattle left this valley en route to markets at the mines, and numerous pack and wagon trains from the town of Walla Walla carried freight for the mining markets. For supplying the mines with provisions, Walla Walla had, as a correspondent wrote from Florence in August, 1862, "the advantage of Oregon by the difference in freight from Portland to Walla Walla," and for that reason, as he told the people of the Walla Walla community, "every available acre [of their land] should be used next season by ... [their] farmers."[67] But Walla Walla had eager competitors in the trade to the mining districts.

[66] *Weekly Oregonian*, April 26, 1862; *Washington Statesman*, May 3, June 14, 1862.
[67] *Washington Statesman*, Sept. 13, 1862.

By 1863, trade to the mines in Idaho was brisk and competition was keen, for in the Boise Basin, in the late spring of that year, beef was selling at twenty-five cents a pound. Early in March a team of eighty-two pack mules left The Dalles for the Boise mines with freight valued at six thousand dollars, and in December, 1863, when several teams were leaving Walla Walla with freight for Boise, pack trains also were leaving Umatilla for Boise with freight being carried at the rate of forty cents a pound. Meanwhile, two trains of provisions, one of fourteen ox teams and the other of twenty-three wagons, had arrived at Bannock (later Idaho City) from Salt Lake City. The first of these, which arrived in October, brought flour "and almost every article in the grocery and provision line needed in the mines." Its coming lowered the price of flour to twenty-four cents a pound, although "Oregon flour" continued to bring twenty-seven cents a pound. The second of these trains, which arrived from Salt Lake City several weeks later, carried a great deal of flour, which cost $3.50 a hundred pounds in Salt Lake City and which brought $31.00 a hundred pounds in Bannock. These routes are highly important to our present study, for ordinarily the routes of pack teams and of freight wagons were also followed by drovers. Presumably, one of the above-mentioned routes from Oregon and Washington had been used by General Joel Palmer, of Yamhill County, Oregon, who was at Bannock City in July, 1863, with a band of cattle to be slaughtered.[68]

A year later the competition in the trade of both livestock and goods to the Idaho mines was still strong. Early in April of 1864 large bands of cattle, some of which were headed for the Boise and Owyhee mines, were moving between The Dalles and Walla Walla; a few days later Stone and Boggs started from Walla Walla with a herd of cattle for Boise; and late in May of that year "Ball and Russel's train of ox-teams" was en route from Walla Walla for Boise. Also in that year, the direct trade from California to the Boise mines had become noticeable, and in May, 1864, according to the editor of a Sacramento newspaper, the use of the "trail

[68] Ibid., April 18, 1863; Morning Oregonian, Oct. 31, Dec. 9, 19, 30, 1863; Oregon Argus, Aug. 10, 1863.

from Red Bluff" to these mines was "unabated." On this route during the first two weeks of May in that year, "2,300 head of cattle and 5,500 head of sheep . . . passed through Battle Creek, all bound Boiseward. The Goose Creek route is the one most generally taken." In August of 1864 another party from California reached Boise via this route, with several hundred head of cattle, having lost a considerable number in an Indian attack in southern Oregon.[69]

By May, 1865, several large droves of cattle had been started from Walla Walla toward Boise, and at about the same time the Eugene *Review* reported that "two large droves . . . [had] crossed the Cascades from the Willamette . . . [that] spring—one by the McKenzie and the other by the Middle Fork Road." In that year also, as Jack Splawn has told us, several hundred head of cattle were driven from the Yakima Valley to the mines in Idaho.[70]

But 1866 provides a most interesting glimpse of the widespreading competition for the trade to the mines in Idaho and in Montana. In the early days of May, an editor in Sacramento affirmed that wagon trains from California had reached Owyhee, and that the editor of the *Idaho World* was therefore exulting in the belief that the Oregon Steam Navigation Company "was got." Some two weeks later the same Sacramento editor was saying that 28 teams, "carrying 145,716 pounds of freight, had left Red Bluff for Idaho," traveling by "the Tehama county wagon road to Susanville"; and on June 22 he quoted from a letter in which the editor of the *Walla Walla Statesman* was told that cattle, horses, and sheep were on the way to the Blackfoot mines in Montana by the way of Lake Coeur d'Alene, in northern Idaho. Also in 1866, as Jack Splawn tells us, Benjamin Snipes drove 1,000 head of cattle from Yakima to the Blackfoot mines. About the middle of July the editor of the *Walla Walla Statesman* noted that William McEnnery had just brought up from southern Oregon 300 head

[69] *Washington Statesman*, April 2, 23, May 27, 1864; *Sacramento Daily Union*, May 19, Sept. 9, 1864. On the trade from California to the mines in Idaho in 1864, see also the *Shasta Courier*, Feb. 27, March 12, 1864, and Throckmorton, *Oregon Argonauts*, p. 262. But in this trade California had competition from the Mississippi Valley. *Napa Register*, Napa City, Calif., Sept. 24, 1864, quoting the *Boise News*.
[70] *Walla Walla Statesman*, May 12, 1865; Splawn, *Ka-mi-akin*, pp. 221-24.

of cattle which he intended to "winter" at his place in the upper
Walla Walla Valley, and then planned to drive them to the Blackfoot mines in the spring of 1867; and a few days later the same
editor published a letter in which the author asserted that Wallula was "full of goods for Blackfoot," and that these goods were
"being rapidly hurried away on pack trains."[71]

A few weeks later, in Virginia City, the editor of the *Montana
Post* commented on the arrival, between September 23 and 26, of
twenty-four wagons bringing to Virginia City goods from places
as far distant as Nebraska City, Omaha, St. Joseph, and Great Salt
Lake; and, in November, 1866, he noted the arrival in Virginia
City of provisions and goods from Great Salt Lake and the arrival
in Helena of "a large quantity of goods" brought from Walla
Walla "on the backs of mules."[72]

Finally, in a memorial in which the legislature of Washington
Territory implored the Congress to improve the Mullan Road so
that it could be used by wagons, we find a summary statement
about the movement of livestock and goods during 1866 from the
Columbia River to Montana. Here the assertion is made that, between January 1 and November 15, 1866, five thousand head of
cattle had been driven from Walla Walla to Montana, and that
six thousand mules "had left the Columbia River and Walla Walla
loaded with freight for Montana."[73] Some of this freight, no
doubt, had been carried from White Bluffs, for the Surveyor-General of Washington Territory reported that "a considerable part of
the trade of the Columbia River" since the opening of the mines
in Montana, "instead of ending at Wallula," had been carried up
the river to the neighborhood of White Bluffs.[74] A year later, as
the era of placer mining in the Pacific Northwest was drawing to
a close, trading to some of the mines in this region was brisk.
From March to June, 1867, steamers were busy transporting cattle
and other livestock up the Columbia, and in March of that year
The Dalles *Mountaineer* quoted a man who was well "posted" in

    [71] *Sacramento Daily Union*, May 8, 22, June 22, 1866; *Walla Walla Statesman*,
July 13, Aug. 17, 1866; Splawn *Ka-mi-akin*, p. 289.
    [72] *Montana Post*, Sept. 29, Nov. 3, 10, 24, 1866.
    [73] *Statutes of the Territory of Washington, 1866-67* (Olympia, 1867), p. 237.
    [74] Commissioner of the General Land Office, *Report* (1866), p. 498.

such matters to the effect that at least three hundred thousand dollars would be paid during that season to the "cow counties" west of the Cascades for cattle to be taken "east of the mountains."[75]

Week by week the *Oregonian* chronicled this movement, affirming as early as March 30 that the driving from the Willamette Valley had become "immense." During the week of April 13, steamers carried from Portland to The Dalles 430 head of cattle, 500 head of sheep, and 135 head of horses and mules. At the beginning of May, cattle were "still coming," another big drove having arrived in Portland from the Willamette Valley "to be taken up the Columbia"; and on May 11 the *Oregonian* said that, during the preceding week, steamers carried from Portland to The Dalles 1,000 head of cattle and large numbers of other livestock. Four weeks later it reported that 607 head of cattle, 1,887 head of sheep, and some horses and hogs arrived at The Dalles from Portland during the first week in June. As early as mid-March a perceptive observer in Wallula remarked that the spring "droves of cattle" were beginning to come in. Already, he said, more than 600 head from the Willamette Valley had passed Wallula on the way to the Nez Percé country, and he had heard that others, "destined for this country," were being brought from Portland. Moreover, he continued, "Cattle which have wintered in this vicinity . . . will soon be put on the move for the Montana market, . . . [and] cattle from the Yakima Valley will take the same route." Some cattle in this eastward movement of 1867 were destined for the Boise country. In Boise City on May 10, 1867, a correspondent remarked that horses in that market were "very high," and that cattle also were in demand; but he believed that there were "sufficient droves on the road to make a change in that quarter."[76]

The extent of the eastward movement of livestock to mining markets in 1867, as revealed in a report of the federal government in 1868, was described succinctly in these words:

From the first of March to the 15th of July there were shipped on steam-

[75] Quoted in the *Weekly Oregonian*, March 30, 1867.
[76] *Ibid.*, April 20, May 4, 11, June 8, 1867; *Walla Walla Statesman*, March 22, May 17, 1867.

boats from Portland to [The] Dalles 12,191 head of cattle and horses, 6,284 head of sheep, and 1,594 head of hogs. There has no doubt been an equal number driven across the Cascade Mountains during the months of July and August, all intended for feeding, accumulating, and marketing . . . in the different mining camps of Idaho, Montana, Washington, eastern Oregon, and British Columbia.[77]

By the end of 1868, much of the excitement arising from placer mining in the Oregon Country east of the Cascade Mountains had subsided; and a year later the first continental railroad was completed, causing the greater part of the trade to markets in western Montana to move northward from railheads in Utah.[78] Accordingly, the year 1868, which marked the beginning of a new era in the economic history of Montana, witnessed also, interestingly enough, the beginning of a new era in the economic history of the Pacific Northwest. In that region, the area of pasture land west of the Cascades—especially in the Willamette Valley—was shrinking, and the area of cultivated land was expanding; and the great open expanse between the Cascades and the Rockies was emerging as an area which, for nearly two decades, would have as one of its principal concerns the breeding of cattle and other livestock. To the rise of this new country we must now give attention.

[77] Browne, *Report on Mineral Resources*, p. 580.
[78] *Montana Post*, Sept. 25, 1868, quoting the *Chicago Tribune* of Sept. 4, 1868; *ibid.*, Oct. 30, 1868; Alton B. Oviatt, "Steamboat Traffic on the Upper Missouri River," *PNQ*, XL (April, 1949), 104-5; Throckmorton, *Oregon Argonauts*, p. 275. See also William E. Lass, *A History of Steamboating on the Upper Missouri River* (Lincoln, Neb., 1962), and on "Freighting Northward" from Utah, see also the *Corrine Daily Utah Reporter*, Aug. 17, 1870, April 5, 1873.

CHAPTER III

The Rise of Transcascadia

The intermontane country of the Pacific Northwest, an area that had been acquiring a peculiar significance during the affluent years of placer mining, is here being called Transcascadia. The reason is not far to seek, for this area—stretching eastward from the Cascades to the Rockies, northward from the forty-second to the forty-ninth parallel, and lying, for the most part, within the drainage system of the Columbia River and its tributaries—possesses neither the physiographical nor the economic unity that would suggest for it a more appropriate name. In the opinion of physiographers, the heart of this area is the Columbia Intermontane Province, of which the principal subdivision is the Columbia Basin. Adjoining this province on the north are the Okanogan Highlands, a subdivision of the Rocky Mountain Province, which also includes northern and central Idaho and western Montana; and adjoining it on the south is a part of the Basin and Range Province extending "northward of the Nevada-Oregon boundary for about 160 miles, and . . . [embracing] not far from 16,000 square miles of the central and southern portions of Oregon."[1] The totality of all this diversity,

[1] Otis W. Freeman and Howard H. Martin (eds.), *The Pacific Northwest: An Overall Appreciation* (2nd ed.; New York, 1954), pp. 65-78, 79-87; Israel C. Russell, "A Geological Reconnaissance in Southern Oregon," *Fourth Annual Report of the United States Geological Survey . . . 1882-3* (Washington, D.C., 1884), p. 435.

the middle and the upper Oregon of earlier years, in this study, is being called Transcascadia. Here, on uplands and lowlands, on grasslands and sagelands, cattle in large numbers roamed freely the year round in scattered districts of a cattlemen's kingdom which flourished during the 1870's and much of the 1880's. It is here that we find the setting of the story which will now be told in this book.

In contrast to western Oregon and western Washington, the emerging Transcascadia was a land of light and variable rainfall, as it also was a land of great distances and striking contrasts. Its people knew no rainy season, but they did know of hot and thirsty lands, of rough and weary country wherein the shadow of a rock made glad the heart of a sojourner; and they also knew of dusty and exhausting ways to markets afar off. Moreover, people coming into Transcascadia perceived the contrast between timbered mountains and great open spaces, much of which was suitable only for pasture; but presently they would learn that some of the open country of their new home—especially the Walla Walla Valley and the fertile hills of the Palouse country in the eastern part of the Columbia Plateau—could be farmed without irrigation. They would perceive, also, that Transcascadia was a country not then effectively united by any one system of transportation. Because obstructions had made impossible the unbroken navigation of the Columbia River and its principal tributary, the Snake River, not all the people of this intermontane country could be served well by this system of rivers; but the people of the Columbia Basin, who had been served effectively, albeit expensively, during the 1860's by the company which controlled the navigation of these rivers, would continue during the 1870's to depend upon this company and thus look westward to Portland and to Puget Sound. The people of southeastern Oregon and of southern Idaho, however, people who had been served only in part by means of these rivers during the 1860's, would continue, more intently during the 1870's than in preceding years, to look eastward to Utah and southward to Nevada and California.

In other words, what had been true in respect to transportation in this intermontane country during the lush years of placer mining would continue for many years thereafter to be emphatically true of the Columbia Basin; but what had during this same time been true of southeastern Oregon and southern Idaho— areas which then had looked westward, eastward, and southward —would be only partly true after the completion of the first transcontinental railroad in 1869. For then Kelton and other towns in Utah began to serve the people of southern Idaho, as well as communities in western Montana, and then also Winnemucca, a town in northern Nevada, emerged and, for a few years, flourished as the economic capital of a large trading area comprising southeastern Oregon, southwestern Idaho, and a part of northern Nevada—an area which may conveniently be called the Winnemucca province. Presently we shall learn more about Winnemucca and the province that it served.

Notwithstanding its diversity, however, Transcascadia came to possess for the people of western Oregon and western Washington both a practical and an emotional unity as the eastern frontier of their settlements—a country standing in relation to them much as, in the eighteenth century, the piedmont and the Great Valley of Virginia had stood in relation to the people in the tidewater region of Virginia. In brief, the movement of people and their livestock across the Cascades from the valleys of western Oregon and western Washington was, in effect, "an eastward movement" of colonization—a reversal of the traditional American westward movement—an aspect of the first occupation of the transmontane country of the American far Northwest. Here, especially during the 1870's and 1880's, three streams of migration were converging: one coming overland from the East, another moving upward from California, and still another running eastward from the more recently settled country west of the Cascades. Of these, the most interesting, and for this study the most significant, was the one last named. To those who watched people from the valleys of western Oregon moving their cattle and other livestock by boat up the Columbia River, or driving their herds or flocks through the passes of the Cascades to grazing lands beyond, it must have appeared that "Old Oregon" was breaking up and moving eastward to Transcascadia, just as, earlier in that century, it had appeared to observers on the Atlantic seaboard that "Old

America" east of the Appalachians was breaking up and moving westward into the valley of the Ohio.[2]

In any event, Transcascadia did then become the "back country" of western Oregon and western Washington; and as such it acquired its first significance to the people west of the Cascades as their great pasture land. Even as late as April, 1887, the editor of the *Morning Oregonian*, observing that large numbers of young cattle were being shipped from the Willamette Valley to ranges east of the Cascades, remarked that the Willamette Valley had "become a sort of nursery for the ranges of the Inland Empire ... [for] calves can be raised here much better than there, while cattle cannot be matured as well in the Willamette as on those ranges."[3] This editor neglected, however, to remind his readers that such a migration eastward from the Willamette Valley and from other valleys of western Oregon had been in progress for more than twenty-five years, and that for more than a decade before 1887 western Oregon had been looking to the ranges of eastern Oregon for its supply of beef, just as, during the same period, the region of Puget Sound had been looking to the ranges of eastern Washington for its supply of beef.[4] Thus had the situation in the Oregon Country changed since the autumn of 1846, when, apart from a few fenced farms, the Willamette Valley was "a common range for cattle,"[5] and when the region of Puget Sound, still an open country, had but recently become American territory.

How many head of cattle and of other livestock had entered Transcascadia for the purpose of stocking ranges during the 1860's we have no means of finding out.[6] The number, however, appears to have been large. As early as April, 1861, the *Weekly Oregonian* reported that "numerous herds of cattle ... [were]

[2] See Morris Birkbeck, *Notes on a Journey in America, from the Coast of Virginia to the Territory of Illinois* (London, 1818), p. 25.

[3] Portland *Morning Oregonian*, April 25, 1887.

[4] Because the "east side" was so well suited for cattle raising, David Newson, in July, 1871, advised the keeping in western Oregon of only enough cattle for home use. Salem *Willamette Farmer*, July 29, 1871.

[5] "Report of Lieutenant Neil M. Howison on Oregon, 1846: A Reprint," *OHQ*, XIV (March, 1913), 52. Published originally in 30th Cong., 1st sess., H. Misc. Doc. 29.

[6] See, however, Earle K. Stewart, "Transporting Livestock by Boat up the Columbia, 1861-1868," *OHQ*, L (December, 1949), 251-59.

seeking pasturage in the upper country. This cattle trade ... is credited exclusively to the Willamette and Columbia valleys." Moreover, on October 4, 1862, an editor in Walla Walla estimated that seven thousand head of cattle had been brought into Oregon and Washington by immigrants crossing the plains in that year, and three weeks later the editor of the *Morning Oregonian* esti- mated that forty-six thousand head of cattle had entered Trans- cascadia from the west in 1862. Accordingly, on November 1, 1862, the editor of the Walla Walla *Washington Statesman*, by adding to the forty-six thousand head received from the settle- ments west of the Cascades those that had been "brought from below, and the large additions that have come in *via* the plains," concluded that there were then in Transcascadia more cattle than had been there before the devastating winter of 1861-62. As live- stock continued through subsequent years to come into this coun- try from both the east and the west, cattle were also being driven in from California. For example, in August, 1869, an observer in Salem, Oregon, in a communication to the editor of a newspaper in Sacramento, remarked that "many trains" were coming north from California, "searching for permanent homes in this valley, and the country of the Lakes, belonging part[ly] to your State, is filling up with a vigorous and energetic people who will follow agriculture somewhat, but devote themselves principally to stock raising."[7]

For a description of Transcascadia's pastoral resources, we turn to revealing passages written early in 1882 by the Reverend Har- vey K. Hines, a Methodist minister who had served his church east of the Cascades for many years, and who had watched the emergence, and at the time of this writing was witnessing some evidence of the decline, of pastoral Transcascadia. In language no doubt then familiar to all the inhabitants of the American Pacific Northwest, he wrote on the one hand of the "bunch grass country" and on the other hand of the "sage brush" country, say- ing on January 5, 1882, that

What we would call the "bunch grass country" is that lying between the

---

[7] *Morning Oregonian*, Oct. 22, 1862; Walla Walla *Washington Statesman*, Oct. 4, Nov. 11, 1862; "C," writing on Aug. 21, 1869, in the *Sacramento Daily Union*, Sept. 4, 1869.

Cascade and Blue mountain ranges, a distance east and west of 150 miles in round numbers, and from the Coeur d'Alene mountains to the high ridges that run from the Blue mountains westward, about a hundred miles south of the Columbia river, a distance north and south of not less than 250 miles. There are tracts within these limits that may be called "sage brush land," as a large part of the Yakima valley and the lower Snake river valley; but, in general, with these exceptions, it is covered with a comparatively clean growth of bunch grass. This country is in general two inclined tables, one sloping downward from the north, and the other from the south, and the Columbia river forming the line of their meeting. These tables are not plains but hilly slopes cut by streams and ravines, but with a general inclination as stated. The whole of it, with the exception of the Yakima valley, has also a westward inclination to conform it to the flow of the Columbia river which has a rapid current, and is the only drainage of that vast region.[8]

Two weeks later he turned his attention to another part of Transcascadia and remarked that

What we would call the "sage brush country" lies mostly east of the Blue mountains, and extends over nearly the whole of the main tributary valleys of the Snake river. . . .

Powder river valley, the great valley of Snake river from the mouth of Burnt river to Fort Hall, a distance of say four hundred miles, and with a width of fifty miles; and the Malheur plains and hills sweeping southward around the southern end of the Blue Mountain range, are mainly of this character. There are limited exceptions to this description, as where the hills rise to a great altitude they are covered with bunch grass, or in the lower bottoms along the streams they are set with either rye grass or a native red top and clover. Nor is the sage all the same. What is called the white sage predominates in some extensive tracts; but generally the black or gray sage gives a dull and leaden aspect to the landscape.

. . . This white sage is not the predominating characteristic of the sage brush land, but rather the exceptional. It is found in some large tracts, as on the north side of the Yakima river, but it is generally in small places, scattered here and there through all the sage brush region.

It may be said [that] this white sage furnishes remarkably nutritious winter forage for cattle, and the places where it flourishes best, are a kind of winter haven for the herds of the "cattle kings."[9]

[8] From an editorial entitled "The Bunch-Grass Land," in the Portland *Pacific Christian Advocate* of Jan. 5, 1882, quoted in the *Willamette Farmer*, Jan. 13, 1882.
[9] From an editorial entitled "Sage-Brush Land," in the *Pacific Christian Advo-*

What Hines called the bunch-grass country is essentially what many persons today would call the Columbia Basin—the middle Oregon of the early pioneers—and what he called the sagebrush country is essentially southeastern Oregon and the Snake River Valley east of the Blue Mountains. Apparently he omitted from his classification not only the northern and northeastern parts of the old Oregon Country, consisting of the Okanogan Highlands, northern Idaho, and western Montana, but also both the "desert" and the "Lake" country of south-central Oregon.

The first era of the colonization of Transcascadia was, as we have seen, an aspect of the mining advance into the Pacific Northwest; and by 1869 men and cattle were widely dispersed through this intermontane country of bunch grass and sagebrush. So rapid, indeed, had been the movement of cattle into this country after its opening late in 1858 that, by the time of the federal census of 1860, there were several thousand head of cattle in Wasco County, the only county in Oregon east of the Cascades at that time; and, north of the Columbia River, there were thousands more in the three counties of Washington Territory east of the Cascades—Klickitat, Yakima, and Walla Walla.[10] And the number was increasing.

The Walla Walla Valley, in the rich country of the Cayuse Indians, had, as we have learned, aroused the enthusiasm of the editor of the *Oregon Spectator* as early as 1848. Ten years later it had become a powerful loadstone which was attracting stockmen and settlers with their cattle and other livestock. On February 19, 1859, the *Weekly Oregonian* predicted that a "large amount of stock would be driven from the Willamette Valley to Walla Walla the coming season," and four days later the Portland *Standard* affirmed that "a very considerable emigration [was] flowing into

cate of Jan. 19, 1882, quoted in the *Willamette Farmer*, Jan. 20, 1882. For an excellent description of the white sage, see the report of E. S. Davis, surveyor-general of Nevada, on Oct. 8, 1872, in Commissioner of the General Land Office, *Report* (1872), p. 176. "After an occurrence of frost," Mr. Davis wrote, "horses, cattle, and sheep feed upon it with great avidity. It possesses great value for winter feeding."

[10] Portland *Weekly Oregonian*, Feb. 19, May 7, Oct. 8, 1859; *Sacramento Daily Union*, June 1, 1859, quoting the Portland *Daily News*; San Francisco *Daily Alta California*, June 20, 1860; *Eighth Federal Census*, 1860, Vol. II, *Agriculture* (Washington, D.C., 1864), pp. 120, 182.

... [the] rich lands" of the Walla Walla Valley. "From present indications," it said, there would be in this valley before the end of spring more than two thousand persons, many of them emigrants from the Willamette Valley.[11]

On April 2 of that year, the Reverend Henry H. Spalding, describing a very severe winter in Linn County, remarked that large numbers of people were "calculating" to leave that county for the "Nez Perces & Walla Walla countries"; and on April 25 General W. S. Harney, reporting from Fort Vancouver to the Assistant Adjutant General in New York City, affirmed that "some two thousand industrious and thriving settlers" were already in the Walla Walla Valley. One who had come from western Oregon, James W. Foster, had acquired a land claim at the base of the Blue Mountains, six miles east of the recently established army post called Fort Walla Walla.[12] By August, 1859, W. W. Chapman, surveyor-general of Oregon, reported that emigration from the Willamette Valley, from California, and from the Atlantic states was "tending" toward the region between the Cascades and the Blue Mountains, and that "thousands of cattle and horses" were also wending their way there. Within a month, he said, more than a hundred settlers were reported to have entered the Grande Ronde prairie. Finally, on the last day of September, 1859, a newspaper of Olympia, Washington, in commenting on the large immigration to Oregon and Washington, remarked that the Walla Walla Valley was reported to be "full of emigrants, having good American cattle and horses," and that other immigrants had taken claims on the Yakima and Klickitat rivers, "and all through the country, from the Dalles to the Simcoe reserve."[13]

The movement into Transcascadia continued through 1860. Before the end of August, a newspaper in Olympia quoted the Portland *Advertiser* as having learned that there were "fully forty thousand head of cattle in the Walla Walla and other valleys east

[11] Quoted in the *Sacramento Daily Union*, March 7, 1859.
[12] American Home Missionary Society, "Oregon Letters, 1859" (MSS in the Library of the Chicago Theological Seminary); Secretary of War, *Report* (1869), 36th Cong., 1st sess., S. Ex. Doc. 2, II, 96; James W. Foster to his father, May 19, 1859 (MS in the Philip Foster Collection, Oregon Historical Society, Portland).
[13] Commissioner of the General Land Office, *Report* (1859), p. 346; Olympia *Pioneer and Democrat*, Sept. 30, 1859.

of the Cascades." Many of these no doubt were in Klickitat County and the Yakima Valley, into which, as we have seen, cattle had first been driven during the preceding year; and farther south, near the northern border of California, cattle were being grazed, as early as the winter of 1858-59, in what today is Klamath County, Oregon. But settlement here did not begin until after 1860.[14]

During the next few years, stockmen and settlers moved rapidly into widely dispersed districts of eastern Oregon, taking with them large numbers of cattle. There were cattle in northeastern Oregon during the severe winter of 1861-62, and, as we already have learned, many thousand head of cattle were presumed to have been driven eastward across the Cascades during the summer of 1862. There was no abatement of the movement. On February 20, 1864, the editor of the *Pacific Christian Advocate* wrote that, during the preceding week, "over four hundred passengers went up the Columbia, and some five hundred head of cattle and horses." Before the summer of 1864 was ended, it was reported that a band of cattle had been stolen in the "Harney Lake Valley." A year later cattle were said to be grazing on Indian Creek, near Canyon City, on the South John Day River, and, farther east, in the Weiser Valley of Idaho Territory; and in the winters of 1865-66 and 1866-67 cattle were reported to be dying in the Grande Ronde and Powder River valleys.[15]

By this time, moreover, cattle were widely dispersed in the country north of the Columbia River. At Dalles City, the principal "port of entry" of the Columbia Basin, large bands of sheep, horses, and cattle were crossing the Columbia River late in November, 1864, "to be driven to the rich pastures on the Yakima, Attanum and Keetatas." This, according to the editor of the *Daily Mountaineer*, was "a move in the right direction," for some of the

[14] *Pioneer and Democrat*, Aug. 24, 1860; A. J. Splawn, *Ka-mi-akin, Last Hero of the Yakimas* (2nd ed.; Portland, Ore., 1944), p. 287; *An Illustrated History of Central Oregon....* (Spokane, Wash., 1905), pp. 931, 938; *An Illustrated History of Klickitat, Yakima and Kittitas Counties...* (Chicago, 1904), pp. 93-94.

[15] Captain George B. Currey to the Acting Assistant Adjutant General, July 25, 1864, in *The War of the Rebellion: A Compilation of Official Records of the Union and Confederate Armies*. Series I (Washington, D.C., 1897), L, Pt. 1, 323; Salem *Oregon Statesman*, Jan. 23, 1865; *Walla Walla Statesman*, Jan. 5, 1866; Commissioner of Indian Affairs, *Report* (1867), pp. 95-96.

cattle then crossing the Columbia were "stock-cattle," whose owners intended "to locate" for the purpose of breeding live-stock. There were, he continued, "already fifteen families on the waters of the Yakima," and this number, he believed, would soon increase, because the "force of circumstances" would cause an overflow of livestock from the Willamette Valley "into this new country." In mid-August of 1866 this same editor, impressed by the continuing movement "up the Columbia" of livestock, espe-cially sheep, expressed the view that there would presently be an outpouring of livestock from the overstocked Willamette Valley into Washington Territory. There were then, he remarked, "about forty settlers on the waters of the Yakima." In the meantime, the Surveyor-General of Washington Territory had reported, in July, 1866, that the valleys of eastern Washington were gradually filling up with farmers, who expected to find markets for their products in mining districts northward and eastward.[16]

Meanwhile, south of the Columbia River, Indians drove away about three hundred head of cattle from Indian Creek, near Can-yon City, "in the mining region of the Blue Mountains," in Au-gust, 1865, and later in that year, and in 1866, they made other depredations upon cattle in northeastern Oregon and southern Idaho. In February, 1866, for example, they took cattle from Miller's ranch near the mouth of the Burnt River, cattle and horses from Hall's ranch in the Jordan Valley, and hundreds of head of livestock from Owyhee County, in southwestern Idaho; and in November of that year they drove cattle from a ranch on the South Fork of the John Day River and from the ranch of Dean and Bayley, on Dixie Creek, in Idaho Territory.[17] Thus we learn of widespread operations of cattlemen in northeastern Ore-gon and in southwestern Idaho; but their activities were not lim-ited to these areas. Farther south, cattle were grazing in the Lake region of Oregon. On September 1, 1866, Captain F. B. Sprague, writing from Fort Klamath to an editor in Jacksonville, remarked that, although the magnificent valley of Goose Lake was not yet

[16] The Dalles *Daily Mountaineer*, Nov. 24, 29, 1865; *Oregon Statesman*, Dec. 11, 1865; The Dalles *Weekly Mountaineer*, Aug. 17, 1866; 39th Cong., 2nd sess., H. Ex. Doc. 1 (Serial 1284), II, 498. See also the *Oregon Statesman*, July 9, 1866.
[17] Commissioner of Indian Affairs, *Report* (1867), pp. 95-101.

settled, Surprise Valley was "being very thickly settled." Here, he said, grain and vegetables of all kinds could be "grown in great abundance."[18]

Evidence of further expansion of cattle breeding in Transcascadia, and of the increasing prosperity of men engaged in this business, is revealed in records of 1867. North of the Columbia, as early as 1865, Yakima County had been organized, and by February, 1867, reports from the Yakima Valley not only disclosed the fact that there were "several large bands of stock in that valley," but also expressed the belief that "a large number of cattle would be driven there from the lower country during the coming spring." By the early summer of that year, news had reached The Dalles that cattle worth more than $150,000 had been sold in the Yakima Valley during the preceding year. Meanwhile, in the country south of the Columbia and Snake rivers, reports of Indian depredations in 1867 called attention to losses of cattle from places as widely separated as Ray's farm on Reynolds Creek in Owyhee County, Idaho, Clamo and Cooper's ranch on the John Day River in eastern Oregon, and Sinker Creek in southwestern Idaho.[19]

During the next two years, the expansion of the cattle business east of the Cascades was noticeable on both sides of the Columbia. By September, 1868, there was feverish buying of cattle in the Walla Walla Valley, and money was so plentiful there that it had given a "new impetus" to "all branches of business," and had created a general feeling that an "era of prosperity" was at hand. More than a month earlier it was reported that several prominent men had taken claims north of the Snake River, and in December, 1869, it was reported that a considerable number of families had settled on Union Flat, in present-day Whitman County, Washington.[20] Furthermore, by midsummer of 1869, a newspaper in Olympia, Washington, reported that William Wagner, of Yelm

[18] Jacksonville *Oregon Sentinel*, Sept. 16, 1866.
[19] *Walla Walla Statesman*, Feb. 22, June 14, 1867; Commissioner of Indian Affairs, *Report* (1867), pp. 101-2.
[20] *Walla Walla Statesman*, Aug. 7, Sept. 25, 1868, Dec. 4, 1869. On Sept. 15, 1869, the *Morning Oregonian* reported that the country lying east of the Colville Road, "from the mouth of the Palouse river to the Spokane river," was "attracting the attention of settlers."

Prairie, had set out with his family to engage in the "cattle raising business" in the Yakima Valley. For this purpose he was driving "about 100 head of cattle through the Nachez Pass." In that
year, moreover, the practice of driving cattle from the Yakima
Valley to the Kittitas Valley for summer grazing was begun, and
farther eastward parties from the Powder River Valley were buying stock cattle from ranchers in the Walla Walla and Umatilla
valleys.[21]

Meanwhile, the business of raising livestock in Wasco County,
Oregon, had become extensive by the spring of 1868. A settler
remarked on May 28 that, for the most part, the leading markets
of the Pacific Northwest were supplied with beef and mutton
from the grass-covered hills of Wasco. Even cattle dealers as far
away as Victoria, he was "credibly informed," were buying cattle
in the Willamette Valley, shipping them up the Columbia River
to be fattened on the Wasco hills, and then reshipping them down
the river for transfer to ocean steamers, which would carry them
to Victoria. In September of that year, E. L. Applegate, surveyor-
general of Oregon, reported that the country of north-central
Oregon bordering the Columbia, as well as the part drained by
the John Day, Deschutes, and Crooked rivers, was partly settled;
and in July, 1869, B. F. Prine, "just in from Ochoco Valley," told
the editor of the *Mountaineer* that new settlers "from west of the
mountains" were constantly arriving in the Ochoco Valley, and
that more than "two thousand head of horned cattle and several
thousand head of sheep" were then grazing in that area. An
editor in Salem, Oregon, learned that 10,656 head of cattle were
grazing in Umatilla County, farther up the Columbia.[22] Nearly
two years later, in August, 1871, Eunice Robbins wrote from
"Ochoco," saying, "Ochoco is settling up fast. New families are
coming in nearly every day, and many of the old settlers are selling their ranches at a large price—and moving farther back into
the mountains. Lower Ochoco has adopted the name of Prine

[21] Olympia *Echo*, Aug. 13, 1869; *Walla Walla Statesman*, Nov. 13, 1869; *Illus-
trated History of Klickitat, Yakima and Kittitas Counties*, pp. 238-39.
    [22] L. L. Rowland to A. J. Dufur, May 28, 1868, in A. J. Dufur, *Statistics of the
State of Oregon* . . . (Salem, Ore., 1869), p. 47; Commissioner of the General
Land Office, *Report* (1868), pp. 326-27; *Weekly Mountaineer*, July 20, 1869;
Salem *Oregon Weekly Statesman*, Oct. 29, 1869.

City and is quite a village for this part of the country."[23]

Equally interesting developments were taking place at this time in south-central Oregon. As early as the winter of 1867-68, Fairchild and Dorris, of Siskiyou County, California, had grazed nearly two thousand head of cattle near Fort Klamath and had reported that the range was the best one "this side of the Sierra Nevadas." In January, 1868, Captain F. B. Sprague wrote from Link River, saying that there were settlers in that neighborhood, and that, with one or two exceptions, they were all from Jackson County, Oregon; by mid-June of that year a newspaper in Jacksonville could say that settlers were "flocking into the Klamath Basin from every direction." By September, the Indian war in that area having ended, settlers were beginning to enter the Goose Lake Valley, a country which Captain Sprague had praised lavishly. The migration to this country increased in 1869, most of the new settlers coming from the Rogue River Valley. By mid-April of that year, Robert Whittle, a resident of Little Klamath Lake, reported that a stream of immigrants was moving to the Goose Lake country. They were, he said, "principally Oregonians," and they all were taking with them "more or less stock." A few days later a newspaper in Yreka, California, noted a constant migration from the Rogue River Valley to the Goose Lake Valley, and early in May, 1869, Nat Langell, who had just returned from the Lost River, reported in Jacksonville that he had met ten wagons, all "bound for the Goose Lake Valley." By late September it was reported that a heavy frost had destroyed vegetables and vines in this valley, but that those who went there to raise stock were satisfied with the country. On the last day of September, 1869, a newspaper in Yreka reported that about "900 head of cattle and 100 head of horses" would be wintered in the Goose Lake Valley.[24]

[23] "Kate L. Robbins Letters" (MSS in the University of Oregon Library, Eugene).

[24] *Oregon Sentinel*, Feb. 29, Sept. 5, 1868; Eugene *Oregon State Journal*, Feb. 29, 1868; *Walla Walla Statesman*, Oct. 9, 1868; Commissioner of the General Land Office, *Report* (1868), p. 331; *Oregon Sentinel*, April 3, 10, 17, May 1, 1869; *Yreka Weekly Union*, April 17, 1869; *Morning Oregonian*, March 26, April 15, 21, May 26, Aug. 4, 1869; *Yreka Journal*, April 22, Sept. 23, 30, 1869. On Aug. 10, 1870, the *Morning Oregonian* reported "a population of over 300 in Goose Lake valley."

While these things were happening in south-central Oregon, the occupation of southeastern Oregon was beginning. On September 15, 1868, E. L. Applegate reported that settlers were beginning to enter the Harney Lake Valley, and in the same year John S. Devine, with the backing of W. B. Todhunter of Sacramento, came up from California and established the celebrated White Horse ranch at the site of the former Camp C. F. Smith.[25] In subsequent years, as we shall see, cattle and other livestock came in large numbers into what we now call Malheur and Harney counties of southeastern Oregon, a subject to which we shall give attention presently. Thus we see that, as the decade of the 1860's was giving way to that of the 1870's, the colonization of Oregon east of the Cascades was acquiring considerable momentum. Indeed, as early as August, 1869, it appeared to an observer in Salem, Oregon, that "All the valleys east of the Cascades, on the waters of the Deschutes, . . . [were] being rapidly settled. Our borders are increasing. Southern, Central, and Southeastern Oregon are commencing to be known."[26]

By this time, moreover, the breeding of cattle for beef was becoming widespread in the Idaho Territory. In 1867 a correspondent in Owyhee and an editor in Idaho City were praising the pastoral and the agricultural resources of their territory, and early in October, 1869, a newspaper in Salem, Oregon, quoted the editor of the Boise *Statesman* as saying that "a great interest is being taken in stock grazing in Idaho. Some are selling lands and property and purchasing cows to take up new claims in unoccupied valleys." Also in that year, or possibly in December, 1868, the occupation of the Raft River Valley by stockmen began, and in the autumn of 1869 "large bands of Texas cattle" were brought into western Idaho. In announcing the arrival of these animals, the editor of the *Walla Walla Statesman* expressed the hope that the Pacific Northwest might escape "a visitation of the disease [Texas fever] that . . . [had] decimated the herds of

[25] Commissioner of the General Land Office, *Report* (1868), p. 327; George Francis Brimlow, *Harney County, Oregon, and Its Range Land* (Portland, Ore., 1951), p. 54; Giles French, *Cattle Country of Peter French* (Portland, Ore., 1964), p. 94.
[26] "C," writing on Aug. 21, 1869, in the *Sacramento Daily Union*, Sept. 4, 1869.

Iowa, Illinois, and nearly all the northwestern states."[27] Before
the end of 1869, the Washington Territorial Legislature had enacted, over the veto of the Governor, a law prohibiting the introduction into Washington Territory of "Texas cattle, or cattle affected with what is known as the Texas cattle disease or Spanish
fever." This law was praised by The Dalles *Mountaineer*, which
also expressed the hope that the legislature of Oregon would
enact a similar law regarding *cultus* cattle.[28] The implication of
such legislation will be dealt with in another context.

But, whether they were *cultus* or *kloshe*, several thousand head
of Texas cattle were grazing in Owyhee County, Idaho, in October, 1869; and in subsequent years other herds of such cattle
were brought into Idaho. Whatever the effect of Texas cattle
upon herds in this territory may have been, the cattle of the
Pacific Northwest, in general, were not affected by their coming.
In any event, by the summer of 1870, stock raising had become
"a growing interest in the Bruneau Valley," where, during the
preceding winter, "many thousand head" of cattle had been
safely pastured without shelter. Stockmen were learning the
value of Idaho's sage lands. "It has been discovered," wrote the
Surveyor-General of Idaho on August 22, 1870, "that the white
sage, after the maturity of its seeds in the fall, is sought for by
cattle in preference to grass. . . . As more than one-half of the wild
sage in the center and southern portions of the Territory is of this
species, and the climate in winter generally mild, the prospects
are that cattle will be raised here to supply the neighboring
country."[29]

The stage was now set for the rapid development of cattle
breeding throughout Transcascadia. In September, 1871, the Surveyor-General of Idaho could report that, as "the grazing lands

[27] *Ibid.*, Feb. 17, 1867, quoting Silex of Owyhee; *ibid.*, Oct. 2, 1867, quoting
the editor of the Idaho City *Idaho World*; *Oregon Weekly Statesman*, Oct. 8,
1869; *Burley Bulletin* (Idaho), Aug. 26, 1926; a paper on the cattle industry in
south-central Idaho, prepared in 1960 by Leslie L. Sudweeks for Mrs. Robert
Helms, Grants Pass, Oregon; *Walla Walla Statesman*, Oct. 23, 1869. See also the
letter of Seth Catlin to A. W. Webb, dated at Silver City, Ida., on Oct. 12, 1869,
in the Idaho State Historical Society, *Sixteenth Biennial Report, 1937-38* (Boise,
1938), p. 49, and Leslie L. Sudweeks, "Early Agricultural Settlements in Southern
Idaho," *PNQ*, XXVIII (April, 1937), 137-50.
[28] *Laws of Washington, 1869*, pp. 404-5; *Weekly Mountaineer*, Jan. 4, 1870.
[29] Commissioner of the General Land Office, *Report* (1870), pp. 135, 137, 437.

of the neighboring states [Oregon and Nevada] are eaten out," cattle from there were being driven to "the extensive pasture lands" of Idaho. During the past year, he said, many thousand head had been driven into this territory, "where both summer and winter ranges are excellent, and the raising of cattle highly profitable." And, loyal Idaho citizen that he had become, he also remarked, for good measure, that "nearly all the settlers who arrived here three or four years ago in destitute circumstances are now prosperous, all owning more or less stock."[30]

But, with due respect for such utterances, we must recognize that, at the beginning of the 1870's, there was still plenty of room for enlarging the business of cattle breeding in Oregon and Washington. Apparently no fear of "eaten-out" pastures troubled the thoughts of either R. W. Hamilton, of Polk County, Oregon, or a group of men in Port Townsend, Washington, one of whom was Allen Francis, formerly United States consul in Victoria. Mr. Hamilton sold his farm in Polk County during the winter of 1869-70, and in the spring of 1870 he bought a claim in Wasco County, where he "could engage in cattle raising to advantage"; and the group of men left Port Townsend early in August, 1870, for Seattle, "*en route* to the Yakima Valley, where they propose[d] to secure suitable range and go into the stock raising business on an extensive scale."[31]

There were other migrations from western Oregon to regions east of the Cascades in 1870. In June a man who had returned to Yreka, California, from a trip through southeastern Oregon reported that "great numbers of cattle and sheep" from the Willamette, Umpqua, and Rogue River valleys had been driven through the Lake country to the Pit River, the Goose Lake Valley, and the state of Nevada. Nor was this all. By July 1 Liggett and Burch had left Polk County to prospect for a good stock country in southeastern Oregon, and during the same month five families brought cattle, sheep, and horses from the Willamette Valley and settled on Rock Creek, in Wasco County, Oregon.[32]

[30] *Ibid.* (1871), p. 210.
[31] *Oregon Weekly Statesman*, May 13, 1870; Olympia *Washington Standard*, Aug. 13, 1870.
[32] *Yreka Weekly Union*, June 24, 1870; *Oregon Weekly Statesman*, July 1, 1870; The Dalles *Mountaineer*, Aug. 13, 1870.

Meanwhile in the north, bands of cattle were moving into the upper country, either by boat on the Columbia River or by trail across the Cascades; and during 1870 more stock raisers went north of the Snake River into present-day Whitman County, Washington. To encourage the movement up the river by boat, the Oregon Steam Navigation Company, early in that year, reduced its rates for carrying livestock from Portland to The Dalles. Late in that year the Reverend Elbridge Gerry, with the complacency of a down-east Yankee, wrote from Oregon City, saying that significant changes were taking place in the Willamette Valley. People of a "better class" were coming in and were replacing the older residents, who were "selling out, and moving east of the mountains, or into Washington Territory."[33] While Mr. Gerry was no doubt thanking God for ridding the Willamette Valley of undesirables, the editor of the Roseburg *Plaindealer* was wondering at the folly of stock raisers who persisted in going east of the Cascades when there were such splendid opportunities for them in Josephine County.[34]

The remarks of these two men—watching the course of events in northern and southern Oregon, respectively—may serve as the prologue to an account of a remarkable "eastward movement" of people and livestock from western Oregon to eastern Oregon and eastern Washington during the 1870's. Because this movement followed the pattern of transportation of the preceding decade, the editor of The Dalles *Mountaineer* could watch with interest and, being acceptably literate, describe with clarity what went up and down the Columbia River during that decade.

Immigration to this section of Oregon [he told his readers on March 11, 1871] has now fairly set in. Almost every evening the O. S. N. Company's steamer *Idaho* arrives here loaded down with cattle and horses, and also a large list of passengers. The winter has been particularly severe on livestock in western Oregon, owing mostly to its having been so wet, and most of the stock raisers who can sell out are coming to this side of the mountains.

[33] *Weekly Mountaineer*, March 29, 1870; *Oregon State Journal*, Feb. 5, April 30, 1870; New York *Home Missionary*, XLIII (February, 1871), 235. The *Morning Oregonian* of April 28, 1871, reported as follows: "Stock raisers are driving herds into the country between Snake and Spokane rivers. 5,000 head have crossed over since last fall from this side."
[34] Quoted by the *Mountaineer*, March 11, 1871.

This important and exciting movement was explained in a slightly different way by an articulate correspondent in Salem, writing to an editor in Sacramento on April 20, 1871, that,

As the Willamette Valley settles up and the old families find half a dozen boys to provide for, it is a very common thing to send some of them east of the mountains to locate, and eastern Oregon is becoming every year more and more a stock raising country, which is its natural use. The cattle of the Willamette are purchased when young and taken up the Columbia, and are brought back several years after, well fatted beef for the butcher stalls of our cities.[35]

The eastward migration of people and livestock continued during 1872, and as late as June 1 of that year an editor in Walla Walla could say that the Willamette Valley was "sending cattle, sheep and horses to the grazing fields of Eastern Oregon by every boat." But by this time a parallel movement, one of even greater size than that on the Columbia River, was well under way. To escape the high cost of transportation by water, some migrating stockmen and farmers were driving their herds and flocks eastward through passes in the Cascade Mountains. "Hundreds and thousands of cattle are annually driven from the Willamette Valley east of the Cascades, and fatted for market," remarked the editor of the Baker City *Bedrock Democrat* on January 31, 1872; and early in August of that year an editor in Sacramento, after scanning the Oregon newspapers of August 3, remarked on the "surprisingly large numbers" of livestock being driven across the mountains to eastern Oregon. "It is estimated," he said, "that 40,000 head of cattle have been driven over the Lebanon and Ochoco road this season already."[36] And thus the movement continued, more or less consistently, into the decade of the 1890's, during which time a considerable number of immigrants came into Transcascadia from or by way of California, as well as in wagons from states east of the Rockies, thus increasing the number of people and livestock in this intermontane country.

Many of the cattle, horses, and sheep that crossed the Cascades during the early 1870's went into Wasco County, the John Day country, and districts in northeastern Oregon, and many ranges

[35] *Sacramento Daily Union*, May 3, 1871.
[36] *Walla Walla Union*, June 1, 1872; *Sacramento Daily Union*, Aug. 7, 1872.

soon became crowded. By February, 1878, stockmen from Umatilla, Baker, Grant, and Wasco counties were driving their herds to ranges in the Wallowa Valley, and they were being joined by "quite a number" of stockmen from western Oregon, who were "astonished to find [in the Wallowa Valley] so large a country with the best stock range they . . . [had] ever seen."[37]

But from 1873 forward much of the cattle and sheep and some of the horses entering Transcascadia were directed toward the vacant or sparsely occupied grasslands and sagebrush lands in south-central and southeastern Oregon. By the summer of 1873, after the end of the Modoc War, the Klamath Lake country and the Link River country were settling rapidly. Most of the cattle and other livestock that entered these and other parts of south-central Oregon came from southwestern Oregon; but some were driven up from the neighborhood of Yreka, California. By November, 1873, there were as many as four thousand head of cattle in the Chewaukan Valley, and a year later there were about six thousand head of sheep and two thousand head of cattle in the Summer Lake Valley, which was overstocked. Here cattle were selling "very cheap."[38]

Thereafter, until at least the early 1880's, cattle were driven from Lane, Douglas, Josephine, and Jackson counties into the Lake country of Oregon. In October, 1875, cattle were numerous in the Chewaukan, the Summer Lake, and the Silver Lake valleys, but there still were several valleys "toward the Idaho boundary" which were not occupied by white men. By January, 1878, I. D. Applegate, a "large" cattleman of Lake County, was selling cattle to be taken to the market in San Francisco. Between 1880 and 1882, there was a heavy movement of both cattle and sheep from southwestern Oregon into Lake County. "Large numbers of

[37] A letter from the Wallowa Valley, dated Feb. 28, 1878, in the *Morning Oregonian*, March 7, 1878. On Sept. 20, 1879, W. E. Wilson, writing from "Crown Rock," Wasco County, advised Mrs. Malinda Gibson, of Jefferson, Oregon, to invest her money in cattle. "The cattle business," he said, "is certainly profitable in this country. I have never heard of any one making a failure." Letter owned by Mrs. J. Orin Oliphant, Salem, Oregon.
[38] *Weekly Mountaineer*, July 19, Sept. 16, 1873; *Yreka Union*, Nov. 15, 1873; *Morning Oregonian*, Nov. 23, 1874, May 23, 1876. A record which Philip Rigdon made of the movement of cattle eastward from western Oregon on the Oregon Central Military Road between 1871 and 1877 is now owned by the Oregon Historical Society, Portland.

cattle and sheep," says the Jacksonville *Oregon Sentinel* of July 21, 1880, "are being driven into Lake County, the last band being that of Stevens of Douglas County, numbering about 500 head."[39]

On the progress of this movement a year later, the evidence is abundant. During 1881, the Applegate brothers drove two hundred head of cattle from the Rogue River Valley to their ranch in Lake County, and M. H. Drake moved six hundred head from Jackson County to the Klamath country. In Jacksonville it was reported in April that F. M. Plymale would start soon for the Lake country with a band of cattle gathered in the Rogue River Valley, and that thousands of cattle, purchased in the Umpqua Valley, would soon be driven through Jackson County "to southeastern Oregon."[40] Early in May "ten droves of cattle," numbering between three thousand and four thousand head, passed through Ashland on the way to the Lake country, each herd being in charge of seven or eight horsemen. In Salem on May 13, 1881, the *Willamette Farmer* quoted the *Jacksonville Times* as saying that "Castle Bros. passed through the [Rogue River] valley last week with their large band of cattle, numbering 500 or 600. A. A. Fink also passed through with his band of 500, all bound for the plains of Lake and Grant counties from Douglas. Nearly every farmer in Josephine county has contributed more or less to the cattle drive, which has left considerable money there. As much can be said for Jackson county."

Evidence for 1881 and 1882 of the "outpouring" of cattle and other livestock from southwestern Oregon is presented in another Jackson County newspaper, the Jacksonville *Oregon Sentinel*, which reported on June 18, 1881, that a band of ten thousand sheep, owned by the Brummel Brothers of Douglas County, had recently passed through the Rogue River Valley on the way to Lake County. On September 3, 1881, the *Sentinel* affirmed that H. B. Black had driven to Lake County a band of cattle which he

---

[39] *Sacramento Daily Union*, Feb. 16, June 14, 1875; *Morning Oregonian*, June 14, Oct. 4, 1875, Jan. 29, May 7, 14, 1878; *Yreka Union*, July 14, 1877. On Lake County, Oregon, as a good pastoral country, see a statement by Orson A. Stearns, of Linkville, on Nov. 28, 1879. 46th Cong., 2nd sess., H. Ex. Doc. 46, p. 466.

[40] *Morning Oregonian*, March 9, 16, 1881; *Oregon Sentinel*, April 30, 1881; *Willamette Farmer*, April 15, 1881, quoting the *Jacksonville Times; ibid.*, May 13, 1881, quoting the *Ashland Tidings*.

intended to fatten for the California market.[41] On May 27, 1882, the same newspaper told its readers that Matt Obenchain would start the next day for his ranch on Sprague River with a band of two hundred cattle which had been gathered for the most part on the Butte Creek range. This drive, it was presumed, might be the last large one of the season.

This was not the end of the eastward movement of cattle from the Rogue River Valley. Although on March 7, 1883, the *Morning Oregonian* affirmed that, because of the "home demand," there would be "fewer cattle driven from the Rogue river valley to the bunch grass plains than for many years past," a letter from Linkville (now Klamath Falls) dated May 24, 1883, informed the editor that "several hundred head of cattle . . . [had] passed in the last few days en route from Rogue river valley to the bunch grass country."[42]

Meanwhile, stockmen were using southeastern Oregon, a region which, as the Surveyor-General of Oregon wrote in 1879, "comprises about one-fourth of the entire area of the state," to fatten cattle for the markets of "California, Utah, Nevada, and most of southern Oregon." The term *southeastern Oregon* undoubtedly comprehended what in this study is being called south-central Oregon and, in addition, the area then comprising Lake, Grant, and Baker counties. The occupation of what had become Grant and Baker counties, in the north as well as in the south, had proceeded steadily from the late 1860's forward. In the north—that is, in the drainage area of the Malheur River and more especially in the area contiguous to present-day Ontario—David Dunbar in 1869 began to raise cattle near the Snake River, southeast of the present site of Ontario, and Con Shea ran herds on Cow Creek, north of the Jordan River; and in the south, as we have seen, a Californian named John S. Devine, with a considerable herd of cattle and the financial backing of W. B. Todhunter, established southeast of Steens Mountain a ranch which spread across the line separating present-day Harney County from present-day Mal

[41] The *Morning Oregonian* of May 10, 1881, reported: "Within four days of last week ten droves of cattle, amounting to between 3000 and 4000 head, passed through Ashland on their way to the Lake country, each drove being in charge of from seven to eight horsemen."

[42] *Ibid.*, March 29, 1883.

heur County. During the next four years, the occupation of this large area continued more rapidly. Among the stock raisers who began operations in the north were Joseph W. Morton, on lower Willow Creek, in 1870; George W. Brinnin, at the mouth of the Malheur River, and William K. Stark, a few miles farther south, in 1871; and Joshua L. Cole, on lower Willow Creek, in 1872. Meanwhile, in the south, other stockmen were establishing themselves—in 1870, Mace McCoy in the western part of Diamond Valley; in 1871, James Abbott and H. Whiteside on Alvord Creek, A. H. Robie in Diamond Valley, and Philip Mann near Mann Lake; and in 1872, John Catlow, formerly of Silver City, Idaho, on Trout Creek, and Thomas Prather, Stilly Riddle, John Boone, and John Chapman in other parts of this large region. But, as the sequel would show, the most notable stockman who entered the present-day Harney County in 1872 was Peter French, who, with the financial backing of Dr. Hugh J. Glenn, drove up from California a herd of twelve hundred head of cattle and established the famous P ranch in the valley of the Donner und Blitzen River.[43]

During the middle years of the 1870's, other stockmen moved into southeastern Oregon. Among them were the Venators, George A. Smyth, John S. Miller, Joe Cooksey, Frank McLeod, Peter Stenger, Thomas Whiting, W. D. Kiger, Maurice Fitzgerald, James Sheppard, and Amos W. Riley and James A. Hardin, the two men who established the OO ranch a few miles west of Harney Lake. Others, including the well-known William Hanley, came somewhat later, and, before the end of the 1870's, the enterprise of breeding cattle was flourishing in the Harney Basin.[44]

As early as May 17, 1873, the *Owyhee Avalanche* quoted John Minear, who recently had visited Silver City, as saying that there were about ten thousand head of cattle in the Steens Mountain

[43] Secretary of the Interior, *Report, 1879* (Washington, D.C., 1879), I, 854; Jacob R. Gregg, *Pioneer Days in Malheur County* ... (Los Angeles, 1950), pp. 90, 98, 101-2, 116-18, 218-19; Brimlow, *Harney County*, pp. 54-58; French, *Cattle Country of Peter French*, p. 43; Silver City *Owyhee Avalanche*, Sept. 7, 1872; Burns *East Oregon Herald*, Sept. 12, 1889; Burns *Times–Herald*, Feb. 13, 1904.

[44] Brimlow, *Harney County*, pp. 58-65; French, *Cattle Country of Peter French*, *passim*.

country, and when Minear again visited Silver City, the *Avalanche* of September 6, 1873, quoted him as saying that "a large number of stockmen" had recently settled in the neighborhood of Steens Mountain, and that "all the stock-range in that locality" had been "taken up and occupied." About a year and a half later, the Corvallis *Democrat* learned that there were a few settlers, seven ranches, and about seven thousand head of cattle and more than four hundred horses in the Donner und Blitzen Valley.[45]

During the next five years, the cattle in southeastern Oregon increased rapidly. We may safely assume that this growth was owing in part to other drives of cattle like the one which John and William Hanley made in May, 1879, when they drove five hundred head from Jacksonville to the Harney Valley for pasturing during the summer. And we may also be fairly certain that among the stockmen of this region who, as the Surveyor-General averred in 1879, were supplying beef to markets in adjoining states as well as to markets in southern Oregon, the foremost was Peter French, who, as the *Morning Oregonian* learned from a "Harney letter" in October, 1879, was "out with a large force of men collecting all his cattle and driving them to Stein's [Steens] mountain,[46] where he has two large enclosures—one of 25,000 acres and the other of about 15,000." Duly impressed by this information, the editor of the *Morning Oregonian* remarked that "Pete, who is a self-made man, is one of the most enterprising men in Grant County. He started ten years ago in the stock business with a very small capital, and now he is worth, at the lowest estimate, $200,000."[47]

In the meantime, while some stockmen were occupying the ranges of Oregon east of the Cascades, other settlers had been advancing into the grasslands of eastern Washington and the panhandle of Idaho. They pressed into the Klickitat country, the Yakima Valley, the Kittitas Valley, and other areas on the eastern slopes of the Cascades; they entered the Palouse country, the

[45] Quoted in the *Morning Oregonian*, March 30, 1875.
[46] The name *Stein Mountain*, although once widely used, has been displaced in correct usage by the name *Steens Mountain*. This mountain was named in honor of Major Enoch Steen, of the U. S. Army. Lewis A. McArthur, *Oregon Geographic Names* (3rd ed.; Portland, Ore., 1965), pp. 573-74.
[47] *Morning Oregonian*, Oct. 24, 1879; *Oregon Sentinel*, May 28, 1879.

Big Bend country, the Okanogan Valley, and the Colville Valley; and they pushed into the unoccupied places of eastern Washington south of the Snake River. By the opening of the 1880's, moreover, the grazing of cattle on open ranges was being hampered by farming operations in both the Yakima and Klickitat countries, in the Palouse country, and in the Walla Walla Valley.

The business of breeding cattle, well started in the Yakima Valley by 1869, expanded steadily during the decade of the 1870's. As early as June, 1872, it was reported that this country was overstocked, and a month later a newspaper in Walla Walla, informed by a report of a recent visitor to Yakima County, affirmed that that country was "fast settling up," and that the Yakima Valley was "full of stock." This newspaper had also learned from "a different source" that the wheat crop of the Yakima Valley was estimated at thirty thousand to forty thousand bushels. Nevertheless, in September of that year more persons were leaving the "west side" with stock for the purpose of settling in the Yakima Valley. At the beginning of March, 1873, Charles Schanno of Yakima City said that there were about twenty thousand head of cattle in the Yakima Valley; and, somewhat more than a year later, a correspondent writing from Yakima City to a newspaper in Walla Walla affirmed that the Yakima Valley, "from the mouth of the river to its head," was occupied by settlers and "devoted to stock raising." The people of this valley, he said, numbered 1,026, and the cattle thereof numbered 25,785.[48]

Four years later Yakima County was still an important country for cattle. In June of 1878, a correspondent could say that Yakima, although well adapted for cattle and horses, was a country ill-adapted to the breeding of sheep because of its sagebrush and its deep snows in winter. There were, he said, large herds of cattle in the country, the largest of them being owned by Ben Snipes, the Indian Department, J. B. Huntingdon, Phelps and

---

[48] On July 1, 1880, according to the federal census of 1880, there were 457,099 head of cattle in Oregon east of the Cascades. *Tenth Federal Census, 1880*, Vol. III, *Agriculture* (Washington, D.C., 1883), p. 1088. See also Splawn, *Ka-mi-akin*, chap. xxxiv; *Mountaineer*, June 29, 1872; *Walla Walla Union*, July 27, 1872; D. J. S., writing from Kittitas, W.T., Aug. 1, 1872, in the *Morning Oregonian*, Aug. 14, 1872; Seattle *Weekly Intelligencer*, Sept. 2, 1872; *Walla Walla Union*, March 1, 1873; Baker City *Bedrock Democrat*, May 13, 1874. See also Gretta

Wadleigh, C. M. Walker, and P. L. Willis. Some fifteen months later, in September, 1879, the returns of the assessor of Yakima County showed that there were about 22,665 head of cattle, 4,205 horses, and 2,994 sheep. Of greater significance for the future of this country, however, was the publication in the *Spokan Times*, in November of that year, of a report in which a Yakima newspaper said that about 225,000 bushels of grain had just been harvested in Yakima County. This report, the editor of the *Spokan Times* pointed out, showed that the Yakima country was "fast settling up, and the acreage in grain steadily increasing."[49]

Meanwhile, in the Klickitat country, which cattlemen had entered as early as 1859, cattle were reported in the summer of 1877 to be "ranging everywhere over the rolling hills," and to be receiving slight attention. But this country, according to the editor of the Vancouver *Independent*, was "overstocked." Nevertheless, nearly two years later, at least one precinct on Alder Creek, where six years earlier the Indians had had full possession, was occupied by thirty-five voters, who owned six thousand head of cattle, sixteen thousand sheep, and about five hundred horses. But by the late spring of 1880, "large stock owners" who had for several years been ranging their stock in the "upper portion of Klickitat County" were reported to be so much "alarmed at the rapid settlement of the country" that they were gathering up their herds with the intention of "driving them east."[50] At the time of the taking of the federal census of 1880, however, the ranges in Klickitat County appear to have been less exhausted than those in Yakima County, which were reported to be "well eaten out." In Yakima County the fencing of valleys was "becoming the rule," and the prediction was freely offered that the day of "great stock ranging" was almost finished there, except as it

Gossett, "Stock Grazing in Washington's Nile Valley," *PNQ*, LV (July, 1964), 120.

[49] Krito, writing on June 6, 1878, for the *Morning Oregonian*, June 14, 1878; *Spokan Times*, Sept. 25, Nov. 27, 1879.

[50] Splawn, *Ka-mi-akin*, p. 131; *Tacoma Herald*, July 14, 1877, quoting W. Byron Daniels, editor of the Vancouver *Independent;* Portland *West Shore*, IV (February, 1879), p. 57; *Morning Oregonian*, May 11, 1880, quoting the *Klickitat Sentinel*.

might be "carried on in connection with farming."[51]

North of the Klickitat and Yakima countries lay the Wenatchee country, which, as the *Walla Walla Statesman* was told in the summer of 1876, was "an excellent stock country." This information came from H. M. Bryant, who was "just in from the Wenatchee country," where for several months he had been "in charge of a band of stock."[52]

Of all the grazing areas east of the Cascades, the best by far was the Great Plateau of the Columbia, politically organized by 1880 as Spokane and Whitman counties. From the Spokane and Columbia rivers on the north, this plateau extended southward to the Snake River, and from the Big Bend of the Columbia in the west it extended eastward through the Idaho panhandle to the Bitter Root Mountains. This region once provided large and continuous areas of pasturage, although the plateau is broken in the west by deep coulees running southwestwardly from the Columbia and, east of these, by extensive channeled scablands. In general, this plateau is rough, rising in elevation "from the Columbia eastward"; and in the 1870's its best pasture lands lay east of the 119th meridian. As we read in the Gordon Report,

The southeast portion of Spokane and Whitman counties, or about one-fifth of the entire section of the great plain of the Columbia, comprising all that country bordering the Palouse river and its tributaries, is, perhaps, the best pasturage of the territory, but it is rapidly passing into the possession of farmers. Bunch-grass is here abundant. The middle part of Whitman county along the main Palouse and the higher country in the east furnishes superior summer range, from which stock can pass in winter to the milder and drier pastures of western Whitman.[53]

Into this country "beyond Snake River," during the 1870's and 1880's, stockmen and farmers moved in steady procession with their cattle and other livestock to take possession of what, to many of them, seemed to be a promised land. Most of them

[51] Clarence W. Gordon, "Report on Cattle, Sheep, and Swine, Supplementary to Enumeration of Live Stock on Farms in 1880," in *Tenth Federal Census, 1880*, Vol. III, *Agriculture*, p. 1088.

[52] *Walla Walla Statesman*, July 1, 1876.

[53] Gordon, "Report," p. 1089; J. Harlen Bretz, "The Channeled Scablands of the Columbia Plateau," *Journal of Geology*, XXXI (November-December, 1923), 617-49. It should be remembered that at this time Whitman County included present-day Adams County.

passed through Walla Walla, then the largest town in Washington Territory, and from there the editor of the *Walla Walla Union* chronicled this advance, much as the editor of the *Mountaineer* at The Dalles chronicled the advance up the Columbia of many of these people. To the editors of these two newspapers the student of the early colonization of the Columbia Basin is much indebted.

On April 22, 1871, the editor of the *Walla Walla Union* observed that the "country between the Snake and Spokane rivers seems now to be the favorite region with stockraisers, and the valleys that skirt the small streams in that section are fast filling up with this class of settlers. We are told that not less than 500 head of cattle have been taken across Snake river at the different ferries since last Fall."[54] Most such cattle, no doubt, were headed for the Palouse country, an area which had been filling up rapidly during the preceding months, and an area where, before the end of 1872, some persons who had come to graze cattle had decided to remain to raise wheat. But some of the immigrants in 1871 may have headed northward into the Spokane country,[55] which then was a part of Stevens County, and still others may have turned westward into the Big Bend of the Columbia; and certainly by 1872 some of the people in this northward advance were turning eastward into the Idaho panhandle north of Lewis-

[54] While the fiftieth anniversary of the organization of Whitman County was being observed, J. B. Holt, of Pullman, Wash., a pioneer of 1871, prepared a list of the settlers of Whitman County at the time of its organization on Nov. 29, 1871. This list was published in the Spokane *Spokesman-Review*, Jan. 15, 1922. See also the recollections of J. B. Holt, published in the *Spokesman-Review*, May 1, 1932, and the recollections or sketches of other pioneers of Whitman County in the *Spokesman-Review* of Dec. 4, 1921, and Sept. 17, 1922. Mrs. W. E. Baskett's "History of the Early Whitman County Pioneers" was published in the *Colfax Commoner* of July 16, 1920.

[55] On Sept. 9, 1872, the surveyor-general of Washington, L. P. Beach, reported as follows: "During the last two years the Palouse country has been rapidly settling up, and those who first located in that section, for the purpose of grazing stock, have found that the soil produces abundance of all grains and vegetables, and many have taken up lands, and now have farms in a fine state of cultivation." Commissioner of the General Land Office, *Report* (1872), p. 241. On the advance of settlers into the Spokane country in the early 1870's, see the recollections of J. F. Spangle in the *Spokesman-Review*, July 4, 1926, and the recollections of Mrs. Laura E. Tyler in the *Cheney Free Press*, April 2, 1915. Mrs. Tyler came with her family by wagon from Eugene, Oregon, in the autumn of 1880, to the newly founded town of Cheney, Wash.

ton. In 1872 I. C. Matheny drove a large band of horses and cattle from the Willamette Valley into the Paradise Valley, in which the town of Moscow would be laid out. Two years later a buyer of livestock was in Lewiston, in eager quest of about fifteen hundred head of cattle.[56]

The heavy immigration into the Palouse country in 1872 was followed in 1873 by one that was perhaps equally large. However that may have been, in March, 1873, the editor of the *Walla Walla Union*, impressed by the number of "teams and families" from the Willamette Valley that were then passing through Walla Walla, and having been told that in 1873 there would be a heavier emigration from that valley than ever before, remarked that "Webfoot" was becoming "too old a country for them." But, whatever the reason may have been, the migration of 1873 continued as predicted; and late in November a correspondent in Colfax, Washington, informed the readers of the *Walla Walla Union* that, although immigrants were "steadily coming in," there was still room in the Palouse country "for thousands more." The best place for the stock raisers, he said, was the western part of Whitman County,

on the waters of the Snake river and the lower Palouse, where it is warmer and the snow disappears more rapidly, from the effect of the Chinook winds. The eastern part of the county is better adapted to farming. The soil is not only of a heavier, richer nature, but it is also more convenient to timber and will admit of large settlements in bodies, where school and church privileges can soon be had.

It was in the country "between the Palouse and the Columbia" that Joseph Freeman had a herd of eleven hundred head of cattle, which wintered without loss in 1872-73; and it was here, as the editor of the *Walla Walla Union* affirmed in January, 1873, that hundreds, or perhaps thousands, of other cattle were doing as well as Freeman's cattle.[57]

[56] On the beginning of settlement in the neighborhood of Cow Creek, see *An Illustrated History of the Big Bend Country* . . . (Spokane, Wash., 1904), p. 755, and on the early settlements in Idaho north of Lewiston see the Colfax *Palouse Gazette*, Oct. 13, 1877, Oct. 10, 1879. See also the Lewiston *Idaho Signal*, April 13, May 11, 1872. In August, 1878, the assessor's returns showed that in Nez Percé County, Idaho, there were 3,925 cattle, 3,672 horses, and 14,590 sheep. *Palouse Gazette*, Aug. 16, 1878.

[57] *Walla Walla Union*, Jan. 25, March 29, December 6, 1873.

For years thereafter, through the later 1870's and beyond, new-comers to the country north of the Snake River, some from the East but perhaps many more from western Oregon, passed north-ward through Walla Walla. We know that in 1874, and again in 1877, immigrants came to the Palouse country from the Willam-ette Valley by the McKenzie River route, and we also know that, in March, 1878, an editor in Walla Walla estimated that 1,200 families had crossed the Snake River to enter Whitman and Stevens counties in 1877. This movement was continuing in 1878, and in August the assessor's returns show that Whitman County had 16,800 head of cattle, 30,000 sheep, and 5,000 horses.[58]

During the next three years, there appears to have been no lessening of this movement. On May 22, 1879, the editor of the *Spokan Times* affirmed that the tide of immigration flowing into Washington Territory was "large beyond precedent." Although some of the immigrants were going to the Puget Sound Basin, many more were settling in eastern Washington, which, as he said, was being occupied with remarkable rapidity. Somewhat more than a year later, E. M. Downing, who had recently arrived in Colfax from the East, said that he had passed on the North Platte River "100 emigrant wagons bound for Eastern Washing-ton," and the people in this party told him that they were "on the way to cultivate the rich cereal producing lands of the north-west." In August of 1880, according to a newspaper in Lewiston, Idaho, there were in Whitman County 35,000 head of cattle, 10,000 horses, and 72,782 sheep. The effect of this inpouring of people and livestock upon the stock-breeding interest in the Palouse country was stated succinctly in an editorial in the *West Shore* in August, 1881, which said that for a decade "the Palouse country, in consequence of its luxuriant growth of bunch grass everywhere found, and its equable climate, has been the Mecca

[58] On May 29, 1877, the *Morning Oregonian* reported that teams were "passing through Pendleton daily, bound for the Palouse country," and on May 20, 1878, it remarked that not a few persons were "going from Lane county [Oregon] to the Palouse country." On this subject see also the *Pacific Christian Advocate*, Oct. 18, 1877, March 28, July 11, 1878; *Sacramento Daily Union*, May 11, 1874; *Palouse Gazette*, Oct. 27, 1877, March 16, 1878; Dayton *Columbia Chronicle*, Aug. 17, 1878.

of stock raisers. The great fertility of the soil and its unfailing yield has, however, given the lands a value which is rapidly displacing the large herds of cattle which once grazed on these lands."[59]

Before the end of the 1870's, much of the immigration into the country north of the Snake River was headed for the Spokane country. In August, 1879, a newspaper in Walla Walla observed that five families from Harrisburg, Oregon, had passed through Walla Walla a few days earlier "with ox teams on their way to the great Spokan[e] Country," and in November the *Walla Walla Union* observed that immigrants were daily coming through Walla Walla in large numbers, some by the railroad and others with "long trains of teams, from all points between Northern Minnesota and Southern Texas"; and their principal destinations were "the Palouse and Spokan[e] countries." As a result of this migration, business improved in the little town of Spokane Falls, which, as the editor of the *Spokan Times* promised on March 25, 1880, would "soon have three restaurants for the feeding of the hungry emigrants." In part, this increasing migration to the Spokane country was stimulated by the construction of the Pend d'Oreille division of the Northern Pacific Railroad, which reached Spokane Falls on June 30, 1881.[60]

In the meantime, cattlemen had extended their interests northward and northwestward of the Spokane country into the Okanogan and Colville valleys. In December, 1877, F. W. Perkins, writing for the *Palouse Gazette,* affirmed that the Okanogan country was "unsurpassed" as a winter range for cattle, and, as if

---

[59] From Central Ferry on the Snake River, Hawk Eye wrote in the autumn of 1879 as follows: ". . . there is a very heavy travel across the river, both local and immigrant. Since the 9th of Aug. 145 emigrant families have crossed at this ferry to the Palouse country. The large portion of them are from Oregon, California, and Kansas." *Dayton News,* Nov. 15, 1879. A few weeks earlier H. Thielsen, writing from Walla Walla, told Henry Villard that, if he and his associates wished to get "extra fine lands and town sites," it was important that they act at once, for, as he said, "it is almost incredible with what avidity the lands are taken up in the Palouse country wherever stakes are set by the Engineers." Thielsen to Villard, Sept. 6, 1879, in Villard Papers, Box 56, Folder 396 (MSS in the Widener Library, Harvard University). See also *Morning Oregonian,* June 23, July 20, 28, Aug. 5, Nov. 29, 1880; *Lewiston Teller,* Aug. 27, 1880; *West Shore,* VII (August 1881), 208.

[60] Quoted in the *Spokan Times,* Aug. 28, Nov. 20, 1879; *ibid.,* June 30, 1881.

to prove this assertion, the firm of Phelps and Wadleigh, in the spring of 1881, sold to Benjamin E. Snipes of The Dalles their herd of 12,000 head of cattle, which had been ranging in the Okanogan country; and more than two years later Yakima Valley cattlemen were still grazing herds in the Okanogan country. Farther eastward, in the Colville Valley, cattle became so numerous that, in the spring of 1881, a buyer was there to purchase several hundred head.[61] So much, then, for the northern country.

Some of the stockmen in the stream of people and livestock that had been moving northward from the Snake River had turned westward from the Palouse country to seek ranges in the Big Bend of the Columbia River, some on Cow Creek, but perhaps many more on Crab Creek. According to an agent of the *Spokan Times*, this country was not suitable for agricultural pursuits, but was "one of the finest stock countries to be found." As early as 1871, stockmen were beginning to occupy this country, and by 1874, and especially by 1875, others were moving in; but even by the middle 1870's the stock then grazing in this country had not made "much impression on the pastures," which, it was alleged, could support many times the number of animals occupying them.[62] During the next few years, the settlement of this country proceeded more rapidly. By 1878, among numerous other stockmen, Samuel Johnson, William Bingham, and Daniel Drumheller had ranches in this country, and in the spring of 1880 the *Walla Walla Union* reported that Bingham and Drumheller had sold their bands of cattle, numbering about twenty-five hundred head, to other stockmen, who intended to keep them in the Crab Creek country "for stock raising purposes." The federal census of 1880 shows that there were more than thirty stock raisers in this part of the Big Bend country, and among them were all the persons mentioned above.[63]

[61] *Palouse Gazette,* Dec. 15, 1877; Boise *Idaho Weekly Statesman,* March 26, 1881; Ellensburg *Kittitas Standard,* Sept. 8, 1883; *Spokan Times,* May 12, 1881.
[62] *Illustrated History of the Big Bend Country,* pp. 67-68, 755; *Spokan Times,* June 5, 1879; *Walla Walla Union,* Oct. 3, 1874, Nov. 13, 1875.
[63] Tacoma *Weekly Ledger,* Sept. 3, 1880; *Walla Walla Statesman,* Sept. 21, 1878; Thomas W. Symons, *Report of an Examination of the Upper Columbia River and the Territory in Its Vicinity, in September and October, 1881 . . .* 4th Cong., 1st sess., S. Ex. Doc. 186, pp. 122-23; *Walla Walla Union,* March 20, 1880; *Compendium of the Tenth Census* (Washington, D.C., 1883), pp. 918-19.

Not all the cattle and other livestock which came into the Columbia Basin during the 1870's were driven to ranges either in the Yakima country or on the Columbia Plateau; a considerable number entered the older Walla Walla country, more especially that part of it which, on November 11, 1875, was organized as Columbia County. In the summer of 1879 this county was supposed to have twenty thousand head of cattle, twenty-five thousand head of horses, and "several thousand head of sheep." But the federal census of 1880 tells us that, in Walla Walla and Columbia counties, "rapidly increasing farming interests ... [had] crowded out free range."[64]

Elsewhere in the Pacific Northwest the process of colonization was proceeding. While some stockmen were occupying the ranges of Oregon and Washington during the 1870's, others were driving their herds to ranges in Idaho south of the panhandle. In the 1870's, as had also been the case in the 1860's, some herds came to this large part of that territory from Oregon, others from Texas, and still others from Nevada and California. By January, 1872, cattle were fattening on "rich and extensive pastures" near Malad City, and in October it was reported that five settlers had about six thousand head of cattle on Raft River, an area which was said to be "a splendid range, both for Winter and Summer." Two of these settlers were J. Q. Shirley and Andrew Sweetser, who, in 1866, had "located a section" near Fort Hall. This land they subsequently surrendered to the United States in exchange for six sections of land on Raft River, near the mouth of Cassia Creek. By 1870 other stockmen were moving into the Raft River area, and by 1876, according to the federal census of 1880, Cassia County was suffering from overstocking, and especially along the Raft River and on Goose Creek many of the "water privileges" were fenced.[65]

At the opening of the 1870's herds of cattle were brought into southwestern Idaho from Texas. In 1870 Con Shea, Tom Bugbee,

---

In May, 1881, the firm of Wilson and Drumheller was grazing cattle in the region of Crab Creek. *Spokan Times,* May 19, 1881.

[64] *Spokan Times,* May 29, 1879; *Tenth Federal Census, 1880,* Vol. III, *Agriculture,* p. 1089.

[65] *Corrine Daily Reporter,* Jan. 8, 1872; *Sacramento Daily Union,* Oct. 23, 1872;

and General Philip Kohlheyer brought Texas herds into Owyhee
County; and in 1871, and again in 1873, David Shirk helped to
drive herds from Texas into this region. But, according to the
Gordon Report accompanying the federal census of 1880, no
cattle from Texas entered Idaho after 1874.[66] By that time,
thanks to the depression, plenty of good cattle could be bought
cheaply in Oregon and in Washington.

During the next few years, the number of cattle in Idaho
increased greatly. Large numbers of cattle were driven into
Idaho, larger numbers were driven through Idaho, and considerable numbers were bought in Idaho and driven out of this
territory. According to the tenth federal census, "several large
cattle owners moved their herds into Idaho in 1875," and in
August of the next year the *Morning Oregonian* affirmed that the
" 'cattle on a thousand hills' scattered all over Idaho never looked
fatter and better."[67] Somewhat earlier in 1876, according to The
Dalles *Mountaineer* of May 13, "Mr. Shirley, from Petulama,
Cal.," bought from James Reynolds of Walla Walla twelve hundred head of fine cattle, which were to be taken to the "Raft River
regions, adjacent to the new mines." Thereafter, cattle continued
to enter Idaho—some to pass through this territory en route to
Montana or Wyoming, some to remain and graze on ranges
already fully stocked or overcrowded. In March, 1878, "another
cattle buyer" from Idaho was seeking two thousand head of
cattle in the Rogue River Valley, and before the end of that year
the Governor of Idaho was fearful lest the encroachment of
cattlemen on the Big Camas Prairie, in Alturas County, might
cause trouble with the Bannock Indians. During the summer of
1880, from "eight to ten thousand stock cattle" grazed on this

---

Jennie B. Brown, *Fort Hall on the Oregon Trail: A Historical Study* (Caldwell,
Ida., 1932), p. 336, quoting the *Reminiscences of Alexander Toponce, Pioneer,
1839-1923* (Ogden, Utah, 1923), p. 139; *Tenth Federal Census, 1880*, Vol. III,
Agriculture, p. 1096.

[66] Silver City, Ida., *Avalanche*, Sept. 24, Oct. 29, 1870, reprinted in the Idaho
State Historical Society, *16th Biennial Report* (1937-38), p. 48; Martin F. Schmitt
(ed.), *The Cattle Drives of David Shirk from Texas to the Idaho Mines, 1871
and 1873* (Portland, Ore., 1956), pp. 50-99 *passim*; *Tenth Federal Census,
1880*, Vol. III, *Agriculture*, pp. 1080, 1098; *Morning Oregonian*, Nov. 10, 1869,
quoting the *Walla Walla Union*.

[67] Gordon, "Report," 1094-99; *Morning Oregonian*, Aug. 13, 1876.

prairie, which was a favorite place for trail drivers to rest their cattle en route to Wyoming.[68]

Before the end of 1879, the Surveyor-General of Idaho reported that interest in stock raising in that territory was "large and constantly growing." He estimated that in western Idaho twenty thousand head of cattle had been sold "for the Eastern markets" during that "season," and that probably as many more had been sold in the northern and eastern parts of this territory. A year later he reported that both stock raising and agriculture in Idaho were "increasing in importance each year," and that immigration was "steadily flowing into this Territory." By 1880 both Cassia County and Owyhee County were reported to be well stocked with cattle of superior quality, but by that time, in the Weiser Valley, in the northern part of Owyhee County, and perhaps elsewhere in the territory, farmers were coming "to plant, fence, and irrigate."[69]

As Idaho moved into the decade of the 1880's, its ranges were well stocked with cattle, horses, and sheep. On February 3, 1881, the *Omaha Daily Republican,* without giving the source of its information, affirmed that "Idaho . . . [had] 450,000 cattle, 60,000 horses, and 60,000 sheep"; and on December 31, 1881, the Governor of Idaho reported that some 35,000 head of cattle were annually marketed from the ranges of Idaho.[70] Like placer mines of earlier years, the bunch grass and the white sage of Idaho had become valuable natural resources.

But in Idaho, as elsewhere in Transcascadia, the uncontrolled extension of the business of breeding cattle for beef during the golden years of the 1860's and the early 1870's presently brought upon cattlemen a distressing depression. Although broadly speaking it ran parallel to a great depression throughout the nation, a depression which no doubt intensified and lengthened the one in the Pacific Northwest, the period of hard times experienced by

[68] *Morning Oregonian,* March 12, 1878; report of the Governor of Idaho, June 13, 1878, 45th Cong., 3rd sess., H. Ex. Doc. 1 (Serial 1850), p. 1105; *Tenth Federal Census, 1880,* Vol. III, *Agriculture,* p. 1097.

[69] *Report of the Surveyor-General of Idaho Made to the Secretary of the Interior for the Year 1879* (Washington, D.C., 1879), p. 12; Commissioner of the General Land Office, *Report* (1880), p. 959; *Tenth Federal Census, 1880,* Vol. III, *Agriculture,* pp. 1096, 1098.

[70] 47th Cong., 1st sess., H. Ex. Doc. 1 (Serial 2018), X, 1090.

cattlemen in Transcascadia had its own sufficient cause—the lack of adequate markets. The increase in the number of cattle was accompanied by a decreasing demand for beef in the mining camps which was not offset by the increasing demand for beef in Portland, Victoria, and the towns in the Puget Sound Basin. Moreover, although more army posts were established in the Pacific Northwest as settlements spread, they were poor substitutes, as markets, for the formerly flourishing mining camps. Accordingly, by 1873, as Jack Splawn, a Yakima Valley cattleman, tersely remarked, the cattlemen east of the Cascades were "up against it."[71] For them the dark days then beginning would last until the end of the 1870's.

At the opening of the 1870's, prices for cattle in Transcascadia were so good, and confidence ran so high, that in February, 1871, the editor of the *Mountaineer* became so boastful that he almost shouted defiance. "If," he exclaimed in February, 1871, "there is any legitimate business on the Pacific Coast that can beat cattle raising for money making, we don't know it." As late as August, 1872, cattle prices in eastern Oregon, southeastern Washington, northern Idaho, and distant Montana continued to justify this boast; but by mid-December "cattle of all kinds" were selling in the Walla Walla Valley "at lower prices than ever before." This decline in prices, as the editor of the *Walla Walla Union* inadequately explained, was "owing mainly to the fact that Texas cattle . . . [had] been brought into Montana, Nevada, Idaho, and eastern Oregon in such quantities that those markets . . . [were] supplied." But, Texas cattle or no Texas cattle, the trend of prices continued downward, and in September, 1876, the editor of the *Mountaineer,* now completely sober, noted that "beef on foot" at The Dalles was selling at a cent and a half a pound.[72] No doubt the bottom here was now well scraped; elsewhere the situation was not, and perhaps never had been, so bad.

Our knowledge that the downward trend of the average price

[71] Splawn, *Ka-mi-akin*, p. 291.
[72] *Mountaineer*, Nov. 5, 1870, Feb. 25, Sept. 2, 1871; *Walla Walla Statesman,* Nov. 19, 1870; *Sacramento Daily Union*, July 26, 1872; *Idaho Signal*, Aug. 31, 1872; Rossiter W. Raymond, *Statistics of Mines and Mining in the States and Territories West of the Rocky Mountains* (Washington, D.C., 1873), p. 259; *Walla Walla Union*, Dec. 14, 1872; *Mountaineer*, Sept. 30, 1876.

for cattle throughout the United States between 1872 and 1880 resembled a like trend in the Pacific Northwest during those years does not deepen our understanding of the situation confronting cattlemen in Transcascadia during the 1870's. To understand how prices varied in that region, we must turn to the fading pages of the newspapers of the American Pacific Northwest during those troubled years. Here, from week to week, and in some places from day to day, we may trace the downward plunge of prices in nearly every community. Whereas in the very heart of the Columbia Basin—at The Dalles and Walla Walla—the price of a cow with calf in 1871 ran from forty to forty-five dollars, the *Walla Walla Union* in December, 1872, was listing good cows at twenty five dollars each. But this was only the beginning. Everywhere in that vast region, as the months went by, men who spoke for the cattle interest complained of the low price of beef. In June, 1873, for example, the editor of a Boise newspaper heard that at The Dalles beef was being sold from butchers' carts for three to six cents a pound, which prices, he noted drily, were "certainly cheap enough"; and in July of that year an editor in Sacramento heard that the Indians in eastern Oregon were complaining of the hard times, saying that they could not "sell a single pony for anything like its value." In March, 1874, cattle were selling in Walla Walla at ten dollars a head, and in the same month the editor of the *Willamette Farmer* affirmed that stock raising was at a low ebb in the Willamette Valley.[73]

By the spring of 1876, however, the price of steers, in both the Yakima Valley and the Walla Walla Valley, was "looking up." But, in general, the depression persisted. In the spring of 1878, large numbers of "heavy cattle" were sold in eastern Washington for not more than eighteen dollars a head. In Prineville, a town in an old cattle district of central Oregon, cattle "from yearlings up" were selling in the fall of 1879 for ten to twelve dollars a head, "with calves thrown in." Even as late as the spring of 1880, four-year-old steers were selling in the Kittitas Valley for not

[73] *Walla Walla Statesman,* Aug. 26, 1871, quoted by the *Mountaineer,* Sept. 2, 1871; *Walla Walla Union,* Dec. 14, 1872; *Idaho Tri-Weekly Statesman,* June 12, 1873; *Sacramento Daily Union,* July 18, 1873; Laramie, Wyo., *Daily Sentinel,* March 16, 1874; *Willamette Farmer,* March 28, 1874.

more than twenty dollars a head. But in June, 1881, cattlemen
in Wasco, Oregon, were being offered twenty-one to twenty-two
dollars a head for four-year-olds, but were generally "holding out
for higher prices,"; and in May, 1883, an editor in the Rogue
River Valley asserted that, because the cost of cattle had advanced so much, only "the wealthy" could eat beef in Jacksonville, Oregon.[74] For cattlemen in Oregon, happy days had come
again.

But for more years than they liked to recall, they had suffered
much discomfort. Wherever they looked, they saw herds increasing and prices declining. Nor were they comforted by their
knowledge that the newspapers were concerned about their
plight, for they knew that editors' writings could raise the price
of steers as little as cattlemen's grumbling. Everyone, of course,
knew the solution of the problem: either reduce the size of herds
to the demand of the market, or increase the demand of the
market to the size of the herds. But how?

In June, 1875, the editor of the *Walla Walla Union* said that,
because of the low cattle prices during the preceding three or
four years, "nearly everybody" had tried to sell his cattle so that
he could turn his attention to something else; and this very fact,
he pointed out, had further depressed the market. But, affirming
that "hundreds and thousands of cattle" had gone, or soon would
go, out of the country, he looked for an improvement in the
situation. But there were others, he continued, who sought different means of decreasing their herds, "and to this end thousands
of cows and heifers are being spayed. We hear of one man in
Umatilla county who has spayed 600 head of his cattle; so that
in a very short time cattle will probably be high here again."[75]

But the optimism of this editor appears to have been ill-
founded. No available evidence shows that there ever was, during
the 1870's, a widespread spaying of cattle in Transcascadia; and,
as we shall learn in subsequent chapters, the evidence hardly

[74] *Walla Walla Union*, Feb. 26, March 4, May 11, 1876; *Palouse Gazette*,
May 11, 1878; *Yakima Record*, March 20, 1880; *Idaho Weekly Statesman*, June
25, 1881; *Oregon Sentinel*, May 5, 1883. The Chicago *Breeders' Gazette*, I (Jan.
26, 1882), 210, quotes the *Willamette Farmer* as saying that the price of cattle in
Portland, Ore., advanced during 1881 from $10 to "about $15" a head.
[75] Quoted by the Whatcom *Bellingham Bay Mail*, June 19, 1875.

shows that, during the early 1870's, a vast number of cattle were moved out of the Pacific Northwest. By the summer of 1875, thousands, but probably not many thousands, had been driven out.

Though generally unwilling to resort to measures of desperation, considerable numbers of Pacific Northwest cattlemen, more especially those operating in the Columbia Basin, after years of lengthening shadows, looked wistfully upon an experiment which offered them at least a possibility of getting markets beyond their own region. That experiment consisted in preserving beef for an export trade. This was not a new idea in the Columbia Valley, for many years earlier the Hudson's Bay Company had packed beef in barrels for export from the Columbia River, and, just before the beginning of the depression of the 1870's, the matter of preserving beef in commercial quantities had been a subject of comment in some Pacific Northwest newspapers. What was new at this time was the idea of putting up beef in tin cans. It was an intriguing idea. If, as one Oregonian asked, Australians could put up beef in tin cans and send this product to Great Britain, why could not Oregonians do likewise? Moreover, a beef-canning enterprise could be set on foot in Oregon without the investment of new capital, for the salmon canneries on the lower Columbia River were idle for a part of each year.

Given the situation then existing—surplus cattle, knowledge of canning, and equipment for canning—it would have been astounding had no one attempted in those difficult years to preserve beef on a commercial scale in the valley of the Columbia. Possibly as early as 1873, and certainly by 1874, an experiment in canning beef was begun on the lower Columbia, and the venturesome undertaker of this experiment was hailed as a public benefactor. But the praise was premature, for the enterprise appears to have been so unsuccessful that the firm which undertook it did not resume this operation in 1875.[76] The firm that pioneered in beef canning on the Columbia River was probably John West

[76] On this subject in general, see J. Orin Oliphant, "A Beef-Canning Enterprise in Oregon," *OHQ*, XXXIV (September, 1933), 241-54. "In 1873 and also in 1874 considerable beef and mutton was canned for export, but owing to losses was discontinued." *Weekly Mountaineer*, Dec. 2, 1876, quoting from the Portland *Commercial Reporter* of November 30.

and Company, which, in September and October, 1874, was canning both mutton and beef.[77] There is some reason for thinking that it lost money on this venture, less reason for thinking that it began operations as early as 1873, and virtually no reason for thinking that it resumed its experiment in 1875.

But interest in such a project persisted, and in 1876 several firms were canning beef on the Columbia River, the principal one being that of August C. Kinney, which put up thirteen thousand cans of beef in 1876. At least some of the canning in 1876 was done under contract to send the finished product to England. In this year probably forty thousand cases of beef and mutton were put up by canneries on the Columbia River, and most of this output was probably sent to England. But the output of canned beef in Oregon in 1877 appears to have been slight, the reason being that the hoped-for market in Britain did not materialize. In subsequent years, the canning of beef in Oregon seems to have been slight.[78]

Such an enterprise had been begun at an unpropitious time, for in the mid years of the 1870's a fresh-meat and live-cattle trade between the eastern United States and Great Britain left little opening for the sale in Great Britain of beef canned in Oregon. Nor was this all. American beef canned in Chicago had been growing in favor in Great Britain since 1864, and by 1876 it was displacing Australian canned beef in the British market. The epitaph of the beef-canning enterprise in Oregon appeared in an extract from the Dickson and Renwick (Glasgow) Report quoted in the London *Economist's* "Commercial History and Review of 1878." It reads as follows: "Oregon meats, including beef, mutton and sundries, have been closed out privately, and at auction, at figures resulting in large losses to packers and importers. The goods were, so far as the meats are concerned, of good quality and honestly packed. The soups and sundries lacked the character of the meats." In the same report it was observed that compressed corned beef, although introduced less than three years before, had grown amazingly in public favor in Great Brit-

[77] *Morning Oregonian*, Sept. 11, Oct. 29, 1874; *Willamette Farmer*, Oct. 16, 1874.
[78] Oliphant, "Beef-Canning Enterprise," 249-52.

ain, and that Chicago had maintained its supremacy as the seat of the trade in this product.[79]

Thus ended in failure an interesting experiment which, as some hoped, would help to lift the depression which had settled on the ranges of Transcascadia. Although this was not to be, the canning of meats in Oregon did not cease altogether; and in subsequent years some beef canned in Oregon did go to England; but, while the enthusiasm for the canning of beef was at its height in the valley of the Columbia, the attention of some thoughtful persons in this region turned hopefully toward a market which appeared to be opening east of the Rocky Mountains. Accordingly, in an effort to understand the lifting of the depression which, for nearly a decade, had bedeviled the cattlemen of Transcascadia, we turn our attention, once again, to the subject of marketing cattle that were either bred or matured on the ranges of the Oregon Country east of the Cascade Mountains.

[79] *Ibid.*, pp. 252-54.

CHAPTER IV

Westward and Southward to Markets

INCREASINGLY, as their markets in northern and northeastern mining camps dwindled, stockmen in the Columbia Basin turned to markets in the lower Columbia Valley and the basin of Puget Sound. By and large, the cattle could be moved from their pasture to these markets along the routes by which most livestock had entered Transcascadia—that is, along the Columbia River, and overland through passes in the Cascade Mountains. It must be remembered, however, that the movement of cattle and other livestock eastward into Transcascadia through passes north of the Columbia River had been relatively slight; most of the cattle, horses, and sheep that entered this country from the west came from the valleys of western Oregon, either up the Columbia River on steamboats or through passes in the Cascades south of the river. But this was not so in respect to the movement of cattle and other livestock westward from the grasslands east of the Cascades. This traffic used two of the passes north of the Columbia River, the Naches and the Snoqualmie; but, except for the Barlow Road, the routes through the mountains south of the Columbia seem not to have been much used for driving cattle westward from Transcascadia. The reason is not far to seek, for cattle from the ranges of eastern Oregon south of the Columbia Basin—in what then were the large counties of Lake, Baker, and Grant—tended to move southward to markets in Nevada or California. To this subject we shall presently return. Our immediate

115

concern is the marketing of cattle fattened on the grasslands and sage lands of the Columbia Basin.

Naches and Snoqualmie passes gave the cattlemen of the Yakima Valley easy access to the country of Puget Sound; and cattle and other livestock could also be driven through these passes from the Okanogan Valley, the Big Bend east of the Columbia River, the Palouse country, northern Idaho, and the Walla Walla country, as well as from Wasco and Umatilla counties, and elsewhere in northeastern Oregon. The Barlow Road provided passage through the mountains from the Columbia Basin ranges lying south of the Columbia River. Moreover, from all the ranges of the Columbia Basin, whether north or south of this river, cattle could be shipped down the Columbia on steamboats from The Dalles to help supply the demand for fresh meat in Portland, in the rising towns and cities in the Puget Sound Basin, and in Victoria. It is with the movement of cattle from the Columbia Basin to all these markets that the first part of this chapter will deal.

Of the two northern passes, the more important for the cattle trade, from the late 1860's to the late 1880's, was Snoqualmie Pass. Through this pass ran a trail (later a road) which was deeply cut by the hoofs of cattle which had been fattened on ranges in the Columbia Basin. But, as we shall see, the Naches Pass during those years also helped to maintain communication between the settlers on Puget Sound and their vast pasture lands east of the Cascade Mountains.

The value of a road which would connect Puget Sound with the region "in which Dr. Whitman lived" was perceived as early as 1844 by Peter H. Burnett. Writing from "Fallatine Plains, Oregon," on December 8, 1844, a little more than a year after his arrival in that country, he remarked that, "when the second region of Oregon shall swarm with cattle[,] as it will in 20 years from this moment, they will be driven to Puget's Sound and there slaughtered. In fact that point will command all the trade of the second and third regions of Oregon, as the carriage by land will be safer and less expensive than the transportation down the dangerous Columbia."[1] By "second region" and "third region,"

[1] Jefferson City, Mo., *Jefferson Inquirer*, Nov. 26, 1845.

Burnett meant all the Oregon Country east of the Cascade Mountains, the country which was frequently called by early pioneers in Oregon "middle Oregon" and "upper Oregon," and which, in this work, has been called Transcascadia.

The vision and the prophecy of Burnett were not lost on his contemporaries in the Oregon Country, and by 1867 travel by both Naches Pass and Snoqualmie Pass had become relatively easy. Naches Pass, as we have seen, had been used by a westward moving train of immigrants as early as 1853, and no doubt was used by immigrants to some extent thereafter.[2] Through this pass was constructed a military road from Fort Steilacoom to Wallula, a road described in some detail, in 1868, by J. Ross Browne, who also observed that during the preceding year a road had been opened from Seattle "across the Snoqualmie Pass" into the Yakima Valley. These two roads came together at the Yakima County seat, which was at "Colonel Thorp's claim on the Yakima, near the mouth of the Atahnam, and not far from the old Catholic mission."[3] Browne's testimony, at least as to the Snoqualmie Pass route, is fully substantiated by contemporaneous newspaper reports, of which one from the Seattle Weekly Intelligencer of October 7, 1867, tells us that "the wagon road over the Snoqualmie is now completed," and that it was hoped that some means would be "at once adopted with a view to reap the advantages which it is claimed the road possesses." From this and an earlier issue of the Weekly Intelligencer we learn that this road would shorten the time and decrease the expense of travel from Walla Walla and Umatilla to Seattle, and that it would open up a wagon trade between Seattle and the eastern hinterland. In December, 1868, the editor of this newspaper was of the opinion that in 1869 measures would be taken to provide the Seattle market "with beef and flour from Walla Walla county direct, by way of the Snoqualmie Pass."[4]

This hope was in part realized. As early as May, 1869, the editor of an Olympia newspaper wrote that "Mr. M. R. Tilley

[2] Elva Cooper Magnusson, "Naches Pass," WHQ, XXV (1934), 176-79.
[3] J. Ross Browne, Report on the Mineral Resources of the States and Territories West of the Rocky Mountains (Washington, D.C., 1868), pp. 562, 564, 567.
[4] Seattle Weekly Intelligencer, Sept. 16, 1867, Dec. 7, 1868.

arrived at Seattle, on Wednesday last, with sixty head of fine cattle from the Yakima country. He came over the Snoqualmie Pass, which he represents as in good condition for crossing. . . . From Seattle the cattle were brought up by the steamer *Eliza Anderson*."[5] In November of that year the same editor asserted that "by the *Hunt* of this evening sixty head of cattle arrived from Seattle, where they were driven from over the mountains. The order of cattle shipments," he said, "is reversed."[6]

How great the movement of cattle from the Yakima Valley to Puget Sound may have been during 1869, there appears to be no way of determining; but it is certain that the Seattle butchering firm of Booth, Foss and Borst drove several bands across the mountains. Writing of this firm's activities, the editor of the *Weekly Intelligencer* tells us on July 19, 1869, that "Messrs. Booth and Foss left here last week for the eastern side of the mountains, for the purpose of driving over another large band of cattle for this and Port Townsend markets." In October the editor of the Olympia *Pacific Tribune* announced that "Mr. Borst, of the firm of Booth, Foss & Borst, meat and cattle dealers of Seattle, arrived at that place on Thursday last, from Yakima Valley, with 75 head of cattle and 600 sheep," and that Mr. Borst would probably make another trip that fall. Finally, in reporting near the end of that year what probably was the last such drive of the season, the editor of the *Weekly Intelligencer* told his readers that "Mr. Booth, of the firm of Booth, Foss & Borst, arrived here last Monday morning from the valleys east of the Cascade Mountains, bringing upwards of 200 head of stock. . . . Four head of cattle were lost on the trip"; and he concluded that, considering "the lateness of the season, the trip was a very successful one."[7]

Between 1870 and 1874 there was a considerable movement of cattle from the Columbia Basin to the country west of the Cascades, much of it by way of the Columbia River. Nevertheless, during those years many cattle were driven westward through Snoqualmie Pass. Because the demand for beef at the

[5] Olympia *Pacific Tribune*, May 29, 1869.
[6] *Ibid.*, Nov. 13, 1869.
[7] *Pacific Tribune*, Oct. 16, 1869; *Weekly Intelligencer*, Dec. 6, 1869.

mines lying north and east of the Columbia Basin had shrunk to the vanishing point, cattlemen of the "Inland Empire" were coming to depend heavily upon the markets of western Oregon, western Washington, and western British Columbia. Presently they were to learn a bitter truth: that their enterprise was so expanded that these markets could not absorb the output of their ranges.

Owing to the scarcity of information, it is impossible to tell how much of the trade in cattle from the Columbia Basin to Puget Sound between the beginning of 1870 and the end of 1873 was carried on by way of Snoqualmie Pass; but we can be fairly certain that several hundred head of cattle were driven westward through this pass during each of those years. Toward the end of October, 1870, an editor at The Dalles learned on good authority that more than twelve hundred head of cattle had already during that year been driven from the Yakima Valley to Puget Sound, and that several hundred more would be "sent over the mountains" before the winter set in.[8] In December cattlemen in the Yakima Valley were anticipating that "buyers from the Sound country" would cross the mountains early in the next year to purchase cattle for the Puget Sound and Victoria markets. How many cattle were bought in the Yakima Valley in 1871 for the "Sound country" the evidence at hand does not reveal, but there is no reason to suppose that there was any slackening of the trade. On the contrary, there is sufficient evidence to warrant the belief that the markets of Puget Sound were beginning to draw cattle from a very wide area of the "eastern" country, for in September, 1871, the editor of an important newspaper at The Dalles wrote that, on the preceding Sunday, "a drove of 200 head of fat beef cattle were ferried across the Columbia river at this point, . . . bound for a market on Puget Sound, by way of the Snoqualmie Pass." "This," he remarked, "is the commencement of what in the course of time will be the route to market of thousands of our cattle."[9]

Whether this trade was large or small in 1871, there can be little doubt that the movement of cattle westward through Sno-

[8] The Dalles *Weekly Mountaineer*, Oct. 22, 1870. "Beef cattle for Puget Sound markets are now driven from Yakima"—Portland *Morning Oregonian*, Oct. 22, 1870.

[9] *Weekly Mountaineer*, Dec. 17, 1870, Sept. 7, 1871.

qualmie Pass in 1872 was fairly large, for in November of that year it was reported that Booth, Foss and Borst "of the Sound" had "monopolized" the buying of beef cattle in the Yakima Valley during the preceding summer, their purchases having amounted to 850 head. But the reference to "monopolizing" of buying of this firm must not be taken at face value, for the *Weekly Intelligencer,* in August, 1872, informed its readers of the arrival of "D. A. Neeley, Esq., of the firm of Snyder & Co., of the City Market, . . . in this city on Friday last, with 45 head of fine beef cattle from Kittitas Valley." While he was in that part of the country, "he purchased several lots of cattle for their market, aggregating in the whole over 400 head, which will be brought here this summer and fall."[10]

By the summer of 1873, however, the story was beginning to change; the trade in cattle through Snoqualmie Pass was slowing down. As late as July 5, 1873, a Kittitas Valley correspondent for the *Walla Walla Union* wrote that as yet only a small band of cattle had been driven from there to Puget Sound, and he estimated that at least a thousand more beef cattle in that valley were ready for market. "Our main dependence for a market is Seattle and the Sound country generally"; and then he remarked: "We need a good road over the Cascade Mountains very much." In a later letter, dated September 22, 1873, he observed that "butchers of Seattle" had recently taken over the mountains a large drove of cattle. The price they gave for two-year-olds, he said, was nineteen and twenty dollars, which was "low compared with the prices that ranged a year ago."[11] Here, then, was the cause of the slackening of the cattle trade: cattlemen of the Columbia Basin were now compelled to dispose of their cattle in a buyer's market. The effects of the depression now setting in we have dealt with, at some length, in the preceding chapter.

Because of the "hard times," the movement of cattle westward from the Columbia Basin was probably not very large during 1874 and 1875. No doubt in both those years some cattle passed on the Snoqualmie trail to markets in Puget Sound, as in former years; but, because of the low prices, stockmen east of the Cas-

[10] *Ibid.,* Nov. 9, 1872; *Weekly Intelligencer,* Aug. 19, 1872.
[11] *Walla Walla Union,* July 19, Oct. 4, 1873.

cades seemed reluctant to part with their cattle.[12] But in July, 1874, it was reported in Sacramento that "plenty" of fine beef cattle were entering "the Sound country" by way of Naches Pass, and a few days later a small band of cattle was said to have crossed by this route. Nearly a year later, on May 14, 1875, a correspondent wrote from the Kittitas Valley, saying that no sales had yet been made that spring, but that butchers from Puget Sound were expected as soon as the mountains could be crossed. He had not heard anything about the prices they would offer. In November, 1875, the *Morning Oregonian*, without mentioning the route they used, affirmed that Phelps and Wadleigh, cattle dealers of Seattle, had "driven out of the Yakima Valley . . . [in that] year over fifteen hundred head of beef cattle to supply their markets on the Sound."[13]

For several years after 1876 the number of cattle driven westward through Snoqualmie Pass mounted, and there were a few reports of bands of cattle being driven from the Yakima Valley through Naches Pass into Pierce County; also, as early as 1876, bands of sheep and an occasional drove of hogs were reported to be traveling westward through Snoqualmie Pass.[14] In 1877, driving through this pass began in February, a fact which led a Kittitas correspondent, who knew that the pass was seldom open before May 1, to express the belief that, "by a little exertion on the part of those engaged in driving," the Snoqualmie trail could be kept open all winter, thus allowing cattlemen east of the mountains to feed their cattle during the winter and dispose of

[12] A correspondent of the Walla Walla *Spirit of the West*, writing of Kititass [*sic*] Valley, said that "the grangers will borrow money before they will sell their beef for less than 4 cents per pound net." Whatcom *Bellingham Bay Mail*, Sept. 4, 1875.

[13] *Sacramento Daily Union*, July 25, Aug. 3, 1874; Tacoma *Weekly Pacific Tribune*, Aug. 7, 1874; *Walla Walla Union*, May 22, 1875; *Morning Oregonian*, Nov. 15, 1875.

[14] "Mr. Jas. Longmire has just returned from east of the mountains with a large band of cattle. He came through the Natchez Pass and reports it in good condition." *Bellingham Bay Mail*, Oct. 21, 1876. See also the *New Tacoma Herald*, Oct. 27, 1877, quoting the *Olympia Transcript*, and the *Morning Oregonian*, Oct. 13, 1879, quoting The Dalles *Inland Empire; Weekly Intelligencer*, June 3, 1876; Seattle *Weekly Pacific Tribune*, Sept. 22, 1876; *Walla Walla Union*, Aug. 12, Oct. 21, 1876. The *Morning Oregonian* of Oct. 26, 1876, reported that the "last and largest drove of cattle that ever came over the Snoqualmie Pass crossed last week. They were from Yakima, for a Seattle firm."

them as soon as they were ready for market. In August, 1877, it was reported that Seattle butchers were slaughtering about three hundred head of cattle a month—cattle which they were obtaining from the Yakima and Kittitas valleys; and at about the same time it was widely reported in the press of Washington Territory that more than three thousand head of cattle had been driven from the Yakima Valley to the sound within a period of one hundred days, and that the driving would continue.[15] During that year, there appeared prominently in the news of the cattle business the name of George F. Smith, a man who for several years thereafter would be actively engaged in driving cattle through Snoqualmie Pass. Before the end of February, 1877, according to an editor at The Dalles, Smith "took a drove of cattle directly across the mountains . . . from the Yakima country to Seattle." In that year also we read that Phelps and Wadleigh, who since at least 1869 had been interested in the cattle business in eastern Washington, increased enormously their holdings in the Columbia Basin.

For 1878 the record of the cattle trade through Snoqualmie Pass is less satisfactory than that of the preceding year, but there is no reason to suppose that this trade was falling off.[16] We do know that the movement during 1879 was considerable, for in November the *Walla Walla Union*, quoting the Seattle *Weekly Intelligencer*, affirmed that four thousand head of cattle had been driven through this pass from the Yakima country in 1878. "This drive," the *Union* continued, "shows what the Pass and road will be capable of when opened, they being only partially opened at present."[17]

[15] Letter from "Kittitass," dated May 10, 1877, in the *Walla Walla Union*, May 26, 1877; *Dayton News*, Aug. 10, 1877, quoting the Seattle *Puget Sound Dispatch;* letter from "Yakima, W. T.," August 8, 1877," in the *Weekly Mountaineer*, Aug. 18, 1877; Port Townsend *Puget Sound Weekly Argus*, Aug. 31, 1877, supplement. See also the comment on the need for a better road through the Snoqualmie Pass in the *Weekly Pacific Tribune*, Oct. 31, 1877.

[16] *Weekly Mountaineer*, March 3, 1877; *Lewiston Teller*, May 12, 1877; letter from Kittitas, dated June 28, 1874, in the *Walla Walla Union*, July 4, 1874. A. J. Splawn affirms that Phelps and Wadleigh entered the cattle business in the Yakima Valley in 1869. *Ka-mi-akin, Last Hero of the Yakimas* (2nd ed.; Portland, Ore., 1944), p. 290.

[17] *Weekly Intelligencer*, June 1, 1878; *Tacoma Herald*, June 21, Sept. 20, 1878; *Bellingham Bay Mail*, May 18, 1878; *Walla Walla Union*, Nov. 29, 1879.

One lot of cattle that followed this trail westward in October of 1879 was disposed of in a manner interesting to those concerned about the developing cattle business in the Pacific Northwest.[18] According to the recently established *Tacoma Ledger* (quoted in the *Yakima Record* of May 15, 1880), the steamer *North Pacific* had brought from Seattle to Tacoma

thirty head of large cattle, for shipment on the Northern Pacific Railroad, half to Portland for H. Johnson, and the other half to Astoria for Warren & Eaton. Another shipment of sixty will be made today. This is said to be the first shipment of cattle from Puget Sound for the Oregon market, and shows their appreciation of good beef. The cattle were raised by Phelps & Wadleigh, at Okanogan, about twenty miles south of the British Columbia line, east of the Cascade Mountains, driven through the Snoqualmie Pass last October and stall fed at Thomas Alvord's, White river. The Indian chief Moses looks after the interests of Phelps & Wadleigh, on the cattle range near Okanogan, and is no doubt well paid for his trouble.

By the summer of 1880, cattle from the Columbia Basin were bringing higher prices in Puget Sound markets than in the preceding year. Before the middle of June, the editor of the *Yakima Record*, observing that Bayless Thorp was getting ready to start through Snoqualmie Pass with a small band of cattle, remarked that prices of cattle were "manifesting a tendency upward," and predicted that the boom would "continue indefinitely." Early in July the *Walla Walla Union*, affirming that the prices offered for "good two-year-old steers" had advanced from twelve dollars in 1879 to a new level of fifteen dollars, ascribed this advance to "the heavy draw made by the spring drives east." The driving of livestock through Snoqualmie Pass in that year was in full swing before the end of June, and it continued well into the autumn, Indians sometimes being employed as drovers. Even heavier, perhaps, if the newspaper reports may be trusted, were the movements of the next two years, notwithstanding the heavy losses of cattle east of the Cascades during the winter of 1880-81 and the continual movement of cattle eastward from the Columbia Basin. Late in August, 1882, an editor in Seattle predicted that, before

[18] In the autumn of 1879, the *Inland Empire* said that Phelps and Wadleigh were keeping "large bands of cattle about the Okanogan, from which they supply their Yakima herds as fast as they become depleted by drives to Puget Sound." Quoted by the *Morning Oregonian*, Oct. 13, 1879.

the end of the season, the cattle drive "from Yakima county to Puget Sound" would number forty-five hundred head, as compared with thirty-five hundred head during 1881; and he most certainly knew that a few weeks earlier S. R. Geddis, a veteran drover of the Yakima country, had declared that no fewer than sixty thousand head of cattle had been purchased in eastern Washington during the spring of 1882 and driven to eastern markets.[19] Some of the cattle driven westward across the Cascades in 1882 went by way of Naches Pass. The Olympia *Courier,* for example, reported that "Mr. A. M. Miller and drovers arrived on Saturday with seventy-three head of beef cattle from the Wenas valley, via Naches Pass." The cattle came through in good condition.[20]

The years 1883 and 1884 were especially significant for the driving of livestock westward through Snoqualmie Pass, largely because the trail was kept open during the winters of 1882-83 and 1883-84. During the first of these winters, driving was steady and apparently heavy. The *Yakima Record* of February 10, 1883, quoted from the *Oregonian* of January 29 a despatch saying that "men, horses and cattle" were "crossing the Cascade mountains by the Snoqualmie pass every day," and that two "droves of cattle came through last week in fine order from Kittitas and Yakima valleys, without losing a single animal." This, he remarked, was "the first winter an effort was made to keep the pass open, and so little difficulty . . . [was] experienced, that its closing will not again be permitted."

The movement of livestock through this pass in 1883 must have been very large. So great, indeed, was the demand for beef and other meat in Puget Sound communities that buyers from Yakima County ranged far and wide in the Columbia Basin making

[19] *Yakima Record,* June 12, 19, 26, July 17, 31, Oct. 16, 1880; *Walla Walla Union,* June 3, 1880; Tacoma *Weekly Ledger,* Sept. 1, 1882, quoting the Seattle *Weekly Post-Intelligencer; Yakima Record,* June 17, 1882, quoting the *Seattle Chronicle.* For further details on this subject, see the *Yakima Record,* Oct. 7, 21, Nov. 11, 1882, and the *Weekly Post-Intelligencer,* June 23, July 21, Aug. 18, Sept. 29, Oct. 13, Nov. 10, 1882.

[20] Quoted by the *Yakima Record,* Aug. 26, 1882. Naches Pass was presumably used enough to rouse the ire of an editor in Seattle, who declared in the autumn of 1882 that the Snoqualmie Pass was "the only practical pass." *Ibid.,* Nov. 18, 1882, quoting the *Weekly Intelligencer.*

purchases for those markets. In March, 1883, such buyers were reported to be in northern Idaho, and throughout the summer and the autumn of that year Yakima County stockmen brought down hundreds of cattle from the Okanogan Valley, many of which were intended for the markets of Puget Sound. In April, 1883, the editor of the *Yakima Signal*, excited by what he was seeing from day to day, wrote that, since the Yakima country was now sending off "a band of several hundred cattle every few days," one must conclude that "the folks over at Seattle and down at Portland must be doing some tall eating to get away with so many of our bovines." But, as long as the price of beef remained high, the people of Yakima, he believed, would "try to stand it."[21]

He was not the only excited editor. The editor of the Vancouver *Clarke County Register* declared on August 2, 1883, that large droves of beef cattle were "coming to the Sound over the Snoqualmie Pass," and on September 27 he said that fat beef cattle in large numbers were being driven "across the mountains from Eastern Washington to Puget Sound." Other newspaper stories confirm in detail the foregoing reports of a heavy movement of cattle through Snoqualmie Pass in that year, a movement which continued steadily through February, 1884, and perhaps much beyond that time. If this pass was closed at all during that winter, it was soon reopened, for late in May, 1884, bands of cattle were coming through it to Seattle.[22]

The success achieved in keeping Snoqualmie Pass open during the winter of 1882-83 was no doubt an important factor in hastening the completion of a wagon toll road intended to strengthen the economic partnership of Seattle and the Yakima Valley. Judging by the evidence now available, the "road" that had been opened through Snoqualmie Pass in 1867 was little more than a trail, serviceable for moving herds and flocks, and pack-trains, but not for the passage of vehicles. The need for a better road

[21] *Yakima Record,* March 10, 1883, quoting the *Walla Walla Statesman,* and Nov. 17, 1883; *Yakima Signal,* April 7, May 26, June 30, July 28, Sept. 22, Oct. 13, 1883; Ellensburg *Kittitas Standard,* June 30, 1883.

[22] *Yakima Record,* March 24, Dec. 29, 1883, Feb. 2, 1884; *Yakima Signal,* March 10, April 21, May 26, Sept. 22, 1883; *Kittitas Standard,* June 30, 1883, quoting the *Weekly Post-Intelligencer; ibid.,* July 14, Aug. 18, Sept. 8, 29, Oct. 20, Nov. 3, 1883, Jan. 19, 26, 1884; *Daily Tacoma News,* May 29, 1884.

was voiced more than once after 1867, but not until 1883 was such a project pushed to completion, and then apparently largely because of the enterprise of a few men, including George F. Smith. There were "about 70 men at work at different points on the road across the mountains," declared an Ellensburg newspaper in September, 1883. "This force must be paid and it is hoped that those who have subscribed will settle, to enable the company to go on with the good work."[23] Later in that month an Olympia newspaper remarked that

Mr. Walter A. Bull is canvassing our city in behalf of a wagon toll road leading from a convenient point, perhaps Ellensburgh, in Yakima county to the Sound, by way of Snoqualmie Pass. Most of the road is now finished on the east side, and a large force of men is hard at work on this slope. Calculations based on the transportation of stock from Eastern Washington to the Sound, for the last year, warrant the conclusion that the annual revenue of the road when finished will reach $12,000 from tolls alone. Mr. Bull is selling certificates of stock with coupons attached for the payment of toll. This stock is just what should be in the hands of those who are largely engaged in the cattle trade between Sound points and Yakima county.[24]

By late November, 1883, a Tacoma editor, relying upon the *Ellensburg Localizer*, said that the Snoqualmie wagon road was so well advanced that sleds could make the trip over the mountains whenever the snow fell; and two weeks later, relying upon the *Yakima Signal*, he announced that "the enterprising firm of Smith Bros. & Co." had purchased the interest in this project previously held by Walter A. Bull, and that it would push the work forward to completion. "The road is now open for wagons and sleds through the entire range to Puget Sound and stations have been established along the road to accommodate travel."[25]

As late as February, 1884, Snoqualmie Pass was open for the passage of cattle, but heavy snow made general travel through it impracticable. Before the end of May, however, men who had just driven cattle through this pass remarked that the road was

[23] Tacoma *Daily Ledger*, April 15, 1883; *Kittitas Standard*, Sept. 8, Nov. 24, 1883. "On or about the 20th inst. the Smith Bros. & Co. will start a band of not less than 150 head of fine beef cattle for Seattle. They will go over the toll road, which is now completed within five miles of Lake Kichelas." *Ibid.*, Aug. 18, 1883.
[24] *Kittitas Standard*, Sept. 22, 1883, quoting the *Olympia Transcript*.
[25] *Daily Tacoma News*, Nov. 28, 1883, quoting the *Ellensburg Localizer*; *ibid.*, Dec. 13, 1883, quoting the *Yakima Signal*.

"in good condition, with the exception of a stretch of ten miles near the summit, which . . . [needed] some considerable work done on it to make it passable for wagons." By early June, however, George F. Smith had a force of men at work on this road, and on June 26 he appealed to the people of Seattle for aid "in the completion of the Snoqualmie Pass wagon road."[26] Thereafter the history of this road is somewhat obscure, but presumably there continued to be considerable travel on it.[27] On April 21, 1886, a correspondent at Snoqualmie, writing to the editor of the *Weekly Post-Intelligencer,* affirmed that this toll road had been open to the public for three years; that it was a well-graded thoroughfare; that a force was then reducing its grades; and that it would be open about June 1 of that year.

The advantages to both Seattle and the Yakima Valley of such an all-year road were easy to comprehend. The snow on the road could be packed so hard that in ordinary winters the driving of cattle through the pass need not be interrupted. With such a route available, stockmen in the Kittitas and Yakima valleys could fatten their cattle during the winter and move them to market at such times as would be most profitable to them. Without an all-year route, they were compelled either to drive all their marketable cattle to Puget Sound before winter, and thus run the risk of forcing down prices, or else to move such stock to market during the winter and spring months by the roundabout and expensive route down the Columbia River and thence overland to Puget Sound. A further objection to the latter route was the fact that some of the cattle sent by boat and train were severely bruised in transit. Furthermore, an all-year road across the mountains could be expected to offer both Seattle and the Yakima Valley the advantage of an exchange of commodities by wagon traffic. By the growth of such a trade Seattle and the whole Yakima country could expect to move forward together to

[26] *Ibid.,* Feb. 15, 1884, quoting the Seattle *Post-Intelligencer; ibid.,* April 19, 1884, quoting the *Yakima Signal; ibid.,* May 29, June 19, 1884; *Morning Oregonian,* June 21, 1884; *Weekly Post-Intelligencer,* June 26, 1884. For toll rates in force on the Snoqualmie wagon road, see the *Daily Tacoma News,* Aug. 22, 1884, quoting the *Ellensburg Localizer.*
[27] *Weekly Post-Intelligencer,* June 4, July 2, Aug. 27, Nov. 19, 1885, May 6, 1886. The author of an article in the last-named issue of this newspaper said that George F. Smith had projected this road.

more prosperous times. Finally, without much reading between the lines, one can perceive that such a road was contemplated as part of a higher strategy by which Seattle, and also Tacoma, hoped to forge ahead of their formidable rival on the Willamette River. A good road through Snoqualmie Pass would counteract to a great extent the enormous power of the Columbia River route to draw the productions of the whole Columbia Basin toward Portland. An arrangement that would profit either Seattle or Tacoma, each aspiring to ascendancy on Puget Sound, could not be expected to please Portland; but it is not a matter of record that restless citizens of either Seattle or Tacoma, or of the Yakima Valley for that matter, spent restless nights worrying about the well-being of Portland.[28] But we do know that in those years Seattle and Tacoma—the former favoring Snoqualmie Pass and the latter Naches Pass—did expend considerable energy in hating each other and in generating a climate of opinion that would nourish their later controversy about the "right" name of the mountain which Captain George Vancouver, without malice aforethought, had called Rainier. In the early years of controversy between Seattle and Tacoma, Yakima was more or less consistently neutral on the side of Seattle.[29]

But stockmen of eastern Washington and eastern Oregon, whatever their wishes may have been, confronted the hard fact that, during severe wintry weather, the Columbia River route had a decided advantage over all its competitors. When the Cascade passes were choked with snow, and when the Barlow Road was impassable because of mud, the river route ordinarily would

---

[28] *Weekly Astorian,* Oct. 20, 1877; *Kittitas Standard,* June 30, Nov. 24, 1883. On Feb. 9, 1884, the editor of the *Kittitas Standard,* having learned that two drovers had recently taken their cattle through Snoqualmie Pass, wrote as follows: "It will now be in order for the Oregonian and other papers opposed to the direct route across the Cascades to entirely overlook this news item," but, he added, "let the contrary be the character of the published news concerning this section" and such news would quickly be republished in both Portland and Tacoma.

[29] During 1883, the editor of the *Daily Ledger* frequently expressed his contempt for Seattle by calling it Yeslerville. In January, 1884, he predicted that Tacoma, after the completion of the Cascade division of the Northern Pacific Railroad, would become not only "the largest city in the Territory," but also "the great supply point" for eastern Washington. Tacoma *Daily Ledger,* Jan. 15, 1884.

be open.[30] For this reason, during all the years that the Snoqualmie road was used for driving cattle, the Columbia River remained an important and at times indispensable alternate route
from the ranges of the Columbia Basin to the markets of Puget
Sound. This route involved no extraordinary difficulty, for once
the cattle were on the lower reaches of the Columbia, those that
were destined for western Washington could be turned northward into a trail beaten out in earlier years by band after band of
cattle that had passed from the valleys of western Oregon into
the Puget Sound Basin. As early as 1870, cattle were leaving
The Dalles by boat for markets on Puget Sound and in Victoria,
as well as in western Oregon.[31] From 1873 forward, cattle could
be taken northward on the Northern Pacific Railroad from Kalama to Tacoma. From the Kalama *Beacon* of June 14, 1873, we
learn that

On Wednesday last, another invoice of beef cattle from east of the mountains, several car loads, was shipped from here on the train to Puget Sound.
We are informed that cattle shipments from east of the Cascades via Columbia river and railroad to the Sound is about closed for the season, as
stock in British Columbia and the Sound country is getting into merchant-
able condition. Stock up the Columbia get fat in the spring about two
months earlier than cattle on the ranges about the Sound, which causes a
spring demand for beef cattle by this route. During two or three months in
the fall, the Snoqualmie trail leading over the Cascades from Yakima valley,
is open as a cattle drovers' route, by which the fall beef supply reaches the
Sound in the vicinity north of Seattle, at which city the leading butchers of
the Sound are located.[32]

Notwithstanding the high prices charged by the Oregon Steam
Navigation Company, The Dalles, formerly a cattle-receiving

[30] During severe winters, the navigation of the Columbia River below The
Dalles would sometimes be blocked by ice. Such was the case during the winters
of 1879-80 and 1880-81. James B. Hedges, *Henry Villard and the Railways of the
Northwest* (New Haven, Conn., 1930), p. 86.

[31] J. Orin Oliphant, "The Cattle Trade on Puget Sound, 1858-1890," *AH*, VII
(July, 1933), 129-49. "Messrs. Booth and Tilly, of Puget Sound, bought of T.
Johnson and Wm. Connell, of Rockland, and Messrs. Fisk and Walker, of Klick-
itat, W. T., one hundred and fifty head of fat beef cattle, which they shipped on
the steamer *Oneonta* yesterday destined for the Puget Sound market." *Weekly
Mountaineer*, May 2, 1870.

[32] Quoted by the *Weekly Intelligencer*, June 21, 1873. This story, of course,
does not correctly portray the situation as it existed a few years later.

port, now of necessity became a cattle-shipping port and prospered by such trade, even during the years of the depression.[33]
As the 1870's glided by, cattle and other livestock were brought
to this port from such distant parts of the Columbia Basin as the
Palouse country and northern Idaho. Early in 1877, the editor of
the *Weekly Mountaineer* estimated that the "live stock shipment
made from ... [The Dalles] to the markets below for the year
just past, was 10,000 head of mutton sheep, and 6,000 head of
beef cattle; besides about 1,000 head of hogs. Nearly all these
animals were sold from R. B. Hood's Stock Yards and were
shipped by the O.S.N. Co's boats."[34]

As the prices of beef began to soar in the early 1880's, the
winter driving of cattle to The Dalles increased. To this point
cattle in larger numbers than ever before came not only from the
Okanogan Valley, by way of the Yakima Valley, but also from
northern Idaho and from places in Oregon as far away as Prineville.[35] Encouraged by the higher prices, cattlemen made winter
drives to The Dalles under hazardous conditions. A Yakima newspaper in December, 1880, reported that Jack Splawn of Yakima
City started from the Yakima Valley

with a drove of eighty head of beef cattle for the Portland market, and arrived in Rockland last Thursday night, where he was river-bound. The ice
was not strong enough to bear the weight of his cattle, and was sufficient
to stop the ferry-boat from running. The above we clip from last Tuesday's
Dalles Times. Since then, however, the ice blockade on the Columbia has
been broken, and we have no doubt ere this Portlanders are enjoying our
juicy steaks.

[33] At the beginning of 1874, an editor at The Dalles was regretting that the
lack of a wagon road "down the river" would impose a heavy burden on stockmen to get their cattle to market. Estimating that at least 100,000 head of cattle
"must be transported down the Columbia River to find a market," he continued:
"These could be driven down the river, if there was a wagon road, at a cost of
about $5,000; to take their cattle down the river by rail and boat will cost
$30,000, making a difference to the stockmen of about $25,000, or one quarter of
what it will cost to make the road." Quoted by the Salem *Willamette Farmer*,
Jan. 17, 1874.
[34] *Walla Walla Union*, July 17, 1874; letter from The Dalles, dated April 28,
1875, in the *Willamette Farmer*, May 7, 1875; *Weekly Mountaineer*, March 4,
1876, quoting the *Oregonian* of March 1; *Walla Walla Union*, Aug. 5, 1876;
Lewiston Teller, Jan. 13, 1877; *Weekly Mountaineer*, Jan. 6, Feb. 17, 24, 1877.
[35] *Yakima Record*, May 29, Dec. 11, 1880, Jan. 15, 1881, March 17, 31, April
7, 21, 1883; *Weekly Mountaineer*, July 1, 1880; *Yakima Signal*, March 24, 31,

But the experience of another Yakima cattleman, who risked a winter drive to The Dalles two years later, was more fortunate. In January, 1883, as another Yakima newspaper tells, "Ben Snipes, the cattle king of the northwest, drove 180 head of beef cattle from his ranch on the lower Yakima a few days ago and then took them across the Columbia on the ice at Rockland."[36]

As late as the summer of 1883, The Dalles was still an important cattle town, but the days of its glory as a river port for cattlemen were numbered, for by this time a considerable portion of eastern Washington had access to a railroad. Jack Splawn recalled, in his memoirs, that in 1881 he sent out the first trainload of cattle on the Northern Pacific from the country north of the Snake River, and that the building of the railroads presently put an end to the long and dangerous winter drives to The Dalles.[37] But such drives were not ended by 1883, for during that spring large numbers of cattle were being driven to The Dalles, some of them by Jack Splawn himself, for shipment to markets on the west coast.[38] Many of these cattle, however, were being sent on from The Dalles by train rather than by boat.[39] By the latter part of the 1880's, when cattle could be sent by rail at any time of the year from various inland points to markets on the west coast, the long winter drives to The Dalles from eastern Washington and northern Idaho were no longer necessary.[40]

By 1883 the cattle industry of the Pacific Northwest, like other aspects of the economy of this region, was in a state of rapid transition. For several years, as we have seen, settlers had been

---

April 7, May 26, 1883; Vancouver *Clarke County Register*, June 7, 1883.

[36] *Yakima Record*, Dec. 18, 1880; *Yakima Signal*, Jan. 27, 1883.

[37] Splawn, *Ka-mi-akin*, p. 295.

[38] *Willamette Farmer*, June 15, 1883, quoting the *Goldendale Gazette; Yakima Signal*, March 24, 31, June 2, 1883; *Yakima Record*, March 17, 31, April 7, 1883.

[39] The *Yakima Signal*, Feb. 2, 1884, quoted the *Tacoma News* as follows: "The local markets present no peculiarly interesting features. The beef supply is principally from Yakima county, where cattle are fed for the Sound market, and driven to The Dalles, coming thence by rail. They cost 5 cents live weight at Yakima, and it costs $5 a head to transport them to Tacoma."

[40] *Yakima Record*, Feb. 25, 1884; *Walla Walla Union*, April 18, 1855, April 17, May 8, 29, 1886, May 19, 1888, March 23, April 13, 1889. It is interesting to observe that choice cattle for the use of the "gold spike" party in Portland, in September, 1883, had been sent to that city by rail from Sprague, Washington. *Walla Walla Union*, Sept. 15, 1883.

moving into the "Inland Empire," and by 1879 the farm products of the Walla Walla and Palouse countries had increased so much that they were choking the facilities for transporting them down the Columbia River.[41] The time was ripe, therefore, for the construction of railroads in this area; and during the 1880's the building of railroads in the Columbia Basin was rapid. In 1879 the Northern Pacific began work on its Pend d'Oreille division, starting at Ainsworth, on the Snake River, and by midsummer of 1881 had completed this division as far east as Spokane Falls. Meanwhile the Oregon Railway and Navigation Company, successor to the Oregon Steam Navigation Company, was building a line on the south side of the Columbia, between Portland and Wallula. In 1880 the Northern Pacific had contracted with the O.R. & N. for the use of this line,[42] and therefore it put aside for the time being any plan that it may have had for building a division from the Columbia River to Puget Sound via the Yakima Valley. By extending to Portland the line which it had completed in 1873 between Tacoma and Kalama, the N.P. would give itself, by use of the facilities of the Oregon Railway and Navigation Company, a through route from the East to Tacoma. On September 8, 1883, the Northern Pacific Railroad, under the aggressive leadership of Henry Villard, was "completed," an event which caused much rejoicing in the Pacific Northwest.[43] In the meantime, the Oregon Railway and Navigation Company had been extending its lines, and before the end of 1884 it had a road through northeastern Oregon that connected at Huntington, Oregon, with the Oregon Short Line, a subsidiary of the Union Pacific. It had also been building in eastern Washington, and

[41] Francis H. Cook, *The Territory of Washington* (Cheney, Wash., 1925), pp. 7-10.
[42] Northern Pacific Railroad, *Annual Report... September 24, 1879* (New York, 1879), p. 14, and *Annual Report... September 15, 1881* (New York, 1881), p. 27. See also the Colfax *Palouse Gazette*, Oct. 10, 1879, and the Cheney *Northwest Tribune*, May 27, 1881. On the Oregon Railway and Navigation Company, incorporated on July 13, 1879, see Irene Lincoln Poppleton, "Oregon's First Monopoly–the O.S.N. Co.," *OHQ*, IX (1908), 298, and Hedges, *Henry Villard*, pp. 72-73.
[43] Northern Pacific Railroad, *Annual Report... September 15, 1881*, p. 29; Hedges, *Henry Villard*, p. 79; *New York Tribune*, Sept. 8, 9, 1883. See also the message of the Governor of Washington Territory, Oct. 3, 1883, to the legislature. *Council Journal* (Olympia, Wash., 1883), p. 29.

between 1881 and 1889 it acquired lines that extended from Connell (Palouse Junction) through Colfax and Pullman to Moscow, Idaho, and from Walla Walla through Whitman County to Spokane Falls. Meanwhile the Northern Pacific had built branch lines in the easternmost part of Washington Territory, one southeastward from Marshall into the Palouse country and the other westward from Cheney into the Big Bend of the Columbia.[44] With the rapid settlement of the country stimulated by such building of railroads, many ranges of the Columbia Basin were quickly transformed into farming land, and the breeding of cattle in the easternmost part of the Columbia Plateau soon became only an aspect of diversified farming.

The completion of the Northern Pacific in 1883, and the connection of the Oregon Railway and Navigation Company with the Union Pacific in 1884, gave to the stockmen of the Columbia Basin two railroads to eastern markets, besides a through line to Puget Sound. Consequently, after 1884 they were less interested in a wagon road through Snoqualmie Pass than ever before. To some extent, however, this road continued to be used for the movement of livestock westward to Puget Sound after 1884. Certainly it was used as late as 1886, and no doubt to some extent thereafter. But by the middle of the 1880's this route was beginning to lose its significance, even for the stockmen in the Yakima Valley, for the Northern Pacific was now making rapid progress in building its long-deferred Cascade division. Work had begun as early as 1883, and before the end of 1884 fifty miles of track had been laid, twenty-five miles from Tacoma eastward and twenty-five miles from the Columbia River westward. By December, 1884, the new towns of Pasco and Kennewick were reported to be booming, and Ainsworth was gasping for breath; and by December 16, 1884, the laying of tracks had been completed westward to Yakima City. At the end of its fiscal year, June 30,

---

[44] Henry Villard, *The Early History of Transportation in Oregon* (Eugene, Ore., 1944), pp. 96-97; Nelson Trottman, *History of the Union Pacific: A Financial and Economic Survey* (New York, 1923), pp. 180-82; Oregon Railway and Navigation Company, *Sixth Annual Report of the Board of Directors ... June 30, 1885* (New York, 1885), pp. 8-9; Railroad Commission of Washington, *First Annual Report to the Governor* (Olympia, Wash., 1907), pp. 98-100; *Northwest Tribune*, Oct. 11, 1889.

1887, the Northern Pacific could proudly announce the completion of its Cascade division and its emancipation from a "dependence upon the Oregon Railway & Navigation Company for an
outlet to the tide water of the Pacific, which was prejudicial to its
interests and unworthy of its position as a great Trans-continental
Road." Such rejoicing is understandable to one who recalls that,
at that time, the Oregon Railway and Navigation Company was,
by lease, a part of the Union Pacific system.[45]

In the meantime, cattle and other kinds of livestock had also
been moving southward from the Oregon Country to markets in
Nevada and California. This movement, as we have seen in an
earlier chapter, began in the late 1840's and probably never
ceased entirely, even when the demand for meat in the northern
mining camps was at its height. Our records of the early 1860's
show small shipments of livestock, including some cattle, from
the Columbia River to San Francisco, and they also disclose an
attack by Indians, near the head of Pit River, on a group of men
en route in 1861 from Oregon to Washoe with a band of 850 head
of cattle.[46] For the next few years the record of such movements
is slight. It is probable that some of the cattle sent southward in
those years came from ranges in eastern Oregon south of the
Columbia Basin, but it is more likely that, before 1870, most of
them were driven southward from the valleys of western Oregon.
For several years after the early 1870's, however, there was, as we
shall see, a considerable movement of cattle and other livestock
from southeastern Washington and northeastern Oregon to the
state of Nevada. But during the 1870's and 1880's the ranges of
Oregon east of the Cascades and south of the Columbia Basin,

[45] Weekly Post-Intelligencer, June 14, July 2, Aug. 27, Nov. 19, 1885, May 6,
13, Aug. 26, 1886; Northern Pacific Railroad, Report of the President . . . September 20, 1883 (New York, 1883), p. 29, and the Annual Report of the Board of
Directors . . . September 18, 1884 (New York, 1884), p. 12; Northern Pacific
Railroad, Annual Report of the Board of Directors . . . September 17, 1885 (New
York, 1885), p. 11; Northwest Tribune, Dec. 26, 1884, quoting the Yakima Republican; Northern Pacific Railroad, Annual Report of the Vice-President and
General Manager . . . for the Fiscal Year Ending June 30th, 1887 (New York,
1887), pp. 3-4; Hedges, Henry Villard, p. 145.
[46] Portland Daily Advertiser, Dec. 17, 18, 1860, Feb. 2, 1861; Morning Oregonian, March 22, 1861; Lieutenant John Feilner to J. H. Kellogg, Aug. 13, 1861,
in the War of the Rebellion, Series I (Washington, D.C., 1897), L, Pt. 1, 22;
Morning Oregonian, Jan. 14, Feb. 7, 1863.

those of Idaho south of the Salmon River, and those throughout the state of Nevada were, broadly speaking, as much the pasture lands of Californians as the ranges of the Columbia Basin were the pasture lands of those who lived in Portland or in the Puget Sound Basin.

By 1867, the trade in livestock and cattle products from the Pacific Northwest to Nevada and California was entering a new period of boom. In May a band of seven hundred head of cattle and a flock of one thousand sheep passed southward from the Umpqua Valley through the Rogue River Valley. Some of the cattle were headed for the market in San Francisco; but most of the cattle and all the sheep were headed for markets in the Washoe country in Nevada. Also in 1867, a considerable quantity of beef in barrels, together with a large number of hides, was shipped from the Columbia River to San Francisco. Near the end of June an editor in Jacksonville, Oregon, observing that a band of three hundred head of cattle from the Umpqua Valley had recently passed through the Rogue River Valley, remarked that, during the preceding spring, more than five thousand head had passed through that valley on the way either to California or to Nevada; and toward the end of October a correspondent in Salem, Oregon, reported that it had "been estimated" that, from "Eastern Oregon and from Idaho," twenty thousand head of cattle and one hundred thousand head of sheep had left Oregon during "the past season by the southern portal."[47]

This southward movement of livestock continued. Other cattle, some from the Willamette Valley, passed through the Rogue River Valley to California in 1868, and in the winter of 1868-69, as an editor in Nevada subsequently wrote, James A. Hardin drove a band of five hundred head of cattle from the Willamette country to Mendocino County, California. The movement of livestock southward from western Oregon appeared to be especially large in 1869. As early as April, livestock buyers were creating excitement near Cottage Grove by their purchases of horses, cattle, and sheep for the market in California, but a month later

[47] Jacksonville *Oregon Sentinel*, May 18, June 29, 1867; Portland *Weekly Oregonian*, August-November, 1867, *passim*; Jacksonville *Southern Oregon Press*, March 2, June 27, 1867; *Sacramento Daily Union*, Oct. 22, 1867.

a buyer from Nevada, while passing through the Rogue River Valley with about seven hundred head of cattle from Douglas County, Oregon, reported that there were "plenty of cattle yet in the Umpqua Valley at reasonable prices." In May a newspaper in Eugene City not only reported that a large drove of young cattle had passed through that place en route to the Pit River country in California, but also remarked that cattle were becoming scarce and dear in the Willamette Valley. Early in June, 1869, several bands of "fine horses" from Oregon passed through Shasta, California, "bound for the lower counties"; and, at the end of that month, a band of about two hundred fifty head of cattle from Josephine County passed through the Rogue River Valley on the way to San Francisco. But the most significant report of the movement of cattle and other livestock from western Oregon in 1869 appeared, at the beginning of June, in the leading newspaper of Portland. Here we read that

Many good horses have been purchased [in Oregon] for the California market, and we judge that not less than 30,000 head of cattle have been purchased in Western Oregon this spring and driven away. A Jacksonville paper says that fully 15,000 head have been driven through that place. . . . [But] it is becoming more difficult to obtain live stock, especially in the Willamette Valley; and probably soon it will be necessary to bring cattle from beyond the Cascade Mountains to supply the market of Portland. It is understood that cattle are yet abundant in some of the eastern counties and in the Yakima Valley in Washington Territory. The consumption of cattle, at Portland, is now from 200 to 250 head a month.[48]

No doubt many of the thirty thousand head of cattle sold in western Oregon in that year were driven toward the "northern" mines, but it may be safely assumed that most of the fifteen thousand head that passed through Jacksonville, Oregon, were headed for some southern market.

[48] *Jacksonville Reveille,* July 4, 1868; *Oregon Sentinel,* Oct. 3, 1868; Eugene *Oregon State Journal,* April 17, May 22, 1869; *Oregon Sentinel,* May 8, July 3, 1869; *Shasta Courier,* June 12, 1869; Harvey W. Scott, *History of the Oregon Country,* compiled by Leslie M. Scott (Cambridge, Mass., 1924), III, 73-74, quoting the *Oregonian* of June 3, 1869. P.W.G., writing from Albany, Ore., on March 26, 1869, said: "A number of Californians are here buying sheep, cattle and horses. The price of horned cattle has been steadily increasing for some years throughout the stock-growing regions of the State." *Morning Oregonian,* March 29, 1869.

By 1870 new trends in the cattle trade from the Oregon Country to California were becoming evident. Buyers from the south continued to purchase cattle in southwestern Oregon, but in June of that year the San Francisco *Scientific Press* observed that cattle were coming to San Francisco from

almost every mountain-ward quarter. Some 220 head recently arrived via railroad from Idaho. Another and a still larger band is en route from the same locality, if they have not already arrived. The C.P.R.R. Co. have built a large corral near the freight depot at Winnemucca, Humboldt county, for the more convenient keeping and loading of cattle on the cars. Heretofore cattle reaching the line of the road near that point have been driven fifty miles along the road to reach a convenient point of shipment.

Not only was Winnemucca now beginning to emerge as an important shipping point for cattle, but the cattle trails leading there were lengthening. In September of 1870, buyers from Nevada made "large purchases" of cattle in Umatilla County and, to the great satisfaction of an editor in Walla Walla, were trying to "pick up any loose bands" they could find in the Walla Walla Valley. Two months later eight cars containing two hundred twenty-seven head of beef cattle were being sidetracked and unloaded at Reno, Nevada, in order that the cattle might be fed and watered. This was the first consignment of two thousand head which had been bought in Baker County, Oregon, and "driven to Winnemucca via Quin[n]'s river valley" for shipment to Dunphy and Hildreth in San Francisco.[49]

The trade now beginning from southeastern Washington and northeastern Oregon would, by the spring of 1878, bring from citizens in the northern part of Grant County, Oregon, a plea to the federal government to set apart from the Malheur Indian Reservation "that part of Harney Lake Valley east of Silvies river." Here, the petitioners affirmed, was an area, unused by the Indians, which lay "athwart the mountain passes which lead from the vast stock country, to its north, to the Pacific Railroad."

[49] Silver City, Ida., *Owyhee Avalanche*, June 25, 1870, quoting the *Scientific Press; Walla Walla Statesman*, Oct. 1, 1870; Reno *Nevada State Journal*, Nov. 30, 1870. In midsummer of that year, a buyer from Lake County, California, purchased "several hundred head of cattle in Jackson County," Oregon. Salem *Oregon Weekly Statesman*, July 1, 1870.

Harney Valley, they declared, was "the Bosporus of all the stock region north of the Blue Mountains as far as the English possessions," and if the white men's cattle were kept from crossing this reservation, "another and less direct and more expensive route of exit must be sought." The "difference in cost of reaching market," they affirmed, would "be a standing and arduous tribute falling upon the stock men for only an ideal benefit to the Indians." In a subsequent chapter we shall learn more about Oregon cattlemen and the Malheur Indian Reservation.

Meanwhile, the southward trade in cattle and other livestock from the Oregon Country had continued and prospered, and the Central Pacific Railroad had become increasingly important as a carrier of such livestock. From June 30, 1870, to June 30, 1871, it carried 11,374 head of beef cattle from Nevada to San Francisco.[50] By then Winnemucca was taking the lead as a shipping point for cattle, and it would retain that position well into the 1880's, serving southeastern Oregon and southwestern Idaho, as well as northwestern Nevada.[51] For a few years it was the economic capital of a pastoral province as important to San Francisco as the Yakima Valley was to Seattle, or as Wasco and Umatilla counties were to Portland. Speaking broadly, the cattle-shipping season for Winnemucca began in the early autumn and lasted into the late spring, and winter driving of cattle from Grant County to Winnemucca could be as disagreeable as winter driving from the Yakima Valley to The Dalles. During the months of summer, shipments of cattle from Winnemucca were, ordinarily, infrequent.

Although some of the cattle driven from the Columbia Basin to Winnemucca in the early 1870's may have been beef cattle ready for market, the evidence now available persuades one to believe that, through 1874, most of the cattle purchased by Nevada buyers in eastern Washington and northeastern Oregon

---

[50] E. S. Davis, surveyor-general of Nevada, report of Sept. 20, 1871, in the Commissioner of the General Land Office, *Report* (1871), p. 226; Henry T. Williams (ed.), *The Pacific Tourist* . . . (New York, 1876), p. 191. "Winnemucca is indeed establishing a reputation as a shipping point, not only for cattle, but for freight generally." Carson City *Daily State Register,* Jan. 17, 1871, quoting the Winnemucca *Humboldt Register* of Jan. 14, 1871.

[51] *Morning Oregonian,* April 6, 1878, quoting the *Grant County Times.*

were wanted, at least partly because of their superior quality, for breeding or stocking purposes. In 1872 hundreds of cattle were driven from the upper Willamette Valley to market in Washoe County, Nevada, and a year later eager buyers from Nevada were purchasing cattle by the hundreds in the Walla Walla Valley and Umatilla County; and in midsummer of that year two buyers from Arizona were in northeastern Oregon seeking more than two thousand young heifers.[52] Thanks to the depression which now was setting in, cattle and other livestock in the Columbia Basin were selling for low prices.

Perhaps in part for this reason, buyers from Nevada and Arizona were purchasing cattle and other livestock in Walla Walla and in Union County, Oregon, in 1874. Also in that year a hundred horses, mostly brood mares from Idaho, arrived in Mohave County, Arizona; and in November eight hundred head of cattle from Owyhee County, Idaho, were sent to San Francisco by rail from Mill City, a shipping point a few miles west of Winnemucca. Late in that year at least three thousand head of cattle were sent from Lake County, Oregon, to markets in Nevada and California; and, on December 11, 1874, the *Daily Sentinel* of Laramie, Wyoming, could report, as an encouragement to cattlemen in southeastern Oregon, that the Central Pacific Railroad had "finished its cattle corral at Winnemucca."[53]

The cattle from the Walla Walla Valley and northeastern Oregon that were used for stocking ranges in Nevada were part of a larger movement of stocking cattle into that state. From the Gordon Report accompanying the federal census of 1880, we learn that cattle and sheep ranchers were fleeing from drought in California to new ranges in Nevada as early as 1870; and from California, as well as from Oregon and Texas, stocking cattle continued to move into Nevada until 1874, when, as we also learn from the Gordon Report, "Texas importations ceased, and Cali-

---

[52] *Yreka Weekly Union*, May 18, 1872; Reno *Nevada State Journal*, Nov. 23, 1872; *Walla Walla Union*, May 17, June 28, 1873; *Weekly Mountaineer*, May 24, July 12, 26, 1873; *Sacramento Daily Union*, June 13, July 11, 1873; *Willamette Farmer*, July 5, 1873.
[53] *Walla Walla Statesman*, March 14, 1874; *Walla Walla Union*, May 30, 1874; *Sacramento Daily Union*, June 29, Dec. 24, 1874; Baker City *Bedrock Democrat*, July 8, 1874.

fornia also ceased to supply any large number." In fact, as this report also tells us, the ranges of Nevada had now become so crowded that several large cattle owners moved their herds into Idaho in 1875, and still others drove theirs either into southeastern Oregon or into Montana.[54]

Nevertheless, cattle and sheep in considerable numbers, as well as horses in somewhat smaller numbers, continued during 1875 to leave southeastern Washington and northeastern Oregon for Nevada, and some of these animals were bought for stocking purposes. In the spring of that year, while some buyers were in the Walla Walla Valley acquiring horses and cattle for Nevada and Montana, other buyers were in Umatilla County purchasing cows and steers for Nevada. Before the end of June in that year, the *Walla Walla Union* could say that

> A number of bands of cattle left the [Walla Walla] valley within the last few days. Dan Drumheller has taken one band of 1000 head over to Grande Ronde, where they will remain until they are joined by four or five hundred more being bought up here, when all will be taken to Nevada. A number of other bands are now making up and will start in a few days. Those who have come over the mountains lately, say that there seems to be almost a string of cattle from this valley across the Blue Mountains. . . .

While these cattle were moving to Nevada, bands of horses from The Dalles and the Grande Ronde, a drove of two thousand head of sheep from western Oregon, a considerable number of cattle from Umatilla and Wasco counties, and one thousand head of cattle from Puget Sound were being driven to Nevada. Also, at the same time, bands of cattle were moving to California from northern Idaho and from Lake County in south-central Oregon.[55]

More significant for the future, however, was the fact that, in 1875, cattle in considerable numbers were being driven from

---

[54] Clarence W. Gordon, "Report on Cattle, Sheep, and Swine, Supplementary to Enumeration of Live Stock on Farms in 1880," *Tenth Federal Census, 1880,* Vol. III, *Agriculture* (Washington, D.C., 1883), p. 1059.

[55] *Weekly Mountaineer,* April 3, 1875; *Morning Oregonian,* March 17, April 21, 22, June 15, 30, 1875; *Walla Walla Union,* April 24, June 5, 26, 1875; La Grande *Mountain Sentinel,* June 5, 1875; *Oregon State Journal,* April 10, 1875; Winnemucca *Silver State,* June 7, Nov. 10, 1875; *Willamette Farmer,* May 7, June 25, 1875; Virginia, Nev., *Daily Territorial Enterprise,* Aug. 25, 1875; Boise *Idaho Weekly Statesman,* Sept. 18, 1875.

southeastern Oregon and southwestern Idaho to Winnemucca
to become a part of the increasing shipments to San Francisco.
In July of that year, freight teams returning from Silver City,
Idaho, were bringing large quantities of hides to Winnemucca,
and the editor of the Winnemucca *Silver State* could rejoice because not "all that class of freight" was being transported from
Idaho to San Francisco by way of the Columbia River.[56]

During the next ten years, Winnemucca rose to its zenith as a
cattle-shipping town and as a center for the distribution of merchandise throughout the large area that it served, although it
divided the trade of southwestern Idaho with Kelton, Utah.
From early 1875 through 1876, cattle in large numbers were
sent by rail from Winnemucca to San Francisco, and no inconsid-
erable part of these shipments were cattle from southeastern
Oregon or southern Idaho.[57] On November 20, 1876, the *Morning Oregonian* quoted The Dalles *Mountaineer* as saying that,
during the last year, no fewer than thirty-six thousand head of
cattle had "been driven from Eastern Oregon and Eastern Washington down towards the Pacific Railroad," some to be sent east
and others to be sent to San Francisco. In this issue the editor
also remarked that a "large stock raiser" of Wasco County had
refused an offer of twenty-eight dollars a head for one thousand
head of cattle delivered at Red Bluff, California, on the ground
that cattle were worth as much as that at The Dalles.

Even more important for Winnemucca was the year 1877, for
then cattle in considerable numbers were driven there from the
Steens Mountain country and elsewhere in southeastern Oregon
for shipment to San Francisco; and, at the same time, buyers
from Nevada were seeking beef cattle as far west as Jackson
County, Oregon, and as far east as the Payette Valley in Idaho.
We do not have a full account of the movement of cattle from
the Oregon Country to Winnemucca in 1877, but there is good

[56] *Silver State,* July 6, 18, Sept. 11, Oct. 23, Nov. 18, Dec. 3, 1875.
[57] *Idaho Weekly Statesman,* Nov. 8, 1879; Leslie L. Sudweeks, "The Raft
River in Idaho History," *PNQ,* XXXII (July, 1941), 305. Some indication of an
extensive movement of cattle southward to Winnemucca may be found in the
following references: *Idaho Weekly Statesman,* Sept. 23, 1876; *Weekly Mountaineer,* Oct. 14, 1876; *Silver State,* Sept. 22, Oct. 7, 17, Nov. 4, 9, 22, Dec. 4,
1876.

reason to think that this movement was very large, for we learn from respectable sources that more than thirty-three thousand head were shipped from this point in that year.[58]

During the next two years, many head of cattle, mostly from southeastern Oregon, were sent by rail from Winnemucca, and of these the greater number were consigned to markets in San Francisco. Also in those years a considerable number of cattle were driven to California from Lake County, Oregon.[59] But there was, as the editor of the *Silver State* pointed out, a significant "turn in the tide of the cattle-shipping business" in 1879. Two years earlier he had reported that cattlemen of the Winnemucca province were interested in an experimental shipping of dressed meat from Winnemucca to Chicago. Presumably nothing came of this experiment, but on April 9, 1879, he reported that "Pete French and other stock raisers in the Stein [Steens] mountain country" had sold twelve thousand head of cattle to N. R. Davis of Wyoming, who would drive them through Idaho and Utah to Colorado. Although he was pleased by this large sale, he was truly elated when he learned, a few weeks later, "that some fifteen hundred head" of cattle would be shipped eastward from Winnemucca. "Should this business prove remunerative to the purchasers," he remarked, "it will be of great advantage to stock owners in this part of Nevada, as it will give them a market east and make them independent of San Francisco, to which all the beef cattle from this part of the country have hitherto been shipped." Significantly, after hearing later in that year that other cattle had been shipped eastward from Winnemucca to Iowa, he remarked that stockmen in the Winnemucca province were "not so dependent on San Francisco as they used to be."

But such desired emancipation was still in the future, for in the autumn of 1879 and early winter of 1879-80 Peter French, W. B. Todhunter, Catlow and Johnson, Harper Brothers, Evans

[58] *Morning Oregonian*, Nov. 20, 1876; *Walla Walla Union*, Nov. 25, 1876; *Willamette Farmer*, Dec. 1, 1876. See also *Oregon State Journal*, July 28, 1877; Boise *Semi-Weekly Idahoan*, Aug. 17, 1877; Boise *Idaho Tri-Weekly Statesman*, Sept. 20, 1877; *Silver State*, Aug. 11, 18, Sept. 5, 8, 22, 1877, Oct. 26, 1878.
[59] *Silver State*, Sept. 10, 1877, Sept. 9, Oct. 26, 1878; *Owyhee Avalanche*, Feb. 9, Sept. 2, Nov. 2, 1878; Jacksonville *Democratic Times*, July 26, 1878; *Morning Oregonian*, Aug. 16, 1878; *Yreka Union*, Nov. 9, 1878.

Brothers, and other cattlemen of southeastern Oregon, as well as cattlemen of southern Idaho, were, as usual, shipping cattle in considerable numbers to San Francisco.[60] During the later months of 1880 similar shipments were made by these men, by Colonel James A. Hardin, William Shirk, Berrott and Stauffer, and others who operated in the Winnemucca province; and of the many thousands of cattle sent by rail from Nevada to California in that year, some twelve thousand had been driven into Nevada from southern Oregon and southern Idaho. Nor was this all. The greatest number of the cattle driven into California during that year came "from Nevada, Oregon, Idaho, and Utah, in the order named as regards importance." A large proportion of the thousands of head of cattle driven from Oregon into Nevada and California in 1879 and 1880 came from Lake County.[61]

In 1881 a few thousand head of cattle were shipped east from Winnemucca, but, as in earlier years, most of the cattle leaving Winnemucca by rail went to California. Of the 8,211 head sent on trains from Winnemucca in August, 1881, only 1,361 went eastward. During that whole year, trains carried 22,699 head from Nevada to California, and 6,683 head to eastern destinations. Fully two-thirds of those transported by rail from Nevada to California were, as the editor of the *Silver State* observed, shipped from Winnemucca. Also, as in earlier years, cattle by the thousands were driven from Lake County, Oregon, to California in 1881.[62]

Other shipments of cattle went eastward from Winnemucca

[60] *Silver State*, Jan. 6, March 19, July 2, 25, Aug. 25, Oct. 2, 23, Nov. 4, 5, Dec. 2, 1879; *Oregon Sentinel*, Jan. 8, 1879; *Idaho Tri-Weekly Statesman*, July 29, Nov. 20, 1879; *Morning Oregonian*, July 28, 1879; Canyon City *Grant County News*, Aug. 16, Sept. 11, 13, Nov. 15, 1879; *Weekly Mountaineer*, Oct. 8, 1879.
[61] *Silver State*, Jan. 14-Dec. 29, 1880, *passim*; *Tenth Federal Census, 1880*, Vol. III, *Agriculture*, pp. 1030, 1045, 1070, 1096, 1101; *Morning Oregonian*, July 14, Sept. 1, 1879; Lakeview, Ore., *State Line Herald*, Nov. 8, 1879, March 20, July 10, 24, Aug. 7, 14, Sept. 4, 18, 1880; *Yreka Union*, Nov. 8, 1879; *Northwest Tribune*, Sept. 1, 1880; *Morning Oregonian*, Aug. 14, Sept. 21, 1880; *Willamette Farmer*, Dec. 10, 1880.
[62] *Silver State*, May 30-Aug. 8, 1881, *passim*. "During the month of January, the cattle shipments from here to California aggregated 2,322 head, and during the present month, to date over 1,000 head were shipped." *Ibid.*, Feb. 18, 1881. See also *ibid.*, March 19-Dec. 19, 1881, *passim*. In September, 1881, "Derby & Co." shipped from Winnemucca to San Francisco 20,000 pounds of dressed beef. *Ibid.*, Sept. 24, 1881. See also the *Morning Oregonian*, July 8, 13, 27, 1881.

in 1882. On February 22 the editor of the *Silver State* made no effort to conceal his elation when he reported what he believed to be "the first shipment of fat cattle" eastward from Winnemucca. Previously, he affirmed, the cattle sent eastward had been stocking cattle. Early in January of 1882, as an editor in southern Idaho learned, buyers "for the Eastern trade" were at "Winnemucca and other points on the Central Pacific Railroad," endeavoring to buy all the marketable stock available "and competing actively with California dealers," who were "buying extensively." The "general inference," he said,

is that the large purchases are based on speculation. Many cattle are being kept near San Francisco, with the intention to fatten for the market in the early spring, in the hope of large margins, which idea seems well founded. Dealers from every point predict a substantial rise, but what they base their calculations upon they decline to divulge. The winter thus far has been easy on stock, and growers will, with the predicted increased prices, more than make up their losses of last winter.[63]

During 1882, however, the main trend in the movement of cattle by rail from the Oregon Country was, as it had been in earlier years, toward California, mostly by way of Winnemucca. By early November of this year, Todhunter and Devine had sent to California seven thousand head of cattle from their ranges in Grant County, Oregon. Other consistent shippers to California were Frank Sweetser and his brother, who had, in August, 1882, bought George Berrot's and Fred Stauffer's cattle, horses, and ranches in Nevada and Oregon, together with their property in Winnemucca. Still other cattlemen of Oregon were contributing to this movement, for late in 1882 a Grant County newspaper reported that "large numbers of beef cattle" were being driven from the southern part of this county to Winnemucca for shipment to San Francisco.[64] During the winter of 1882-83, the cattle shipments from Winnemucca were nearly as heavy as they had been during the preceding winter; but, significantly, as the editor of the *Silver State* remarked in March, 1883, whereas

[63] *Silver State,* Feb. 27, 1882; *Idaho Tri-Weekly Statesman,* Jan. 17, 1882.
[64] *Morning Oregonian,* Nov. 11, 1882; *Silver State,* Aug. 29, Oct. 28, Dec. 12, 1882; Portland *Oregon and Washington Farmer* (December, 1882), p. 8, quoting the *Grant County News.*

"several hundred head of fat cattle" had been shipped eastward from Winnemucca a year earlier, "not a car-load . . . [had] been sent in that direction during the past Winter."[65] But, despite the heavy shipments of cattle by rail from Oregon to California in 1882, the driving of Oregon livestock to California was by no means ended. During the summer of that year, as the *Morning Oregonian* reported, five thousand head of cattle, mostly beef steers from the Prineville country, about seven thousand head of mutton sheep from the Umpqua Valley, and one thousand head of sheep from the Rogue River Valley were being driven to California.[66]

Shipments of cattle from Winnemucca to California were heavy during the seasons of 1883-84 and 1884-85, and as late as July, 1885, the editor of the *Silver State* was complaining because, as he said, the cattle raisers of Nevada (and, by implication, all other stockmen who used Winnemucca as a shipping point) "were almost wholly dependent upon San Francisco for a market." A few days earlier he had reported that one of their number, N. H. A. Mason, had gone east for the purpose of arranging with the railroad for a rate that would permit him to "get into the Chicago market with Nevada and Oregon beef." How successful his mission was we do not know, but we are told that, before the end of the summer, a new market for cattlemen of the Oregon Country had opened in Omaha. On this subject the *Silver State* quoted the *Omaha Journal* as follows:

G. B. Green, of the Omaha Union Stock Yards, has returned from an extended tour through Utah, Idaho and Oregon. He was absent about twenty-five days, hunted and fished, and visited the cattle ranges of the northwestern Rocky Mountains and saw in Oregon some of the finest grass cattle on the globe. He says there are about 20,000 head up there that will come to these yards this season. Cattle from these points heretofore have been shipped to San Francisco, but the opening of the Utah Northern and Oregon Short Line have changed their routes and opened a new field in this direction that promises to be of great importance to that region, and of much interest to Omaha, as she will catch the cream of all that vast interest.

---

[65] *Silver State*, March 2, 1883.
[66] *Morning Oregonian*, June 21, 22, 1882. For details of the movement of cattle from the Oregon Country through Winnemucca during this year, see the *Silver State*, 1882 *passim*.

Mr. Green says they are raising some of the finest grass cattle in that upper country he ever saw. One Omaha gentleman, L. R. Bolles, who went with Mr. Green, bought about 5,000 head of these fine Oregon cattle and will ship them to the Omaha yards. Green & Burke will probably handle them. Mr. Bolles heretofore has been shipping from Utah. One lot of from 2,500 to 3,000 head were purchased of Overfelt & Co., whose ranges are largely in Baker and Grant counties, Oregon. This firm owns about 40,000 head of cattle and horses in that upper country.[67]

The glory that had been Winnemucca's was now passing, and presently Ontario, Oregon, would become a greater cattle-shipping point than Winnemucca had ever been. The beginning of this transition was not lost on the editor of the *Silver State*, who, on March 20, 1886, reported that, during the season ended on March 1 of that year, 18,741 head of cattle had been shipped from Winnemucca and other points in Humboldt County. "This," he said, "shows a falling off of a few thousand head from the shipments of the previous year, caused by northern cattle-men shipping to Chicago over the Oregon Short Line."

But San Francisco and other cities in California continued to need beef, and, despite the prediction of W. B. Todhunter and L. Godchaux in August, 1886, that "at least 25,000 head of cattle" would be sent in that year by rail from southeastern Oregon and southwestern Idaho to "Chicago and other eastern markets," California continued for several more years to receive from eastern Oregon and southern Idaho large numbers of cattle by way of Nevada. Such cattle were driven to the railroad in that state from the ranges of Peter French, Todhunter and Devine, Miller and Lux, Hardin and Riley, Stauffer and Sweetser, N. H. A. Mason, David L. Shirk, L. Godchaux, and others in Oregon, as well as from the ranches of many cattlemen in southern Idaho.[68] California also continued to receive, during the later years of the 1880's, cattle, sheep, and horses driven overland

[67] For shipments of cattle from Winnemucca in 1884, see the *Silver State passim*, and the Cheyenne *Northwestern Live Stock Journal*, Sept. 12, Nov. 14, 1884. For such shipments in 1885, see especially the *Silver State* for that year.
[68] For the movement of cattle through Winnemucca during the last half of the 1880's, see, besides the *Silver State* for those years, the *Northwestern Live Stock Journal*, Oct. 14, 21, 1887, Sept. 14, 21, Oct. 26, 1888; the Burns *East Oregon Herald*, Oct. 11, 18, 25, Nov. 15, 22, 1888, Aug. 1, Sept. 26, 1889, Jan. 2, 9, Feb. 27, 1890; and the *Morning Oregonian*, May 3, 1889.

from "the hills and valleys" of Lake County, Oregon. The pattern of marketing, however, was subject to changes as additional miles of railroad were laid. In January, 1888, the *West Shore* told its readers that cattle from all parts of southeastern Oregon were being driven to shipping points in the Shasta Valley of California. Here, "principally at Montague, Gazelle, and Edgewood, where large stock yards ... [had been] provided," cattle trains were loaded for southern markets. But the practice of driving cattle and other livestock from the Oregon Country to California continued for years after the need for such driving had passed away. Stockmen who thought that the rates for sending their cattle by rail were excessive, or men not otherwise gainfully employed, believed that it was worth their while to make such long drives of livestock. In September, 1885, an editor in Prineville reported that G. H. Churchill of Waldron had "started on Thursday of last week for California with thirty head of fine young geldings." Five years later S. J. Newson started for California from the Prineville country with a drove of young mules; and nearly two years later a band of six hundred head of cattle that Jesse D. Carr had bought in Klickitat County, Washington, passed through Prineville en route to Modoc County, California. As late as September, 1903, C. J. Johnson drove from the Prineville country a band of more than seven hundred head of cattle to California.[69]

But neither the men who drove cattle from the Oregon Country to markets in Nevada and in California, nor those who drove cattle to shipping points on the Central Pacific Railroad, contributed appreciably, during the late 1870's and the early 1880's, to the lifting of the troublesome depression from the ranges of Transcascadia. How this depression was lifted the next chapter will endeavor to tell.

[69] Portland *West Shore*, XII (June, 1886), 178-79, and XIV (January, 1888), 47; Prineville *Ochoco Review*, Aug. 30, 1890, May 7, 1892; Burns *Times-Herald*, Feb. 6, 1904.

CHAPTER V

Markets Beyond the Rockies

BETWEEN the middle 1870's and the middle 1880's, most of the surplus cattle on the ranges of the Oregon Country were sent to newly found markets east of the Rockies. To reach these markets, some of the cattle were driven southward to Nevada and sent eastward by rail from there; but by all odds the greater number were driven on trails leading through the Snake River Valley to passes in the Rocky Mountains.

Beyond the Rockies, more often than not in Wyoming, the cattle were disposed of in various ways. A few went by rail directly to Chicago, but many more were carried by trains, or were driven, to the corn-growing states of Nebraska, Kansas, Iowa, and Missouri. Here they were fattened for markets in the Middle West. Beyond doubt, however, the greater number of cattle in this movement found temporary homes on the ranges of Montana, Wyoming, Colorado, Nebraska, Kansas, and even Dakota; and it was the contribution of the Oregon Country to the stocking of these ranges with cattle superior to Texas cattle that must be set down as a significant consequence of the movement of cattle eastward from the Pacific Northwest. We should never forget that the stocking of the northern Great Plains was not achieved entirely with cattle from Texas and from the East, as some persons have believed; it was achieved, to no slight extent, with cattle from ranges west of the Rocky Mountains.[1] What the Oregon Country contributed to the stocking of these ranges this chapter, among other things, will endeavor to make clear.

The story of the long drives of cattle eastward from the Oregon Country is as fascinating as the story of the Texas cattle drives; but the fact should be repeated—indeed, it should be emphasized—that the driving of cattle and other livestock to distant markets was not a phenomenon peculiar to American frontiers west of the ninety-eighth meridian. Such drives had been made earlier on other American frontiers. During the 1770's and 1780's, for example, herds of cattle from the deep south were driven northward to Pennsylvania through the back country of the Carolinas; and, as late as September, 1795, a tan yard in Salem, North Carolina, was having difficulty in getting an adequate supply of saddle-leather "because so many cattle . . . [were] being driven to Philadelphia."[2]

West of the Allegheny Mountains, as early as 1802, settlers in Kentucky were driving horses to markets in South Carolina and other southern states, and were sending cattle east to Virginia to be fattened for markets in Baltimore and Philadelphia; and in 1805 settlers in southern Ohio were driving their beef cattle to markets in Baltimore. Driving of this sort continued through many years. In the spring of 1814, it was affirmed in Baltimore that "great herds of cattle and hogs" had been driven there from Ohio, and in June, 1817, a newspaper in Baltimore said that a band of cattle from Chillicothe, Ohio, had arrived in New York "in fine order."[3] Thereafter, for a generation or more, cattle, horses, mules, and hogs were driven from the Ohio Valley eastward to markets in Baltimore, Philadelphia, and New York, and southeastward to

[1] J. Orin Oliphant, "The Cattle Trade from the Far Northwest to Montana," *AH*, VI (April, 1932), 69-83, and "The Eastward Movement of Cattle from the Oregon Country," *AH*, XX (January, 1946), 19-43.

[2] Adelaide Fries (ed.), *Records of the Moravians in North Carolina* (Raleigh, N.C., 1925-43), II, 835; IV, 1869; V, 2204; VI, 2544.

[3] F. A. Michaux, *Travels*, Vol. III in R. G. Thwaites (ed.), *Early Western Travels* (Cleveland, 1904), pp. 244-45; Paul C. Henlein, *Cattle Kingdom in the Ohio Valley, 1783-1860* (Lexington, Ky., 1959), p. 103: *Niles' Weekly Register*, VI (May 28, 1814), 210, and *ibid.*, XII (June 28, 1817), 287.

markets in Charleston and elsewhere in the South.[4] Steamboats were used on the Ohio River, as later such boats were used on the Columbia River, and still later on the Missouri River, to carry cattle to market. In March, 1849, for example, an editor in Pittsburgh, observing that "one hundred and ten head of fine large fat cattle," intended for the "eastern market," had been brought up the Ohio River from Kentucky on the steamer *Schuylkill*, expressed the opinion that Kentucky was likely "to become the successful rival of Ohio for cattle." Even the coming of the railroads did not immediately stop the driving of livestock from the Ohio Valley to distant markets.[5]

Precisely when the driving of cattle from the Oregon Country to destinations east of the Rockies began, we do not know; but any person having knowledge of earlier American frontiers could have predicted that the movement of cattle from the East to frontiers west of the Rockies during the 1840's and later would be followed, sooner or later, by a reverse movement of cattle from these newer frontiers to markets in more fully developed communities east of these mountains. From American frontiers cattle could be driven, at slight expense, long distances to markets. But probably no person at that time would have predicted that a new frontier, located between the older settlements east of the Rockies and the newer settlements west of these mountains, would be partly stocked by cattle and other livestock driven eastward from the Oregon Country.

Be that as it may, livestock was presently moving from the Pacific Northwest to ranges east of the continental divide, as well as to markets in the Middle West. To the best of our knowledge, horses preceded cattle in this movement. As early as November, 1869, the editor of a newspaper in Ottawa, Kansas, could say that W. C. Myer had "just arrived from Ashland Mills, Oregon,

[4] F. J. Turner, "The Colonization of the West," *AHR*, XI (1905-6), 322-23; Sunbury, Pa., *Public Inquirer*, May 16, 1822; Chillicothe, Ohio, *The Supporter and Scioto Gazette*, Feb. 19, 1824; *Baltimore Patriot*, July 29, 1826; Salisbury *Western Carolinian*, Sept. 15, 1829; Boston *Christian Watchman*, Dec. 26, 1834; Columbus, Ohio, *Cross and Journal*, Oct. 21, Nov. 18, Dec. 2, 1842; Philadelphia *Christian Chronicle*, Sept. 7, 1846; *New York Weekly Tribune*, May 21, 28, June 25, 1842.

[5] Pittsburgh *Daily Commercial Journal*, March 4, 1849; *New York Weekly Herald*, Jan. 10, May 23, 1857.

with a drove of two hundred horses, and is pasturing them within two miles of this place." Mr. Myer, he remarked, had been "five months making the trip." Less than a year later, buyers from Montana spent six thousand dollars in the Walla Walla Valley for horses and mules which they intended to drive to Colorado. "This is about the first large sale of this kind of stock ever made in this Valley," the editor of the *Walla Walla Statesman* remarked, "and is certainly indicative of the great stock market which is fast assuming vast proportions in our midst." Some four years later, when the entire Oregon Country was feeling the pinch of depression, an editor in Iowa wrote that a "drove of 200 ponies and colts from northeastern Oregon—1,800 miles away—passed through . . . [Council Bluffs, Iowa] to the Missouri Valley and points east." This drove had consisted originally of about twelve hundred head, but had, on its journey eastward, been greatly diminished by "disease and Indians—principally the latter."[6]

The driving of these and perhaps other bands of horses eastward may have prepared the way for moving cattle eastward from the Oregon Country. In any event, an editor in Walla Walla could report in January 1875, that "a number of stockmen from abroad . . . [were] in this Valley with the money to buy stock"; and in May of that year another editor in Walla Walla could say that among the cattle buyers then "scouring" the Walla Walla Valley was a man "buying up all of the thoroughbred cattle that he could get with a view of taking them to Wyoming Territory." Six weeks later this editor wrote exultantly that

On Wednesday a band of some hundreds of cattle that have been purchased in this country started for Wyoming Territory. The greater portion of them were common cattle or mixed bloods, but there were also some [of] the finest blooded animals in the valley. This thing of buying thoroughbred stock here to drive so far east shows that Walla Walla is the cheapest place in which to purchase any kind of cattle.[7]

[6] Salem *Oregon Weekly Statesman*, Nov. 12, 1869, quoting the *Ottawa Republic*; *Walla Walla Statesman*, Aug. 27, 1870; *Sacramento Daily Union*, Aug. 31, 1874, quoting the Council Bluffs *Nonpareil*.
[7] Boise *Idaho Weekly Statesman*, Oct. 9, 1875; *Walla Walla Statesman*, Jan. 8, 1875; *Walla Walla Union*, May 22, July 3, 1875.

Meanwhile, cattle and other livestock for the use of white men had been passing from Oregon into Montana since at least the summer of 1868, and in June of 1870 "an old Siskiyouan" was preparing to drive to Montana from northern California some 400 horses, as well as "some 2,000 or 3,000 head of sheep" which he had purchased recently in Oregon, and which he then was keeping in the neighborhood of Link River. At the same time, W. W. Boone was starting "for Montana with 80 head of beef cattle" from Polk County, Oregon. Some three years later, in July, 1873, buyers from Montana were looking for "stock" in the Walla Walla Valley, and in November it was reported that "large numbers of horned cattle, sheep and horses" were being bought in the Walla Walla Valley "for Idaho and Montana ranches." Early in the spring of 1875, buyers of cattle, horses, and mules for Montana and Nevada were again in the Walla Walla Valley, and in August 2,300 head of sheep, "pasturing on the Touchet," were sold "for the Montana market at $2.50 a head." During the course of that year, "numerous herds of horses, cattle, and sheep" were being sent into Montana from Oregon, Texas, and Colorado in sufficient numbers, in the opinion of the Surveyor-General of Montana, "to swell the figures fully one-third."[8]

Thus it appears that, by 1875, a movement of livestock eastward from the far Northwest was getting under way. How many head of cattle were so moved in that year it is impossible to determine, but there is some reason to think that the band for Wyoming mentioned above was not the only one driven eastward from the Oregon Country in 1875. The editor of the *Walla Walla Union,* in January, 1878, said that "three years ago" a certain "Mr. Lang," of Kansas, had visited Walla Walla, and had been so much impressed by the cattle that he bought "quite a band" of them, which, presumably, he drove across the Rockies.[9] This man

[8] *Oregon Weekly Statesman,* July 1, 1870; *Walla Walla Union,* July 26, 1873, March 27, 1875; *Sacramento Daily Union,* Aug. 3, Nov. 3, 1873; The Dalles *Weekly Mountaineer,* Aug. 28, 1875; Commissioner of the General Land Office, *Report* (1875), p. 230; John Owen, *Journals and Letters . . .* ed. by Seymour Dunbar and Paul C. Phillips (New York, 1927), II, 139; *Yreka Weekly Union,* June 24, 1870.

[9] *Walla Walla Union,* Jan. 19, 1878.

subsequently became well known in the Oregon Country as a member of the firm of Lang and Ryan, a firm which for several years, as we shall see, annually bought large herds of cattle and drove them to destinations east of the Rockies. Finally, as further justification of the statement that the movement of livestock eastward from the Oregon Country began in 1875, one may call attention to a special report on the livestock industry in the far West that was made for the federal census of 1880, a report which affirms that, because of the demand "for the past six years" for cattle from the far Northwest to "stock ranges in Wyoming, Nebraska, and Montana," stockmen in the Oregon Country had "more generally turned their attention to disposing of young cattle to purchasers from other grazing states and territories." Consequently, as this report tells us, a "system of sales to special drovers and of personal drives to Wyoming and Colorado was . . . inaugurated in 1875." But this report also affirms, emphatically, that in the spring of 1876 the demands for livestock in Wyoming, Colorado, Nebraska, and Montana, "where cattle occupy open ranges, *first induced a general driving out of cattle from Oregon and Washington to assist in stocking these regions.*"[10]

Evidence in abundance will prove the assertion that a "general driving out" of cattle from the Oregon Country had begun by 1876. Perhaps because the cattle business in Montana was still suffering from the depression, the demand there, in 1876, was largely for horses. But it was otherwise in Wyoming and Nebraska. In January, 1876, Galusha B. Grow, of Susquehanna County, Pennsylvania, was in Boise for the purpose of buying "a thousand or twelve hundred head of cattle" to drive to Wyoming Territory, where he intended to fatten them for the market in Chicago. Presently other buyers from the East were in the Columbia Basin, where, early in February, "an Arkansas man" bought in the Walla Walla Valley five hundred head of cattle which he intended to drive eastward; and later in that month the editor of The Dalles *Mountaineer*, learning that buyers in

[10] Clarence W. Gordon, "Report on Cattle, Sheep, and Swine, Supplementary to Enumeration of Live Stock on Farms in 1880," in the *Tenth Federal Census, 1880*, Vol. III, *Agriculture* (Washington, D.C., 1883), pp. 1080-81. Italics are mine.

the counties east of Wasco were purchasing "cattle and horses to drive east and to the overland railroad," advised stockmen of that region not to be in a hurry to sell. But perhaps the greatest excitement among cattlemen in the Columbia Basin during 1876 was aroused by the arrival in Portland, in the early spring, of two buyers—one from Omaha and the other from Cheyenne— who purposed to buy about ten thousand head of cattle "for the East and the rapidly filling country in and around the Black Hills."[11]

So great, indeed, did the concern of cattlemen in the Oregon Country become in that year about markets to the eastward that several cattlemen in the Columbia Basin began to drive their own cattle to shipping points on the Central Pacific and Union Pacific Railroads. One of these cattlemen was Dan Drumheller, who, as an editor in Walla Walla reported late in May, 1876, had "left for Cheyenne, taking with him 3,400 head of cattle." This band was composed of "cows, steers, and cattle of all ages." But he was neither the first nor the only one to make such a drive in that year. A few days earlier, according to an editor in Pendleton, "Adams and Reynolds" had left that place "en route to Wyoming with about two thousand head" of cattle. So lively, indeed, was the eastward movement of cattle from northeastern Oregon that, by early June of that year, the Union *Mountain Sentinel* was willing to predict that livestock worth $100,000 would be driven from the Grande Ronde Valley that season—"to say nothing about estrays."

In the spring of 1876, "Mr. Lang," a purchaser of the preceding year, who now appeared to be associated with a man named Shiedly (or perhaps Shadley), was again buying cattle in the Columbia Basin. By early May he had collected about three thousand head on the Touchet River, and he was desirous of increasing this number to four thousand or even five thousand head. Presumably he did so, for an editor in Pendleton remarked, before the end of May, that "Shiedly and Lang" had purchased about four thousand head of cattle, and that within a few days

[11] *Weekly Mountaineer*, Feb. 19, April 1, July 29, 1876; *Helena Daily Herald*, July 29, 1876, quoting the *Missoulian* of July 26; *Idaho Weekly Statesman*, Jan. 29, 1876; *Morning Oregonian*, Feb. 10, 1876.

they would start driving this herd to Cheyenne. Happily, we have the diary of a lad of seventeen, William Emsley Jackson, who, with his fifteen-year-old brother, Lorenzo Dow Jackson, participated in this drive.[12]

William Jackson left La Grande on May 23, "to go with Lang and Shadl[e]y's cattle to Cheyenne, Wyoming." The next day he overtook "the herds on Clover Creek and went to driving with Lang's herd on May 24, for $30.00 a month." Because Jackson lost his notebook after the first few days, and did not replace it until the "end of the first month," we learn nothing about this drive until June 23, when he left Lang's herd to begin cooking, at $40.00 a month, for Cox, the "foreman of the stock herd of 1400 cattle." The cattle of Lang and Shadley were moving toward Cheyenne in at least two herds.

This memorable day for Jackson—June 23, 1876—was not a pleasant one for the men on this drive, for they encountered "Dirt, dust and sage brush, no grass and no water all the way." There would be more unpleasant days on this drive, and there would be more than enough "dry camps." We have, however, few details of the journey until June 28, when the drovers passed Shoshone Falls. Eight days later the herd which Jackson accompanied, now south of the Snake River in Cassia County, Idaho, crossed Goose Creek. Here the mosquitoes were so bad that Jackson and his companions "barely escaped being eaten alive, by losing a night's sleep and putting in the time fighting these blood-letting insects." But they all survived this ordeal, and on July 8 they camped on Raft River. Four days later they were at American Falls, where they "bade farewell to Snake River."

From American Falls the drive proceeded in an easterly direction, passed the Fort Hall Indian Agency on the way to Soda Springs, where it turned southeast and passed through Georgetown and Montpelier in Bear Lake County, Idaho. On July 31 it crossed the Wyoming-Idaho line, "which was marked by a stake every half mile," and from here it proceeded to the Union Pacific

---

[12] *Walla Walla Statesman*, May 27, 1876; Union, Ore., *Mountain Sentinel*, June 10, 1876; *Morning Oregonian*, May 23, 1876, quoting a "Pendleton paper"; *Weekly Mountaineer*, May 6, 1876; J. Orin Oliphant and C. S. Kingston (eds.), "William Emsley Jackson's Diary of a Cattle Drive from La Grande, Oregon, to Cheyenne, Wyoming, in 1876," *AH*, XXIII (October, 1949), 260-73.

Railroad at Black's Fork, where, on August 12, Mr. Lang shipped "400 head of beeves to Chicago."

The drive of the remaining cattle moved eastwardly, roughly on the route of the present-day U. S. Highway 30, crossed the continental divide through Bridger's Pass on August 27, passed through Rawlins, and presently entered the Laramie Plains. On September 3, near Wagon Hound Creek, it passed "a herd of about 500 cattle from Marsh Valley, Idaho," which was proceeding to Laramie, and four days later Jackson and his associates were within sight of Laramie City. By September 11 they were within eighteen miles of Cheyenne, and three days later William Emsley Jackson and his brother boarded a train in Cheyenne, headed for Omaha; from there they intended to proceed to Illinois for the purpose of visiting their former home.[13]

The number of cattle moved eastward from the Oregon Country in 1876 will probably never be known.[14] We do know, however, that in September Elwood Evans, a prominent citizen of Washington Territory, said in a speech at the Centennial Exposition in Philadelphia that already in that year more than 10,000 head of cattle had been driven from the Pacific Northwest to points east of the Rockies, "principally into Wyoming." We also know that, toward the end of that year, an ambiguous story that was making the rounds of newspapers in Washington, Oregon, and northern California affirmed that, during 1876, "not less than 36,000 head of beef cattle had been driven from Eastern Oregon and Eastern Washington down towards the railroad," some of which were "going East and some to San Francisco." More specifically, in 1876 one drove of cattle that had been trailed from The Dalles entrained at Cheyenne for an eastern destination, and

[13] Oliphant and Kingston (eds.), "Jackson's Diary," pp. 261-73. About a year later, a "forwarding agent" of the Union Pacific Railroad, in a poster dated at Fort Bridger on July 2, 1877, directed persons moving cattle eastwardly from western Montana or from Idaho, and passing Soda Springs and Bear Lake, to "cross over" into southwestern Wyoming and go down the Little Muddy almost to its junction with the Big Muddy, where there was good pasture near the stockyards. From this place they could either ship their cattle "at greatly reduced rates" or sell them to the agent. This poster is reproduced in Gene M. Gressley, *Bankers and Cattlemen* (New York, 1966), opposite p. 75.

[14] See, however, Agnes Wright Spring, *Seventy Years: A Panoramic History of the Wyoming Stock Growers' Association* (Cheyenne, Wyo., 1943), pp. 46-59.

another drove, which had been trailed from southeastern Oregon, passed through Wyoming to Ogallala, Nebraska, before entraining for an eastern destination. Equally specific is the assurance that, at the end of the summer of 1876, there arrived by train in Chicago a band of 400 head of cattle "direct from Washington Territory." They had been driven "600 miles from the ranges where they were bought to a point 350 miles west of Cheyenne, on the Union Pacific Railroad, from which point they came by rail to Chicago." They were part of a band of 2,600 head that had been bought in Washington and Oregon for the market in Chicago.[15] Conceivably, they could have been the cattle shipped by Lang from western Wyoming on August 12.

Such, then, is our present knowledge of the driving and the shipping of cattle eastward from the Oregon Country in 1876. But, however large the number sent eastward in that year, and whatever the destinations of such cattle may have been, this fact is well established: observers of these drives in that and subsequent years were fully persuaded that the effective beginning of the eastward movement of cattle from the Oregon Country dates from the year 1876.

For 1877 the movement of cattle eastward from Oregon, Washington, and Idaho appears to have been principally into, or through, Wyoming. In preparation for the drives of that year, cattle buyers were reported to be "quite numerous in Eastern Oregon" as early as December, 1876. But the low prices they were offering seemed unattractive to many cattlemen. At the beginning of February, 1877, however, "outside parties" had obtained on Camas Prairie, in northern Idaho, more than one thousand head of cattle at prices ranging from ten dollars for two-year-olds to fourteen dollars for three-year-olds, and eighteen dollars for four-year-olds.[16]

But, if the information published in contemporary Pacific

[15] Elwood Evans, *Washington Territory* . . . (Olympia, 1877), p. 49; *Seattle Weekly Pacific Tribune*, Nov. 24, 1876; *Yreka Union*, Dec. 2, 1876; Ernest Staples Osgood, *The Day of the Cattleman* (Minneapolis, 1929), p. 50, citing the *Cheyenne Daily Leader*, Sept. 14, Oct. 27, 1876; *Walla Walla Union*, Sept. 16, 1876, quoting the Chicago *Stock Journal* (meaning, perhaps, the *Weekly Drovers' Journal*).

[16] *Morning Oregonian*, Dec. 20, 1876; *Lewiston Teller*, Feb. 3, 1877.

Northwest newspapers may be trusted, we know that during 1877 cattle were bought for eastward drives principally in northeastern Oregon, eastern Washington, and northern Idaho, and that at least one of the principal purchasers of such cattle was the firm of Lang and Ryan. This firm consisted of G. W. Lang, a drover who, as we have seen, had been buying cattle in the Oregon Country since 1875, and his new associate, Matt Ryan. The accounts of this firm's operations in the Pacific Northwest in 1877 are not altogether clear, and some of them are somewhat conflicting. An editor in Walla Walla says that, by the middle of February, 1877, Mr. Lang had acquired in the Walla Walla Valley two thousand steers, four or five years old, at an average price of twenty dollars a head. Two months later an editor in Lewiston, Idaho, said that Mr. Lang had ferried some eight hundred head of cattle across the Snake River, and by early May an editor in Walla Walla had learned that Lang and Ryan had paid ten to twenty dollars a head for twenty-six hundred head of cattle and some four hundred head of horses north of the Snake. This herd had already been started to Kansas. It is possible, of course, that this firm bought in 1877 more cattle than it intended to drive eastward in that year. Whatever the fact may be, an editor in Boise, on the last day of May, 1877, reported to his readers that

Messrs. Lang & Ryan crossed Snake river a few days ago at Kenney's Ferry and came up the Boise valley to Fouche's Ferry at Boise river, where they crossed with 3,300 head of beef cattle—steers ranging from two to five years old—which they drove up Indian creek to the Overland Road, where they are now encamped. The cattle were bought in Walla Walla valley, and will be driven to Nebraska, where, after selling a portion of the herd, the remainder will be stall-fed for the Chicago and other eastern markets.[17]

Whether the cattle here mentioned were originally intended for Kansas or for Nebraska is of little moment, for, about three and a half months after crossing the ferry on the Boise River, Lang and Ryan, now near Laramie City, Wyoming, sold to J. T. Allen of Kansas City, Missouri, "2,000 head of the best of the fine herd of cattle which they drove from Washington Territory this

[17] *Walla Walla Statesman*, Feb. 17, 1877; *Lewiston Teller*, April 4, 1877; *ibid.*, May 12, 1877, quoting the *Walla Walla Statesman*; Boise *Idaho Tri-Weekly Statesman*, May 31, 1877.

year, numbering 3,000 head in all." Mr. Allen, who agreed "to pay in the neighborhood of $80,000 for this purchase," intended to ship the cattle to Kansas City. We are not told what was done with the remaining cattle in this herd. All we know about this matter we learn from the *Walla Walla Union* of November 2, 1877, which says that "G. W. Lang, who last spring bought and drove from this country 3000 head of cattle, has returned for more. The cattle he drove last spring are now being corn fed in western Missouri."[18]

Whatever may be the truth about Lang and Ryan's operations in the Pacific Northwest in 1877, the editor of the *Willamette Farmer*, on May 11 of that year, was persuaded, as a consequence of an investigation made by W. S. Newberry of Portland in the upper Columbia Valley, that

a regular trade . . . [had been] established between Kansas ranches and stock men and the cattlemen of Eastern Oregon, and [that] already this Spring several parties of cattle buyers . . . [had] gone through the Upper Country from the Dalles to Palouse, purchasing beef cattle to drive East. One firm [perhaps Lang & Ryan] had purchased 2,700 head and was still buying, and others were in the field making large purchases.

These cattle are started Eastward by way of Boise and Snake river, through Utah, and are driven all the way to Kansas by easy stages, reaching there, some of them, early in the Fall. Later in the season those that are in good order are shipped East by rail, and the rest are wintered in Kansas ready for shipment the next Spring, as soon as they are in good condition. Some of these buyers have purchased stock in Oregon for three years past, and it is becoming an old settled business, one that will grow and increase and that calls for the improvement of stock to make it as profitable as it should be to the ranch men of Oregon and Washington.

What all this means is not entirely clear, for in the newspapers of the Oregon Country no specific mention has been found of herds of cattle moving from the Oregon Country *through Utah* to Kansas in 1877. If herds of considerable size were moved to Kansas through Utah, it is odd that this fact was ignored by editors who frequently mentioned the fact that cattle were passing through Idaho into Wyoming. But this oversight, if such it was, is less important than the knowledge conveyed to us that

[18] *Cheyenne Weekly Leader*, Sept. 20, 1877; *Weekly Mountaineer*, Nov. 10, 1877.

Lang and Ryan did not monopolize the driving of cattle eastward from the Oregon Country in 1877. We are not told how many drovers were engaged in this business, but we do know that the Boise *Idaho Weekly Statesman* announced on May 5, 1877, that Eb. Pinkham and O. P. Johnson would soon leave the Boise Valley for the Black Hills with "about 2,000 head of cattle," and we also know that it announced, on October 6 of that year, that Pinkham had sold his cattle in Rawlins, Wyoming, and that Johnson "had bargained for his." Nor was this all. On March 14, 1877, a resident of Ada County, Idaho, Jacob Bloomer, reported that he had received from interested "parties" in Nebraska inquiries about the opportunities for buying cattle in Idaho and in places farther west, and on September 22 of that year the *Morning Oregonian* announced that John Moore, who had been driving cattle for Portland butchers for several years, had gone to Harney Lake "for the purpose of driving 1,200 head of cattle eastward for the Chicago market."

One herd of some three thousand head of cattle, not specifically described in the newspapers of the Oregon Country in 1877, was gathered in that year by "Rice and Montgomery" in the Crab Creek region and on Snake River, and was driven eastward. We learn of this drive from Charles Albert Smith, a resident of Spokane, who in 1944 related some of his experiences, as a boy of fifteen, on this drive, which took him from Crab Creek in central Washington to Black Eagle Rock in eastern Idaho. Among other things, he said:

We went through Walla Walla and over the Blue Mountain road to La Grande in Oregon and then out through the Burnt River country to Snake River at the Applegate Ferry. There we swam the cattle across Snake River and then we went on to Payette River and from that point to Boise City, where we camped near the reservoir. From Boise we went on east to Big Camas Prairie and from there on to Wood River and then to Black Eagle Rock on the Snake River where we crossed the river for the second time. There my boss met eastern buyers and sold the cattle. . . . Counting the cook, there were eleven in the outfit that drove the cattle from Crab Creek to Black Eagle Rock. We had good luck with the cattle and lost practically none.[19]

[19] From a typed copy of a statement made in 1944 by Charles Albert Smith to Professor C. S. Kingston of Cheney, Washington.

Within the year 1877, two editors in Oregon may have succeeded in stimulating momentarily the pride of their readers by hinting at the possibility of new markets, one in England and the other in Chicago, for cattle bred in the Oregon Country. On May 29 the *Morning Oregonian* announced that Philip Houghton, of Baker, had sold five hundred head of cattle, which would be driven to Winnemucca and sent from there by rail to Jersey City, where they would be "butchered for shipment to England." From this band may have come "the 400 head of large beef cattle" which the *Weekly Mountaineer*, at the end of the summer, said had been driven from Oregon during the preceding spring to the "Overland railroad," and sent by way of Chicago to New York, from which port they were shipped across the ocean to "tickle the palates of the Johnny Bulls."[20] So much for the prospective English market. The possibility of opening a new market in Chicago was envisaged when the editor of the *Weekly Mountaineer* announced, in the early autumn of 1877, that there had been a sale in Chicago of "150 of Eastern Oregon beef steers ... [which] had been grazed in Kansas." These steers, he remarked, had brought more than three times as much as "a lot of Texas cattle"; but, since he had no knowledge of the cost of getting steers from Oregon to "the Chicago market," he was uncertain whether such a venture would be profitable.[21]

All told, the editorial outlook in Oregon, Washington, and Idaho in respect to the marketing of cattle from the Oregon Country was, during 1877, decidedly optimistic. To the editors of this region it seemed that at long last the isolation of their country was being broken, and that better times for the cattlemen of Transcascadia were not far off. The prospect of an improvement in economic conditions in Idaho provoked some editorial scolding. Early in June of that year, an editor in Boise, annoyed at what he considered a lackadaisical attitude of the stockmen of Idaho, relieved his feelings by writing an editorial in which he said:

It is truly astonishing that the stock raisers of Idaho, who have at command unlimited and unsurpassed ranges for the production of the best

[20] Quoted by the *Walla Walla Union*, Sept. 22, 1877.
[21] Quoted *ibid.*, Oct. 6, 1877.

quality of beef, do not turn their attention to this branch of business and help supply the markets. Every season men of means visit this Territory in search of cattle to drive to the railroad to be turned into beef, but who invariably are compelled to go to the west to find them. The price of beef is steadily increasing, and the supply never surpasses the demand. Only a few days since a band of two or three thousand head of cattle passed through here which came from Eastern Oregon and Walla Walla, and which would have been purchased in Idaho could they have been procured. And such is the case every year. Why do not our stock-raisers devise some way to keep this money here in place of allowing the country below us to gather it up?[22]

In 1878, despite the disturbance created by the war with the Bannock Indians,[23] more cattle appear to have been driven eastward from the Oregon Country than in 1877; and not all these cattle entered Wyoming. At least one herd of one thousand head was driven from Oregon to Montana, and more than one herd was started from the Pacific Northwest to Colorado. On September 16 of that year, an editor in Colorado Springs went "overboard" when he announced that one hundred thousand were "said" to be on the road to Colorado. Because cattle in Oregon were much cheaper than in Colorado, he thought that a considerable profit might be made by driving cattle from Oregon to Colorado. By November 9, however, having become fully calmed, he announced that the Bowling Brothers, under considerable difficulty because of Indian trouble, had recently brought fifteen hundred head of cattle from Oregon to Colorado. Unhappily, we do not know exactly how many head of cattle entered Colorado from the Oregon Country in 1878.[24]

Once again the firm of Lang and Ryan in 1878 attracted more attention than any other buyer of cattle in the Oregon Country. Before the end of January, it had bought thousands of cattle from ranges north of the Snake River and from ranges in Wasco

[22] Boise *Semi-Weekly Idahoan,* June 8, 1877.

[23] The *Idaho Weekly Statesman,* July 6, 1878, reported that "Stewart and Son, of Grande Ronde Valley, Oregon," started eastward with three thousand head of beef cattle, but, at the mouth of the Malheur River, gave up the undertaking and turned "their stock loose on the range until the war is over."

[24] Granville Stuart, *Forty Years on the Frontier* ... ed. Paul C. Phillips (Cleveland, 1925), II, 98; Colorado Springs *Weekly Gazette,* Sept. 28, Nov. 9, 1878. See also *Morning Oregonian,* Jan. 23, April 30, June 5, 1878; Colfax *Palouse Gazette,* May 11, 1878; *Cheyenne Weekly Leader,* Aug. 1, 1878.

and Umatilla counties in Oregon. But the journalistic accounts of these transactions are not easy to harmonize, for editors tended to claim larger purchases in their respective localities than the facts would seem to warrant. We can be fairly certain, however, that this firm made purchases in the Yakima and Kittitas Valleys, the Palouse country, the Walla Walla country, eastern Oregon, and northern Idaho. As early as January 19, 1878, the editor of the *Walla Walla Union* averred that Mr. Lang had told him that, "up to the present time," his firm had purchased, principally in the Yakima and Crab Creek countries, 12,000 head of cattle "at an average of $13 per head." The cattle thus purchased would be gathered in the spring and driven to Colorado, and from that state all the beef cattle would be shipped to Missouri to be fattened for market. The remaining cattle would be driven to Missouri the next year.[25]

Regardless of where this firm bought its cattle, what it paid for them, and what was said about the route of its drive in 1878, about the middle of May, when the eastward-bound herd of Lang and Ryan was nearing the western border of Idaho, an editor in Boise wrote as follows:

Mr. Eldridge Farnham arrived here Thursday, having come up from the Walla Walla country in the employ of Messrs. Lang & Ryan, who are now near the mouth of the Malheur, seventy-five miles from here, with a band of sixteen thousand head of cattle, destined for Cheyenne, Wyoming Territory. Two thousand head of these cattle were purchased in northern Idaho, and the balance in the Walla Walla count[r]y and in Umatilla and Wasco counties, Oregon.[26]

Despite the annoying discrepancies which appear in the foregoing accounts, there is abundant evidence to give us a glimpse of a large and continuing flow of cattle in 1878 from the Oregon Country to Wyoming and to points east of that territory. In February of that year, the Portland *Standard* announced that the firm of Everding and Company, "with eight men as drivers," was scouring the Umatilla and the Grande Ronde valleys to get thirty-seven hundred head of "beeves" to drive to Cheyenne. In March, eastern buyers were reported to have purchased fifteen thousand

[25] Quoted by the *Morning Oregonian*, Jan. 23, 1878.
[26] *Idaho Weekly Statesman*, May 18, 1878.

head of cattle in the Yakima country, and also in that month "several hundred head of cattle" were taken across the Snake River from Camas Prairie in northern Idaho and headed toward Cheyenne. In May, David Harer and Son gathered in Whitman and Stevens counties and started to Wyoming more than three thousand head of what the editor of the Colfax *Palouse Gazette* called "the finest cattle that ever left the Palouse country"; and, at the same time, the editor of the *Walla Walla Statesman* was telling his readers that, besides the thousands bought by Lang and Ryan, four other firms—Spratly and Everhardy, Haley and Company, Rand and Company, and Insley and Company—had bought sixty-five hundred head of cattle in the "immediate vicinity" of Walla Walla. On the basis of these and of other purchases, this editor estimated that "fully 30,000 head" of cattle would be driven from that "country" during the season of 1878, and that most of the cattle so driven would go to Leavenworth, "from which place they would be sent by rail to the large cities of the eastern states."[27] Somewhat earlier, relying on a report by D. M. Franch of The Dalles, the editor of the *Astorian* remarked that it was "probable" that at least one hundred thousand head of beef cattle would be driven eastward from Oregon and Washington during 1878.[28]

Still other evidence, some from the Oregon Country and some from Wyoming, supports the conclusion that there was a considerable movement of cattle eastward from the Pacific Northwest in 1878. On September 17, C. S. Bush, who had left Walla Walla with a drove of cattle "some time ago," wrote from a point near Rawlins to tell the editor of the *Walla Walla Statesman* that, in November, he expected to return to Walla Walla to "buy more cattle." Years afterward, in a book published in 1904, Charles J. Steedman told of helping to drive a herd of cattle from Oregon to Wyoming in 1878 and of seeing three other herds moving eastward.[29]

[27] *Weekly Pacific Tribune*, Feb. 13, 1878, quoting the Portland *Standard;* Morning Oregonian, Feb. 25, March 12, 1878; Whatcom *Bellingham Bay Mail*, March 23, May 25, 1878; *Lewiston Teller*, March 23, 1878; *Palouse Gazette*, May 11, 1878.
[28] Cited by the Salem *Willamette Farmer*, March 20, 1878.
[29] *Weekly Astorian*, Oct. 12, 1878; Charles J. Steedman, *Bucking the Sage*

That a great many of the eastward-moving cattle remained at least for a while in Wyoming, we can scarcely doubt. The editor of the *Cheyenne Daily Leader*, after observing on July 25, 1878, that the "cattle interests on the plains and [in] the Rocky Mountain region" were receiving large accessions of cattle from the far West, announced on September 12 that a large herd of cattle from the Columbia River had arrived at "Schwartze's ranch on Pole creek." Two days later he said that, during last year and "this season," many thousands of cattle were "shipped and driven east from Utah and other territories." On September 29 he predicted that more than "a hundred thousand head of cattle" would be driven into Utah and Wyoming from Oregon before the season closed, and on October 18 he announced that Lee and Blewitt had arrived on the Little Laramie with sixteen hundred head of "beef and stock" cattle from Oregon.[30] Finally, if further proof be needed of a substantial eastward movement of cattle from the Pacific Northwest in 1878, one may turn to the reports for that year of two western governors. On October 14 Governor E. P. Ferry of Washington Territory reported, perhaps somewhat imprecisely, that large numbers of cattle from Washington Territory were "annually driven to the Union Pacific Railroad and thence transported to Chicago," and a few days later Governor John W. Hoyt of Wyoming Territory reported that young cattle from Oregon and the western territories were preferred in Wyoming to young cattle from Texas. Governor Hoyt also quoted prices showing that cattle from Oregon and the western territories were worth more in Wyoming than cattle from Texas.[31]

By the beginning of 1879, as the *Kentucky Live Stock Record* pointed out, cattlemen and others increasingly recognized that "a great change" was taking place in the cattle trade of the nation, "and that more . . . [was] promised in the immediate future."

Brush, or the Oregon Trail in the Seventies (New York, 1904), p. 231 and *passim*.

[30] Reprinted in John K. Rollinson, *Wyoming Cattle Trails* . . . (Caldwell, Ida., 1948), pp. 332-35. Two years later the *Omaha Daily Republican*, June 24, 1880, announced that "Lee & Blewett, of Fremont, Nebraska, have been on the road a month with 10,000 cattle which they are driving from Oregon and Washington to the prairies. . . ."

[31] 45th Cong., 3rd sess., H. Ex. Doc. 1, IX, 1121.

It also said that the feeding grounds were "being transferred from Texas to the great buffalo plains," and that "the central portions of the continent, with the Pacific States [and Territories], . . . [were] becoming the leading producers of beef."[32] A year later the boom precipitated by this "great change" was at its height, as we learn from the Gordon Report accompanying the tenth federal census. Here we are told that one of the reasons for the driving of large numbers of cattle into Wyoming in 1880 from Oregon, Washington, Idaho, Utah, and Colorado was "the demand for stock-cattle in Montana, Wyoming, Dakota, and Nebraska, especially in Wyoming, where 100,000 head were located in the new country from the Big Horn mountains to the little Missouri river." Of the 364,010 head of cattle brought into Wyoming in 1880, only 160,920 were sent out of this territory, and of these about 60,000 head went to Chicago.[33]

The role that Utah and the Pacific Northwest were playing in the cattle boom that was starting on the high plains was explained in 1880 by an interested Englishman, William A. Baillie-Grohman:

The general public voice declares the Oregon and Utah breed to be far superior to Texas cattle; and while the earlier ranchemen [sic] in Colorado, Wyoming, and Montana had only the latter, the Oregon cows driven to the two last-mentioned Territories in 1879 outnumbered Texas stock at least three or four times. At first it was greatly doubted whether cattle raised on the Pacific slopes, and especially in the damp, moderately warm climate of Oregon,[34] could possibly stand a Wyoming or Montana winter with its terribly severe snowstorms. Experience, however, has established not only that Oregon stock can withstand great climatic hardships, but also that they flourish on Wyoming soil. As both Utah and Oregon cattle fetch comparatively much higher prices in Chicago and other great markets, those breeds are now the prime favorites; and, as a natural consequence of the vastly increased demands, cows in Oregon have risen quite seventy-five per cent in value in the last four or five years.[35]

[32] Reprinted in the Philadelphia *National Baptist*, Feb. 6, 1879, p. 7, under the heading, "The Cattle Drives of 1878."

[33] Gordon, "Report," p. 1018.

[34] Baillie-Grohman apparently did not know that the climate of eastern Oregon and eastern Washington is drier than that of the Willamette Valley and Puget Sound.

[35] First published in "Cattle Ranches in the Far West," *Fortnightly Review*, XXVIII, n.s. (October, 1880), 447, and reprinted with some emendations in

Accordingly, from 1879 through 1883, the eastward movement of cattle from the far Northwest to Montana, Colorado, and especially Wyoming was one of great importance. Perhaps the largest herd moved eastward from the Oregon Country in 1879 was the one, mentioned in an earlier chapter, which N. R. Davis bought from Peter French and other breeders of cattle in southeastern Oregon and drove to Colorado. To move this large herd, it was necessary to divide it into numerous bands and to employ a large outfit to take charge of them. The editor of the Winnemucca *Silver State* described the character and size of this outfit as follows:

Yesterday A. A. Jordan arrived here, and is now preparing to drive the cattle east. He has brought two car loads of horses and several wagons here, and has already engaged twenty-five men, and will require as many more to complete the outfit. A band of 150 horses purchased in California, is being driven across the country to Stein [Steens] Mountain. The outfit will be here in a few days and go direct to Stein Mountain, where the cattle will be divided into three or four drives and started east to their destination.

A few weeks later this editor reported that another outfit, consisting of "twenty-five men, four wagons, and eighty horses," had left Winnemucca the day before for the Steens Mountain country to help drive to Colorado the cattle belonging to N. R. Davis.[36]

Elsewhere in the Pacific Northwest there was extensive buying of cattle for the eastern markets in 1879. The firm of Lang and Ryan was once more a leading buyer, and the firm of Rand and Briggs perhaps bought as many more. Moreover, numerous references to substantial purchases by other buyers in Oregon, Washington, and Idaho may be found in the newspapers of this region.[37] In May the editor of the Boise *Idaho Weekly Statesman*

William A. Baillie-Grohman, *Camps in the Rockies* . . . (London, 1882), p. 346. On the cattle boom, see Ernest Staples Osgood's *Day of the Cattleman* (Minneapolis, 1929), chap. iv.

[36] *Morning Oregonian*, May 2, 1879; Winnemucca *Silver State*, April 9, May 16, 1879.

[37] *Walla Walla Union*, Jan. 18, 1879; *Morning Oregonian*, Jan. 23, May 21, 30, Aug. 8, 1879; Seattle *Weekly Intelligencer*, May 31, Nov. 8, 1879; *Spokan Times*, June 19, 1879; *Idaho Weekly Statesman*, March 29, April 27, May 22, June 14, 1879; Oxford *Idaho Enterprise*, July 31, 1879; *Idaho Tri-Weekly States-*

made an interesting estimate. Relying on the observation of I. W. Garrett of Boise, who, during a recent trip into Grant County, Oregon, had seen "several immense herds of cattle" advancing from eastern Oregon into southern Idaho en route to eastern markets, he conjectured that not fewer than one hundred thousand head of cattle would be driven eastward from Oregon and Idaho in 1879.

There are several herds of these cattle [he wrote], ranging all the way from 10,000 to 1,000 head now crossing or near the [Snake] river, and many others coming. . . . All these cattle are driven across Idaho at a heavy expense to the purchasers, and at a serious inconvenience and some damage to the country passed over. They crowd the ferries and crossings, get mixed up with the cattle on the range, requiring much labor and care on the part of resident stockmen to prevent their own cattle from being driven off. This cattle trade is constantly increasing. . . . People are just beginning to awake to the immense value of the magnificent cattle ranges which cover a large portion of Idaho and Eastern Oregon. Purchasers are attracted to this region by the superior quality of the beef and the camparitively [sic] easy terms upon which cattle can be bought. . . .[38]

This editor's estimate may not have been far wrong. In October, 1879, the Surveyor-General of Idaho calculated that forty thousand head of cattle had been sold in Idaho during that season for the eastern markets,[39] and on January 25, 1881, a correspondent of the *Chicago Times,* writing from the Kittitas Valley in Washington Territory, asserted that the firm of Lang and Ryan had driven eastward, "by the way of Boise City and Cheyenne," twenty thousand head of cattle in 1879.[40] Assuming that the two foregoing estimates are approximately correct, it would not be unreasonable to suppose that at least one hundred thousand head of cattle were driven eastward from Oregon, Washington, and Idaho during 1879.

In that year some of the cattlemen of Idaho, doubtless profit-

---

man, June 10, Sept. 4, 13, Oct. 21, 1879; *Lewiston Teller,* June 13, 1879; *Cheyenne Weekly Leader,* June 19, Aug. 14, 1879; Canyon City *Grant County Times,* June 28, Aug. 9, 1879; Chicago *Weekly Drovers' Journal,* March 11, 1880. See also William P. Ricketts, *50 Years in the Saddle* (Sheridan, Wyo., 1942), pp. 34-65.

[38] *Idaho Weekly Statesman,* May 24, 1879.
[39] 46th Cong., 2nd sess., H. Ex. Doc. 1 (Serial 1911), X, 438.
[40] Quoted in the New Tacoma *North Pacific Coast,* May 16, 1881.

ing by the experience of cattlemen in Oregon and Washington, drove their own stock to points of entrainment on the Union Pacific Railroad. But the editor of the *Idaho Tri-Weekly States-man* was nettled because not every one of them had done so. Taking his cue from a report made to him by Solomon Jeffries of Weiser City, who had just returned from driving eight hundred head of beef cattle to Cheyenne, he read a lecture to the cattlemen of Idaho on the economics of the cattle business, saying,

During the present summer [1879] several large herds of cattle have been sold in this section of Idaho to Eastern dealers and driven to Cheyenne and other points on the railroad. Those who sold got what they considered a fair price at home, but they might have realized much more by driving their own cattle to market. There is never any trouble or delay in disposing of good beef cattle at the railroad or in the markets of Omaha and Chicago. There is nothing whatever to prevent our cattle raisers from marketing their own stock and pocketing all that can be made in the business.

The cattle trade from this region is fast attaining immense proportions. Among the causes of this are the constantly growing demand for beef in the Eastern markets, and the fact that beef raised here is of a superior quality to that raised in Texas or anywhere east of the Rocky Mountains.

Another mistake which stock raisers make in this country is in keeping cattle of marketable age over the winter. The winters here, while they are generally mild and favorable to the keeping of large herds on range without much care, are uncertain enough to make it a matter of prudence to dispose of the surplus and marketable stock before the winter sets in. If cattle raisers would adopt the plan of driving and shipping their own stock and disposing each season of all the cattle ready for market they would not only save all that the outside dealer makes by the buying and driving, but they would also save all that is liable to be lost by keeping too many cattle over winter.[41]

Whatever may have been the effect of this scolding, the driving of cattle eastward from the Oregon Country reached its culmination in 1880. So large was the movement in that year that observers on both sides of the Rocky Mountains were excited about it.[42]

[41] *Idaho Tri-Weekly Statesman*, Oct. 21, 23, 1879.

[42] Gordon, "Report," p. 1081. A correspondent in Portland, Ore., writing to an editor in Sacramento on May 6, 1880, said: "The country east of the [Cascade] mountains has been flooded this season with cattle buyers, who have purchased all the saleable stock of cattle and many horses, and are now gathering their herds together to drive them east." *Sacramento Daily Record-Union*, May 6, 1880. The *Idaho Enterprise*, March 18, 1880, predicted that Lang would drive

No one knows precisely how large it was, and contemporaneous estimates vary. Perhaps the most trustworthy was that of the federal census of 1880, which estimated that Wyoming received 62,000 head of cattle from Washington Territory, 58,300 from Oregon, and 50,000 from Idaho Territory.[43] Yet there were other estimates or enumerations, none of which should be ignored, that put the number still higher. Some of these we shall now examine.

Early in 1881, the editor of a newspaper in the heart of the cattle country in northeastern Oregon offered some evidence to support his belief that more than two hundred thousand head of cattle moved eastward from the Pacific Northwest in 1880.

On the Sweetwater in Wyoming at one station, a record is kept of all stock driven over the route during the past year, and this record shows that the surprisingly large number of 170,000 head passed through the Rock Creek station. These came from Oregon, Washington and Idaho, but the majority from the eastern portion of our state. There are other routes, which will increase this number probably 70,000.[44]

This record, with its accompanying estimate, shows a somewhat larger number than a record said to have been made in Idaho a few months earlier by "Judge Peck" of Big Camas Prairie, who reported to the editor of the *Idaho Democrat* that "180,000 head of cattle, 50,200 head of sheep, and about 2,000 head of horses" had passed through this prairie in 1880 on the way to eastern markets.[45]

Estimates made east of the Rockies disclose similar inconsistencies. In June, 1880, a Chicago stock journal reprinted from a Kansas City trade journal a prediction that an "unprecedented" number of cattle would be driven eastward from the Pacific Coast in 1880. This prediction reads as follows:

"40,000 head of cattle from Oregon through Idaho east this spring," and on July 1 of that year it affirmed that as many as 100,000 head of cattle were "on the eastward trail from southern Idaho." On this subject see also the *Grant County News,* July 24, 1880, quoting the *Idaho Enterprise,* and the *Weekly Drovers' Journal,* Jan. 13, 1881, quoting the St. Joseph, Mo., *Gazette.* Of the various newspapers dealing with this movement in 1880, none perhaps has fuller coverage than the *Morning Oregonian.*

[43] Gordon, "Report," p. 1018.

[44] *Idaho Weekly Statesman,* Jan. 22, 1881, quoting the *Baker County Reveille.* This story was also reprinted in the *Willamette Farmer,* March 11, 1881.

[45] *Willamette Farmer,* Oct. 29, 1880, quoting from the Boise *Idaho Democrat;* also reprinted in the *Idaho Enterprise,* Oct. 28, 1880.

The Oregon cattle drive, says the Kansas City *Price Current,* promises to be a very important factor in the Western cattle market this season. Mr. J. W. Gamel arrived at Kansas City last week from a visit to the cattle country along the Union Pacific Railroad. He says the number of cattle driven in and shipped Eastward from the Pacific Coast this year will be unprecedented. The drive is placed by some as high as 200,000. Col. Carter, of the firm of Coe & Carter, Omaha, has just returned, where he has contracted for 10,000 cattle and will ship them in by rail to his range in Wyoming, he having obtained a freight rate of $6 per head. J. M. Taylor is driving 15,000, Messrs. Lang & Ryan a large number, the Gillespie boys of our city have a herd, and there are a number of others driving whose names Mr. Gamel was unable to obtain.[46]

On January 31, 1881, this journal reprinted an estimate from the St. Joseph, Missouri, *Gazette,* which put the 1880 drive from Oregon, Washington, and Idaho into Wyoming at "about 150,000 head, which found a ready market."[47]

Whatever it may have been, the number of cattle sent eastward from the Pacific Northwest in 1880 was very large.[48] To provide cattle for this movement, there was extensive buying on all the ranges of that region. Once again the most widely advertised buyer in the Columbia Basin was the firm of Lang and Ryan, whose enormous herd of 1880 was drawn from the ranges of Oregon, Washington, and Idaho. Early in March the *Morning Oregonian* published the names of the cattlemen of eastern Oregon and Idaho who had sold to Lang and Ryan, as well as the number of cattle involved in each sale. These sales aggregated 24,800 head. But this total does not include several thousand head of cattle that Lang and Ryan obtained in Washington Territory. It seems likely that a subsequent estimate of "over 30,000" as the size of the herd that they drove eastward from the far Northwest in 1880 was not an exaggeration.[49]

[46] Chicago *Weekly Drovers' Journal,* June 10, 1880.

[47] *Ibid.,* Jan. 13, 1881.

[48] *Grant County News,* July 24, 1880, quoting the *Idaho Enterprise.* One estimate, based upon purchases by eight firms or individuals, put the number of cattle to be driven eastward in 1880 from eastern Oregon at 100,800 head. Portland *West Shore,* VI (April, 1880), 104.

[49] *Morning Oregonian,* March 9, 1880; *Yakima Record,* March 3, July 31, 1880; *Weekly Mountaineer,* March 11, 1880. For a Texan view expressing in 1880 the belief that the competition of Oregon with Texas and Colorado in the markets of the Middle West would be one of short duration, see the Chicago

The driving of so large a herd required a considerable force of men and horses, and the preparations for this undertaking aroused interest in the Middle West as well as in the Pacific Northwest. In June, 1880, the *Weekly Drovers' Journal* of Chicago copied from the *Willamette Farmer* a description of these preparations (without making known the fact that the *Farmer* had borrowed this description from the *Morning Oregonian*). The *Oregonian's* account of the preparations for this drive reads as follows:

To drive these [cattle of Lang and Ryan] to the Yellowstone country, where they will winter, will require 800 head of horses and the services of 120 men. Most of these "cow boys" are Kansas men, who have been in the employ of this concern for the past six years. Forty wagons accompany the drive, and about 160 stand of loaded rifles will always be on hand, good for about 3000 shots at any band of hostile Indians that may attack them. The drive will be cut up into three squads or bands of cattle, the first lot having two days start of the third. This brings them in easy range of the rear from the front. In April they will begin to gather up for the start, and by the 25th of that month the greatest body of cattle ever banded together will be slowly marching eastward. Up to the twentieth of June the drive will be about nine miles per day, but as the heat of summer comes along they will decrease it to about five. Therefore a steer travels no more on a drive of this kind than he would upon the range, and is sure to be in good order when he reaches the Yellowstone, as there is abundance of bunch grass as soon as the Grande Ronde river is passed.[50]

An account of a smaller drive eastward from Oregon in 1880 is of particular interest because it is based on a report by E. O. Grimes, "the foreman of the herders of Todd, Coleman & Co.'s cattle band" in that year. After making the drive to Wyoming and returning in a wagon, Mr. Grimes related his experiences to the editor of *The Dalles Times*, who reported to his readers as follows:

Mr. Grimes started from Prineville on the 14th of last June, having two droves of cattle numbering in the aggregate 3,150, belonging to Messrs. Todd, Coleman & Co., he being foreman of the band of twenty-one herders, including eight Indians. The route was as follows: From Prineville, by way of Camp Harney, to Snake river, which they crossed at Steele's ferry; from

National Live-Stock Journal, XI (December, 1880), 541, quoting the *San Antonio Express*.
[50] *Morning Oregonian*, March 9, 1880.

this point they proceeded by way of Big Camas Prairie to Wood river, in Idaho; they then crossed the Snake river again at Eagle Rock, and followed what is called the Soda Springs route.... They crossed the Rocky Mountains at the South Pass, and, arriving at Sweet Water, followed down that river to Rock Creek station, one hundred miles west of Cheyenne, where the cattle were put on cars and shipped to Council Bluffs. . . .

The cattle, after being shipped to Council Bluffs, Mr. Grimes informs us, are driven into some of the valleys near the Missouri river, and fed during the winter on corn, fodder and hay. In the spring they are taken up and stall-fed and soon placed on the market for beef.[51]

Owing at least in part to the devastating effect of the winter of 1880-81 on herds throughout the entire Pacific Northwest, the movement of cattle from that region in 1881 appears to have been relatively slight. According to an estimate printed in the *Morning Oregonian,* the losses of cattle during that winter were 83 per cent in the Yakima Valley, 78 per cent in Klickitat County, 62 per cent in Wasco County, and 55 per cent in Umatilla and Walla Walla counties. Such estimates no doubt are extravagant, but there is no denying the fact that, everywhere in the Pacific Northwest, the winter losses were very heavy. Nevertheless, there were some sales to eastern buyers in both eastern Washington and eastern Oregon in 1881, and an official report made in 1885 affirms that there was a large drive of cattle from Washington and Oregon to northern ranges in 1881.[52] However much one may doubt such an affirmation, there is no denying the fact that, early in 1881, buyers from the East, among whom were "Mr. Lang and son," were seeking cattle in various parts of the Oregon Country: in the Crab Creek country, in the Prineville region, on the north fork of the John Day River, in southern Oregon, and in the Jordan Valley.[53] But the widespread excitement in 1880 about the sales of cattle was now noticeably absent. Only one large

[51] Quoted in *ibid.,* Jan. 11, 1881.
[52] *Ibid.,* March 7, 1883; U.S. Bureau of Animal Industry, *Second Annual Report* (1885), p. 296.
[53] *Morning Oregonian,* Jan. 5, April 20, June 8, 1881; *Weekly Intelligencer,* March 5, 1881, quoting the *Walla Walla Union; Idaho Weekly Statesman,* March 19, July 30, 1881; *Willamette Farmer,* April 15, 1881; *Sacramento Daily Record-Union,* May 2, 1881; Silver City *Idaho Avalanche,* May 28, 1881. A letter from the Jordan Valley, dated May 25, 1881, affirms that in this valley cattle buyers had obtained fewer cattle than they had expected to get. *Idaho Avalanche,* June 4, 1881.

drove of cattle moving eastward in that year—that of Lang and Ryan—was specifically reported in the newspapers. On February 10, 1882, the *Willamette Farmer* quoted the *Grant County News* as saying that "Lang & Ryan purchased 20,000 head of cattle in this county last year and drove them to Eastern markets. These were mostly purchased in the northern part of the county, along the John Day and its tributaries. The southern and central portions of the county, where the bulk of the cattle are, finds *[sic]* its market for beef in San Francisco." The total evidence now available does not, however, warrant our attempting to estimate the size of the eastward drive of cattle from the Oregon Country in 1881. Apropos of this matter, it is significant to note that, in November, 1881, the Governor of Wyoming reported to the Secretary of the Interior a "falling off in the export supply [of cattle] of the Pacific States and Territories."[54]

The number of cattle in the eastward movement from the Pacific Northwest in 1882 was no doubt considerably larger than that of 1881. Prices were rising, and where cattle once had been plentiful few were now for sale; the owners of marketable cattle in 1882 were thinking twice before disposing of their stock. Some of the excitement of 1880 seems to have returned, as eastern buyers, perceiving that the ranges of Oregon and Washington had less to offer them than in earlier years, scoured northern and southern Idaho for marketable cattle. "Cattle men are arriving in this city in large numbers and are being distributed to the various ranges as fast as they arrive," the Boise *Idaho Weekly Statesman* affirmed on March 18, 1882. "Yesterday's stage brought half a dozen, who will drive from the Weiser and Payette ranges." A week later this newspaper reported that several buyers were in Lewiston, where they were preparing to drive cattle from northern Idaho to eastern markets.[55] In May, 1882, the *Lewiston Teller* estimated that about ten thousand head of cattle and about fifteen hundred horses would be driven from two counties of the Idaho panhandle and from two counties of

---

[54] 47th Cong., 1st sess., H. Ex. Doc. 1 (Serial 2018), 1059.
[55] Vancouver *Clarke County Register,* March 16, 1882; *Idaho Weekly Statesman,* March 24, 31, 1882.

eastern Washington "by four or five purchasing companies." Estimates of the number of cattle purchased in eastern Oregon for eastern markets varied, but none of them was less than thirty-five thousand head. By the end of June, 1882, the *Morning Oregonian* was persuaded to believe that one hundred thousand head of cattle had already moved eastward past Boise City, and it presumed that these cattle had been obtained in about equal numbers from Oregon, Washington, and Idaho.[56]

But the eastward movement of livestock from the Oregon Country in 1882 was not entirely a movement of cattle. Some eastern drivers bought both horses and sheep in considerable numbers in order to fill out their quotas. This change in the composition of the drives is well illustrated by the experience of the firm of Lang and Ryan, which, by the early part of February, 1882, was reported to have gathered "about 13,000 head" of cattle to be driven eastward,[57] and again, a few weeks later, to have the largest band—"twelve to thirteen thousand head"—of those driving cattle eastward.[58] At about the same time, Matt Ryan wrote from Leavenworth, Kansas, to the Kansas City *Price Current*, saying that "the Oregon cattle drive promised to be a light one" that year, because cattle were getting scarce there. "My boys," he said, "will drive 18,000 cattle, 10,000 sheep and some 1,500 horses. They say they could get no more cattle so bought horses. Two of them went over the Blue Mountains to British Columbia to try and get cattle, but could find none."[59] It appears, however, that, although Ryan's "boys" did not achieve their quota for cattle, they exceeded their quota for sheep. On June 29, 1882, after Ryan had gone to the Oregon Country to help with the eastward drive, the editor of the *Idaho Tri-Weekly Statesman* remarked that "Mr. Ryan, of the Kansas City stock firm of Lang & Ryan, was in town yesterday. He is superintending a drive of 12,000 head of cattle. He also has from 20,000 to

[56] Colfax *Washington Democrat*, May 5, 1882, quoting the *Lewiston Teller; West Shore*, VIII (June, 1883), 139, quoting the *Grant County News; Weekly Drovers' Journal*, July 20, 1882, quoting the *Morning Oregonian* of June 30, 1882.

[57] *Pataha City Spirit*, April 1, 1882.

[58] *Willamette Farmer*, Feb. 10, March 31, 1882.

[59] *Weekly Drovers' Journal*, May 22, 1882.

30,000 head of sheep under his control on the road."[60]

Another herd of more than usual interest was gathered in southeastern Washington in the spring of 1882, and driven to a ranch in what is now South Dakota. Oddly enough, we first encounter the purchaser of this herd in a story in the Vancouver *Clarke County Register* of March 16, 1882. Here we read that "J. Haft, of Dakota, is in the vicinity of Pomeroy buying cattle to drive east." A book published in Colorado seventy-four years later says that James Haft and William Henry Bayless, on January 16, 1882, had formed a partnership to trade in cattle in Dakota, and that, soon thereafter, Mr. Haft went into the Pacific Northwest to buy cattle. He arrived in Walla Walla on February 3, 1882, and by February 12 he was buying cattle in Pomeroy in what must be called a seller's market. All told, he bought about 1,100 head of cattle, paying a dollar more for yearlings and for two-year-old steers in the last 500 than he had paid for the first 375 head that he had bought. The scarcity of cattle is revealed in a letter which he wrote from Pataha City on March 6, in which he said that, two years earlier, there were three times as many cattle in that country as were there in 1882.

Mr. Haft took his cattle across the Snake River at White's Ferry, drove them over the Coeur d'Alene Mountains, and on through Montana, going by Missoula and passing south of Helena and Deer Lodge en route to Miles City, from which place he proceeded to the Dakota ranch of Haft and Bayless, where he arrived on October 30. He lost about a hundred head of cattle on the journey.[61]

How many cattle were driven eastward from the Oregon Country in 1882 we shall probably never know. We can affirm, however, that fewer cattle were trailed eastward from this region in that year than in the record year of 1880, and that the number of both horses and sheep moving eastward in 1882 had become

[60] An interesting sidelight on this drive is revealed by the following story: "Lang & Ryan, the well-known drovers, have secured the services of a band of negro minstrels, genuine darkies, to aid in driving their cattle across the plains. The minstrels are to sing to the cattle at night to keep them quiet." *Clarke County Register*, March 30, 1882.

[61] Maurice Frink *et al.*, *When Grass Was King* (Boulder, Colo., 1956), pp. 76-82.

surprisingly large. The new tendency in this trade may be illustrated for one part of the Oregon Country by quoting from the *Grant County News,* which estimated that of the livestock worth $2,000,000 that had been exported from eastern Oregon in 1882, three-fourths—"4,000 horses at $35, 55,000 cattle at $18, 200,000 sheep at $1.85"—had been driven to eastern markets. Notwithstanding the fact that the price of cattle had doubled, the editor of this newspaper said that stockmen were more eager to increase their herds than to sell at current prices.[62]

The eastward drive of 1882 was the last important one from the Pacific Northwest. It is true that, in the spring of 1883, buyers from the East were seeking cattle and horses in Idaho, but, in general, they encountered a scarcity of cattle. It is true also that a letter dated in Lewiston on May 27 told the editor of the *Idaho Weekly Statesman* that the county of Nez Percés was "full of horse and cattle-buyers," and that several "large bands of each" and lots of "scattering ones" had been sold. Because of these sales, "lots of $20 pieces" had been left, and money could "be considered easy."[63] But elsewhere in the Oregon Country, in Washington as in Oregon, beef cattle had become scarce. On this subject the *Morning Oregonian,* in its issue for May 29, 1883, remarked that

Cattle-buyers, who heretofore have operated largely in Oregon, find it impossible to gather herds this spring. Almost all the salable stock has been sold or contracted to the home market, while productive cows and heifers are not for sale at any reasonable price. . . . The only parts of this state where great droves of cattle still feed on the range is the region about Prineville, in the central part of the state, and in Lake county. The famous ranges of eastern Oregon are being fast settled and cut up into farms, and Wasco has become almost solely a farming region.

One who is not yet persuaded that the large drives of cattle eastward from the Pacific Northwest had by now become a thing of the past is referred to a report dated November 10, 1883, in which Governor William Hale of Wyoming remarked that formerly "large herds of cattle were driven each year to Wyoming

[62] Reprinted in *West Shore,* VIII (June, 1883), 139.
[63] *Idaho Weekly Statesman,* June 9, 1883.

from Oregon and the Territories of the Pacific slope, but these drives from the west have now almost entirely ceased."[64]

Interestingly enough, as we learn from newspapers published in Idaho, Utah, and Wyoming, the main trail through Idaho to Wyoming was clogged in 1884 with sheep moving eastward from Oregon.[65] In that year editors in the Oregon Country said little or nothing about cattle on this trail.

During the years of the large cattle drives to Wyoming and Colorado—that is, from 1879 through 1882—other drives of cattle, horses, and sheep were being made from the far Northwest to Montana. Two routes led to Montana. The northern route, which was the Mullan Road, was constructed by the army of the United States to connect Fort Benton on the Missouri River with the newly established Fort Walla Walla in southeastern Washington. The southern route ran through southern Idaho by way of Boise almost to the eastern border of this territory before turning northward into western Montana. Both of these routes were used by drovers, but the Mullan Road lost its significance for the cattle trade after the completion of the Northern Pacific Railroad in 1883.

Large numbers of cattle were driven over both of these roads, especially between 1880 and 1883. According to the Gordon Report, the number of cattle driven into Montana from Oregon and Washington in 1880 exceeded 26,000 head; and a well-informed contemporaneous observer asserted that 60,000 head of cattle and 100,000 head of sheep were driven from Oregon and Washington to the ranges of Montana in 1881. During the next two years, such drives, although not slight, appear to have been smaller. The two years 1880 and 1881, therefore, saw the peak, but not the end, of the driving of cattle from the far Northwest to Montana. Thereafter this traffic continued, just as it did to Wyoming and Colorado, but before the end of 1883 the movement by rail was beginning to supplant the movement by trail. This change the vice-president and general manager of the Northern Pacific Railroad revealed in his annual report in 1885, when he wrote

[64] 48th Cong., 1st sess., H. Ex. Doc. 1 (Serial 2191), XI, 576.
[65] *Tacoma Daily Ledger*, June 3, 1884; *Salt Lake Daily Tribune*, June 5, July 12, Aug. 20, 1884; *Idaho Weekly Statesman*, June 7, 1884.

that, whereas in 1883-84 the company had "forwarded from eastern terminals 77,320 head and from Washington and Oregon
3,100 head," in 1884-85 the offer of special rates had "developed
an important movement" from the western divisions of the road.
"There have been shipped from stations west of the Rocky Mountains," he said, "34,740 head of cattle, 3,360 horses, and 24,400
sheep" during the preceding fiscal year.[66]

When the Oregon Short Line was completed, before the end of
1884, cattlemen of the Columbia Basin could ship their stock
eastward on either of two railroads. Moreover, to reach their
older markets west of the Cascades, they had three options: they
could drive their cattle through passes in the Cascade Mountains; they could send them by steamboats down the Columbia
River to Portland or to Kalama; or they could send them by
train alongside the Columbia River to Portland, and from there,
if they wished, by train to markets on Puget Sound. Cattlemen in
Oregon south of the Columbia Basin—in Lake, Grant, and Baker
counties—as well as those in southern Idaho, could also now
choose between two railroads. They could continue to drive cattle to Winnemucca or to other points on the Central Pacific Railroad and send them to markets either in California or east of the
Rockies; or, if they preferred, as many of them did, they could
drive their cattle northward to Ontario, and from that point send
them by rail either eastward to destinations beyond the Rockies
or westward to markets in the Willamette Valley or on Puget
Sound.[67] Thus the *need* of stockmen of the Oregon Country to
drive their cattle and other livestock to far-off markets no longer
existed; but, as we have seen was the case elsewhere, the *desire*
to make such drives lingered on in the Pacific Northwest through
many years after 1883.

The long drives of cattle eastward from the Pacific Northwest

---

[66] Note 1, above; Northern Pacific Railroad, *Annual Report of the Vice-President and General Manager . . . for the Fiscal Year Ending June 30th, 1885* (New
York, 1885), p. 5. See also the Seattle *Weekly Post-Intelligencer*, April 16,
1885, quoting the *Walla Walla Journal*.
[67] During the summer and autumn of 1885, cattle were being sent eastward
from the Columbia Basin not only by way of the Oregon Short Line from Pendleton, Baker City, and Ontario, but also by way of the Northern Pacific Railroad
from Sprague, Washington. Before the end of August, 1885, an editor in Salem,
Ore., remarked that Ontario "was coming to the front rapidly as a cattle-shipping

contributed to a significant transition in the economic history of both the northern Great Plains and the Pacific Northwest. East of the Rockies the effect of these drives was felt immediately and significantly. Evidence of extensive use of cattle from the Oregon Country to stock the northern Great Plains we have already found in newspapers and in other sources originating west of the Rockies. It remains to examine evidence on this subject in sources originating east of these mountains.

We turn, first of all, to documents and reports issued by, or under the sponsorship of, the government of the United States. The Gordon Report is explicit on this subject, saying that the "great number of animals coming into the territory of Wyoming [in 1880] was owing to the severe preceding winter and to the driving out of cattle by the advance of sheep and agriculture in Oregon, Washington, and Utah, and to the flight of stock from the drought in Colorado." This report also says that there was a great demand for cattle to stock the northern ranges of the Great Plains. Equally explicit on this subject is another federal report, the one prepared in 1885 by Joseph Nimmo, Jr., who, after affirming that the rise of the "range and ranch cattle business" on the northern ranges had provided an "enormous outlet" for young cattle from Texas and from ranges of the Pacific Northwest, remarked that

> Young cattle were, at an early day in this business, driven from Eastern Oregon and Eastern Washington Territory to stock the ranges of Montana, Idaho, and Wyoming. Latterly, however, the surplus product of Eastern Oregon and Eastern Washington Territory has been chiefly needed for local consumption on the Pacific Coast, and for stocking new ranges in Oregon, Washington Territory, and British Columbia.[68]

No less significant than the evidence derived from federal sources is the testimony of men who either were directly interested in the cattle business in Wyoming or who learned much about that business by personal contacts. For example, Thomas

---

point," and that it promised to become "the Cheyenne of the Northwest." Salem *Oregon Statesman,* July 31, Aug. 28, 31, Sept. 4, 1885.

[68] Gordon, "Report," p. 1018; Joseph Nimmo, Jr., "Range and Ranch Cattle Traffic in the Western States and Territories," in 48th Cong., 2nd sess., H. Ex Doc. 267, March 25, 1885 (Serial 2304), pp. 56-57.

Sturgis, a stockman who for several years was the secretary of the Wyoming Stock Growers Association, wrote from Cheyenne on November 21, 1880, saying that the "cattle on these ranges, with the exception of those that came through this year from Texas or Oregon, went into winter in good order—decidedly better than in 1879." Of like import is an observation of another widely known cattleman of Wyoming, John Clay, who wrote in his later years that early in the 1880's he had observed in the Sweetwater Valley "a fine class of cattle, mostly bred up from herds that had come from Oregon and Washington Territories [sic]." Equally important is a report read at a meeting in Edinburgh on July 30, 1883, in which the Swan Land and Cattle Company affirmed that the cattle on its south range in Wyoming were "a good lot, mostly Hereford crosses, and those on the Northwest . . . [were] mostly Oregon Shorthorn crosses." Finally, a statement by Morton E. Post, sometime delegate from Wyoming to the Congress of the United States, has so significant a bearing on this subject that Nimmo appended it to his report on the traffic in range and ranch cattle. According to Post, the range-cattle business in Wyoming began about 1868 or 1870, and from that time until the late 1870's most of the cattle grazed there were brought from Texas. Thereafter, he continues, "the rangemen imported largely from Nevada and Oregon and the Territories of Montana, Idaho, and Utah, and also some from Colorado—mixed herds of cattle. The cattle imported from Utah, Nevada, Oregon, Idaho, and Montana were a good class of cattle. . . . We have practically exhausted the supply of Nevada, Oregon, and Washington Territory."[69]

With this testimony we might rest our case; but there is additional evidence published east of Wyoming and Colorado in newspapers whose editors were under professional obligation to be informed about the cattle trade of the West. One such editor, writing at the beginning of 1881, declared: "Nearly all the cattle men of Wyoming are getting out of Texas cattle and are building up their cow herds and getting young stock from the extreme

[69] *Weekly Drovers' Journal*, Nov. 25, 1880; John Clay, *My Life on the Range* (Chicago, 1924), p. 38; Beecher, Ill., *Breeders' Journal* (September, 1883), p. 545; Nimmo, "Range and Ranch Cattle," pp. 184-87.

Western Country, Idaho, Oregon and Washington Territory. . . ."[70] In like manner, some three years later, the editor of the *National Stockman*, impressed by the increase within a short time of the value of cows in the West, remarked that "with the giving out of stocker supplies in Oregon, Montana, and elsewhere, ranchmen began to see that they must raise their own stockers, and the cow commenced straightway to increase in value. . . ."[71] No less impressed by the changes taking place in the cattle business in the West was the editor of a Kansas newspaper, who said in the summer of 1884 that a remarkable feature of the western cattle business had been the movement westward from eastern or midwestern states of "at least 150,000 head" of young breeding stock and stock steers to Wyoming, Nebraska, Colorado, and Montana. *"Oregon,"* he said, *"which in former times was the chief source of stock cattle supplies for the States and Territories named, has been too closely drained to yield any more for the present."*[72]

There should now be little doubt that cattle from the Oregon Country played a significant role in the stocking of ranges east of the Rockies. At the moment we know little enough about the distribution of cattle from this region on the ranges of Wyoming[73] and elsewhere, but Charles Lindsay's detailed study of the Big Horn Basin in Wyoming provides some valuable information. In his study, Lindsay has shown that, between 1879 and 1884, two herds consisting of fifteen thousand head of cattle were driven from Oregon to help stock that part of Wyoming. These herds belonged to Charles Carter and Henry T. Lovell.[74]

The economic effect on the Pacific Northwest of this eastward movement of cattle was likewise immediate and significant. Within a few years the cattlemen of this region emerged from the dark shadows of a depression into the clear light of a booming prosperity. But the removal of perhaps as many as four hundred thousand head of cattle within a few years had been as upsetting

[70] *Weekly Drovers' Journal*, Jan. 13, 1881, quoting the St. Joseph., Mo., *Gazette*.
[71] Quoted in *ibid.*, March 20, 1884.
[72] Chicago *Breeders' Gazette*, V (June 5, 1884), 884, quoting the Barbara County, Kan., *Index*. Italics are mine.
[73] See, however, *Cattle Brands Owned by Members of the Wyoming Stock Growers' Association* (Chicago, 1882), p. 54.
[74] Charles Lindsay, *The Big Horn Basin* (Lincoln, Neb., 1932), chap. iv.

to some persons as it had been profitable to others.[75] As early as 1881, some persons in the Pacific Northwest were worrying about the prospect of a "beef famine,"[76] and, as the months rolled by, editors in widely separated areas of this country were expressing their deep concern about the rising prices of beef. By May, 1882, the price of beef in Portland had advanced to twenty cents a pound for choice cuts. In October of that year, fat cattle in Wasco County were bringing thirty to thirty-five dollars a head, and, at the same time, steers in the Walla Walla Valley were in demand at forty to forty-five dollars a head. Prices continued to soar during 1883, and every community in the Oregon Country was affected by the rise. "Beef is worth double what it was a year ago, and is worth three times as much as it was three years ago," exclaimed the editor of a Boise City newspaper in March. "Five years ago," the editor of the *Morning Oregonian* remarked on March 7, 1883, "before hungry Kansas men began coming in here to buy cattle for shipment to New York via Cheyenne, there was no very ready sale for average beef at $14 a head. Now the same grade of beef commands from $42 to $50 per head delivered any-where within 200 miles of Portland."[77] By this time, indeed, opti-mism among some cattlemen of the Oregon Country had risen as high as the prices of their cattle. In June, 1883, the editor of the *Kittitas Standard* wrote that cattle now were "as good as gold," and that cattlemen need not worry about "a downward tendency in prices."[78]

For the West as a whole, the greatest significance of the east-ward driving of cattle from the Oregon Country between 1875 and 1883 was the breaking of the isolation of the cattle ranges of the far Northwest. Within less than a decade, cattle from these remote ranges had entered national and international markets,

[75] *Willamette Farmer*, Feb. 17, 1882, quoting the Baker City *Bedrock Demo-crat*. On Jan. 1, 1882, the *Morning Oregonian* estimated that, within the "past six years," Baker and Grant counties had sent out, apart from those which went to market in Portland, considerably more than one hundred thousand head of cattle.

[76] *North Pacific Coast*, May 16, 1881, reprinting a letter from the Kittitas Valley to the *Chicago Times*.

[77] On the subject of rising prices, see Oliphant, "Eastward Movement of Cattle from the Oregon Country," pp. 39-40.

[78] Ellensburg *Kittitas Standard*, June 30, 1883.

and cattlemen of the Oregon Country had been released from their dependence upon local markets and markets in California. Moreover, during those years herds from the far Northwest mingled with herds from Texas and from the eastern states upon ranges in a newer cattle country east of Idaho. By the opening of the 1880's, western cattle drovers knew the trails leading eastward from the far Northwest as well as they knew those leading northward from Texas. By that time the range- and ranch-cattle area of the far West had become a unified area, a fact well known to men of that time, but one which was soon forgotten, and which remained forgotten until it was rediscovered in fairly recent years.

For the Pacific Northwest as a region, the greatest long-range significance was that the clearance of its ranges of surplus cattle disclosed an industry in retreat. By the opening of the 1880's the grazing of cattle on the open ranges in many parts of the Pacific Northwest, more especially in the choicest parts of the Columbia Basin, was nearing its end; here and elsewhere in the far Northwest cattlemen were being crowded hard by sheepmen or farmers—sometimes by both. Before the end of 1883, a railroad, as we have seen, had united the Columbia Basin with the country east of the Rockies, and settlers were swarming faster than ever before into the rich agricultural lands of the Palouse country. But the story of significant changes then in progress in the Pacific Northwest must wait upon our study of other important problems confronting cattlemen on the ranges of the Oregon Country.

CHAPTER VI

Cattlemen and Their Cattle

THE cattlemen who began to drive their herds into Transcascadia toward the end of 1858 took with them a heritage of usages on American frontiers dating from early colonial days on the Atlantic seaboard. Foremost among these, perhaps, was the one implied by a law enacted in Virginia in 1642, and specifically embodied in a law enacted in the old Northwest Territory in 1792—namely, that "the open woods and uninclosed grounds within the territory shall be taken and considered as the common pasture or herbage of the citizens thereof saving to all persons their right of fencing."[1] This conception of a public domain, freely open to the cattle and other livestock of all the settlers, made the idea of a "lawful fence" an important one on every American frontier. The right to fence what had been a part of the common pasture meant the right to be fully protected in the use of such land as had been enclosed pursuant to law. It meant, furthermore, that stockmen using the common pasture would be liable for the depredations their cattle or other livestock committed in fields enclosed by lawful fences. Eventually, as we shall see, the problem of fencing became an important one in Transcascadia.

Equally important, no doubt, were other usages or practices

[1] William W. Hening (ed.), *The Statutes at Large: Being A Collection of All the Laws of Virginia* (New York, 1823), I, 244; T. C. Pease (ed.), *The Laws of the Northwest Territory, 1788-1800* (Illinois State Historical Library, *Collections*, Vol. XVII) (Springfield, Ill., 1925), p. 84.

accepted, with or without the sanction of law, by settlers on early American frontiers and brought by their spiritual heirs in later times to the ranges of the Oregon Country. One of these, as we already have seen, was the practice of permitting cattle and other livestock to roam freely the year through, without shelter and without special attention in winter. Still another of these traditional practices was that of determining the ownership of livestock by putting marks and brands on animals, and, to supplement the law, there was the practice of voluntary cooperation by frontiersmen not only for the purpose of "rounding up" their cattle periodically, but also for the purpose of protecting their livestock from predatory animals and thieves.[2]

Nevertheless, despite a common heritage of ideas and practices, stockmen did not operate with precise uniformity everywhere in Transcascadia. In the Columbia Basin, for example, large herds of cattle were not numerous. Here, moreover, the associations of cattlemen tended to be localized, and here farmers were soon encroaching on the ranges. In the Winnemucca province, on the other hand, not a few men emerged as "cattle kings." Land for farming without irrigation was not plentiful here, and large-scale cattlemen, some of whom were not restricted in their operations to ranges in one state or territory, were not helped much by local associations. They lived in a larger sphere of endeavor than that of cattlemen in the Columbia Basin. Differences such as these we must keep firmly in mind if we wish to understand fully the history of grazing cattle on the open ranges of the Oregon Country.

Our knowledge of the sizes of herds grazed in the Columbia Basin, whether in eastern Washington, northern Idaho, or the northeastern part of Oregon drained by tributaries of the Columbia River, is fragmentary and not always precise; but it appears from the evidence available that herds of great size were exceptional anywhere in the Columbia Basin. A sale of twelve thousand head of cattle in the Okanogan country, reported to have

[2] Wesley N. Laing, "Cattle in Seventeenth-Century Virginia," *Virginia Magazine of History and Biography*, LVII (April, 1959), 159-62; Pease (ed.), *Laws of Northwest Territory*, p. 46; F. A. Michaux, *Travels*, Vol. III in R. G. Thwaites (ed.), *Early Western Travels* (Cleveland, 1904), p. 134.

been made in the spring of 1881 by Phelps and Wadleigh of Seattle to Benjamin E. Snipes of The Dalles was perhaps unique. It attracted widespread attention in the Pacific Northwest.[3] Phelps and Wadleigh would have been recognized anywhere in the Oregon Country as "cattle kings," as would Snipes, who at times numbered his cattle by perhaps tens of thousands.[4] In the Columbia Basin, Snipes occupied a place comparable to that of Peter French, W. B. Todhunter, Sparks and Tinnin, and several other cattlemen in the Winnemucca province. But, whereas Ben Snipes appeared to walk before other cattlemen in his province, there were lesser operators in the Columbia Basin, who, thanks no doubt to the courtesy of editors of newspapers, were also designated "cattle kings." For example, Nick McCoy, John Clemens, E. McDaniel, and perhaps others were mentioned, at one time or another, as Yakima cattle kings.[5] But, whatever the character of the evidence that we examine—whether it be reports of sales, reports of movements of livestock, or estimates of cattle in a given locality—we arrive at the same general conclusion about both cattle and cattlemen in the Columbia Basin: in the aggregate, cattle were numerous, but cattlemen owning very large herds were few in number. In the Columbia Basin many herds north of the Columbia River consisted of only a few hundred head each, fewer herds consisted of twenty-five hundred head or more, and still fewer consisted of five thousand head or more.

Available information about specific herds, north and south of the Columbia, confirms our judgment on this subject. North of this river, the cattleman who described at length for the Gordon Report his operations in the Yakima country claimed no more

[3] *Spokan Times,* March 31, 1881; Boise *Idaho Tri-Weekly Statesman,* March 22, 1881.

[4] On Benjamin E. Snipes, see Seattle *Weekly Pacific Tribune,* May 19, 1876; Seattle *Weekly Post-Intelligencer,* March 16, 1883; *Yakima Signal,* Jan. 27, June 9, 1883; Charles J. Steedman, *Bucking the Sage Brush, or the Oregon Trail in the Seventies* (New York, 1904). There is no critical biography of Snipes, but see Robert Ballou, *Early Klickitat Valley Days* (Goldendale, Wash., 1938), pp. 177-92, and Roscoe Sheller, *Ben Snipes: Northwest Cattle King* (Portland, Ore., 1957), *passim.*

[5] *Yakima Weekly Record,* April 7, 1883; Portland *Morning Oregonian,* May 21, 1880; Ellensburg *Kittitas Standard,* July 21, 1883.

than two thousand head of cattle, and another cattleman, describing for this report his operations in the Klickitat country, said that his herd was not larger than five thousand head. South of the Columbia, the herds of the Columbia Basin of which we have knowledge differed little in size from the herds in the Yakima and the Klickitat countries. According to a story based on information given by "Mr. Summerville," for the firm of Breyman and Summerville of Prineville, Oregon, his firm, which possessed five thousand head, and the firm of Mays and Son, which possessed ten thousand head, were among the "heavy owners" of cattle in the southern part of Wasco County in December, 1881.[6] These men undoubtedly would have been recognized anywhere in the Columbia Basin as cattle kings. Accordingly, we may conclude, tentatively, that in the Columbia Basin a man whose cattle numbered at least five thousand head would, in the opinion of editors of newspapers in this region, have been unquestionably a cattle king. But such a title, like that of "colonel" in Kentucky, was perhaps sometimes bestowed on men for reasons that now pass understanding.

In the Winnemucca province, however, royal status in the bovine kingdom was not so easily come by. Here, it is true, there were many owners of cattle, particularly during the early years of occupation, whose herds were small; but here also there were owners whose herds varied in size from relatively small to relatively large. In this province, owing in part to the scarcity of arable land, a few men succeeded in accumulating herds of considerable size. The capital for such enterprises came, in large measure, from California. In south-central Oregon large herds of cattle were held in present-day Klamath and Lake counties,[7] and

[6] The Dalles *Weekly Mountaineer*, Feb. 24, 1872; Olympia *Washington Standard*, May 1, 1875; Portland *West Shore*, IV (February, 1879), 57; Hugh Small, *Oregon and Her Resources: From Personal Observation and Investigation* (San Francisco, 1872), p. 56; Clarence W. Gordon, "Report on Cattle, Sheep, and Swine, Supplementary to Enumeration of Live Stock on Farms in 1880," in the *Tenth Federal Census, 1880*, Vol. III, *Agriculture* (Washington, D.C., 1883), pp. 1089-91; Salem *Willamette Farmer*, Dec. 16, 1881.

[7] J. F. Wharton, during the course of a journey from California northward through southeastern Oregon in 1879, wrote that Warner Valley was then "divided into five or six extensive stock ranches, and held by as many men, who raise numerous herds of horses, cattle, sheep and hogs, at no earthly expense,

in southeastern Oregon even larger herds were held in the country now comprising Grant, Baker, Harney, and Malheur counties.[8] In these counties, as well as in the Idaho counties lying directly eastward, were to be found, from the late 1870's through the 1880's, some of the real cattle kings of the Pacific Northwest. Various sources provide evidence of the extent of their holdings and the ramifications of their interests: successive stories of heavy movements of cattle from southeastern Oregon to Winnemucca, Nevada; governmental reports concerning the trespassing of cattle on the Malheur Indian Reservation; reports of purchases by which some cattlemen enlarged their holdings; and descriptions occasionally encountered of the large ranches or ranges of cattlemen in this region. But, whatever the source of our knowledge respecting them, we need not doubt the importance of the operations of cattlemen like Peter French and Dr. Hugh James Glenn, W. B. Todhunter and John S. Devine, Miller and Lux, Colonel James A. Hardin, Amos W. Riley, J. C. Abbott, Hock Mason, Arthur Langell, Jesse D. Carr, Con Shea, W. F. Summercamp, Sparks and Tinnin, and others. Such men were widely known as large-scale cattlemen.

As the years of the 1870's went by, the tendency toward consolidation of interests became noticeable among cattlemen in southeastern Oregon. We have already learned that in 1872 Peter French, the partner and later the son-in-law of Dr. Hugh James Glenn, the "wheat king" of California, had arrived in southeastern Oregon with a herd of cattle from California. By 1879 he was managing two large ranches—the P Ranch and the Diamond Ranch—on a range near Steens Mountain in what is now Harney County.[9] In 1882 Glenn and French enlarged their holdings in

save the trouble of branding them and driving them to market." *Weekly Colusa Sun*, Nov. 29, 1879.

[8] *Morning Oregonian*, Oct. 12, 1876, Sept. 26, 1877, March 2, 1880, June 22, Aug. 22, 1882; Wallis Nash, *Two Years in Oregon* (New York, 1882), p. 111; Small, *Oregon and Her Resources*, p. 56; Salem *Willamette Farmer*, Feb. 17, 1882, quoting the Baker City *Bedrock Democrat*. In 1885 it was reported that there were about 200,000 head of cattle in Grant County, Oregon, "some firms having as many as 40,000." *West Shore*, X (April, 1885), 125.

[9] Winnemucca *Silver State*, Dec. 12, 1879. The Frenchglen post office, established in the early 1920's near the P Ranch, honors, with a misspelling of the name of one of them, the owners of this ranch. Lewis A. McArthur, *Oregon Geographic Names* (2nd ed.; Portland, Ore., 1944), pp. 216-17, 405.

this region by purchasing for $102,000 the interests of John Cat-
low in the area of Steens Mountain. Dr. Glenn was shot to death
in California in 1883, but French continued his large-scale operations in breeding cattle in southeastern Oregon until he too was
shot to death in 1897.[10]

More important, perhaps, than the Glenn-French interests
were those of Todhunter and Devine, whose headquarters were
at the Whitehorse Ranch, on Whitehorse Creek in present-day
Harney County. To this country, as we already have learned,
John S. Devine had come from California as early as 1868, and
here he had remained as the partner of W. B. Todhunter, also of
California, in a stock-breeding enterprise. Todhunter provided
the capital for this partnership, and perhaps for this reason he
did not hesitate to push himself into public notice. More often
than not he was so mentioned as to give the impression that he
was the sole owner of what he and his partner possessed. However this fact may be accounted for, the Todhunter-Devine interests expanded rapidly. In the autumn of 1880 these men
bought for sixty-five thousand dollars the stock ranch of Abbott
and Whiteside near Fort Harney, and in the spring of 1882 they
were said to possess more than twenty thousand head of stock
cattle, distributed among four ranches, three in southeastern Oregon and one in northwestern Nevada. In the spring of 1881, they
were supposed to have branded nine thousand calves, and during
the "season" of 1882 they were said to have sent more than six
thousand head of beeves to market. They increased their holdings in the spring of 1883 by purchasing for seventy-five thousand dollars the cattle and ranges of G. B. Crowley and Captain
Whiteside at Steens Mountain. Others at this time credited them
with even larger holdings, and there were complaints that both
Todhunter and Glenn were monopolizing a vast area in Oregon.[11]
Having suffered severe reverses, Todhunter was obliged to make

[10] *Morning Oregonian*, Feb. 25, 1882; Silver City *Idaho Avalanche*, March 18,
1882; *Silver State*, Feb. 20, 1883; *San Francisco Chronicle*, Dec. 29, 1897; Giles
French, *Cattle Country of Peter French* (Portland, Ore., 1964), pp. 103, 151-52.
[11] French, *Cattle Country of Peter French*, p. 94; *Morning Oregonian*, Oct.
6, 1880, Jan. 1, 1883; *Silver State*, March 31, 1882, March 30, 1883; D. H.
Stearns, *Oregon Papers, No. 11* (supplement to the *Daily Evening Telegram*,
Portland, Ore., 1882), p. 6.

an assignment of his property in May, 1887. The deed which he gave specified, among other things, forty-three thousand head of beef cattle valued at more than eight hundred thousand dollars and other property in Oregon, and "lands in Nevada and town property in Winnemucca" valued at considerably more than one million dollars. As an editor in Baker City, Oregon, remarked concerning it, "The deed calls for more property than any deed ever recorded in Eastern Oregon, the full estimate being $2,230,000." The editor of the *Sacramento Bee*, observing the extensive holdings in California, Nevada, and Oregon of this financially embarrassed cattle king, predicted that Todhunter would still have "a snug fortune" after all his creditors were satisfied. Whether this prediction was or was not justified, Todhunter had retired from the stock business in Oregon by the spring of 1889, and, as we shall see, Devine had become a member of the largest livestock enterprise that Oregon thus far had known.[12]

Men like Glenn and French, or like Todhunter and Devine, were, properly speaking, cattle kings of Oregon who had interests extending beyond the bounds of this state. There were other men, however, who were primarily cattle kings in other states or territories, but who also had extensive interests in cattle breeding in Oregon. Such, for example, was Colonel James A. Hardin, the cattle king of Humboldt, whose holdings in Oregon, Idaho, Nevada, and California account for his becoming a vice president of the National Stock Growers' Association in 1884. A "leading Nevada cattle baron," Hardin was associated in the firm of Riley and Hardin with Amos W. Riley and John Taylor, California capitalists.[13] Also in this category were Miller and Lux, butchers

[12] *Silver State*, May 24, 1887, quoting the Baker City *Democrat; Morning Oregonian*, May 11, 1887; Eugene *Oregon State Journal*, May 14, 1887; *Willamette Farmer*, May 13, 1887; Boise *Idaho Weekly Statesman*, May 21, 1887; *Sacramento Bee*, quoted by the Chicago *Weekly National Live-Stock Journal* (May 31, 1887), p. 346; Miles City, Mont., *Stock Growers Journal*, June 1, 1889, p. 2, quoting from the *Silver State; Morning Oregonian*, Aug. 23, 1900; Burns *Times-Herald*, April 12, July 19, 1902; Edward F. Treadwell, *The Cattle King, A Dramatized Biography* (New York, 1931), *passim;* Jacob R. Gregg, *Pioneer Days in Malheur County* . . . (Los Angeles, 1950), p. 217; French, *Cattle Country of Peter French*, pp. 115-18.
[13] *Silver State*, Dec. 14, 1885, quoting the St. Louis *Globe-Democrat*. On the rise of the four largest herds and ranches in Harney County, Oregon—those of Todhunter and Devine, French and Glenn, Riley and Hardin, and the Pacific

and cattlemen, whose principal holdings were in California, but whose properties in Nevada and Oregon were extensive. In 1882 it was reported that these men had bought herds from Harper and McMahon in Baker County (two thousand), Leslie on the Owyhee River (about four thousand); Dreslers and Clara on the Burnt River (about one thousand), and Charles Bedker in Cow Valley (about fifteen hundred); they also were collecting as many small herds as they could get, offering as much as thirty-two dollars a head for three-year-old steers.[14]

Some seven years later consolidation in cattle-breeding enterprises in southeastern Oregon reached a culmination when, in the early summer of 1889, an editor in Winnemucca reported that "the Todhunter ranch and Miller & Lux and N.H.A. Mason's ranches and cattle, all in Oregon," had been consolidated. He had been told that the new firm consisted of Miller and Lux, N.H.A. Mason, and John Devine, and that W. B. Todhunter had retired from "the stock business in Oregon."[15] Soon thereafter an editor in Cheyenne told his readers that Miller and Lux had about seventy-five thousand head of cattle in eastern Oregon, and that they were moving twenty thousand young steers from Oregon to "maturing ranches" in California.[16] On September 26 the Burns *East Oregon Herald* published an article entitled "Harney Valley," which affirmed that this recently formed enterprise, known as the "Pacific Live Stock Association [Company]," was "perhaps the strongest on this coast if not the strongest in the world. Their dominions extend from Grant county, Or., to the southern confines of California. They can travel hundreds of miles from here in a southerly direction and camp every night on their freeholds."[17]

Meanwhile, enlargement of ranches and consolidation of herds had characterized the progress of cattle breeding in southern

Livestock Company—see Margaret Justine Lo Piccolo's "Some Aspects of the Range Cattle Industry of Harney County, Oregon, 1870-1900" (M.A. thesis, University of Oregon, 1962).

[14] *Walla Walla Union*, Sept. 9, 1882, quoting the La Grande *Mountain Sentinel*.
[15] *Stock Growers Journal*, June 1, 1889, quoting the *Silver State*.
[16] *Ibid.*, July 20, 1889, quoting the Cheyenne *Northwestern Live Stock Journal*.
[17] On the rise of the Pacific Livestock Company, see "The Property of Miller & Lux," in the *National Live-Stock Journal*, April 19, 1887, quoting the Reno *Stockman*.

Idaho. In 1874, the editor of the *Walla Walla Union* published a letter dated in Silver City on June 15—a letter in which the author affirmed that, within a radius of seventy-five miles of Silver City, there were presumed to be fifty thousand head of cattle, of which "some parties" owned "as many as six and eight thousand head"; and three years later an editor in Boise City wrote gleefully that the country in Idaho south of the Snake River was an excellent range, "where several of the cattle kings of Idaho have thousands of fat cattle ready for the outside markets." By 1880 at least one of these cattle kings, according to the Gordon Report, "controlled the herds of Goose Creek" in Cassia County and had acquired "title to the land for 20 miles above and below his ranch on Salmon Fall river."[18]

Soon the consolidation of cattle holdings in Idaho became especially noticeable,[19] and one instance attracted widespread attention in September, 1883, when a stockmen's journal in Chicago quoted from the Reno *Evening Gazette* as follows:

> The greatest cattle range in the West is now owned by Sparks & Tinnin, of Tecoma, Nev., who have consolidated half a dozen large ranches into one. A year and a half ago they bought two ranches on [sic] Thousand Springs Valley, and made one of them. They bought a lot of land on Goose Creek, running up to Idaho. On the 4th of July they bought out Barley Harrel's ranch in [sic] Snake River, Idaho, for $900,000. This gives them a very safe and large breeding range, running for fifty miles on the Snake, where the winters are not severe, and cows will raise a large percentage of calves and a good ranch with hay and grain near the track, where they can drive their beef cattle in the fall and ship them at their leisure, no matter how hard the winter or how deep the snow may be. They have now 70,000 head of cattle, and they will brand 17,000 calves this fall. They are undoubtedly the largest of the cattle kings of the coast. . . .[20]

The business of Sparks and Tinnin in Idaho grew with the passing months. By the spring of 1886, as we learn from a news-

[18] *Walla Walla Union*, June 20, 1874; *Idaho Weekly Statesman*, June 16, 1877; Gordon, "Report," p. 1096.

[19] As late as 1881, however, one well-informed writer believed that "probably two-thirds of all the cattle in . . . [this] territory . . . [were] divided up into herds not exceeding 500 head." Robert E. Strahorn, *The Resources and Attractions of Idaho Territory* . . . (Boise City, Ida., 1881), p. 74.

[20] Chicago *Weekly Drovers' Journal*, Sept. 6, 1883, quoting the Reno *Evening Gazette*. See also a Wyoming letter to the *Chicago Tribune*, July 7, 1883, quoted by the Beecher, Ill., *Breeders' Journal*, IV (August, 1883), 459.

paper in Cassia County, their Idaho interests had become so
important that John Sparks had "taken up his permanent residence on one of his ranches at Point of Mountain," on Deep
Creek in Cassia County. Their possessions in this county were
now so impressive that the editor of the *Albion Times* was
prompted to say that they "have in the neighborhood of 100,000
head of cattle and their range takes in the entire western portion
of the county, from Rock creek to Owyhee county. Their summer
range extends into the mountains of Nevada, while their winter
range is principally on Warm Creek, Shoshone Valley and Snake
River. They employ fifty or sixty men during the summer season.
The firm is also interested in the stock business in Texas." Incidentally, in 1886 the firm of Sparks and Tinnin was, after the
Central Pacific Railroad, the largest taxpayer in Elko County,
Nevada, its property in this county being assessed at $220,000.[21]

But John Sparks and John Tinnin were not the only large-
scale cattlemen in Cassia County in the mid-1800's. By the
spring of 1885, W. S. McCormick and the Keogh Brothers, at
their recently purchased 4,000-acre ranch on the Raft River, had
more than 6,000 head of cattle and 175 head of good horses and
mules. In August they were reported to have "about 7,000 cattle
and 200 horses." Unlike some ranchers, they put up about 1,000
tons of hay annually for winter feed, and they specialized in
breeding cattle of good quality. Their cattle, we are told, were
"all American crossed formerly with the Devon breed." During
the two preceding years, however, they had been using "thoroughbred and grade shorthorn bulls." Before the end of 1885,
their enterprise had been incorporated under the laws of Utah
as the Raft River Land and Cattle Company, and it was controlled, as the Boise *Statesman* assured its readers, "by McCormick & Co., bankers, Salt Lake City, and the Keogh brothers."[22]

In the spring of 1886, however, the *Albion Times* was still

[21] Cheyenne *Northwestern Live Stock Journal*, March 12, 1886, quoting the
Albion Times; ibid., Oct. 1, 1886, quoting the Elko, Nev., *Independent.* On the
history of the firm of Sparks and Tinnin, see also Charles S. Walgamott, *Reminiscences of Early Days* . . . (Twin Falls, Ida., 1926), I, 14.
[22] *Idaho Weekly Statesman*, April 26, 1884, quoting the *Salt Lake Daily Tribune; Northwestern Live Stock Journal*, Dec. 11, 1885, quoting the Boise *Statesman.*

referring to the above-named enterprise as "Keogh Bros.," who, it said, were "enterprising and thriving cattle raisers" who had come to Cassia County in 1882 and transformed their ranch into "one of the most desirable stock ranches in the territory." According to the *Times*, they now owned more than eight thousand head of cattle, and they had recently added to their herd some "fine thoroughbred Hereford and Durham bulls."

Meanwhile, late in 1885, capital provided largely by men in Salt Lake City made possible the formation of the Omaha Live Stock Company, which would have its headquarters at Howe, in Alturas County. Wallace and Lyman, "the Salt Lake City capitalists," owned two-thirds of the stock of this company, and M. L. Hoyt, formerly of Weiser but now of Rock Springs, owned the other third. The management had made provision for an investment of forty thousand dollars.

By 1886, we may safely say, the breeding of cattle on a large scale had come of age in Idaho. In March the *Albion Times*, in a short and somewhat retrospective survey of the cattle business in Cassia County, remarked that A. D. Norton, who had come there in 1873, now had three or four thousand head of cattle and horses on his range on Rock Creek and Salmon River; that in the same part of this county J. E. Bower and Ed Hardesty had on their "improved ranches" on both Dry Creek and Rock Creek more than one thousand head of graded cattle; that Russell and Bradley, who had large interests in cattle in Elko, Lander, and Humboldt counties in Nevada, also had more than five thousand head of cattle on their "fine ranch" on Dry Creek; that S.R. Gwin, "an oldtimer" in Cassia County, not only had on Marsh Creek a home ranch consisting of "500 acres of beautiful valley land," and on Raft River three other ranches, which he used principally as "meadow land," but also possessed about "12,000 head of cattle and horses of medium grade," and more than a hundred head of "thoroughbred Hereford, Galloway and Polled-Angus bulls"; and, finally, that Sweetser and Pierce, who had formed a partnership in 1880, had "built up" on Clear Creek "one of the most attractive stock ranches" in Idaho—one on which they now were "breeding thoroughbred Hereford bulls to thoroughbred Durham cows and raising their own bulls for the range." They had "some

1400 acres of land under fence in easy access to the finest summer grazing land in the West."

Nor was the foregoing survey complete. From other sources we learn that former Governor G. W. Emery, now residing in Boston, Massachusetts, was rated as "one of the biggest four or five cattle kings" of Cassia County. He had "an excellent stock ranch" on the upper Raft River, and it was "understood" that recently he had bought the "Metcalf ranch."[23]

Elsewhere in Idaho companies had been formed for the purpose of breeding cattle. In 1886 the Promontory Cattle Company, operating in Nevada and in Oneida County, Idaho, bought seven thousand head of cattle from Russell and Bradley in Cassia County, and in 1887 it bought ten thousand head of cattle from Todhunter and Devine in southeastern Oregon. Also in 1886 the Hallack Cattle Company was operating on the Humboldt River and on the east fork of the Bruneau River; and both the Armour Cattle Company and the Idaho Land and Cattle Company were grazing stock on the west side of the Snake River, in the neighborhood of American Falls.[24] So promising, indeed, had the expanding cattle business in Idaho become that, on October 9, 1886, the editor of the *Idaho Weekly Statesman* could say that the cattle business "has grown to wonderful proportions of late years. Where 1,000 head was formerly considered a large band, now bands of 5,000, 10,000 and even 20,000 head are not uncommon. Millions of dollars are invested in stock in Idaho, and the returns from this source excel all others combined."

Some of the cattle kings of the Oregon Country—men like Peter French, Ben Snipes, Henry Miller, and others—traveled much and worked hard at their business. Others, whose contribution to the business was principally the investment of money, lived in comfort in Salt Lake City, Denver, Sacramento, San Francisco, or perhaps in Portland, Winnemucca, Boise City, or in small cities or towns in western Oregon or western Washington. Even some of the large-scale cattlemen who were actively en-

---

[23] *Ibid.*, March 12, 1886, quoting the *Albion Times; ibid.*, Dec. 11, 1885, quoting the *Statesman; ibid.*, Oct. 29, 1886, quoting the *Salt Lake Daily Tribune.*
[24] *Ibid.*, March 23, Dec. 24, 1886; *Idaho Weekly Statesman*, June 4, 1887; *Northwestern Live Stock Journal*, Dec. 24, 1886, p. 13 (list of brands).

gaged in the business of breeding cattle spent the winters away from their ranches or ranges. But there were many others—men of lesser means—who settled in the cattle country, bred cattle on a small scale, and also bought and sold cattle on a small scale. For them life was rigorous, and at least some of them were away from home much of the time.

Such, indeed, was the case with Abner Robbins, who was settled with his family, as early as 1870, on a claim of 160 acres in the Ochoco Valley, about 50 miles from the Warm Springs Indian Reservation. In the opinion of his wife, Kate L. Robbins, Abner was never "idle one moment." Such also was the opinion of his daughter Eunice, who, in August, 1871, expressed the opinion (but not to Abner) that her father could make as much money by staying at home and raising cattle as he could by "buying and selling all the time." Abner thought otherwise. On September 4, 1871, his wife wrote that he had left with cattle for Idaho, and she feared that, in carrying on his business of buying and selling cattle, he "would drive himself to death." Some three years later she wrote that her husband ordinarily would leave home early in the spring and would not get back "till in the winter"; and on February 2, 1875, she wrote that Abner intended to start in March with a band of cattle for Idaho, hoping to be "one of the first into market." He would take with him, she said, more than 100 head of cattle, most of which he had bought. She dreaded the thought of his leaving on such a trip, for, as she remarked, "so much hard driving is beginning to tell on him, for it is a very rough business to follow, driving all day in all kinds of weather and lying on the ground at night with scarcely ever anything to eat but bacon and bread." Nearly three years later, on January 18, 1878, she wrote that Abner was "camped out in the woods" to make rails to be used in fencing a large pasture. After years of low prices for cattle, Abner was expecting better times, because there was now a demand for cattle "by eastern buyers."[25]

[25] Robbins Letters, Kate L. Robbins to her brother, May 27, Dec. 6, 1870, Jan. 19, March 31, 1871; Kate L. Robbins to her mother, Dec. 24, 1870, Sept. 4, 1871, Aug. 18, 1874, Feb. 2, 1875; Kate L. Robbins to her father, Jan. 18, 1878; Eunice Robbins to her grandmother, Aug. 27, 1871, July 7, 1878 (MSS in the University of Oregon Library, Eugene).

Another cattleman who traveled much and endured many hardships was Frank Sweetser, who, after spending a few years in the Raft River country in Idaho, came from Cassia County in that territory to eastern Oregon in the spring of 1879.[26] Here he formed a partnership with Tom Overfelt, but their herd was almost wiped out by the severe winter of 1879-80, an account of which disaster Sweetser wrote to his wife from "Selvies Valley" on April 17, 1880.[27] Subsequently Sweetser established himself as a cattle dealer in Winnemucca, and there he prospered as a member of the firm of Stauffer and Sweetser, which had ranges in northern Nevada and eastern Oregon.[28] But even as late as 1888, Sweetser was away from home much of the time, supervising activities at the ranches and directing the cattle drives to Winnemucca. On September 13, 1888, he wrote to his wife from the Three Forks Ranch on the Owyhee River, saying that he hoped to sell his marketable cattle "to an Eastern party." If he did so, he would "be able to get home much quicker" than if he had "to have them driven to Nevada." Presumably the deal with the "eastern party" fell through, for on September 30 he wrote from Jordan Valley, saying that on the next day he would start a band of five hundred head of cattle to Winnemucca. Nearly two weeks later, all his marketable cattle being now presumably "on the road," he again wrote to his wife from the Owyhee ranch, saying that he intended to hunt deer. "I have not the least idea," he continued, "when I will leave here for Nevada, but will stay as long as I can, as there is lots of work to do here and I want to get as much of it done this fall as I can. Ive got seven miles of wire fence to build this fall and the wire to come from Caldwell yet, and five miles to build in the Spring."[29]

[26] George Francis Brimlow, *Harney County, Oregon, and Its Range Land* (Portland, Ore., 1951), pp. 136, 140; *Morning Oregonian*, July 3, 1879, quoting the Canyon City *Grant County News*.

[27] Frank W. Sweetser to his wife, April 17, 1880. The letters of Frank W. Sweetser are now in the possession of his daughter, Mrs. K. M. C. Neill, of Grants Pass, Ore., and they have been made available to me through the courtesy of Mrs. Neill's daughter, Mrs. Robert Helms, also of Grants Pass.

[28] *Evening Gazette,* Feb. 11, 1960. The letterhead of Stauffer and Sweetser shows that the ranges of these men were situated as follows: Nevada—Grass Valley, Blue Mountain, and Humboldt River; Oregon—Crane Creek, Harney Valley, and South Malheur.

[29] Frank W. Sweetser to his wife, Sept. 13, 30, Oct. 11, 1888.

Difficult as it is to reach satisfactory conclusions as to the holdings of cattlemen in either the Columbia Basin or the Winnemucca province, it is perhaps even more difficult to come by
precise conclusions as to the quality of herds anywhere in the
Oregon Country. Were the range cattle of the Oregon Country
from the 1860's through the 1880's of superior quality, "as good"
as the cattle of Oregon and Washington a generation or two
later,[30] or were they "sadly below par"?[31] This question is not an
easy one to answer, partly because of scanty information and
partly because some of the evidence at our disposal consists of
generalizations based upon limited observations. There can be
little doubt that the quality of the cattle in the Oregon Country
differed from time to time and from place to place, but there is
much reason to believe that from an early date Oregon cattle in
general were much superior to the Spanish cattle which were
the foundation of the first herds in the Willamette Valley.

We have already learned that, during the 1840's and 1850's,
some thoroughbred cattle, together with great numbers of ordinary American stock, came overland to Oregon; and that, as
early as 1855, a company was formed in western Oregon for the
purpose of importing blooded stock into the Oregon Country.[32]
Three years later the *Oregon Farmer* was established in Portland.
This magazine, devoted to the interests of farmers and stockmen,
promoted among other things the cause of better stock breeding,
the burden of its message on this subject being that keeping poor
stock was uneconomical. In May, 1859, its editor declared that
the "time is now fully come when the raising of *Cayuse* horses
and *Spanish* cattle *do [sic] not pay* in the Willamette Valley.
Could this portion of the State be purged of the superabundance
of this stock, which has now become a burden, rather than profit

---

[30] This was the opinion of Daniel M. Drumheller, when, as an old man, he
told of his early experiences in the Pacific Northwest. *"Uncle Dan" Drumheller
Tells Thrills of Western Trails in 1854* (Spokane, Wash., 1925), p. 66.

[31] This opinion of the cattle of Washington was expressed in the *Spokan Times*,
May 22, 1879.

[32] See, in general, R. C. Geer, "Blooded Cattle in Oregon," *Willamette Farmer*,
Dec. 10, 1871, and Thomas Cross, "Cattle in Oregon: Historical Sketch and Ac-
count of the Cattle Business at the Present Time," *ibid.*, Jan. 7, 1881. See also the
Portland *Oregon Farmer* for 1858-59, and the Portland *Weekly Oregonian* of
Aug. 4, 1855.

to our citizens, room could be given for better breeds, which are already fast being introduced, and the good work of improvement soon be fairly under way."[33] The good work of improvement proceeded slowly, however, for many Oregonians continued to believe that cows are cows; but during the 1840's and 1850's enough Durham shorthorns were brought into Oregon to establish a preference for that breed that continued as long as the range-cattle industry flourished in the Oregon Country.

The campaign for the improvement of herds in the Pacific Northwest during the 1860's was carried on principally in the Willamette Valley. Superior cattle were exhibited at fairs, additional blooded cattle were imported, and in 1866 a herd of Durham shorthorns that had come across the plains arrived in the valley, a fact which seems to offer conclusive proof that superior cattle were wanted.[34] By the end of this decade, editorial support of better-bred cattle had been enlisted east of the Cascades in the person of the forthright editor of The Dalles *Weekly Mountaineer*, who, in the course of his campaigning for an agricultural fair, came up with this choice contribution to the argument for the better breeding of livestock, saying,

We know one man who declares that he can not afford to raise good stock.—Now we ask him, how much more would it cost to raise a *number one* cow, than it does that miserable sway-backed, thin-flanked *abortion of a cow* that stands looking through that pair of pole bars, at the ghost of a deformed calf in his corral. . . . We believe that experience will show that the good stock costs even less in care and labor than that kind which has to be helped to rise every morning because of disease or scrubby origin.[35]

But more important for promoting the breeding of better cattle than lively editorials was the Reedville Stock-Breeding Farm, established early in the 1870's in Washington County, Oregon, twelve miles from Portland. The owner, Simeon G. Reed, specialized in the breeding of thoroughbred animals, and within a few years his stock had become widely distributed in the Pacific

[33] *Oregon Farmer* (May, 1859), 152.
[34] *Ibid.*, 1861-62 *passim; Walla Walla Statesman*, July 26, Oct. 11, 1867; Lewis F. Allen, "Improvement of Native Cattle," U.S. Commissioner of Agriculture, *Report* (1866), p. 306.
[35] *Weekly Mountaineer*, Sept. 17, 1870.

Northwest.[36] Other Oregonians imported blooded cattle during the 1870's, and before the end of this decade there had been published several reports of the presence of thoroughbred bulls in eastern Oregon, eastern Washington, and southern Idaho.[37] As early as 1877, a correspondent in the Yakima Valley complained to the editor of the Weekly Mountaineer that in the East the view was widely and unjustly held that the range cattle of the Pacific Northwest were of inferior quality, and, as if in justification of the foregoing complaint, an English traveler in Oregon in that year observed that the "horses and horned cattle of the State represent a good average stock, and are continually improved by the importation of blooded animals from Europe and the Eastern States through private enterprise."[38] Presently, as we already have learned, another Englishman, as well as a governor of Wyoming, would affirm that Oregon cattle were much superior to Texas cattle, and that they brought higher prices as stockers of ranges in Wyoming and elsewhere east of the Rockies than were being paid for Texas cattle.[39]

On this subject the survey of the cattle industry in the Pacific Northwest that was made for the federal census of 1880 provides information as interesting as it is pertinent. It was found that thoroughbred bulls introduced into southeastern Oregon had improved somewhat the quality of cattle in that area, but that difficulties inherent in the practice of open-range grazing had prevented extensive upgrading of herds. Some cattlemen would not cooperate in the effort to acquire better bulls for the ranges, and others, although appreciating the advantage of having thor-

[36] Willamette Farmer, Nov. 25, 1871, May 18, 1872, April 24, May 21, 1875; Weekly Mountaineer, Feb. 27, 1873. Reed sold his shorthorn bull calf, named Central Pacific, to Dr. W. F. Tolmie, of Victoria, Vancouver Island, for one thousand dollars. Ibid., Sept. 28, 1872.

[37] During the 1870's, the Willamette Farmer published many notices of such importations. See also Weekly Mountaineer, Jan. 6, 1872, April 5, Nov. 15, 1873; Walla Walla Union, Aug. 24, 1872; Jan. 31, April 18, May 2, 16, 1874, May 8, 1875; Silver City Owyhee Avalanche, May 25, 1872; and especially the Willamette Farmer, June 29, 1872.

[38] Weekly Mountaineer, May 19, 1877; Henry N. Moseley, Oregon: Its Resources, Climate, People and Productions (London, 1878), p. 59.

[39] W. Baillie-Grohman, "Cattle Ranches in the Far West," Fortnightly Review, n.s., XXVIII (1880), 447; 45th Cong., 3rd sess., H. Ex. Doc. 1 (Serial 1850), IX, 1160, quoting Governor John W. Hoyt.

oughbred bulls on the ranges, held back for fear that their indifferent or tight-fisted competitors might reap where they had
not sown. In Idaho, according to this survey, cattle generally
were found to be of good quality, showing few traces of Spanish
or Texan strains. In Owyhee County the cattle were of exceptionally good quality. The general improvement of the cattle in
Idaho was attributed to the fact that several of the ranges were
amply supplied with blooded bulls. Similar conditions were observed also in eastern Washington. In Klickitat County, for example, Shorthorn bulls had had a noticeably good effect on the
cattle, and this improvement had, to some extent, counteracted
the evil effect of deteriorating ranges. Shorthorn bulls and cows
had likewise improved the quality of range cattle in the Yakima
country, but there, as elsewhere in the Pacific Northwest, cattle
were said to be decreasing in weight, and at least one cattleman
expressed the opinion that the improvement of range cattle was
not profitable.[40]

Notwithstanding the indifference of some cattlemen, there was,
during the 1880's, considerable grading up of the herds in the
Oregon Country. Doubtless the shrinking of the grazing area,
the shift in some districts to the breeding of cattle as an aspect
of farming operations, and a growing tendency for large opera-
ters to use enclosures altered considerably the outlook of cattlemen in the Pacific Northwest. But, whatever the reason for the
accelerating improvement of stock in this region may have been,
we read in the newspapers of that decade numerous reports of
the importation of blooded cattle into northeastern and southeastern Oregon, eastern Washington, and various parts of
Idaho.[41] Several kinds of blooded cattle were brought in, including the Hereford, but the Durham shorthorn, the early favor-

[40] Gordon, "Report," pp. 1080, 1082-83, 1090-91.
[41] *Spokane Falls Chronicle*, Aug. 17, 1881; *Waitsburg Times*, July 22, 1882;
Yakima Signal, Feb. 24, 1883; *Pomeroy Republican*, June 16, 1883; *Walla Walla
Union*, May 8, 1886; *Silver State*, April 14, 1880, Oct. 21, 1882; *Idaho Tri-
Weekly Statesman*, April 17, 1886; Chicago *Breeders' Gazette*, V (Feb. 28, 1884),
313; Cheney *Northwest Tribune*, May 20, June 3, July 22, 1886; *Spokane Falls
Review*, Sept. 30, 1886; Chicago *Weekly Drovers' Journal*, May 18, 1882; *Lewis-
ton Teller*, May 7, 1885, July 22, 1886, June 2, 1887, May 31, 1888; "Report of
the Governor of Washington Territory," Oct. 15, 1887, in 50th Cong., 1st sess.,
H. Ex. Doc. 1 (Serial 2541), X, 941-42. As early as 1883, the Idaho Fine Stock

ite in the Oregon Country, was still in the lead as late as 1886, according to an article in an early report of the United States Bureau of Animal Industry. This same article affirms that, between 1877 and 1886, there were reported in Oregon 501 head of thoroughbred cattle, in Washington 172 head, and in Idaho 126 head. If these figures and the returns of the eleventh federal census are correct, the increase in the number of "improved" cattle in the Oregon Country during the latter half of the 1880's was remarkable indeed, for in 1890 Oregon had 3,687 head of recorded purebred cattle, Washington 2,129 head, and Idaho 1,285 head. Of the one-half or higher grade of cattle, Oregon possessed 39,965 head, Washington 20,809 head, and Idaho 10,225 head.[42]

It may well be, therefore, that the editor of the *Morning Oregonian*, writing at the beginning of 1889, was not far wrong in his summary account of this matter when he said:

Inquiry as to the condition of the stock on the ranges east of the Cascades shows that constant improvement has been made in excellence and breeds. Many importations of shorthorns, Polled Angus and Herefords have been made, and range cattle are being graded up and improved in quality. Only within a few weeks there have been brought to locations in Wasco several car-loads of fine stock of the best breeds. While the shorthorn has a settled place and hold on the cattlemen of that region, there is beginning to be a liking for the hornless breeds. . . . There is hardly a trace left of the old Spanish cattle that had possession in the earliest days. The cattle that were brought across from the frontier by the pioneers of the forties were fair ordinary stock, American cattle of what we now call the common stock. . . . Gradually the range cattle have improved by the infusion of full blood through the introduction of thoroughbred males, until the herds that now roam the limitless ranges of Eastern Oregon and [Eastern] Washington are high grades in many instances and good beef stock in all. . . .[43]

Other reports, some of which we have already examined, lead one to conclude that the cattle of Idaho in the later 1880's were

Breeders' Association was importing blooded cattle from the eastern states. *Idaho Tri-Weekly Statesman*, Nov. 24, 1883.
[42] E. W. Perry, "Number and Value of Pure-Bred Cattle in the United States," U.S. Bureau of Animal Industry, *Fourth and Fifth Annual Reports, 1887-1888* (Washington, D.C., 1889), pp. 339-58; *Eleventh Federal Census, 1890: Report on the Statistics of Agriculture* (Washington, D.C., 1895), pp. 282, 303, 312-13.
[43] *Morning Oregonian*, Jan. 1, 1889.

fully equal in quality to those of Oregon and Washington.[44]

In the management of herds—whether large or small, whether in the Columbia Basin or the Winnemucca province—the ways of cattlemen in the Oregon Country were not strikingly dissimilar. Unfortunately, the information on this subject before 1880 is little enough, perhaps because newspaper editors found little "news value" in things generally familiar. Only travelers unacquainted with the practices of a cattle country or agents sent to gather specific information on the operations of cattlemen could be expected to record facts about the management of cattle herds that people of a later time, who know little or nothing about a cattle economy, would like to know. Accordingly, despite extensive investigation, only two accounts—both skimpy—have been found of cattle ranges or ranches in the Oregon Country during the period before 1880. One of these was situated in eastern Washington, and the other in southeastern Oregon.

In 1875 the editor of the *Willamette Farmer* obtained from a "fellow-townsman, Mr. M. Fisk," the following information about a ranch which Fisk and Walker owned in Washington Territory, "about fifty miles above the Dalles":

> Chapman's Creek [he said] puts into the Columbia there, and about three miles up the creek is a small valley containing about 300 acres of rich arable soil. Here the ranch is located, and here they have a fine farm for grasses, vegetables and cereals, with a good orchard, but that is the only arable land within the circuit of fifteen miles around, and as a consequence there is no other settlement to interfere with them in all that distance. The cattle of Fisk and Walker ought to number at least a thousand head, but there is no easy means of counting them. They are inhabitants of a range 200 miles in extent, at least some of them stray over that extent of country.[45]

Some four years later J. F. Wharton, accompanied by E. W. Cameron, traveled from Colusa, California, through southeastern Oregon into Washington Territory, visiting en route the two

[44] James L. Onderdonk, *Idaho: Facts and Statistics* . . . (San Francisco, 1885), pp. 66, 84. In the autumn of 1879, an editor in Boise attributed, in part, the rapidly growing cattle trade in his neighborhood to the fact that the beef raised there was "of a superior quality to that raised in Texas or anywhere east of the Rocky mountains." Quoted by the *Morning Oregonian*, Oct. 29, 1879.

[45] *Willamette Farmer*, May 14, 1875.

ranches of Glenn and French in the Steens Mountain country. From Mr. Wharton's diary kept on this trip we learn that

It [*i.e.*, the P Ranch] is a stock ranch, and covers an area seventy-five miles long by twenty miles wide. If it were not, Dr. Glenn, you know, would have nothing to do with it. The Doctor has never seen it, however, and probably never will. He has a partner, Peter French, who stays at the ranch and runs the business. Mr. French was not at home, being absent in Portland on some Government business, but we were taken in charge by his major domo, or overseer, and kindly and hospitably entertained. There are two ranches on the range, the P ranch here in this valley,[46] and the Diamond ranch—so called from the brands used—some twenty-five miles further on, in the valley of Keiger Creek.[47] These streams and valleys are so similar that a description of one is a description of both. The streams rise on the west side of Stein [Steens] mountain and flow in a northwesterly course, and sinking or spreading into broad marshes go to contribute to the waters of lakes Malheur and Harney.

The valleys are thirty or forty miles long and from six to twelve miles in width. The soil is wonderfully fertile; the climate is not excessive, and fine grain and vegetables are produced in abundance every year, and of the best quality. The gently sloping hills are covered with bunch grass, and the wild grass of the valley will produce a ton and a half of hay to the acre. Here are rich and beautiful homes for 500 families, with ample stock range for all. Glenn and French hold this vast body of land by the right of undisturbed possession. We were told by his [*sic*] bookkeeper that no part of the immense track [*sic*] of land over which their 25,000 head of cattle roam has ever passed any kind of title. It is true it would be a little unsafe for a settler to go into this country and attempt to make a homestead, for all such are treated as interlopers, and quickly invited to emigrate. . . .[48]

Our earliest generalized view of the practices of cattlemen throughout the Oregon Country—whether they operated on a large or a small scale—comes to us in the Gordon Report. Here we learn something about their ways of acquiring land, their using of ranges in common, their capital outlays for ranching equipment, their shifting of cattle between summer and winter ranges, and their widespread practice of letting cattle fend for themselves in winter. Cattlemen, and especially those whose op-

[46] The P Ranch was in the valley of the Donner und Blitzen River, south of Burns and west of Steens Mountain, in present Harney County. McArthur, *Oregon Geographic Names*, p. 405.

[47] A misspelling of Kiger Creek, so named by the wife of Ruben C. Kiger, who lived in this country between 1874 and 1878. *Ibid.*, p. 290.

[48] *Silver State*, Dec. 12, 1879, presumably copied from the Colusa, Calif., *Sun.*

erations were on a small scale, generally held by homestead right, by pre-emption, or sometimes by the right of first occupation only, a small tract of land adjacent to a watering place. If water were scarce, a cattleman might fence his holding to monopolize a large range; but on ranges where water was plentiful and herds were rather small it was not unusual for the cattle of several owners to mingle freely together. Investments in ranching equipment, in comparison with the outlays for cattle, were small. Labor costs were low, and when, as sometimes was the case, cattle merely drifted between summer and winter ranges, the demands on the pocketbook of the cattleman for herdsmen's wages were not heavy.[49]

Usually an investment of a few thousand dollars provided ample equipment for carrying on even a large cattle-breeding enterprise. A home ranch equipped with a house or cabin for herders, stables for horses in active winter service, and a few corrals for branding stock was considered sufficient. If the range were large, branding corrals were built at several convenient places. As a rule, a small area of meadow land was enclosed to provide hay for saddle horses, and there might also be enclosed pastures for horses kept for purposes of breeding. Some owners, having learned the value of storing up hay for emergency winter feeding, enclosed rather extensive hay-producing areas. Such men, however, were exceptional, and over against them may be set a few other men who seemingly could conduct a cattle-breeding enterprise with virtually no investment at all in ranching equipment.[50]

In the Gordon Report there are brief descriptions of the equipment that two cattlemen of Washington Territory considered necessary for carrying on their operations. One of these men, a Klickitat cattleman, had an investment of $5,600 in land

[49] On the subject of the movement of cattle from summer to winter ranges, and vice versa, see the *Walla Walla Union,* May 3, 1873, Oct. 17, 1874; the *Willamette Farmer,* April 26, 1884; the Portland *Oregon and Washington Farmer* (May, 1883), p. 14; and the Gordon "Report," p. 1081.

[50] Gordon, "Report," p. 1091; John C. Young of Oneida County, Idaho, in the "Report of the Public Lands Commission," 46th Cong., 2nd sess., H. Ex. Doc. 46, p. 337; letter from M. McManamon, Feb. 27, 1878, in the Colfax *Palouse Gazette,* March 8, 1878; *Willamette Farmer,* Dec. 16, 1881.

and ranching equipment. This consisted of 160 acres of land valued at $1,600, buildings and fences worth $2,000, wagons, harness, saddles, and the like worth $500, and horses worth $1,500. With this equipment he managed a herd of 5,000 head of cattle. The other man, who was from Yakima, had found that an outlay of $11,800 would be needed to provide land and ranching equipment to take care of 5,000 head of cattle on his range. This sum would provide buildings, fences, and corrals, horses for handling cattle and for breeding purposes, and 300 acres of land worth $5,000.[51]

The buildings and other equipment in some of the large ranches in southeastern Oregon were not much more assuming, if at all. Concerning ranches in Baker and Grant counties, the Gordon Report says:

In some instances in Oregon the plant embraces more pretentious buildings, a hay claim, and fenced pastures of very considerable extent, but commonly the improvements are limited to merely a comfortable log cabin and a rough stable for half a dozen horses, with open stock-pens adjacent in which to corral and brand cattle. If the herd handled is a large one, and the cattle occupy a large extent of country, several other corrals are generally put up at points convenient to the usual rodeo grounds. At such enclosures the necessary marking and branding of calves can be effected without the trouble and injury to cows and calves of driving them a long distance to the corrals at the home ranch, or of doing this work on the open prairie; the latter practice is always injurious to cattle, as it is apt to over-heat the calves and make the whole herd wild, besides wearing out the saddle-horses unnecessarily. In addition to his buildings and corrals and limited fencing, the large cattle-raiser is possessed of a camp wagon, work animals, harness, and saddles, and a band of well-broken cow-horses sufficient to allow each of his herders several spare animals. With this moderate outlay in equipments the Oregon cattle-raiser is prepared to conduct a business which involves a capital in cattle of many thousands of dollars.[52]

Before the end of the 1870's, large-scale cattlemen in southeastern Oregon and southern Idaho were beginning to increase their holdings of land and to fence, lawfully or unlawfully, large tracts of land. In these regions, and especially in southeastern Oregon, the opportunities to lay hold of land were abundant.

[51] Gordon, "Report," p. 1090.
[52] Ibid., p. 1081.

Everywhere in the West, under conditions that were not onerous, land in small tracts could be acquired from the federal government under the Pre-emption Act of 1841, the Homestead Act of 1862, the Timber Culture Act of 1873, the Desert Land Act of 1877, and the Stone and Timber Act of 1878. Also in the West each state (Texas excepted) had for sale land that had come to it under various grants of the federal government: lands for the benefit of public schools and of higher education, and lands for the promotion of internal improvements.[53] But, apart from the grants of land ordinarily made by the federal government to new states, Oregon had received in 1860 a grant of 286,108 acres of swamp lands; and in 1870 it had established a minimum price of a dollar an acre for these lands, of which sum 20 per cent was to be paid at the time the purchaser made his selection. The remaining 80 per cent was to be paid within ten years, after the purchaser proved that he had fulfilled the conditions on which such lands could be obtained.[54]

Before 1880, no doubt because of the overstocking of the ranges, stockmen in southeastern Oregon were patenting lands by homesteading and by the procedure of pre-emption, purchasing state-owned school lands, and, of particular significance, acquiring lands pursuant to the provisions of the Oregon Swamp Lands Act of 1870. On April 14, 1877, John Catlow sold to the Oregon Stock and Butchering Company 47,000 acres which he had acquired under the Swamp Lands Act, and on September 13, 1877, A. H. Robie and the Oregon and Nevada Stock Growers Association sold to Dr. H. J. Glenn 43,360 acres that had been acquired as swamp and overflow lands. The editor of the *Weekly Mountaineer*, with this purchase in mind, may have been referring to the Glenn-French holdings when, in September, 1881, he wrote as follows: "The stock range of one firm in the south end of

[53] Roy Marvin Robbins, *Our Landed Heritage: The Public Domain, 1776-1936* (Princeton, N.J., 1942), *passim;* Ernest Staples Osgood, *The Day of the Cattleman* (Minneapolis, 1929), pp. 194-95; Benjamin H. Hibbard, *History of the Public Land Policies* (New York, 1924), *passim.*

[54] C. Marc Miller, *An Appraisal of the Snake-Piute Tract, State of Oregon, January, 1879: Case Number 17 Before the Indian Claims Commission* (prepared for the Lands Division, United States Department of Justice; Seattle, Wash., July, 1958), pp. 38-39.

Grant county is 50 miles wide and one hundred and twenty-five miles long. This firm, by taking advantage of the nefarious swamp land laws of Oregon now hold firm possession of the watering places in this vast region, and as effectually keep settlers out as if they had a patent to the whole region."[55]

Glenn and French, however, were not the only large-scale cattlemen in southeastern Oregon to acquire title to swamp lands in this state. On January 1 and 17, 1882, W. B. Todhunter received from the state of Oregon deeds to 34,859.42 acres of swamp lands. These purchases were not overlooked by alert observers in the Winnemucca province. Within a few weeks an editor in Reno, Nevada, affirming that Todhunter now had more than 20,000 head of cattle and more than 100,000 acres of land, remarked that he had obtained patents "last month for 35,000 acres of swamp land in one bunch." Of Todhunter's outfit in general, this editor wrote as follows:

He has about 1,000 bulls and 300 saddle horses. He employs 50 men and puts up 2,500 tons of hay, to guard against hard winters. He keeps 100 work horses and raises grain enough to feed all his saddle and work stock. Besides his cattle he has 700 or 800 stock horses, 4 jacks and 50 stal[l]ions. His stock is divided among four ranches, one known as the White Horse ranch, lying just inside the Oregon line, northwest of Fort McDermitt, where 5,000 head are kept; one in Long Valley, in the northwest corner of Nevada lying along side of Surprise, supports 4,000 head; the Pyramid ranch, lying at the northeast of the lake, has 1,500 and a lot of horses; the Abbott ranch, at Stein's Mountain, feeds 5,000, and Harney Valley 5,000 more. The home ranch is twenty-five miles from a neighbor.

When Todhunter disposed of his holdings in 1887, he had, besides his cattle, 200,000 acres of land and 2,000 horses.[56]

Before and after Todhunter's purchases, the state of Oregon sold swamp lands to other cattlemen of Oregon. In two separate sales—one on July 28, 1880, the other on July 25, 1883—H. C. Owens, a speculator in lands, acquired 121,791.68 acres of swamp lands. Some two years later, on July 30, 1885, Glenn and French bought another parcel of swamp lands consisting of 22,055.67

[55] *Ibid.*, p. 105. The quotation, taken from the *Weekly Mountaineer*, appears under the heading "A Big Range" in the *Palouse Gazette*, Nov. 11, 1881.
[56] Miller, *Snake-Piute Tract*, p. 101; *Silver State*, March 31, 1882, quoting the Reno *Gazette; ibid.*, May 14, 24, 1887.

acres; and on January 22, 1889, E. C. Singleterry and others obtained 8,711.88 acres of such lands. Meanwhile, since 1879, Todhunter and other cattlemen in southeastern Oregon had been buying school lands from their state, and throughout the 1880's they bought numerous small tracts of land from men who, presumably, had acquired title by pre-emption or by homesteading. In the meantime, as we have seen, some cattlemen in southern Idaho had enlarged their holdings of land.

From the evidence now available it appears that, on the best-conducted ranches in eastern Oregon, fencing was becoming general during the 1880's. The Gordon Report asserts that the Glenn-French ranches had more than thirty thousand acres of land inclosed, and that elsewhere in Grant County large areas had been fenced.[57] Still other sources mention similar developments in southern Idaho, and make clear the fact that Todhunter and several other large-scale cattlemen in southeastern Oregon were in trouble in the spring of 1887 because they had run fences on government-owned land.[58]

Like the land and the equipment, the labor that a cattleman needed to operate a ranch in the Oregon Country could be obtained at a moderate cost. At the beginning of the 1880's, cowboys in southeastern Oregon were paid from $35.00 to $40.00 a month, besides board, which, at that time in the Yakima Valley, was said to be worth $20.00 a month. On the large ranches of southeastern Oregon, foremen (majordomos), upon whom fell heavy responsibilities, received wages varying from $60.00 to as much as $125 a month. Ordinary ranch hands in that area were paid $30.00 a month and board. The Klickitat cattleman whose business is described in the Gordon Report kept six men regularly employed, and paid five of them at the rate of $30.00 a month and board. One man, evidently a foreman or principal herder, received

[57] Miller, *Snake-Piute Tract*, pp. 101-2, 104, 106-7, Gordon, "Report," p. 1080. There is need of a detailed study of the subject of fencing in the Oregon Country east of the Cascade Mountains. The introduction of barbed wire into this region undoubtedly had an important effect on the practices of cattlemen in this region.
[58] *Idaho Weekly Statesman*, Aug. 14, 1880; *Silver State*, March 24, 1887. The Salem *Oregon Statesman*, Feb. 8, 1889, quoted the Lakeview *Lake County Examiner* as follows: "Jesse D. Carr is in a fair way to let go of 40,000 acres of govern-

$40.00 a month and board. These men, by constant riding, did all the work that was required. The Yakima cattleman whose business also was described in the Gordon Report employed five men regularly. Four of them received $40.00 a month and board, and one of them received $60.00 a month and board. Additional men, when needed, received $1.50 a day and board. This cattleman needed ten extra men for one month to help round up his cattle for market, and in winter, when the cattle had to be fed, he also needed ten extra men for a month. Because of the cost of labor, some cattlemen believed that a herd containing fewer than 1,000 head was unprofitable. In southeastern Oregon three competent cowboys, it was said, would care for a herd of that size during the season of active work (April to December), except during roundups; and in that area the per capita cost of herding decreased as the size of the herd increased, twelve cowboys, for example, being expected to care for a herd of 8,000, except during a general roundup.[59]

Cowboys of the Oregon Country have not shared the glamour of their brethren of Texas and the Great Plains. No cowboy literature has risen from the ranges of the Columbia Basin; no collections have been made of songs that may have lightened the labors of the men who punched cattle on the trails that led to The Dalles of the Columbia River, or through the passes in the Cascade Mountains, or on the lesser trails that led to the great trail running eastward into Wyoming. Cattle herders in the Columbia Basin, judged by evidence now available, were hard-working and prosaic men. In that area, as we have seen, Indians were sometimes called into service as helpers or drovers, but frontiersmen would hardly have been expected to get lyrical about "lousy" Siwashes. Jack Splawn, himself a cowboy who rode the ranges and the trails of the Columbia Basin, eulogized in his later years the cowboys he had known; but John Minto, an Oregon pioneer,

---

ment land he has fenced on Clear Lake. It will be like pulling teeth for the millionaire to lose so much land that has cost him nothing, but if the government officers do their duty, the settlers of that section will soon have the chance to locate some good land."

[59] Gordon, "Report," pp. 1083, 1090-91.

saw cowboys in a somewhat less favorable light.[60] Before 1880, cowboys from California had come upon the ranges of southeastern Oregon. These men were described as proficient herders, expert horsemen, and skillful ropers. Said to be superior even to the cowboys of Texas, a few of them could, under the direction of a competent majordomo, handle large herds of cattle with good results and with little "wear and tear on their saddle animals." Better equipped and better mounted, they easily eclipsed, in efficiency and picturesqueness, the American and Siwash cowmen of northeastern Oregon and eastern Washington. Not until the great eastward drives of the late 1870's and early 1880's got under way did the people of the Columbia Basin get glimpses of cowboys from ranges beyond the Rockies. These men were objects of interest in the Columbia Valley in 1879, but by 1881 not a few of them were looked upon as corrupters of the trade of cattle herder. ". . . now the American cowboy," wailed an Idaho editor in 1881, "seems to be a bigger thief and ruffian than his Mexican prototype."[61] But that was an overstatement.

For the men who rode the ranges, whether they were cowboys or owners of cattle, the most exacting and exciting labor was that connected with the rodeo or roundup.[62] This institution, as we have seen, flourished wherever cattle had grazed on open ranges, and was a means of getting cattle marked and branded. In the Oregon Country, as in other open-range countries, brands were of various designs. Some consisted of the initials of the owners, others were simple numerical designs, and still others were more or less intricate designs. Occasionally one appeared that was gro-

[60] *Yakima Record*, June 26, 1880, June 17, 1882; A. J. Splawn, *Ka-mi-akin, Last Hero of the Yakimas* (2nd ed.; Portland, Ore., 1944), chap. xxxvi; John Minto, "Sheep Husbandry in Oregon," *OHQ*, III (1902), 237-38.

[61] Gordon, "Report," p. 1083; *Idaho Tri-Weekly Statesman*, Nov. 3, 1881. A letter from The Dalles, dated March 20, 1882, embodies the complaint that in the country tributary to The Dalles "a small but vicious" group of cowboys were becoming as "desperate and lawless as their brethren in Arizona and New Mexico." *Morning Oregonian*, March 21, 1882.

[62] Oddly enough, instead of *rodeo*, the word *rodero* often appeared in the newspapers of the Pacific Northwest. *Walla Walla Union*, May 9, 1874; *Idaho Avalanche*, April 16, 1881; *Yakima Signal*, Oct. 13, 1883; *Kittitas Standard*, Sept. 22, 1883; *Yakima Record*, April 15, 1882; *Northwest Tribune*, July 17, 1885. In the notices of such gatherings examined in the *Silver State*, the word *rodeo* was consistently used. In the course of time, however, this word was generally supplanted by the word *roundup*.

tesque.[63] But whatever it may have been, the design of the branding iron was burned into the hide of the calf, and, at the same
time, the calf was marked—that is, one of its ears was notched or
perhaps cut to a point.[64] For the purpose of marking and branding, it seemed desirable to bring the cattle together periodically.
Out of this need, therefore, the institution of the roundup had
come into being.

Roundups could be conducted either independently by owners
of large herds, or, as was most commonly the case, by the voluntary cooperation of the cattlemen of a particular district, who
acted pursuant to rules of their own adoption or according to
regulations prescribed either by an association of which they
were members or by the legislature of a state or a territory. In the
Oregon Country practices varied, but voluntary cooperation,
often by consent informally given, was widely practiced. Not
more than a few cattlemen were well enough equipped to round
up their own cattle. There appears to have been little regulation
of roundups by statutes in the Oregon Country. As early as 1877,
the Idaho Legislature prescribed a mode of procedure for roundups in certain counties of that territory, but in respect to this
matter Idaho seems to have been unique. No such laws appear to
have been enacted either in Oregon or in Washington. As to
regulation by associations, there was some of that to be sure, but
in the Oregon Country no association of cattlemen ever became
powerful enough to regulate roundups generally.

Ordinarily two roundups a year were held in the Oregon Country, the first one beginning in April or May and lasting, sometimes, for several weeks. The second roundup was held in the late
summer or early autumn, at which time calves that had been
missed in the spring were branded and marked, and beef cattle

[63] *Lewiston Teller*, Aug. 3, 1882; *Spokane Falls Review*, Dec. 16, 1886. On the
subject of brands in Whitman County, Washington, see the *Walla Walla Union*,
Sept. 19, 1885, and on brands in Oregon see the article by Keneth Young, "Sherman County Cattle Brands Tell History of Pioneer Days," in *The Dalles Chronicle*,
Sept. 29, 1948.

[64] There were laws in both Oregon and Washington prohibiting the cutting off
of more than one-half of an animal's ear, and in Idaho there was a law forbidding
the removal of more than one-third of an ear, and also the trimming of an ear to a
point. *Laws of Oregon, 1885*, p. 44; *Laws of Washington, 1871*, p. 103; *Laws of
Idaho, 1880-81*, p. 297.

that were ready for market were separated from the herds. About
the middle 1870's, when Oregon cattlemen began selling cattle
to stockmen east of the Rockies and to buyers from the Middle
West, the spring roundups in the Oregon Country took on a
peculiar importance, for cattle contracted for during the preceding winter were then delivered to the buyers. Spring delivery was
necessary because of the time required to drive cattle from eastern Washington or eastern Oregon to ranges in Wyoming or other
far-distant states or territories, or to get them to Cheyenne or
some other point on the Union Pacific Railroad from which they
could be sent by rail to feeding grounds or to markets in the
Mississippi Valley. Accordingly, at the spring roundups the cattle
that had been sold to eastern buyers were cut out of the herds,
branded with the road brand of the seller, and started toward
their eastern destination, grazing en route.[65]

In the Columbia Basin the practice of holding roundups by
informal voluntary cooperation was all but universal. At the beginning of the 1880's, however, a Klickitat cattleman reported
that the roughness of the country in which his cattle grazed precluded a general roundup there.[66] The practice followed in rounding up cattle in the lower Yakima Valley is thus described:

The work of branding begins about the 1st of May, when an outfit of a
dozen men starts out with a wagon and cook, and camp[s] near some corral
on the range. The surrounding country is ridden over, and all stock handled
and calves branded within reach, the branding pen being used to corral
cows and calves in. After working all the range within reach, the outfit and
wagon go to another corral, 10 or 20 miles distant, and proceed to handle
all the stock in that neighborhood. Thus they go through the range where,

[65] *Yakima Record*, April 15, 1882, May 12, 1883; *Northwest Tribune*, March 2,
1888, quoting the Ritzville, Wash., *Times*; L. U., writing from Jordan Valley, Ore.,
May 1, 1881, in the *Idaho Avalanche*, May 7, 1881; *Oregon and Washington
Farmer* (October, 1882), p. 14, quoting the *Lake County Examiner*; *Kittitas
Standard*, Sept. 22, 1883; *Yakima Signal*, Oct. 13, 1883; Gordon, "Report," p.
1082; *Idaho Avalanche*, June 4, 1881.
[66] The general practice is illustrated by a notice which reads as follows: "We
are requested by Mr. P. J. Flint to announce that the annual spring 'round up' of
cattle on the Lower Yakima will begin at Selah Springs on Wednesday, the 23d of
May, 1883. All who wish to take part are requested to meet at Selah Springs on
Tuesday, the 22d." *Yakima Record*, May 12, 1883. See also Splawn, *Ka-mi-akin*, p.
293, and Gordon, "Report," p. 1090.

at different points convenient to favorite pasture grounds of cattle and to good water, corrals have been located for branding.[67]

In 1883 the spring roundup in the Yakima country was late, for it did not begin until May 23. The cattle then ranging there perhaps did not exceed fifteen thousand head. We do not know how long that roundup lasted, but in June Benjamin E. Snipes still had eighteen men at work branding calves on this range, and it was reported that this work would continue through the summer. Evidently Snipes, like stockmen in an earlier year in the Owyhee River country, was not fully satisfied with the roundup and was supplementing its work by individual effort. The fall roundup in the Yakima Valley in 1883 was completed early in October; and, significantly enough, it was reported that only about twenty men participated, for by this time the number of cattle on this range had been greatly decreased.[68]

In southeastern Oregon, at the beginning of the 1880's, a general meeting of the stockmen of an area of "common occupation" was held each spring for the purpose of organizing a roundup. Such a roundup was carried out under the supervision of one man, whose special knowledge of the stock and the area entitled him to a place of leadership. The roundups in this area, as the Gordon Report makes clear, were never equal in magnitude to those held along the North Platte River, but in general object and in methods of procedure they were identical with those held east of the Rockies.

. . . Camp wagons follow the stockmen through the country "worked," and each day a new camp is made, from which, on the following morning, all the cattle within a radius of eight or ten miles are surrounded and driven to some flat or prairie convenient for rounding them up. While some of the riders keep the stock bunched by riding around the skirts of the herd, others enter the "round-up" on trained horses and separate or "cut out" first the cows and calves. They afterward separate the "dry stock," consisting of all other cattle, provided the stockmen present desire, as is generally the case in the spring, to gather all the animals of their own brand which can be found in order to move them back to their own range, from

[67] Gordon, "Report," p. 1091.
[68] Yakima Record, May 12, 1883; Willamette Farmer, June 15, 1883; Idaho Avalanche, Nov. 12, 1881; Yakima Signal, Oct. 13, 1883.

which they may have drifted during the winter storms. The "round-up," having been thoroughly reviewed or "worked" by all those present who are looking for cattle, is turned loose, and the remaining cattle, consisting of animals belonging to the range and estrays unclaimed by their owners at the time, are permitted again to seek their usual feeding grounds. The cows and calves are now driven to branding pens, usually adjacent to the rodeo ground, where, after the calves are properly marked and branded, they are again turned out on range, or, if belonging to another locality, are held with the other estrays and guarded night and day until enough cattle are gathered to warrant a "drive" to the range where they belong. A "round-up" thus traverses a region of some 75 or 100 miles long by 25 or 35 wide, and by gathering every herd of cattle met with during the daily reconnaissance or "circling in" of the vaqueros engaged in the work, each cattle-owner has an opportunity of finding and restoring to their proper pasture-grounds the cattle of his brand, provided no unusual storms during the winter have drifted his stock beyond the limits covered by the "round-up" in question. The large owners whose cattle range over several counties send men to represent their interests in the various "round-ups" of the neighboring regions. These men accompany, gather, and drive back such estrays of their employer's brand as are recovered.[69]

Men like Glenn and French, or like Todhunter and Devine, monopolizing as they did large ranges for their own stock, conducted their own roundups. Their interest in the roundups like those just described would consist merely in recovering such of their cattle as had wandered away from the ranges to which they belonged.

In Idaho, practices were, in general, similar to those in Oregon and Washington, but in that territory, as we have mentioned above, some roundups were held subject to rules established by law. A statute, passed by the legislature of Idaho early in 1877, provided for the creation in certain counties of stock districts, the appointment therein of stock boards, and the compulsory attendance at the annual roundup of cattlemen affected by the provisions of this act.[70] Because in virtually all the counties exempted from the provisions of this law cattle breeding was an important enterprise, one is inclined to believe that the regulations prescribed by this act were intended to correct conditions in certain

[69] Gordon, "Report," pp. 1081-82.
[70] *Laws of Idaho, 1876-77*, pp. 27-32; *ibid., 1880-81*, pp. 330-35; *Local and Special Laws of Idaho in Force on June 1, 1887*, pp. 135-39.

parts of Idaho that were beyond the power of cattlemen to set right by voluntary cooperation. "Slick-earing" and rustling, for example, may have become intolerable evils in some parts of Idaho.

In the days when cattle were grazed on open ranges, "slick-earing" was a practice somewhat like the practice, during the days of the Volstead Act, of making bathtub gin. Neither activity was respectable or honest, and consequently both were productive of stories that everybody liked to tell, sometimes with rich embellishments. Slick-ears, or mavericks, or whatever other name may have been used to designate them, were calves that turned up without mothers. There were always some of these at every roundup, and what to do with them was, of course, a problem— but one that could be solved by agreement among the cattlemen participating in the roundup.[71] No roundup, however, was entirely efficient. As a Yakima cattleman observed,

Many calves are necessarily missed, and when these leave their mothers, or are weaned naturally, they are called "slick-ears," "sleepers," or "mavericks," and belong to any cattleman who can get his brand on them. In the spring men go out "slick-earing" with lassos and branding-irons on their saddles and secure such calves. The animals are roped and the iron put on, having been heated over a fire of sage-brush or cow-chips. This sort of business has proved the most profitable branch of the enterprise to some cattle-raisers, as they brand more calves than their cows number.[72]

Thus a cattleman who was quick with a lariat and untroubled by a conscience might add considerably to his wealth by slick-earing. It was simply astonishing how productive some ranges were, and how easily one might get started in the cattle business, wrote a correspondent of the *Yakima Record* from the Kittitas Valley in the spring of 1880. "I heard of one man that bought an old cow in the fall," this writer affirmed, "and in the spring came out with said cow and 40 head of calves." A practice inevitable under the conditions of open-range grazing, slick-earing tended to deaden the consciences of some cattlemen, and so, as one

[71] At the spring roundup on the Yakima range in 1883, "it was mutually agreed that one-half of all the 'slick-ears' found should be branded for Snipes & Allen and the other half be divided among the other stockmen." *Kittitas Standard*, June 30, 1883, quoting the *Goldendale Gazette*.
[72] Gordon, "Report," p. 1091.

editor put it, we need not be "surprised if, now and then, a cow-boy kinder sorter persuaded a calf to denounce and abandon its mamma before the natural weaning time."[73] At least this sort of thing did not appear to be extraordinary to a cowboy on the Wasco range, who, in 1882, wrote as follows:

You may know or have heard of "mavericks," "mallet-heads," "bronchos," etc. Well, they are unbranded yearlings; that is, calves that are missed on the spring and fall rides, and so go unmarked, unbranded, but not un-known. There are sharp eyes, swift horses and ready ropes waiting for just such opportunities and soon the broncho is marked and branded. It is only by easy stages that from yearlings the ages dropped until now *anything* unbranded, young or old, is taken, weaned away from its mother, branded and turned out. This nefarious business has assumed somewhat large pro-portions, and stockmen are becoming alarmed. What would you call this business? Up here we mustn't breathe the harsh word that rises to your lips—"It is retaliation: They all do it."[74]

On the ranges men could conveniently pass from the practice of slick-earing to that of rustling, just as in a later time men could easily pass from the practice of making liquor for themselves to that of making it to sell to others. In either case, the practice was naughty, dangerous, and frequently profitable.

To honest cattlemen, however, rustlers were the meanest crea-tures fashioned by the hand of God—"low, brutish things called men," as one editor characterized them.[75] They made sheepherd-ers appear to be respectable persons. Wherever they went, rus-tlers were loathed by honest men; and they went far and operated in devious ways. From the beginning of open-range grazing, they were present in the Pacific Northwest, laying hold of cattle that were not their own. They altered cattle brands and marks, and they laid claim to cattle that were imperfectly branded and marked. If they happened to be drovers, they might put a road brand on cattle they had not bought.[76] All such diverting pas-

[73] *Walla Walla Union*, April 17, 1880, quoting the *Yakima Record*, March 27, 1880; *Yakima Record*, Oct. 1, Dec. 24, 1881.
[74] "The Wasco Range," *Morning Oregonian*, Feb. 21, 1882.
[75] Pomeroy *Washington Independent*, June 5, 1884.
[76] *Walla Walla Statesman*, April 14, 1865; *Owyhee Avalanche*, Oct. 5, Nov. 23, 1867; *Walla Walla Union*, April 11, 1874; *Idaho Tri-Weekly Statesman*, Feb. 23, March 4, 1875; *Lewiston Teller*, Aug. 11, 1877; *Yakima Record*, July 10, 1880; *Spokane Falls Chronicle*, June 20, 1882; *Northwest Tribune*, Feb. 23, 1883; *Walla Walla Watchman*, Feb. 15, July 11, 1884; *Cheney Enterprise*, March 27, 1890.

times as these were, to be sure, refinements of open stealing, of which during the 1880's there were widely voiced complaints— complaints that organized bands of cattle thieves were operating in Idaho, eastern Oregon, the Yakima Valley, and the Big Bend of the Columbia River.[77] By law the property of cattlemen appeared to be adequately protected, but the enforcement of law was not easy in a sparsely peopled and poorly policed country. There were indictments, trials, and convictions of cattle thieves, but of the men who felt called to the profession of stealing cattle no doubt many more escaped detection than served sentences in state or territorial prisons.[78] Cattlemen were not, however, wholly dependent upon the law for the protection of their cattle; they all knew of vigilante ways in mining camps, and they could and did band together to inflict upon evildoers summary punishment. Vigilante action did not invariably mean that a suspected person was informally tried, swiftly convicted, and then informally and quickly hanged. Sometimes men suspected of stealing cattle were warned to leave the country within a period of a few hours, and men so warned were not wise if they delayed their departure. For cattlemen in the Oregon Country did take drastic action on such fellows. More than once the break of day disclosed the body of a suspected rustler hanging from the limb of a tree.[79] How many such actions took place, we shall probably never know. One is left to suspect more than one can prove. No doubt there was more cursing than acting, more threatening than hanging. But the knowledge that enraged cattlemen would deal out justice of their own devising to rustlers undoubtedly served to restrain somewhat men who yearned to appropriate to their own use cattle which were not their own.

Men who were given to slick-earing or rustling were beyond

---

[77] *Yakima Record*, July 10, 1880; *Walla Walla Union*, Nov. 25, 1882; quoting the *Yakima Record*; *Walla Walla Watchman*, July 25, 1884; *Lewiston Teller*, June 4, 1885; *Idaho Weekly Statesman*, Aug. 4, 1883, May 24, 1884, Dec. 3, 1887; *Weekly Oregonian*, Oct. 25, 1889; *Cheney Enterprise*, March 27, 1890.

[78] *Walla Walla Union*, June 7, 1873, April 13, 1889; Vancouver *Clarke County Register*, Nov. 16, 1882; *Spokane Falls Chronicle*, June 27, 1882; *Lewiston Teller*, July 1, 1886, July 18, 1889.

[79] *Weekly Oregonian*, April 9, 1864; *Walla Walla Union*, Nov. 7, 1885; *Seattle Gazette*, April 27, 1865; Whatcom *Bellingham Bay Mail*, June 1, 1878; *Willamette Farmer*, May 17, 1878; *Walla Walla Union*, June 13, 1885.

doubt the worst human enemies of the cattlemen, but they were not their only enemies. There were careless white men who set fire to the bunch grass, and there were malicious settlers who shot down trespassing cattle. In earlier years, it is true, American settlers in western Washington improved their marksmanship by shooting the cattle of the Puget's Sound Agricultural Company, but obviously such conduct, as they believed, ought not to be invoked as a precedent. For were not these cattle the property of a foreign monopoly—British at that? For an American settler to shoot the trespassing cattle of an American stockman—that was another matter, an offense not to be tolerated in a "humane community."[80]

Accordingly, against these and other enemies that might beset them, cattlemen of the Oregon Country needed not only the protection of laws duly enacted, but also the protection of such associations as they might form to safeguard and promote their interest. What the law and the principle of voluntary association did for those who exploited the ranges of the Oregon Country we shall now endeavor to ascertain.

[80] *Lewiston Teller*, Sept. 13, 1878; *Northwest Tribune*, Sept. 15, 1882; *Idaho Weekly Statesman*, July 12, 1884; *Weekly Oregonian*, Nov. 29, 1889; *Idaho Tri-Weekly Statesman*, Oct. 22, 1864; *Walla Walla Union*, Sept. 4, 1875. Also, see the complaint of Dr. W. F. Tolmie to Isaac I. Stevens, governor of Washington Territory, Dec. 27, 1853, in 33rd Cong., 2nd sess., S. Ex. Doc. 37, pp. 14-15.

CHAPTER VII

Cattlemen and the Law

IN THE Oregon Country, as elsewhere in the American West, the authority of the federal government touched in several ways the business of breeding cattle on the ranges of the public domain. It could not have been otherwise, for this government, as owner of the public lands, was the absentee landlord of all stockmen who made use of such lands. Although it made no charge for the use of its lands, the federal government permitted no stockman to acquire by mere occupation a vested interest in any part of the public domain. Like other men, a stockman could acquire, pursuant to the laws dealing with such matters, title to tracts of government-owned lands; but he could not lawfully fence the range that he used on the public domain, and thus exclude from it other stockmen seeking pasture for their herds or flocks. Nor could he lawfully exclude from his range a prospective farmer seeking a quarter section of land pursuant to the Homestead Act. Moreover, since the power to regulate interstate commerce is vested in the federal government, no state or territory could protect the ranges used by its stockmen against "unfair" competition by imposing a tax upon herds or flocks which were being driven through such state or territory. This right of transit was emphatically affirmed by the Supreme Court of the United States in 1903, when it held that a tax imposed by Wyoming in 1895 on all livestock brought into that state "for the purpose of being grazed" was not applica-

221

ble to a band of sheep driven through Wyoming from a point in Utah to a point in Nebraska. As a "subject of interstate commerce," such sheep, the court held, were exempt from this tax, even though "they might incidentally have supported themselves in grazing while actually in transit."[1] Finally, as guardian of the Indians, the federal government retained jurisdiction of Indian reservations, and some of this land in the Oregon Country was highly tempting to cattlemen. This subject, however, will be treated in a later chapter of this book.

If the federal government used the arm of its law primarily for the purpose of restricting the operations of cattlemen, a state or a territory, pursuant to its police power, could use the arm of its law to protect the property of stockmen and to promote their interests as graziers on public lands.[2] The power of a state or a territory to protect stockmen in the possession of their ambulatory property was as broad as the need of stockmen for the protection of such property was great; but, as we have observed in a preceding chapter, the efficiency of a state or a territory in enforcing all its police regulations at times left something to be desired. In such circumstances, cattlemen in the Oregon Country behaved like cattlemen elsewhere in the American West. How they organized themselves to promote their interests we shall see later in this chapter.

Laws enacted to protect the interests of breeders of livestock in the Oregon Country disclose two fairly well-defined trends— first, a similarity in the provisions of many such laws, whether enacted in Oregon, Washington, or Idaho; and, secondly, a recognition of the fact that the special needs of cattlemen in certain areas required laws that were applicable to these areas only. Accordingly, numerous laws, some of general and others of restricted application, were enacted to prescribe penalties for steal-

---

[1] Kelly v. Rhoads, 188 U. S. 1 (1903). On the situation of cattlemen in relation to the public lands of the United States, see in Ernest Staples Osgood's *The Day of the Cattleman* (Minneapolis, 1929) the chapter entitled "The Cattleman and the Public Domain." The laws under which public lands of the United States might be acquired were not well adapted to the needs of the people in the dry country west of the ninety-eighth meridian.

[2] On the subject of law in relation to livestock in a state contiguous to the Oregon Country, see Levi S. Peterson, "The Development of Utah Livestock Law, 1848-1896," *Utah Historical Quarterly*, XXXII (Summer, 1964), 198-216.

ing livestock, to make provision for safeguarding marks and brands by requiring their registration, to protect herds against the onslaughts of disease and the depredations of predatory animals, to provide for the owners of such herds the means to recover damages for injuries done to their animals on account of the negligence of persons engaged in various occupations, and to protect stockmen from suits for damages done by their livestock to the crops of persons whose fences had not been constructed pursuant to law. Cattlemen also received protection of a more subtle character by the imposition of taxes upon cattle brought into a state or territory for temporary grazing, sometimes in order to escape the payment elsewhere of taxes on such livestock. Such laws were intended, in part, to "equalize" competition between resident and nonresident owners of cattle. With all the laws that touched the interests of cattlemen anywhere in the Oregon Country this chapter is concerned.

Early in their respective legislative histories, Oregon, Washington, and Idaho enacted laws making the theft of livestock an offense punishable as grand larceny, and providing that any person convicted of such an offense should be imprisoned from one to fifteen years. This penalty, however, was lessened with the passing years.[3]

To avoid confusion and dishonesty in the use of marks and brands, there must be legal recognition of the exclusive rights of cattlemen to their respective marks and brands. Accordingly, laws were enacted to require some officer in each county to record descriptions of the marks and brands of resident owners of cattle and other livestock. To provide for this service, Oregon Territory, as early as January 12, 1854, was requiring that it should "be the duty of the county clerk of each county, on the application of any person residing in such county, to record a description of the marks and brands with which said person may be desirous of marking his horses, cattle, sheep, or hogs; but the same description shall not be recorded for more than one resident of the same

[3] Matthew P. Deady and Lafayette Lane (compilers), *The Organic and Other General Laws of Oregon . . . 1843-1872* (Salem, Ore., 1874), p. 414; *Laws of Washington Territory, 1854* (first legislative session), p. 83; *Laws of Idaho, 1863-64* (Lewiston, Ida., 1864), p. 447. For a reduction of the penalty, see *The Code of Washington, 1881* (Olympia, 1881), chap. lxix, sec. 833.

county."[4] Section 2 of this law specified that no "two persons, residing within 15 miles of each other" should use the same brand, but, if two persons within a fifteen-mile limit should adopt the same brand, the one having the oldest recorded mark would be given "the preference." Nothing would, however, prevent such persons from "agreeing" which of them should change his mark or brand.[5]

In substance, the foregoing provisions for registering marks and brands persisted in Oregon. An act approved on January 23, 1887, however, authorized the appointment in each county of an inspector of livestock who would be required to keep "record books" in which he should enter "as nearly complete as practicable a description of the marks and brands with which each person in his county marks or brands his horses, cattle, sheep or hogs." This act further provided that in counties where no inspector had been appointed, the county clerk should continue to keep such records.[6]

As early as 1855, the legislature of Washington required the auditor of each county to record the marks and brands presented to him by any person residing in his county, but not to record the same description for more than one person. The person who first recorded his brand would be given the preference in case of duplication. Moreover, unless marks and brands were recorded as thus prescribed, they would not be considered lawful.[7] In its session of 1867-68, the legislature of this territory enacted a law *requiring* the owners of stock in Klickitat, Yakima, and Walla Walla counties to record with their respective county auditors their several marks, brands, and counterbrands. An owner's mark was cut into a piece of leather upon which both his brand and counter-brand were burned. In the trial of any action involving

[4] *General Laws of Oregon, 1843-1872,* p. 660. This provision is the first section of an act approved on Jan 12, 1854.

[5] William Lair Hill (ed.), *The Codes and General Laws of Oregon . . .* (San Francisco, 1887), I, 974.

[6] *Oregon Session Laws, 1877* (Salem, 1877), p. 105. On the laws of Montana and Wyoming dealing with marks and brands, see Osgood, *Day of the Cattleman,* pp. 125-27.

[7] John P. Judson and Elwood Evans (compilers), *Laws of Washington Territory* (Olympia, 1881), p. 3. This compilation consisted of laws not included in the Code of 1881 but which, nevertheless, were believed to be still in force.

the ownership of animals, an auditor's certified copy of the marks and brands of the person claiming such animals would be regarded as prima-facie evidence of ownership by such claimant. In 1875 the provisions of this act were extended to Stevens, Whitman, and Columbia counties, and two years later they were made general for the territory. In the code of 1881, the laws of Washington pertaining to this subject contain substantially the provisions of the above-mentioned laws, although this code specifies that any owner of livestock "may keep a mark, brand and counter-brand, different from the brand of his neighbors, and as far as practicable different from any others." But, having once adopted a mark and a brand, the owner must register them in the office of the county auditor.[8]

Similar laws pertaining to marks and brands were enacted in Idaho, beginning with the first session of the first legislature of that territory, and by 1877 the laws of Idaho pertaining to marks and brands differed little from such laws in either Washington or Oregon. By this time marks and brands were the established means of determining the ownership of livestock running at large in Idaho, and every owner of such livestock was required to "record with the recorder of his county, his mark, brand and counter-brand by delivering to the said recorder his mark cut upon a piece of leather, and his brand and counter-brand burnt upon it, and the same shall be kept in the recorder's office."[9] The recorder in each county, moreover, was required to send transcripts of his recorded marks and brands to recorders in adjoining counties. This was presumably that territory's first law to require the marking and branding of cattle running at large, for on November 3, 1877, the *Lewiston Teller* warned its readers that the legislature of Idaho, at its latest session had "enacted a law making it imperative for any person owning stock, such as horses, mules, cattle, sheep, goats and hogs running at large, to have them branded." Cattle were required to be marked and branded before they were twelve months old.

[8] *Laws of Washington, 1867-68*, p. 43; Frank Pierce (ed.), *Laws of Washington: A Publication of the Session Laws of Washington Territory* ... (Seattle, 1895), III, 698, IV, 808-9.

[9] *Laws of Idaho, 1863-64*, pp. 448-49; *Laws of Idaho, 1876-77*, pp. 32-33.

By this time, moreover, no person was entitled to record in Idaho more than one mark and one brand unless he operated more than one ranch, but a law approved on February 9, 1881, recognized the legality of partnership brands. Presently also the laws of Idaho recognized the right of a resident stockowner to purchase a band of cattle and to have the brand of such cattle recorded in his name. But he was required to use only one brand on the increase of this stock. Finally, in Idaho as in both Oregon and Washington, no stockman was permitted to mark an animal by cutting off more than one-half of an ear.[10]

The recording of marks and brands was the first important step in protecting stockmen in the possession of their livestock. But this was not enough, for marks and brands could be, and frequently were, misused. From the beginning, the defacing of brands and the marking and branding of livestock not one's own were declared to be serious offenses for which severe punishment was prescribed in Oregon, Washington, and Idaho.[11]

To the honest purchasers of branded cattle, the law gave suitable protection by requiring them to be given a counterbrand, the registration of which was required. Counterbranding was, in effect, the equivalent of giving a bill of sale, and was expressly so recognized in Idaho by a law approved on January 12, 1877. This law, among other things, affirmed that

all persons selling or disposing of any cattle which are not intended for slaughter, or any horses, mares, mules, jacks or jennies shall be required to counter-brand them on the shoulder or give a written descriptive bill of sale, and any person failing to so counter-brand said animals or give such written bill of sale, shall lose all benefits of this act, and all rights to use said brand as evidence in any court under this act.[12]

Laws also were enacted to protect stockmen against the unlawful slaughtering of their cattle. In both Washington and Idaho any person regularly engaged in the business of slaughtering cat-

[10] *The Revised Statutes of Idaho Territory . . . in Force June 1, 1887* (Boise City, 1887), p. 179; *Laws of Oregon, 1885*, p. 44; *Code of Washington, 1881*, p. 168.

[11] *Laws of Idaho, 1863-64*, pp. 448-49; *Laws of Washington, 1854*, p. 84; *General Laws of Oregon, 1843-72*, p. 414.

[12] *Laws of Idaho, 1876-77*, p. 34.

tle was required to keep for inspection a book containing not only complete information on the marks and brands of the animals he slaughtered, but also the names of the persons from whom he had purchased such animals. Moreover, an early Washington law required that the hides of slaughtered cattle be kept for twenty days, and an Idaho law, approved on January 12, 1877, required that persons "not regularly engaged in the business of slaughtering cattle" should keep for thirty days, with ears attached and with marks and brands intact, the hides of all the cattle they killed. During that period such hides were subject to inspection by "any owner of cattle." The need for such a law appears to have been great, for on April 8, 1878, the Boise *Idaho Tri-Weekly Statesman*, having been informed of the unlawful killing of cattle in the country "between Boise City and the Payette," called attention not only to the penalty for violating the foregoing law, but also to the penalty for branding cattle not belonging to the person who did the branding. "Cattlemen," it remarked, "request us to inform those liable to violate the above laws to beware, for they will prosecute all offenders to the full letter and extent of the law."[13]

Not only was it important to stockmen that their marks and brands should be duly recorded; it was equally important that such marks and brands should be widely known. A general knowledge of marks and brands not only would facilitate the recovery of animals which had strayed from their accustomed ranges, but would also make more difficult the successful operation of rustlers. Brand books and newspapers—newspapers of general interest as well as newspapers specifically devoted to the interests of stockmen—were the principal media for the dissemination of such information. In such journals stockmen could—and most of them did—advertise both their brands and their ranges; and now and again an alert editor of a newspaper, with one eye on his subscription list and the other on the promotion of an economic enterprise important to his community, might publish a stockmen's column, allowing all his subscribers free use

[13] *Code of Washington, 1881*, p. 444; *Laws of Idaho, 1876-77*, p. 36; *Laws of Washington, 1867-68*, p. 44; Boise *Idaho Tri-Weekly Statesman*, April 9, 1878.

of it for advertising purposes.[14] Some newspapers also played a significant role in the publication of brand books. For example, in 1878 the publishers of the Colfax *Palouse Gazette* were, according to the *Lewiston Teller* of June 28, "at work compiling a book to contain the brands of every stock owner in Nez Perce, Columbia, Stevens, and Whitman counties." This book was published in the fall of 1878.

Journalism and the law became united for the protection of stockmen when the legislative assembly of Washington, on February 4, 1886, prescribed that every county auditor in the territory should compile from his records and give to the publisher of the newspaper doing the county printing, before December 1 of each year, a list of the recorded owners of stock, together with a description of their respective marks and brands, for publication "in three successive numbers of such newspaper during the month of December."[15] One of the consequences of this act was to hasten the revision of a brand book, published in the preceding autumn, that would include the marks and brands recorded in Whitman County, Washington. On March 5, 1886, the publishers of the Colfax *Palouse Gazette* announced that they were printing a "new mark and brand book" which would contain, besides the stock laws of the territory, all the brands on record in Whitman County, "as well as all the brands contained in the book printed last fall." This new book would be given to new subscribers to the *Gazette* who paid a year in advance and to old subscribers who "paid up arrearages and one year in advance." To nonsubscribers it would be sold for $1.50 a copy, but those who had bought a copy of the book printed during the preceding autumn could obtain a copy of the new book for 50 cents. This book was ready for sale by June of 1886. In December of that year, pursuant to law, all the registered marks and brands in Whitman County were published in a four-page supplement to the *Palouse Gazette*.[16]

[14] The Cheney *Northwest Tribune* conducted such a column through several years of the 1880's.

[15] *Laws of Washington, 1885-86*, p. 118.

[16] A list of all the recorded marks and brands in Whitman County appeared in a supplement to the issue of the Colfax *Palouse Gazette* for Dec. 17, 1886, a copy of which I found in the bound file of the publisher.

Legislation dealing with the subject of estrays claimed the attention of lawmaking bodies early in the history of the Oregon Country.[17] Although such laws were amended from time to time, the main principles informing legislation on this subject remained constant, with the result that the comparable laws of Washington, Oregon, and Idaho differed only in details.[18] Accordingly, the provisions relating to estrays in the Washington Code of 1881 may be used to illustrate legislation on this subject throughout the Oregon Country. Here we observe that, subject to the exceptions to be noted, any householder might take up an estray found near his property, but within ten days of so doing he was required to post descriptive notices of such animal in three public places in the county, one of which must be in the precinct in which the estray was taken up. No animal bearing a brand recorded in the county in which the animal was roaming could be considered an estray, and no animal, except one that was either breachy or vicious,[19] could be taken up as an estray between April 15 and December 15. Within ten days after the posting of the notices, the owner might reclaim the animal by paying the costs incurred by the one who took it up; if the owner could prove that the man who took it up knew who owned the animal and did not notify him before posting the required notices, the person taking up the animal could recover nothing from the owner.

If no claimant appeared within ten days after the posting of the notices, the person taking up the estray was required to get the nearest justice of the peace to appraise the impounded animal and report the result of such appraisal to the county auditor, who would then, pursuant to the law pertaining to estrays, make a record of the matter in a book designated as the county Record of Estrays. If the owner did not establish his title within thirty days after the filing of the notice of appraisal with the county

[17] See, for example, *Laws of Washington, 1854*, pp. 380-82.
[18] For purposes of comparison, see the account of the laws on estrays in Montana and Wyoming in Osgood, *Day of the Cattleman*, 125-28.
[19] For early laws on the subject of vicious cattle in the Oregon Country, see *Statutes of a General Nature Passed by the Legislative Assembly of the Territory of Oregon at the Second Session Begun and Held at Oregon City, December 2, 1850* (Oregon City, 1851), pp. 65-66. See also the *Laws of Washington, 1854*, p. 445.

auditor, the estray (after due notice of the intention to do so had been given) would be sold by public auction. The proceeds of such sale were deposited in the county treasury for the benefit of the common schools of the county, but the owner of property thus sold might recover the money by establishing his title to the estray within six months after the proceeds of the sale had been deposited.

To protect owners against the abuse of the right to take up estrays, the law specified that any person taking up an estray should forfeit all right to compensation if he worked, or in any way used, the animal that he had taken up, or if he removed it for more than three days at a time from the county in which it was taken up. Moreover, a person who took up an estray without complying with the requirements of the law in respect to this matter rendered himself liable not only for damages double the value of the animal impounded, but also for the costs of a suit to recover such damages. All moneys collected as fines under the provisions of the law pertaining to estrays were required to be paid into the county treasury for the benefit of the common schools of the county.[20]

The operation in 1868 of the law of Washington then pertaining to estrays may be illustrated by a few entries taken from Book A, Record of Estrays, in Walla Walla County, Washington. Here, among other entries, we read that the action in respect to an estray taken up by W. W. Markham was as follows:

> Taken up by the undersigned living 2½ miles west of Walla Walla City one dark red cow seven or eight years old, brand S on the left hip and E.S. on the right thigh and marked with an under half crop in each ear. Also a small deep lop, said cow came to my premises in June last.
>
> W. W. Markham
>
> Walla Walla Co.
> February 10th, 1868
>
> This is to certify that we have this day appraised the above described cow at $30.00 dollars.
>
> D. M. Coonc
> H. Bergman

[20] *Code of Washington, 1881*, pp. 442-43. See also the *General Laws of Oregon, 1843-72*, pp. 589-91, and the *Laws of Idaho, 1874-75*, pp. 146-49.

Walla Walla March 3rd, 1868.
Territory of Washington
County of Walla Walla

ss

H. Bergman being first duly sworn says he in connection with
D. M. Coonc made the foregoing appraisement and that the same
is just and correct as he verily believes.

H. Bergman

Subscribed and sworn to before me March 3, 1868.

J. H. Blewett
County Auditor

Recorded March 3, A. D. 1868
    J. H. Blewett
    County Auditor

Territory of Washington
County of Walla Walla

ss

J. R. Courtnay being first duly sworn says the above described
estray animal is his property.

J. R. Courtnay

Subscribed and sworn to before
me April 20, 1868

J. H. Blewett
County Auditor

Advertisements calling attention to the fact that estrays had
been taken up appeared frequently in newspapers in the Oregon
Country. As early as July 8, 1854, A. J. Bolon, Indian agent in
the "Yakamaw Valley," Washington Territory, inserted in an
Olympia newspaper descriptive notices of several head of es-
trayed cattle that had been found by an Indian in the Cascade
Mountains during the preceding autumn. Mr. Bolon requested
the owners of these animals to pay the costs incurred in taking
care of them if they did not wish him to "proceed according to
the law regulating waifs and strays."[21] As late as the 1880's, Washington newspapers published estray notices, such as one copied
from a Spokane County paper:

Taken up, Jan. 2, one red and white steer, 2 years old next spring. No
visible brand. Marked, crop off of left ear, underbit. The owner may have

---

[21] Olympia *Pioneer and Democrat*, Aug. 26, 1854.

same by calling at my place 5 miles northwest of Cheney. Also 1 lined black roan and white steer, two years old next spring, slant crop off of left ear and no brand to be seen. Owner can have same by proving property and paying charge.

C. W. Murphy, Cheney, W. T.[22]

In order that hunters of estrays might not accidentally drive off animals not their own, a law of Washington Territory, approved on January 29, 1868, for Walla Walla, Yakima, and Klickitat counties, provided that it should be the duty of all persons hunting estrays in these counties

to drive the band or herd in which they may find their stray horses, mules or cattle, into the nearest corral before separating their said estray animals from the balance of the herd or band; that in order to separate their said stray animals from the herd or band, the person or persons owning said stray [animals] shall drive them out of and away from the corral into which they may be driven before setting the herd or band at large.

One year later the provisions of this act were extended, without the approval of the Governor of the territory, to all the counties of Washington Territory.[23]

A similar statute, enacted in Oregon in 1878, forbade any person not the owner to remove from its habitual range any animal for a "distance of more than ten miles," and a later Idaho law made it a misdemeanor for any person, "not the owner or entitled to the possession" thereof, to remove, "knowingly and wilfully," any "head of live stock away from its usual range," unless he corraled and separated "the same at the first suitable corral that . . . [could] be obtained."[24]

In the late 1870's the legislature of Idaho set on foot in certain counties of that territory an experiment, mentioned in passing in a preceding chapter, which had for its objects the more orderly conduct of roundups and the more effective protection of the property of cattlemen in these counties. This experiment, one of decentralized but required administration, rested on an act approved on January 12, 1877, which instructed the commissioners

[22] *Northwest Tribune*, March 4, 1886.
[23] *Laws of Washington, 1867-68*, pp. 74-75; *Laws of Washington, 1869*, pp. 408-9.
[24] *Laws of Oregon, 1878*, p. 10; *Revised Statutes of Idaho, 1887*, p. 741.

in each affected county to divide their county into not more than twelve stock districts. For each district the commissioners would appoint for one year a stock board of three resident stockowners, of whom one would be designated chairman and another clerk. Between April 1 and August 1 each district would hold the annual roundup, which members of the stock board would attend for the purpose of settling disputes about ownership. Each owner of twenty-five or more head of cattle in a district (dairy and work cattle excepted) was required to attend the district roundup. Roundups in adjoining districts could not be held simultaneously.

Each stock board was required to provide itself with a book of record and with a district brand and a district counterbrand, both of which were to be duly recorded. The clerk was required to keep in the book of record descriptions of all unclaimed livestock, and, after a general roundup in his district, he was to send transcripts of these descriptions to the other district clerks in his county, who were required to record and keep them as a public record.

The foregoing provisions did not apply to the counties of Alturas, Nez Percé, Idaho, Shoshone, Bear Lake, Owyhee, and Boise. Section 13 of this act reads as follows:

Whenever the owner, agent of the owner, or parties in charge of any cattle shall desire to remove such cattle from the range on which they have been running for the space of 10 days or more, to another range ten miles or more distant, they are hereby required to give three days' notice to the stock owners having cattle on such range, before such removal, in order that such stock owners may separate their stock; and the said owner, agent, or parties in possession, shall be further required to gather or round up their cattle for that purpose. . . .[25]

This section did not apply to the counties listed above nor to Ada County.

The foregoing stock-districting law apparently gave satisfaction, for the legislature of Idaho, on January 28, 1881, enacted a similar law for Bear County, and two years later it enacted a slightly modified act providing for the creation of stock districts in Idaho County. The act of 1883 required semiannual roundups in Idaho County, the first one to be held between March 15 and

[25] *Laws of Idaho, 1876-77*, pp. 27-32. See Chapter VI, note 70, above.

May 15 and the second between September 1 and November 1. It also provided for the sale of unclaimed stock thirty days after the end of the roundup. The principle of decentralized administration, however, was fully preserved in the last-named act.[26]

In some counties of Idaho the property rights of cattlemen were subjected to unusual dangers during the late 1870's and early 1880's on account of the driving of many herds of cattle eastward through Idaho from Oregon and Washington. Apparently in an effort to solve a problem which had become acute, the Idaho Legislature enacted an emergency statute, approved on February 9, 1881, requiring that all livestock driven through Idaho Territory carry a road brand. Moreover, this act made it "the imperative duty of every stock-drover or his assistants, each day to carefully search through and examine his herd or drove after driving or moving them over any portion of this Territory, and separate from, and drive and keep away from his herd or drove, all livestock not belonging thereto." Upon the petition of five resident stock raisers, the county commissioners of any county in Idaho were required to appoint, for the purpose of inspection, one or more experienced stockmen to detect violations of this law, or of any other law of the territory relating to livestock. Such officer or officers would be authorized to arrest without warrant any violator of the provisions of this act.[27] The special nature of the problem which this act was intended to solve is revealed by the fact that its provisions did not apply to Nez Percé, Idaho, and Shoshone counties, through which no cattle trails passed. In northern Idaho, the Mullan Road passed through Kootenai County, and in southern Idaho the cattle trails leading to Wyoming ran south of Idaho County. Four years later another Idaho statute, whose enactment may well have been caused by unlawful activities of drovers, made it an offense punishable as grand larceny for a person in Idaho to use, or even to have in his possession, any instrument for "running a brand on any live stock."[28]

---

[26] *Laws of Idaho, 1880-81*, pp. 330-35; *The Local and Special Laws of Idaho Remaining in Force June 1, 1887* (Boise City, 1887), pp. 135-39.

[27] *Laws of Idaho, 1881*, p. 299.

[28] This law, which amended a previous act, was approved on Feb. 5, 1885.

The theft of their livestock was not the only hazard confronting stockmen in the Oregon Country. Everywhere in that vast region—in Oregon, Washington, and Idaho—some lurking disease might at any time strike their herds or flocks. But legislatures possessed a police power not only to protect their stockmen against the importation of domestic animals known to be diseased, but also to require in their respective jurisdictions the segregation of domestic animals stricken with disease. By 1862 in Oregon, and 1866 in Washington, such legislative power was so exercised. In an act approved on November 26, 1869, the legislative assembly of Washington Territory reaffirmed such earlier prohibitions and requirements of segregation, and prescribed appropriate penalties for violations; and in 1873 it enacted, and the Governor of Washington Territory approved, an act empowering any person aggrieved by a violation of the act of 1869 to collect damages in a civil suit before any court of competent jurisdiction. Laws on this subject similar to those of Washington were presently enacted by the legislature of Oregon.[29]

During the late 1860's, an epidemic of "Texas" or Spanish fever was destroying cattle by the thousands in states east of the Rocky Mountains, and in an endeavor to check its ravages several states in the upper Mississippi Valley—notably Missouri, Iowa, and Illinois—enacted drastic laws, even going so far as to prohibit the importation of Texas cattle into their respective jurisdictions. In the autumn of 1869, cattle from Texas began to trickle into the Oregon Country, and fear of Texas fever led the legislative assembly of Washington Territory, on December 1 of that year, to enact over the Governor's veto a law prohibiting "the introduction of Texas cattle, or cattle infected with what is known as the Texas cattle disease or Spanish fever, into the territory of Washington."[30] This law, modeled on the plan of similar laws in Illi-

---

Laws of Idaho, 1884-85, p. 61. Late in June, 1885, an editor in Idaho City reprinted it for the instruction of "growers of cattle" in Idaho, and he admonished all such persons to "take notice of the law passed at the last session of the Idaho legislature relating to branding cattle with a running iron." Idaho Semi-Weekly World, June 28, 1885.

[29] Eugene Oregon Sentinel, Nov. 29, 1862; Laws of Washington, 1865-66, p. 107; Laws of Washington 1869, p. 378; Laws of Washington 1873, p. 482; Laws of Oregon, 1872, p. 121; ibid., 1874, pp. 100-1.

[30] Report of John Gamgee in the U. S. Commissioner of Agriculture, Report on

nois and Iowa, was no doubt prompted by the outbreak of Texas fever in California early in the autumn of 1869 and the simultaneous bringing of some Texas cattle into southwestern Idaho and eastern Oregon. About the danger of introducing such cattle, the *Oregon Weekly Statesman*, in a pointed editorial of September 24, 1869, minced no words. It called attention to the arrival in Idaho of cattle from Texas and urged that caution be used to "prevent the spread of the terrible contagion" through Oregon. "Farmers and drovers," it said, "cannot be too careful in efforts to avoid letting stock follow in the wake of Texas cattle." Whether the danger of such disease was or was not imminent in the Pacific Northwest, the above-mentioned law of Washington Territory evoked favorable comment in both eastern and western Oregon. In January, 1870, an editor in The Dalles not only condemned the importation of "cultus" Texas cattle into Oregon, but also praised the Washington statute prohibiting such importation; and he expressed the hope that the Oregon Legislature would enact a similar law at its next session. Moreover, in February, 1870, it was reported that the managers of the State Agricultural Society of Oregon had adopted a resolution disapproving the importation into Oregon of cattle from Texas.[31]

State or territorial laws prohibiting the importation of cattle from Texas, however, clashed with the delegated power of the Congress to regulate interstate commerce. Such laws, in effect, established embargoes, and consequently obstructed, to some extent, the channels of interstate commerce. As early as December 18, 1869, the editor of the *Walla Walla Statesman* announced that the "law of this character which was vetoed on the ground of unconstitutionality, but subsequently passed over the veto [by the legislative assembly of Washington Territory]," had been rendered null and void by a United States Supreme Court decision invalidating an Illinois law prohibiting the introduction into Illi-

---

the *Diseases of Cattle in the United States* (Washington, D.C., 1871), pp. 82 ff.; U. S. Commissioner of Agriculture, *Report* (1869), pp. 406, 409; Railroad Co. v. Husen, 95 U.S. 465 (1877); *Laws of Washington, 1869*, pp. 404-5.

[31] Salem *Daily Oregon Statesman*, Sept. 24, 26, 1869; Martin Schmitt, "Introduction" to *The Cattle Drives of David Shirk from Texas to the Idaho Mines, 1871 and 1873* (Portland, Ore., 1956), p. iv; The Dalles *Weekly Mountaineer*, Jan. 4, 1870; Olympia *Pacific Tribune*, Feb. 19, 1870.

nois of cattle from Texas. "The court held," this editor continued, "that the Legislature might just as well have prohibited the introduction of Kentucky whiskey or Connecticut clocks."

But, despite this decision, the supreme court of Illinois was not yet persuaded to adopt this view. In 1871 it upheld a statute of Illinois, approved on February 27, 1867, prohibiting the importation into Illinois of either Texas or Cherokee cattle. It reasoned that, if "the enactment is within the police power of the State, then the constitutional question is not involved." Affirming that the power to determine whether "the importation of cattle should be permitted on conditions, or wholly prevented," was a matter "peculiarly within the province of the law-making power," it concluded that the legislature, "by virtue of the police power," had the right to enact the law in question.[32]

Such reasoning the Supreme Court of the United States overruled in 1877, in a decision brought up on a writ of error to the supreme court of Missouri. This case involved the constitutionality of a statute of Missouri, approved on January 23, 1872, which prohibited the bringing into Missouri of any Texas, Mexican, or Indian cattle between March 1 and November 1 in any year. Mr. Justice William Strong, who delivered the opinion of the Court, held that the power of the Congress to regulate interstate commerce is exclusive, and that the statute in question was an unwarranted exercise of the police power vested in the state of Missouri. The unquestioned power of a state to enact laws providing for quarantine or inspection could not be invoked, he said, to justify the regulation of interstate commerce by a state.[33] Accordingly, all such laws as that of Washington Territory prohibiting the importation into that territory of cattle from Texas were unconstitutional.

But the opinion of the Supreme Court of the United States in respect to such prohibitory laws, although unimpeachable from the standpoint of consitutional law, did not solve the problem of the dissemination of infectious or contagious diseases. As a result of this decision, however, prohibitory laws were superseded in

[32] Yeazel v. Alexander, 58 Ill. 254 (1871).
[33] Railroad Co. v. Husen, 95 U. S. 465 (1877). See also Osgood, *Day of the Cattleman*, pp. 163-64.

states east of the Rockies by laws providing for strict inspection and quarantine, and such laws were within the competency of the states to enforce.[34] But for several years laws of this sort were not enacted in the Pacific Northwest. Because cattle from Texas had ceased to come into the Oregon Country by 1874, the fear of Texas fever had subsided there. In the 1880's when there was danger that cattle imported from states in the East might disseminate in the Pacific Northwest the dreaded disease of pleuro-pneumonia, the legislative assembly of Washington Territory was so indifferent to this subject that the Governor of the territory, in his biennial message to this legislature in 1887, after calling attention to the threat of "certain diseases like pleuro-pneumonia," not only raised his voice in warning, but urged upon this body immediate action to protect the livestock of Washington Territory from such diseases. He recommended the passage of laws "modeled after those of other states [sic], where the subject has received due attention, by which the herds and flocks of Washington may be protected from contact with animals from infected districts."[35]

In 1889 the legislatures of both Oregon and Idaho, now aware of the danger of such diseases, enacted laws creating livestock boards or commissions. In principle, these two laws were alike. Each one authorized the establishment of quarantine regulations, the destruction of diseased animals, and the promulgation of regulations to guard against the importation of diseased animals from other states or territories; and each of them provided for some compensation to the owners of animals destroyed by order of the livestock board or commission. In Idaho, the compensation was to be drawn from a county stock-indemnity fund maintained by a special tax of not more than one mill on each dollar invested in livestock within the county; but in Oregon compensation to the owners of diseased animals destroyed pursuant to law was made a general obligation of the state.[36]

Laws intended to protect the herds or flocks of stockmen from

[34] Joseph Nimmo, Jr., *Report in Regard to the Range and Ranch Cattle Business of the United States, May 16, 1885* (Washington, D.C., 1885), pp. 134-37.

[35] Eugene Semple, *Biennial Message, 1887-88* (Olympia, Wash., 1887), pp. 12-13.

[36] The Idaho law was approved on Feb. 7, 1889, and the Oregon law was ap-

diseases were paralleled by other laws intended to help them
protect their cattle and other livestock from predatory animals.
As early as 1854, a law of Washington Territory authorized county commissioners to offer bounties for the killing of wild animals;
and both Oregon and Idaho eventually had similar laws on their
statute books. Such laws, more or less revised from time to time,
continued in force during the period of this study.[37]

The need of collective action to protect their herds against
predatory animals was perceived by settlers in the Willamette
Valley in the early years of colonization; and the so-called "wolf
meetings," held there in the early months of 1843, opened the
way to the formation of the Oregon Provisional Government.
That wolves and other predatory animals were a menace to the
livestock of the early pioneers in Oregon need not be doubted.
As early as February, 1851, the *Oregon Spectator* published a
letter describing a society formed to destroy wolves, cougars, and
panthers in the southeastern part of Marion County, and many
years later John Minto wrote that the "chief enemies of early
home building [in Oregon] were the carnivori, of which the large
wolf was the most destructive," for it attacked "all kinds of
stock." The wolves, he said, "kept range cattle wild and made
swine band together in self defence."[38]

Depredations of wild animals upon flocks and herds in the
Oregon Country continued through many years. Cougars were
killing calves near Oregon City in the summer of 1873; wolves
were killing cattle in Patton's Valley, Washington County, Oregon, early in 1875; cougars were killing cattle in Whatcom County, Washington, in 1883; wolves were killing cattle in Bear Lake
County, Idaho, in 1887; and cougars were killing cattle in central
Oregon as late as 1908. Still other animals at times menaced
herds. Bears perhaps did the greatest damage. They were attacking cattle in Jackson County, Oregon, in the spring of 1874, and

---

proved on Feb. 25, 1889. *Laws of Idaho, 1888-89,* pp. 47-53; *Laws of Oregon,*
1889, p. 93-95.
  [37] *Laws of Washington, 1854,* p. 407; *Laws of Idaho, 1884-85,* pp. 25-26;
Laws of Oregon, 1887, pp. 74-75.
  [38] La Fayette Grover (ed.), *The Oregon Archives* (Salem, 1853), pp. 8-9,
14-15; Oregon City *Oregon Spectator,* Feb. 20, 1851; John Minto, "From Youth to
Age as an American," *OHQ,* IX (1908), 149.

on More's Creek, in Idaho, they were reported to be "killing the calves and hogs off at a lively rate" in September, 1875. Four years later the farmers in one precinct of Pierce County, Washington, were "so harassed" by wild animals that they formed a protective union and established "a cash bounty of $20 a panther or bear killed by a member of the union."[39]

By 1880, grizzly bears were destroying cattle in south-central Oregon. In May it was reported that four grizzlies had killed more than one hundred calves belonging to John Jackson in Lake County, and more than three years later Avery and James of Chewaucan said that grizzly bears were reported to have killed from seventy-five to one hundred head of cattle on the Little Chewaucan within a period of three weeks. Cattlemen there were offering a bounty of thirty dollars "for every bear killed on that range." As late as April, 1886, a grizzly bear that "had been preying upon the cattle to a costly extent" was killed on the Sprague River in Klamath County, Oregon. The death of this bear, we are told, was "not regretted by the ranchers" of that part of Oregon.[40]

Other protective laws were enacted from time to time in the interest of stockmen in the Oregon Country. In Idaho Territory, for example, a law of January 10, 1873, applicable only to Alturas County, required the owners of all quartz mills to fence their dumps and reservoirs that contained substances injurious to the health of livestock; and still another Idaho law, this one of general application, protected the owners of livestock against losses resulting from the carelessness of ranchers to whom such owners had entrusted their herds or flocks.[41]

The annual losses of cattle from the hazards of the ranges in the Oregon Country were not insignificant. According to the Gordon Report, such loss of cattle more than twelve months old

---

[39] Sacramento Daily Union, July 23, 1873; Portland Morning Oregonian, Feb. 6, 1875; Yakima Signal, Oct. 13, 1883, quoting the Whatcom Reveille; Sacramento Daily Union, March 29, 1874; Boise Idaho Weekly Statesman, Sept. 18, 1875; Morning Oregonian, Oct. 29, 1879.

[40] Canyon City Grant County News, May 29, 1880; Salem Willamette Farmer, Nov. 2, 1883, quoting the Lakeview Lake County Examiner; ibid., April 23, 1886.

[41] Compiled and Revised Laws of Idaho, 1874-75, p. 741; Revised Statutes of Idaho Territory, 1887, p. 185.

from the ravages of diseases, predatory animals, and inclement weather was presumed to be 6.3 per cent in Oregon, 14.5 per cent in Washington, and 10 per cent in Idaho.[42]

A new hazard to stockmen of the Oregon County, one which spread rapidly and widely with the passing years, arose with the introduction of railroads into this region. Here was a menace to property interests that required protective legislation. As early as the spring of 1872, the editor of the *Willamette Farmer* complained that trains were killing cattle in considerable numbers in the Willamette Valley, and he urged the enactment of a law to compel railway companies to fence their tracks. Some months later, in the autumn of 1873, the editor of the *Eugene Journal* accused locomotive engineers, rightly or wrongly, of seeming "to delight in killing or crippling cattle and other stock."[43]

As the menace was made more obvious by the rapid building of railroads in Oregon, Washington, and Idaho during the 1880's, public opinion forced legislative bodies in the Pacific Northwest to come to grips with this problem. By November, 1883, the legislative assembly of Washington Territory had enacted a law making railway companies liable "for the full value" of livestock killed or maimed by their trains; but it exempted all such companies from liability if their roads were fenced "with a good lawful fence." Four years later both Oregon and Idaho enacted similar laws. The Oregon law, an emergency measure of February 21, 1887, made railway companies liable for injury to livestock by moving trains on unfenced tracks, and it required such companies to file notices giving adequate descriptions of all livestock so killed. By that year every railroad company operating in Idaho Territory was required to fence its tracks wherever the line of its road was contiguous to private property; but by paying the owners of such lands to make and maintain lawful fences between their respective lands and the railway tracks, a company would escape liability to such persons if one of its trains killed any of their animals. Such companies would be liable, however,

[42] *Tenth Federal Census, 1880,* Vol. III, *Agriculture* (Washington, D.C., 1883), pp. 1083, 1091, 1099.

[43] *Willamette Farmer,* April 6, 1872; *Sacramento Daily Union,* Oct. 10, 1873, quoting the Eugene *Journal.* As late as 1886, trains in Colorado were killing cattle by the hundreds. Denver *Field and Farm,* April 24, 1886.

242   ON THE CATTLE RANGES OF THE OREGON COUNTRY

if, through their own fault, animals were killed by their trains. Each railroad company operating in Idaho was required to keep a record book at a principal station in each county in which it operated, and to enter in this book adequate descriptions of all animals maimed or killed in that county by its trains.[44] By 1887 there was an anomalous situation in Washington Territory. In that year the territorial supreme court held that the Washington laws did not require cattle to be fenced in or herded, and did not require railway tracks to be fenced. Consequently, it was not negligence on the part of the owner to permit his cattle to go upon a railway track, even though he knew that it was unfenced. Nor was a railroad company negligent if it permitted its track to remain unfenced. Nevertheless, as the court held, railway engineers could be expected to do what prudent men should do, and, circumstances permitting, to bring their trains "to a standstill" rather than injure livestock.[45]

Fencing laws touched still other matters affecting grazing interests in the Oregon Country, and consequently the need to determine what constituted a lawful fence was, from an early day, recognized by all legislative bodies in the Pacific Northwest. Although many of the laws pertaining to fencing in Oregon, Washington, and Idaho had only local or regional application, a general principle underlay all of them—namely, that the owners of cultivated fields were debarred from legal actions to recover damages from the owners of livestock which trespassed thereon unless the fields were enclosed with lawful fences.[46] How this principle was applied in three Idaho counties by an act approved on January 7, 1873, the following text will show:

All farming lands used for raising grain, grass, or other agricultural purposes, in the Counties of Nez Perce, Oneida and Idaho, in said Territory, to enable the owner, or possessor thereof, to maintain an action for damages to the same, shall be enclosed with a good and lawful fence, sufficient to

[44] *Laws of Washington, 1883*, pp. 51-52; *Laws of Oregon, 1887*, pp. 51-52; *Revised Statutes of Idaho, 1887*, p. 332.
[45] Timm and Forck v. Northern Pacific Railway Company, 3 Wash. Ter. Rep. 299 (1887).
[46] According to the Winnemucca *Silver State* of June 18, 1880, the Supreme Court of Nevada, in the case of Chase v. Chase, held that, in the absence of a law of Nevada defining a lawful fence, "the fence must be high enough and sufficient in other respects to prevent ordinary stock from breaking into the enclosure. This

secure the crops therein from the encroachments of all kinds of domestic animals.[47]

The introduction of barbed-wire fences into the Oregon Country led to the enactment of additional laws for the regulation of fencing in this region. These laws defined lawful barbed-wire fences, and prescribed remedies for the owners of livestock injured by fences that did not pass the test of legality.[48] Such laws were, perhaps, of more importance to horse breeders than to cattle breeders. Yet by 1885 the Oregon Legislature had enacted a law providing for one kind of barbed-wire fence for the predominantly grazing country east of the Cascade Mountains and another law providing for a different kind of barbed-wire fence for the more highly developed agricultural country west of these mountains.[49]

Although perhaps of less significance to stockmen in the Oregon Country than the problem of enclosed fields, the problem of migratory herds and flocks was as annoying as it was enduring. Herds and flocks owned in one state or territory could not lawfully be prevented from grazing on open ranges of another state or territory; but to taxpaying residents of, say, Washington Territory it seemed unfair that stockmen residing in Oregon could escape taxation by driving their herds or flocks to ranges in Washington and grazing them there during the period of property assessment in Oregon. To prevent such "unfairness," laws were enacted in Oregon, Washington, and Idaho for the purpose of laying taxes on migratory herds and flocks.[50] Besides "equaliz-

said the *Silver State*] is the first decision on the points involved made in this State."

[47] *Laws of Idaho, 1872-73*, p. 26. Ten years later specific acts gave this law effect in the counties of Bear Lake, Cassia, Idaho, and Boise. *Laws of Idaho, 1882-83*, pp. 124, 130, 132.

[48] *Code of Washington, 1881*, p. 227; *Laws of Idaho, 1880-81*, pp. 306-7; *Laws of Oregon, 1885*, pp. 40-41, 113. The barbed-wire fence evoked much discussion, which led to frequent changes in the law pertaining to this matter. See, for example, the *Idaho Tri-Weekly Statesman*, Jan. 15, 1881, and the *Palouse Gazette*, June 4, 1886, quoting the *Pomeroy Times*.

[49] *Laws of Oregon, 1885*, p. 113; *Laws of Oregon* (Special Session, 1885), pp. 40-41. For Oregon see also *Hill's Code, 1887*, II, 1509-15, and for Washington see *Laws of Washington, 1887-88*, pp. 95-96.

[50] *General Laws of Oregon, 1843-72*, pp. 768-69. According to the *Idaho Tri-Weekly Statesman* of Jan 9, 1875, many stockmen of Idaho kept livestock in Oregon or Washington to escape high taxes in Idaho.

ing" the burden of taxation, such laws required the owners o
migratory livestock to pay something for the use of ranges which
it might be argued from the standpoint of abstract justice, tax
paying residents of a state or territory had a better right to use.[51]
Whether justly or not, the legislature of Oregon, as early as 1864
decreed that

> All cattle, sheep, horses, hogs and other stock driven into this state fo
> pasture or to a market from other states or territories, or driven throug]
> this state to a market in any other state or territory, shall be assessed a
> personal property is assessed in this state, in any county where such trans:
> ent stock may be found; and the tax so assessed, shall be immediately co]
> lected from the owner or owners of such transient stock.

But this law also decreed that in any year the owner of migrator
stock would not be required to pay taxes on those animals i
more than one county of Oregon.[52]

Three years later the legislative assembly of Washington Ter
ritory enacted a law declaring that all livestock which remaine
for thirty days in any county should be "liable to taxes equal i
assessment to the stock of actual settlers in said county," but suc
taxes could not be levied in more than one county. On Decembe
2, 1869, a law embodying, *mutatis mutandis*, the language of th
above-quoted law of Oregon, was approved for Washington Te
ritory.[53]

Since, however, the provision making liable to taxation live
stock driven *through* a state or territory to a market beyond wa
of doubtful constitutionality, this provision was omitted from
subsequent statute of Washington Territory, enacted on Januar
29, 1886, to make livestock driven into any county of Washingto
after the first Monday in April subject to taxation as though suc
livestock had actually been in that county at the time of th

---

[51] Such taxes, however, threatened to provoke local "taxing wars." As early
Oct. 14, 1872, the *Sacramento Daily Union* published as one of its "Orege
Items" this short story: "The tax collector of Umatilla county, Oregon, is levy[in
taxes upon cattle from Walla Walla county, Washington Territory, that graze ov
the line. The Walla Wallaians threaten to retaliate."

[52] *General Laws of Oregon, 1843-72*, pp. 768-69.

[53] *Laws of Washington, 1866-67*, p. 142; *Laws of Washington, 1869*, pp. 19
94. The "raiding" or "monopolizing" of ranges claimed by settlers had become
serious a matter by the middle of the 1880's that presently meetings of citize
were held in Whitman County, Washington, and in Grant County, Oregon, to co

annual assessment. A similar law, enacted in Idaho during the legislative session of 1884-85, specifically exempted from assessment "live stock on the trail and being moved through the Territory or out of it." But the Oregon law of 1864 providing for the taxation of migratory livestock remained unchanged not only in the Oregon Code of 1887, but also in the revision of that code published in 1892.[54]

It was one thing to enact laws that would protect the interests of cattlemen; it was something else, in a sparsely settled country, to enforce such laws by the established agencies of government.[55] Consequently, cattlemen on the ranges of the Oregon Country used the experience of men on other American frontiers to solve some of their problems. Here, as in Weld County, Colorado, stockmen would have affirmed that it was proper for them to take such action as might be needed for "the prevention of stealing; the detention and punishment of thieves if stealing occurs; securing better order and method in conducting the collection and handling of stock at the round-ups; and ... [improving] the breed of cattle...."[56] To achieve such objects, cattlemen throughout the American West formed voluntary associations charged with the duty of seeing to it that "justice" was done.

Sooner or later, cattlemen everywhere in the Pacific Northwest came to perceive the advantages of such association. Even the most powerful cattlemen—men so well equipped that they could conduct their own roundups—joined associations for the purpose of promoting and protecting the interests of stockmen. Local associations of cattlemen no doubt often evolved from informal district organizations, or cattle clubs, under whose auspices dis-

sider means to dissuade transient stockmen from "raiding" the "home range" of settlers. *Palouse Gazette*, July 17, 1885; *Morning Oregonian*, Feb. 2, 1888.

[54] *Laws of Washington, 1885-86*, pp. 94-95; *Laws of Idaho, 1884-85*, p. 136; *Hill's Code, 1887*, II, 1311; *ibid., 1892*, II, 1311.

[55] Even in older communities organizations formed for "self-help" persisted long after agencies of law enforcement were well established. On Oct. 20, 1881, the Yankton *Press and Dakotan* announced that the "anti-horse-stealing association of Illinois, Iowa and Missouri would hold their regular annual meeting in Keokuk, Iowa, commencing Oct. 21st."

[56] Remarks of J. L. Bailey, president of the Colorado Stock-Growers' Association, at the meeting held to form the Weld County Stock-Growers' Association. Denver *Rocky Mountain News*, Feb. 16, 1873.

trict roundups were held.[57] Such associations were characteristic of the Columbia Basin, where physiographic and economic conditions were not favorable to large-scale organization.[58] Neither here nor elsewhere in the Oregon Country was there any organization comparable in power to that of the Wyoming Stock Growers' Association, the Colorado Stock Growers' Association, or the Montana Stock Growers' Association.[59] For the period before 1890, no evidence has been found of a state-wide association of stockmen either in Oregon or in Washington; and most certainly there was no association representing the interests of all the cattlemen of both Oregon and Washington.

In contrast to the local or district associations in the Columbia Basin, some larger associations emerged in the Winnemucca province. Cattlemen there formed local and regional associations, as they did elsewhere in the American West. In the spring of 1881, an association of cattlemen in Baker County, Oregon, adopted resolutions opposing the branding of livestock not known to belong to those doing the branding, and favoring the appointment of a judiciary committee to adjust among its members all matters pertaining to the ownership of livestock. A year later the *Prineville News* advised the local association of stockmen to "tax each member, according to the amount of stock owned, to a sufficient amount to import a number of thoroughbreds, to be turned on the range for the general use of all." In Lake County, Oregon, as early as January, 1881, cattlemen were reportedly banding together to offer a five-hundred-dollar reward for the

---

[57] Interestingly, county associations were formed in Colorado as auxiliaries to the Colorado Stock Growers' Association. *Rocky Mountain News*, Feb. 12, April 5, 1873.

[58] Lewiston *Idaho Signal*, Aug. 17, 1872; *Weekly Mountaineer*, June 12, 1875; *Palouse Gazette*, Jan. 6, 1880; *Willamette Farmer*, March 25, 1881; *Walla Walla Union*, Jan. 31, 1882, and May 8, 1886; *Lewiston Teller*, Sept. 9, 1886.

[59] On these and other stockmen's associations, see Osgood, *Day of the Cattleman*, pp. 118-19, 122-23, 132, 135-37, 158-62, and *passim*; Harold E. Briggs, *Frontiers of the Northwest* (New York, 1940), pp. 266-69; Maurice Frink *et al.*, *When Grass Was King* (Boulder, Colo., 1956), pp. 69, 89, 93, 406, 421; *Rocky Mountain News*, April 19, 1871, Feb. 1, 1872, Jan. 6, 1882. As early as January, 1885, the Colorado Stock Growers' Association was reported to have 300 members who controlled 750,000 head of cattle in Colorado. *National Live-Stock Journal*, XVI (January, 1885), 43.

arrest and conviction of anybody guilty of stealing livestock or altering brands.[60]

But Oregon cattlemen operating east of the Blue Mountains, men whose herds grazed along the streams which ran southeastwardly to the Snake River, and cattlemen farther south, whose herds grazed in the country drained by the Owyhee River and its numerous tributaries, were drawn into associations with cattlemen of Idaho and Nevada. In 1883, for example, there was formed in Silver City, Idaho, an association of stockmen from Baker County, Oregon, Owyhee County, Idaho, and Elko County, Nevada. Elsewhere, particularly in southern Idaho, local and regional associations of stockmen were formed, as, for example, the one which was started in Boise in 1875, and which may have been functioning as late as 1886 and 1887 under the name of Central Idaho Stock Growers' Association. As early as the spring of 1884, the Eastern Idaho Stock Growers' Association was operating under the presidency of H. O. Harkness, who also was president of the Commercial National Bank of Ogden, Utah. In that same year the president of the Utah and Idaho Consolidated Stock Association called for the meeting which formed a territorial association of the cattlemen of Idaho. A few years later at least some Idaho cattlemen had interests which drew their attention farther eastward, for early in 1888 the editor of a newspaper in Boise remarked that Idaho would be well represented at the cattlemen's convention which would meet in Denver on March 28.[61]

So much, then, for local and regional associations of cattlemen in the Winnemucca province. But this province also invited large-scale associations which attracted members from more than

[60] *Willamette Farmer*, March 25, 1881; *Morning Oregonian*, Jan. 11, 1881; Portland *Oregon and Washington Farmer* (September, 1882), p. 2, quoting the *Prineville News*.
[61] Wallace W. Elliott and Co., *History of Idaho Territory* ... (San Francisco, 1884), p. 299; *Silver State*, July 9, 1883, Jan. 27, 1886; *Idaho Tri-Weekly Statesman*, May 4, 1875; *Morning Oregonian*, March 23, 1875; *Idaho Weekly Statesman*, Nov. 1, 1884, Jan. 23, 1886, June 11, 1887, March 24, 1888; Cheyenne *Northwestern Live-Stock Journal*, May 2, 1884, Nov. 6, 1885, quoting the Eagle Rock, Ida., *Register*; *Salt Lake Daily Tribune*, Oct. 30, Nov. 2, 1884; *Idaho Semi-Weekly World*, Oct. 31, 1884.

one state or territory. In addition to the Idaho Cattle Growers' Association, referred to above, the Nevada Live Stock Association was formed here in 1884. Of these, the Nevada Live Stock Association was the first in point of time and perhaps also in importance. Formed as an interstate association on February 11 and 12, it sought, without complete success, to absorb cattlemen's associations in Oregon and Idaho. Within a year of its formation, however, its secretary, Frank Sweetser, could report a membership of 177,

including representatives from Idaho, Oregon, Utah, California and Nevada, representing 235,425 head of cattle, 20,379 head of horses, and 48,600 sheep, at an estimated value of $6,696,090. The first work of importance of your Executive Committee after the meeting for organization on the 13th of February, 1884, was to confer with a delegation of the Idaho Stock Growers Association, with a view of consolidating the two Associations, with headquarters at Winnemucca. For some reason we could not come to a satisfactory agreement, and the matter was dropped.[62]

But whether local, regional, state-wide, or interstate in character, cattlemen's associations in the Oregon Country never lost sight of the fact that their primary concern was to protect the property of their members. To accomplish this purpose, one Idaho association planned to keep a record of marks and brands to mark and brand calves at roundups whether their owners were present or absent, to appoint an inspector of cattle to visit herds passing through Idaho territory for the purpose of recovering cattle belonging to members of the association, and to prosecute thieves.[63] So determined was the Nevada Live Stock Association from its beginning "to protect the property of its members, and to prosecute evildoers," that it gave a "general impression," as the editor of a newspaper in Winnemucca averred, "that a thief would run much less chance of being punished if caught stealing a hundred thousand dollars from Uncle Sam than if caught stealing a horse or branding a calf that belongs to a member of the Nevada Live Stock Association."[64] Presumably the Nevada Live

[62] *Silver State*, Feb. 11-12, May 21, 1884, March 4, 1885; *Salt Lake Daily Tribune*, May 28, 1884.
[63] Wallace W. Elliott, *History of Idaho Territory*, p. 299.
[64] *Silver State*, Feb. 13, 1884.

Stock Association was worthy of this encomium, for on April 2, 1884, the *Salt Lake Daily Tribune* remarked that

The action of the Nevada Live Stock Association in hunting down horse and cattle thieves and vigorously prosecuting them will, it is believed, effectually stop the business of stealing stock in northern Nevada. The conviction of Bowden and Lee, at Winnemucca, revealed the existence of a well-organized band of thieves, which had its headquarters in the Juniper ranges—an almost inaccessible portion of country, on the line of Humboldt county and Oregon. The band has now been completely broken up and its supposed leader captured.

A few months later the editor of the *Silver State* learned that the "Nevada, Idaho, and Montana Cattle Growers' Associations . . . [had] appropriated $3,000 to pay detectives to scour the Snake River mountains for cattle thieves, and secure evidence that will lead to there [sic] conviction. The associations are determined to stop cattle and horse stealing, and see that no guilty man escapes."[65]

Until a detailed study of the operations of cattlemen's associations in the Winnemucca province is made, we shall not be certain whether these organizations, in practice, exercised themselves principally to obtain laws more nearly adequate to their needs and to achieve better enforcement of existing laws, or whether they tended to seek justice for themselves by resorting to summary action.

[65] *Ibid.*, Nov. 20, 1885.

CHAPTER VIII

When the Chinook Wind Failed

EVERYWHERE in the American West stockmen faced hazards that could not be removed by the enactment of laws or by the decisions of stockmen's associations. Laws, if properly made and adequately enforced, could prevent the movement of diseased animals from one state or territory to another; and the decisions of stockmen to employ agents to round up rustlers could be given effect. But careless white men or malicious Indians who set fires that swept over ranges; or plants that poisoned the grazing animals of stockmen; or diseases that broke out at random in herds or flocks—these were hazards that were as indifferent to the authority of legislatures as they were to the prestige of stockmen's associations. Such hazards were constant and grim realities to men whose livestock grazed on the open ranges of the Oregon Country.

Intermittently cattlemen in the far Northwest were disturbed by prairie fires. Late in the summer of 1867, "prowling bands of Indians" were reported to be setting fires which, in some places, "entirely destroyed the stock ranges" in the Walla Walla Valley. Eleven years later an editor in Lewiston, Idaho, was complaining that fires "on the prairies" were destroying grass that was needed for feeding cattle during the winter. Between September 9, 1882, and July 12, 1884, newspapers in the Oregon Country told of destructive grass fires at the head of Crab Creek in the Big Bend country of eastern Washington, of heavy fires "on the east end" of the Nez Percé Reservation in northern Idaho, and of complaints of both farmers and stockmen about the burning of grass "on the sage plain between the Boise and Snake rivers." All these fires endangered the winter pasturage of livestock. To those who believed that such fires were "only clearing the land of worthless sage brush," the *Idaho Weekly Statesman* explained on July 2, 1884, that prairie fires "destroy the bunch grass that grows among the brush, and so heat the ground that the grass will not grow again in time for winter pasturage. It is safer and better to leave the sage brush until the land is needed for cultivation, when it can be easily removed." As late as November, 1889, fires in the Warner Valley, in south-central Oregon, ruined a range on which, presumably, three thousand head of cattle could have been wintered.[1]

Perhaps even more disturbing to graziers in the Oregon Country was the persisting hazard of poisonous plants. As early as the spring of 1859, cattle in the Coquille Valley and in Linn County, Oregon, were being poisoned by something which they ate, and two years later the *Oregon Farmer* reported that cattle in various parts of the Pacific Northwest had been killed by eating larkspur. Most of this poisoning seemed to result from eating early spring vegetation,[2] and in the Walla Walla Valley in February, 1874, the wild parsnip was blamed for the death of several head of cattle.[3] A year later, in the Owyhee River country about twenty-four miles from Silver City, Idaho, some cattle died from eating what was "generally supposed" to be larkspur, and by the early spring of 1876 most stockmen "in the vicinity of Snake River" were driving their horses and cattle "away from there to the foot-

---

[1] *Walla Walla Union*, Aug. 16, 1867; *Lewiston Teller*, Sept. 13, 1878; Cheney *Northwest Tribune*, Sept. 15, 1882; Commissioner of Indian Affairs, *Report* (1883), p. 117; Boise *Idaho Weekly Statesman*, July 12, 1884; Portland *Weekly Oregonian*, Nov. 28, 1889.

[2] Portland *Oregon Farmer* (May, 1859), p. 136; *ibid.* (July, 1859), p. 181; *ibid.* (May 15, 1861), p. 146; The Dalles *Daily Mountaineer*, March 30, 1866; Silver City, Ida., *Owyhee Avalanche*, March 8, 1873.

[3] *Walla Walla Union* Feb. 21, 1874. For evidence of the poisoning of cattle in northeastern Oregon and on the Warm Springs Indian Reservation in 1874, see also the Commissioner of Indian Affairs, *Report* (1874), p. 325.

hills in consequence of the appearance of the poisonous weed that turns up regularly every spring."[4]

During the 1880's, the poisoning of cattle from eating weeds in the early spring was widespread in the Pacific Northwest, and both the wild parsnip and the larkspur were blamed. But in 1886, the *Idaho Weekly Statesman* expressed its uncertainty as to which weed should be blamed.

> Stock men [it said] have been driving their cattle back into the foothills for a week or ten days past to escape the poison weed that is so fatal to cattle when eaten by them. This weed, whatever it is, grows only in the low lands, and is injurious to cattle only when it first comes up. A month or six weeks later there is no danger from this weed. Cattle either do not eat it when it grows larger or it looses [*sic*] its deadly effect. There is a difference of opinion what this weed is, some claiming that it is the wild larkspur; but this is disputed by others who claim that it has not yet been discovered what weed it is that kills cattle.[5]

Whatever the dangerous weed may have been, the *Morning Oregonian* asserted in the spring of 1887 that cattle in Grant County, Oregon, were eating wild parsnip, which, it said, was "sure death"; and, at the same time, the Boise *Statesman*, less precise in its utterance, was saying that a "good number of cattle... [had] died from eating poison this spring on Snake river." In January, 1889, Peter Clemens, in Harney Valley, Oregon, was said to have lost ten head of cattle which had eaten wild parsnip.[6]

Investigations by scientists presently confirmed the fact that the larkspur (genus *Delphinium*) and the water hemlock (genus *Cicuta*) (which some stockmen apparently had mistaken for wild parsnip) were the plants which poisoned their cattle. Early in the twentieth century David Griffiths accepted this fact in a bulletin which he prepared for the Bureau of Plant Industry, United States Department of Agriculture, and more than fifty years later this department, in another bulletin, affirmed that a certain spe-

---

[4] Whatcom *Bellingham Bay Mail*, April 24, 1875; Portland *Morning Oregonian*, March 1, 1876.

[5] *Idaho Weekly Statesman*, April 3, 1886.

[6] *Morning Oregonian*, April 5, 1887; Cheyenne *Northwestern Live-Stock Journal*, April 22, 1887, quoting the Boise *Statesman*; Burns *East Oregon Herald*, Jan. 24, 1889.

cies of larkspur (genus *Delphinium*) probably caused "more cattle losses in the western range States than any other poisonous
plant," and that water hemlock (*Cicuta douglassi* being a common species on the ranges of western states) is "probably the
most poisonous plant in the United States."[7] Both of these plants
are commonly found in the country west of the 100th meridian.

Equally widespread in the Oregon Country, at least from the
beginning of the 1880's, was a disease of cattle commonly called
blackleg. As early as the 1860's and the 1870's, newspapers of
Oregon and Washington reported that some unknown disease
was killing cattle here and there in the Pacific Northwest; but
the reports were infrequent, and the losses seem to have been
small.[8] Late in 1880, however, cattle in Baker County, Oregon,
and in the Payette country of Idaho were reported to be dying
of blackleg; and on the last day of that year the editor of the
Willamette Farmer, calling attention to losses from this disease
on "Upper Burnt River," remarked that several sections of the
Oregon Country had suffered severely from blackleg, and he predicted that the malady, if not checked, would "cause a great
financial loss to many stock-raisers."[9]

Presumably the malady was not checked, for the Harney country and the Wallowa Valley, the Snake River country in Idaho,
and the Owyhee country suffered heavy losses from this disease
during the autumn and summer of 1881. The situation was little
better in 1882. By March blackleg had begun its ravages in the
country of the Owyhee River, and subsequently it attacked cattle
not only on the Klamath Indian Reservation, where its ravages
were heavy among the young cattle, but also in both the Yakima

[7] David Griffiths, *Range Conditions and Problems in Eastern Washington,
Eastern Oregon, Northeastern California, and Northwestern Nevada* (Washington,
D.C., 1903), p. 41; U. S. Department of Agriculture, *16 Plants Poisonous to Live-
stock in the Western States* (Farmers' Bulletin No. 2106) (Washington, D.C.,
1958), pp. 26, 47. See also Will C. Barnes, *Winter Grazing Grounds and Forest
Rangers* (Chicago, 1913), pp. 246-73, and Samuel Van Dersal (compiler), *Live
Stock Growers' Directory of Marks and Brands for the State of Oregon, 1918*
(Portland, 1918), pp. 14-16.

[8] Walla Walla *Washington Statesman*, Aug. 1, 1863; Jacksonville *Oregon Sentinel*, Oct. 13, 1866; *Walla Walla Statesman*, March 23, 1872; *Sacramento Daily
Union*, Feb. 16, 1874.

[9] *Idaho Weekly Statesman*, Oct. 16, Dec. 25, 1880; Portland *Willamette
Farmer*, Dec. 31, 1880.

and Kittitas valleys.[10] It was still attacking calves in the lower Yakima Valley in the spring of 1883, and by June it had moved into Columbia County, Washington. Before the end of 1883, this disease was attacking young cattle in such widely separated areas as the Klamath Indian Reservation in south-central Oregon, and Whitman County, Washington.[11]

By 1884, blackleg in the Pacific Northwest appears to have been at its worst, for in that year heavy losses were reported in the Kittitas Valley, Washington, in Grant County, Oregon, and in various places in both Idaho and Montana. In the autumn of that year the *Willamette Farmer* remarked that the "blackleg among cattle east of the Cascades attacks the fattest and healthiest looking. They grow lame in the leg and finally get down and never get up again." After 1884, whether because of hardened indifference to such losses or a lessening of the disease, fewer reports of losses from blackleg appeared in the newspapers of the Oregon Country. But the disease had not been eradicated. In the summer of 1886 it killed cattle in Umatilla County, Oregon, and in Whitman County, Washington; and in October, 1887, it was reported to be attacking cattle in the neighborhood of Baker City, Oregon. Soon thereafter the Federal Bureau of Animal Industry began to distribute a vaccine to protect young cattle from blackleg, and by 1905 the losses had been greatly reduced. Even as late as 1918, however, blackleg was reported to be prevalent on the ranges of eastern Oregon, but by that time vaccination had come to be considered a certain means of preventing this disease.[12]

[10] *Oregon Sentinel*, Aug. 20, 1881; *Willamette Farmer*, July 8, Sept. 16, 1881; Boise *Idaho Tri-Weekly Statesman*, Sept. 15, 1881; Silver City *Idaho Avalanche*, Nov. 12, 1881; Vancouver *Clarke County Register*, March 30, 1882; Tacoma *Weekly Ledger*, Nov. 10, 1882; Commissioner of Indian Affairs, *Report* (1882), p. 137.

[11] *Yakima Signal*, March 24, June 9, 1883; *Waitsburg Times*, June 8, 1883; Pomeroy *Washington Independent*, Aug. 16, 1883; Commissioner of Indian Affairs, *Report* (1883), p. 186.

[12] *Yakima Record*, Feb. 2, 1884; Ellensburg *Kittitas Standard*, July 14, 1883; *Daily Tacoma News*, June 28, 1884; *Northwest Tribune*, Aug. 29, 1884; *Willamette Farmer*, Oct. 3, 1884; U. S. Bureau of Animal Industry, *First Annual Report* (1884), p. 277; *Willamette Farmer*, Nov. 28, 1884, July 16, Aug. 13, 1886; *Morning Oregonian*, Oct. 3, 1887, quoting the Baker City *Democrat*; "Report of the Chief of the Bureau of Animal Industry," U. S. Department of Agriculture,

Enemies such as poisonous plants and deadly diseases were highly exasperating, but the harm they did was slight when compared with the damage inflicted by winter, the greatest of all the enemies of cattlemen in the American West. Here was a foe that relentlessly dogged the heels of cattlemen, a foe that was capricious, implacable, remorseless. Winter laughed at the enactments of legislatures, scoffed at the resolutions of cattlemen's associations, and made sport not only of the suffering of cattle, but also of the helplessness of stockmen who, by neglecting to provide feed and shelter for their livestock, had gambled recklessly with fortune. Habitually, cattlemen of the Oregon Country put their faith in "the natural enemy of frost and snow," the warm-breathed Chinook wind, whose coming inward from the Pacific Ocean made "a sound of delight" in the ears of those who heard it.[13] They invoked this wind when chilly gales from the north and the east, sweeping over snow-crusted ranges and frozen watering places, threatened the destruction of their herds. Agonizingly they cried out, saying, as a rimester tells us,

> Chinook, Chinook, from over the sea,
>   Come hither, come hither, kind friend we pray;
> Great blower of good to my cattle and me,
>   Come blow our hungry troubles away.
>
> Up from the realms of the sultry south,
>   From the glowing isles of spices and palm, . . .
>
> Sweep over the mountains, wild and free,
>   Swoop down this side on hillock and plain;
> O give us thy breath, my cattle and me,
>   Kissing our hopes to life again. . . .[14]

But heavy losses of cattle, one time after another, could not be explained away merely as the consequence of freakish weather—as an act of God that was beyond human understanding. Cattlemen, it is true, could not have prevented the coming of winter's storms, but they could have made adequate provision for the

Annual Report, 1905 (Washington, D.C., 1905), p. 32; Van Dersal, *Directory of Marks and Brands,* pp. 5-6. See also Barnes, *Winter Grazing Grounds,* pp. 288-94.
[13] John Minto, "From Youth to Age as an American," *OHQ,* IX (1908), 380-81.
[14] *Weekly Mountaineer,* Dec. 28, 1872.

care of their livestock in times of extraordinary stress, and occasionally a few of them did. Why more of them did not do so, we are at no great loss to find out. Theirs was a speculative business. With free pastures at their disposal, they invested their money in cattle and sought large returns with a minimum of expense and effort. Moreover, behind them lay a long tradition of mild winters in the Oregon Country, a tradition of cattle keeping fat on grass the year round, needing neither feed nor shelter. And it is not altogether astonishing that such beliefs persisted, even in the face of accumulating evidence that proved them to be false. Winters of extraordinary inclemency, most stockmen believed, would come so infrequently that owners of livestock could afford to take chances; and they were encouraged in this belief by writers who presumably knew whereof they wrote. One of them was J. Ross Browne, who said in 1868 that of "the 16 winters passed in . . . [Washington] Territory the writer has known but three so severe as to render it essential to house and feed stock. The Indians do not pretend to such acts of providence, and they lose but little of their small wealth from exposure or cold. . . . [But the more successful stockmen, he confessed] did provide from two to three months' feed as a general rule."[15]

Some fourteen years later an Englishman who had learned much about raising cattle in Oregon remarked that some of the "provident" cattlemen there collected "one or two hundred tons of natural hay against the severities of winter. It may be that for two or three years the hay will stand unused; then comes the stress."[16]

Cattlemen in the Oregon Country seemed willing to take in stride "normal" winter losses, and, after one severe winter, many of them no doubt toyed with the expectation of "cashing in" before another severe winter should settle down upon their ranges. Accordingly, when disaster did strike again, their only resource, as an Oregon rimester believed, was to forsake their "cards, cigars and wine," and repeat "The Stockmen's Prayer," which, in part, is as follows:

[15] 40th Cong., 2nd sess., H. Ex. Doc. 202 (Serial 1342), p. 548.
[16] Wallis Nash, *Two Years in Oregon* (New York, 1882), p. 111.

O Stockmen's God! O Thou
   To whom we always look
And humbly, trusting bow
   In prayer and praise—*Chinook!*
On thee we more rely
   Than all the hay and straw,
Or barley, oats and rye
   For thy propitious thaw. . . .
O, grant thy winds and rain
   Upon poor us to send,
And we'll not pray again
   Until next fall—Amen.[17]

Stockmen in the Oregon Country were frequently warned of the consequences of persistently neglecting their cattle. Newspaper editors were not remiss in lecturing them on both the bad economics and the gross inhumanity of letting cattle suffer; but their efforts were largely in vain. "This depending on cattle wintering themselves without feed at this day when range [in the Willamette Valley] is eaten out will not do," remarked an editor in Oregon City as early as April, 1859; and a month later the editor of the *Oregon Farmer* asked, "How long will this plan of raising stock without shelter from the cold blasts of winter, and without feed, be continued in Oregon?" A few years later, in the midst of a devastating winter, an editor in Walla Walla remarked that the "experience of the present winter has certainly furnished sufficient argument to induce preparations hereafter, if like results would be avoided."[18]

But preparations thereafter remained inadequate, and "like results" were not avoided. The common view on this subject was expressed a decade later by an editor who, predicting at the beginning of February, 1872, that half of the cattle in the intermontane country of the far Northwest would soon be dead, remarked that, after "three good mild winters," hundreds of people would be "rushing off to these great public pastures to raise cat-

[17] *Weekly Mountaineer*, Jan. 6, 1872. This "prayer," according to the editor of the *Mountaineer*, was written by a man living on Fifteen Mile Creek. It had been first printed in the *Mountaineer* "some four years ago."
[18] Oregon City *Oregon Argus*, March 12, 1859; *Oregon Farmer* (April, 1859), p. 136; *Washington Statesman*, Jan. 25, 1862.

tle and sheep without hay or shelter in the winter." Nine years later, in the depth of a very severe winter, an editor in southeastern Washington, also hoping that cattlemen might profit by costly experience, remarked that there was "nothing to hinder farmers and stockmen from putting up plenty of hay and straw to feed their stock through the winter if they want[ed] to do so."[19]

Presumably most cattlemen did not want to do so. In 1859, a disillusioned editor in Oregon City pointed out that farmers in Oregon "seem to learn little or nothing from experience, and we don't know that they ever will." Time would prove that he was right, for in the valleys of western Oregon, as on the widely dispersed ranges between the Cascades and the Rockies, stockmen generally remained as indifferent to experience of this sort as they continued to be neglectful of the blunt admonitions or the subtle irony of some reporters and editors. From the Antelope Valley, in Wasco County, Oregon, a correspondent wrote on November 26, 1872, saying that, on an average, only one stockman in twenty-five had enough hay "to feed through one storm."[20] More than six years later an editor in Walla Walla, asserting that cattlemen were complaining of few calves to brand, remarked, tongue in cheek, "This again goes to show that cattle will not fare well on 'mild' climate during a hard winter." In February, 1881, a correspondent from the Wallowa Valley, doubting whether the stockmen's losses on account of deep snow and lack of feed would make them wise enough to avoid a recurrence, said: "Stockmen in Eastern Oregon generally prefer to take the chances."[21] During the next few years, most of the cattlemen

---

[19] *Willamette Farmer*, Feb. 3, 1872; *Pataha City Spirit*, Jan. 2, 1881.

[20] *Oregon Argus*, March 12, 1859; *Willamette Farmer*, Dec. 14, 1872. A promotional book which appeared in Oregon at about this time affirmed that "Middle Oregon is really the great western paradise of stock raisers. There rain seldom falls in winter, and the bunch grass, which covers the high rolling plains—almost illimitable in extent, is seldom covered with snow, so as to prevent cattle and horses from subsisting on it." W. L. Adams, *Oregon as It Is: Its Present and Future, by a Resident for Twenty-five Years, Being a Reply to Inquiries* (Portland, Ore., 1873), p. 42.

[21] *Walla Walla Watchman*, quoted in the *Morning Oregonian*, July 15, 1879, and W. J. Dean, writing from Lostine, Wallowa Valley, Feb. 15, 1881, to the editor of the *Oregonian*. A newspaper clipping in the Henry Villard Papers, Box 5 (MSS in the Widener Library, Harvard University).

between the Cascades and the Rockies continued to "take the chances." In Owyhee County, Idaho, as late as January 28, 1888, cattlemen were depending upon the Chinook wind more than upon feed. Remarking on that date that a recent Chinook wind had melted nearly all the snow "on the south side of Snake river as high up as Reynolds creek," the editor of the *Idaho Avalanche* affirmed that this good fortune would "cause the old cows to throw their heels high in the air, and their tails over their backs, as they gambol around and over the valley in search of grass and white sage."[22] Two months later an editor in Grant County, Oregon, after asserting that the loss of stock at the head of the South Fork of the John Day River had been slight, remarked, with gentle irony, that stockmen there, "as a rule, had an abundance of hay," which was "the very best upholstery that can be used for sheep and cattle pelts." It would, he continued, even help "the appearance of horses."[23] As late as 1890, journalists in the Oregon Country were still admonishing stockmen to make provision for the adequate care of their livestock during severe winters.

Stockmen in the Oregon Country, however, had not been unique in the treatment of their cattle. On earlier American frontiers, from the beginnings of settlement in the seventeenth century, stock owners had let their animals feed on the open range the year through; and long before cattle roamed on ranges in the Oregon Country their losses of cattle from exposure and from starvation during severe winters had been persistent and widespread. On February 25, 1823, in the recently formed territory of Arkansas, the editor of the Little Rock *Arkansas Gazette* was saying substantially what editors in the Oregon Country a generation later would be saying—namely, that he was hearing

from almost every quarter of vast numbers of cattle that have died during the late extreme cold weather. The winters in this country are generally so mild that our farmers never think of keeping up their cattle, or providing fodder for them, but turn them into the river bottoms, where they find an excellent range, and keep in good order through the winter....This winter,

[22] *Idaho Avalanche*, Jan. 28, 1888.
[23] *Morning Oregonian*, March 27, 1888, quoting the Canyon City *Grant County News*.

however, has been more fatal to stock of every description, than any that has preceded it for a great many years. . . . A person who came down the Arkansas a few days ago, informs us, that the river bottoms are literally strewed with the carcasses of cattle.

Thus it appears that stockmen in the Oregon Country were the captives of their heritage, as were also the graziers whose herds were ranging contemporaneously on the Great Plains, where the losses of cattle in winter, because of more and larger herds, were even greater than those in the Oregon Country. On the Great Plains, however, thanks to the "big boom" which began at the end of the 1870's,[24] the business of raising cattle became so extensive that losses there during severe winters were large enough to arouse public opinion in the eastern states. Accordingly, as the frightful winter of 1880-81 was drawing to a close, there appeared in the National Live-Stock Journal an editorial entitled "Cattle on the Plains," in which the author, after predicting that "cattle raising on the Plains had reached its maximum," urged federal intervention to prevent barbarous cruelty to animals on the public domain. "It is being stoutly maintained," he said, "that men should not be permitted to use the Government domain for the purpose of rearing vast herds of cattle, for which no possible supply of feed can be furnished against the severe winters that are always liable to occur, and that the Government should interfere to prevent a system under which hundreds of thousands of cattle are annually exposed to death from starvation."[25] Here was a proposal for a "new deal" that would have seemed intolerable to most Americans who were "on the make" in the Gilded Age of the American Republic.

No one knows how many head of cattle died on the ranges of the Oregon Country during severe winters, for no careful count of such losses was made. Some cattlemen, indeed, could not tell

[24] In the summer of 1867, people in New England could read in the highly respected Springfield, Mass., Republican a letter from Central City, Colorado, in which the author affirmed that cattle and sheep did not "require housing" during winter in the southern counties of Colorado, but could find "enough food and nourishment in the bunch grass which grows plentifully along the valley of the Arkansas." Reprinted in the Sacramento Daily Union, Aug. 13, 1867. On the cattle boom, see Ernest Staples Osgood, The Day of the Cattleman (Minneapolis, 1929), chap. iv.

[25] Chicago National Live-Stock Journal, XII (March, 1881), 105.

precisely the extent of their losses because they knew only vaguely how many cattle they owned. Whatever their other shortcomings may have been, Oregon cattlemen in the days of open range grazing cannot rightly be accused of keeping accurate books or of wasting time on a system of cost accounting. They lived before the days of the federal income tax, and they were not threatened with computers. The federal government, in short, did not bother them, except, perhaps, when they fenced government land. Why, then, should they bother themselves? If they failed, their failure was their own business. They could begin again. Since their returns of their cattle to county assessors cannot be taken seriously, neither should their estimates of their losses from winter's storms be taken at face value. Many of them guessed about such losses because they could not do otherwise. Nevertheless, the surviving records seem to show that, through the years, the losses of cattle in the Pacific Northwest because of the rigors of winters were more or less continuous and, in the aggregate, considerable. Such losses varied from district to district, and rose or fell with the changing intensity of winter seasons. But on the ranges of the Oregon Country winter never ceased to threaten; it was the most relentless foe known to the stockmen of this region.

Both in the recollections of pioneers and in contemporaneous writings, three winters in the Oregon Country stand out as exceptionally severe: those of 1861-62, 1880-81, and 1889-90. These were winters of widespread suffering and of appalling loss of cattle. Because of their length and severity, they were remembered; but other winters, damaging but somewhat restricted in their devastations, were soon forgotten. The severity of the winter of 1846-47, for example, was without precedent in the recollection of the oldest Oregonian, but the Oregon Country was then young, and that exceptionally severe winter was shrugged off by the old-timers; and it was of no concern to later comers who had been indoctrinated with the notion that Oregon was a promised land, where much could be obtained with little effort and where livestock needed no care during any part of the year. Also of more than ordinary severity were the winters of 1874-75 and 1879-80; and still others—especially those of 1871-72 and

1873-74—brought anxiety and losses to stockmen in more than one part of the Oregon Country. So often, indeed, did winter threaten the interests of stockmen that, at this distance in time, we wonder that so many of them remained indifferent to their pecuniary interests.

Losses of livestock during severe winters were due principally to insufficient feed, lack of shelter, and, frequently, lack of water. A heavy snowfall was not necessarily dangerous to livestock, for cattle and horses could paw through dry snow to grass beneath it. But alternate thawing and freezing after a fall of snow produced an icy crust on the snow, and then cattle on the ranges suffered severely. Whenever they could, they would huddle together in a sheltered place and be loath to move. Even if, as sometimes was the case, hay had been stacked for their winter feeding, cattle that were scattered over a large range might have starved before they could be got to the place of feeding. Moreover, frozen watering places intensified the suffering of cattle and increased the number that died. Sometimes sheer exposure killed animals in large numbers. Regardless of the precautions that could have been taken, some cattle on open ranges would have died in winters like those of 1861-62, 1880-81, and 1889-90. But through long years most cattlemen of the Oregon Country made little or no preparation to care for their livestock during any winter, and for this reason, when the Chinook wind failed, their cattle suffered and many died.

The winter of 1846-47 was the first one to challenge the cherished belief that, at least in the lower Columbia Valley, there was, as Dr. John McLoughlin had said in March, 1837, "no need to make hay" for cattle.[26] This winter was a revelation, and it should have been a warning. It struck everywhere: west of the Cascades, where cattle were becoming fairly numerous, and east of these mountains, where cattle had not yet become abundant. North of the Columbia River, it killed considerable livestock at the establishments of the Hudson's Bay Company and of the Puget's Sound Agricultural Company; south of this river, it killed much livestock belonging to settlers in the Willamette Valley.

[26] John McLoughlin to Edward Ermatinger, March 3, 1837, OHQ, XXIII (December, 1922), 370.

Here, in January, 1847, the temperature fell below zero, and the artist Paul Kane wrote that the intense cold was "killing nearly all the cattle that had become acclimated."[27] The Reverend George Gary was in the Willamette Valley at this time, and his diary reveals much about the winter of 1846-47. On the morning of January 14, 1847, he wrote that "the poor cattle are suffering and dying, many of them," and on the next day he noted that the "wild beasts (wolves and panthers) are hungry and are making considerable havoc among the cattle." By February 1 he had heard that most of the cattle that came over the mountains in 1846 were dead, and a month later he was writing that the "poor cattle in this land are suffering, many of them unto death." On March 2, 1847, he heard that the winter had been very cold at The Dalles of the Columbia, and on March 11, when "the thermometer at times [was] down to ten degrees below zero," he was writing again that many cattle had died.[28] Meanwhile, at Astoria, the winter had been equally severe. On April 2, 1847, the Reverend Ezra Fisher, a Baptist home missionary who had come overland to Oregon in 1845, wrote from Astoria that his cattle, "which were more than twenty head in the fall, . . . [were] now reduced to two."[29]

East of the Cascade Mountains a similar tale of disaster was recorded. There, at least at inhabited places, the winter was uniformly severe. The Reverend Cushing Eells wrote from Tshimakain on April 6, 1847, of heavy losses of both cattle and horses at his missionary station, among the Indians of that district, and at Fort Colvile. A few days earlier Spalding had written about the loss of cattle at Clearwater and the heavy losses of both cattle and horses by the Nez Percé Indians; and on April 1, 1847, Dr. Whitman said that the winter just ended had been "one of unusual severity throughout the whole country." At Waiilatpu, he continued, his loss had been heavy "in sheep, calves and some

[27] Paul Kane, *Wanderings of an Artist* . . . (Toronto, 1925), pp. 131-32.

[28] Charles H. Carey (ed.), "Diary of Reverend George Gary," *OHQ*, XXIV (December, 1923), 387-94. The Oregon City *Oregon Spectator*, March 18, 1847, reported that the "Rev. A. F. Waller, from the Dalles, has been in our city recently. The weather has been severely and unusually cold in that section of country, and many horses have perished."

[29] Ezra Fisher, "Correspondence," *OHQ*, XVI (September, 1915), 304.

cattle (old cows), colts and horses."[30] Meanwhile, according to John Lee Lewes, the Columbia River was frozen at Colvile, and everybody was "literally buried in snow"—a great "contrast from last Winter, when all was mildness." The deep snow, he continued, had "played fearfull havoc among his horses," but he could not then determine the precise extent of the loss.[31] Indeed, on both sides of the Cascades people were astounded at what seemed to be impossible. The oldest Indians in the country had no recollection of such terrible weather, and consequently neither they nor the white people dwelling in the valley of the Columbia were prepared for the heavy losses they suffered.

Other winters of considerable severity came in the train of this one. In December, 1851, Jesse Applegate wrote that hundreds of animals had died of starvation in the Willamette Valley during the winter of 1848-49; and both Dr. William Fraser Tolmie and John R. Jackson affirmed, in testimony given under oath in 1865, that the winter of 1849-50 had been severe, and that the Puget's Sound Agricultural Company had lost a great deal of livestock at Cowlitz.[32] The severity of these two winters, however, is not attested in reports from other persons throughout the Oregon Country.

But the severity of the winter of 1852-53 is well attested. On December 22, 1852, George Gibbs, writing from Astoria, said that the country "was covered with snow to the depth of over a foot," and predicted that many cattle would perish throughout Oregon.[33] Late in January, 1853, Charles Stevens, of Milwaukie,

[30] Cushing Eells to David Greene, April 6, 1847, in the ABCFM, Letters and Papers, CCXXXXVIII, No. 102, (MSS in the Houghton Library, Harvard University). Dr. Whitman's letter is quoted in William I. Marshall, *Acquisition of Oregon and the Long Suppressed Evidence About Marcus Whitman* (Seattle, Wash., 1911), II, 161-64, 260-61. On Feb. 22, 1847, Henry H. Spalding wrote to A. T. Smith as follows: "This is our eleventh winter in this country and never before have the animals needed fodder. . . . It has been very cold for nearly three months with much snow, two weeks one foot deep which entirely prevented cattle from feeding." (Typescript of this letter in the library of the Presbyterian Historical Society, Philadelphia.)
[31] Coe Collection, MS No. 186 (MS in the Yale University Library).
[32] U. S. Commissioner of Patents, *Report* (1851), p. 472; British and American Joint Commission, *Evidence on the Part of the Puget's Sound Agricultural Company* (Montreal, 1868), pp. 18, 126.
[33] Vernon Carstensen (ed.), *Pacific Northwest Letters of George Gibbs* (Portland, Ore., 1954), p. 32. From St. Helens, Oregon Territory, the Reverend G. M.

said that he believed the "old settlers" who were saying that Oregon was having "one of the hardest winters" ever known in that country. Farther south in the Willamette Valley, Richard Irwin, writing from Benton County on March 22, 1853, affirmed that the past winter was reported to have been "the hardest winter that has ever been known in Oregon. . . . It is supposed, by close calculators, that over ten thousand head of stock died in Oregon from the severity of the winter. Oregonians never cut hay or save fodder for their stock." Nor was this all. A letter dated at Salem on April 14 affirmed that the winter just ended had been an exceedingly hard one for Oregon. "There was much snow and cold rain, and grass was very poor."[34]

North of the Columbia River, the winter of 1852-53 in the Puget Sound country was perhaps even more severe than in the Willamette Valley. Here, as Simpson P. Moses testified in 1867, the snow was "two feet two inches deep for several weeks," and both the settlers and the Puget's Sound Agricultural Company "lost a large portion of their cattle." But the greatest losses were suffered east of the Cascades, especially in the neighborhood of The Dalles of the Columbia, where immigrants of 1852 had left much of their cattle. According to a report made in April, 1853, "the snow fell five feet deep, and lay on the ground seven weeks, which killed 7,000 head of cattle and horses." This contemporaneous report was corroborated, in substance, in 1867 by the testimony of Edward I. Allen, who had learned from "several parties who had herds of cattle" in this area that "most of the cattle east of the Cascades died in that winter."[35] Whatever the number of cattle lost in that winter may have been, the evidence shows that the weather was severe both east and west of the Cascades. It should have persuaded Oregonians to believe that

Perry wrote on Dec. 30, 1852, saying, "Last week a snow fell to the unusual depth of three feet. It was intensely cold. Cattle died by scores, and the suffering of a large number of this season's emigrants was and is most distressing." New York *Christian Advocate and Journal*, XXVIII (March 24, 1853), 46.

[34] Ruth Rockwood (ed.), "Letters of Charles Stevens," *OHQ*, XXXVII (September, 1936), 243; St. Louis *Weekly Missouri Republican*, May 20, 1853; D. N., in the *New York Weekly Tribune*, June 4, 1853.

[35] British and American Joint Commission, *Evidence for the United States in the Matter of the Claim of the Puget's Sound Agricultural Company* (Washington, D.C., 1867), pp. 249, 301.

what had happened in 1846-47 could happen again. But it did not.

For the next six years the winters in the Pacific Northwest were comparatively safe for stockmen. Although there is some evidence of loss of livestock and of damage to crops during the two winters of 1856-57 and 1857-58,[36] few owners of cattle in the Willamette Valley were sufficiently alarmed to heed the editor of the *Oregon Statesman* when, on February 23, 1858, he warned all and sundry that "no cattle grower should be without fodder enough to last, at least a week or two in winter." So indifferent were they to such advice that, once again, they were unprepared to care for their livestock during severe weather early in 1859. Of this ordeal an editor in Oregon City wrote, on March 12, 1859, that it had been "a terrible time on stock," many of which had died, and others had become "candidates for the boneyard." Two weeks later he expressed the belief that at least two thousand head of cattle had died in the Willamette Valley during the preceding six weeks. At the same time, an editor in Olympia, Washington, after remarking on the heavy loss of livestock in Washington Territory on account of severe weather, quoted the Salem *Oregon Statesman* as saying not only that the loss of cattle in the Willamette Valley on account of the "recent severe weather" had been unprecedented, but also that the "cold rains, accompanied with snow and sleet, which . . . [had] prevailed every day for the last six weeks . . . [were] more fatal to stock than the coolest weather, if dry, would be." In April, 1859, the Portland *Oregon Farmer* expressed a similar view.[37]

The winter losses of cattle in the Oregon Country were large enough to attract the attention of a Council Bluffs, Iowa, editor, who affirmed in June, 1859, that the "past season" had been "the most disastrous" that Oregon had ever seen.[38] This, to be

[36] John Owen, *Journals and Letters . . .* , ed. by Seymour Dunbar and Paul C. Phillips (New York, 1927), I, 157. A Baptist newspaper of New York City, the *New York Chronicle*, in its issue of April 18, 1857, affirmed that the "latest accounts from Oregon speak of the severity of the *Winter*, and of consequent damage to crops and cattle."

[37] Olympia *Pioneer and Democrat*, March 25, 1859; *Oregon Argus*, March 12, 26, 1859; *Oregon Farmer* (April, 1859), p. 136. See also the Victoria *British Colonist*, March 19, 1859, and the Salem *Oregon Statesman*, March 15, 1859.

[38] *Weekly Council Bluffs Bugle*, June 1, 1859.

sure, was an overstatement, and perhaps it was made because this editor knew nothing about the winter of 1846-47 in the Pacific Northwest.

The winter of 1858-59 should have prepared Oregon stockmen for the devastating winter of 1861-62, which began with a damaging flood of the Willamette River in December, 1861. But it did not. Because three relatively mild winters had lulled them into forgetfulness, they were ill-prepared to face one of the worst winters in the Pacific Northwest. Optimistic as ever—or perhaps lazy, as the editor of an Olympia newspaper believed—the stockmen of the Oregon Country had made little if any provision for feeding their livestock. This negligence cost them dearly, for during that winter deep snow covered the country, and the watering places froze over.[39] West and east of the Cascades, north and south of the Columbia River, very low temperatures were recorded—"from 5 to 20 below zero" for forty days at The Dalles—and by January, 1862, cattle were dying there by the thousands.[40]

Elsewhere in the country east of the Cascades there were very low temperatures. In Walla Walla, from late December, 1861, to at least January 25, 1862, "the thermometer ... [ranged] from a freezing point down to as low as 29 degrees below zero"; in the Colville Valley, on January 17, 1862, the temperature was thirty-three degrees below zero; and farther eastward, in the Bitter Root Valley, the temperature fell as low as thirty-seven degrees below zero. At about the same time Edward Huggins reported a heavy toll of livestock at Fort Nisqually, and the Reverend J. H. Wilbur told of a "fearful loss" of livestock in Klickitat County, Washington, and in Wasco County, Oregon. On Vancouver Island the loss of livestock was reported to be "terrible."[41] Thus it

[39] Weekly Oregonian, Jan. 25, 1862; Oregon Farmer (Feb. 15, 1862), p. 101; Olympia Overland Press, Feb. 2, 1862; James Watt, "Experiences of a Freighter in the Inland Empire" (Statement made to J. Orin Oliphant, in Cheney, Washington, on Jan. 23, 1926); A. J. Splawn, Ka-mi-akin, the Last Hero of the Yakimas (2nd ed.; Portland, Ore., 1944), pp. 153-54.
[40] H. P. Isaacs to General George Wright, Feb. 11, 1862, in The War of the Rebellion ... Series I (Washington, 1897), L, Pt. 1, 861; Walla Walla Statesman, Feb. 22, 26, 1862; Weekly Oregonian, Jan 25, Feb. 1, 15, 1862; Daniel M. Drumheller, "Uncle Dan" Drumheller Tells Thrills of Western Trails in 1854 (Spokane, Wash., 1925), pp. 64-65; "The Winter of 1861-62," Willamette Farmer, Jan. 2, 1885.
[41] Walla Walla Statesman, Jan. 25, April 12, 1862, quoted in An Illustrated

can be seen that in all the settled parts of the Pacific Northwest the suffering of animals was intense and the loss of livestock was great.

Cattle which lacked both feed and shelter died by the thousands. Late in January, 1862, a Walla Walla editor affirmed that nearly all the cattle which had been driven from the Willamette Valley into the Walla Walla Valley in the preceding autumn had perished, and two months later he declared that the "loss of stock in the Willamette during the past winter was but little less in proportion than that experienced" in the Walla Walla Valley. "It was estimated," he said, "that near one-fourth of the stock in the Willammette [sic] died during the winter." At The Dalles a stockman named John T. Jeffreys, writing in the early spring of 1862, expressed the opinion that nine-tenths of all the stock east of the Cascades had perished. Interestingly enough, this was the percentage of loss estimated, at different times by different persons, for districts as widely separated as the Walla Walla Valley, the vicinity of Lewiston, Idaho, and the Bitter Root Valley.[42] On March 29, 1862, the Washington Statesman estimated the total loss of cattle east of the Cascades at twenty-five thousand head.

Nobody knew whether the foregoing estimate was close to the mark or wide of it, but many persons learned of the tragic consequences of that winter when springtime brought to view a ghastly sight. "Whose duty is it to abate the nuisances that abound on every hand about the whole valley [of Walla Walla] in the shape of dead cattle"? This question an unidentified correspondent put to the editor of the Washington Statesman on March 25, 1862, and then he offered this observation: "You cannot walk out one thousand yards from the main street of Walla Walla but you encounter the festering and decaying carcasses of animals." The editor of the Statesman agreed that such nuisances

History of Southeastern Washington . . . (Spokane, Wash., 1906), p. 91; W. P. Winans, "Stevens County, Washington: Its Creation, Addition, Subtraction and Division" (typed copy is in my possession); Owen, Journals and Letters, I, 238-52; Oregon Farmer, (April 1, 1862), p. 128; Port Townsend North-West, March 22, 1862; Weekly Oregonian, Feb. 22, 1862; British Colonist, March 24, 1862.

[42] British Colonist, April 15, 1862; Weekly Oregonian, March 20, 1862; Washington Statesman, Jan. 25, Feb. 22, March 29, April 12, 1862; Olympia Washington Standard, March 29, 1862.

should be abated, either by individuals or by the county commissioners; but more than two weeks later another unidentified correspondent was complaining to the same newspaper about "piles of dead cattle, in a state of decomposition, here and there upon the commons near the city." He feared that they might "form the exciting cause of maladies malignant in character."[43] Certainly, as the editor of the *Washington Statesman* averred on January 25, 1862, the experience of this winter provided "sufficient argument" for preparations to avoid like results in the future; and in the autumn of 1862 the editor of the *Oregon Farmer* remarked that the boast of the early pioneers—namely, that in Oregon cattle need be neither fed nor sheltered in winter—had been disproved. Old "sleepy" habits, he said, must be discarded, for ranges had become restricted, and cattle should now be fed not only in winter, but also in late summer. But there is little reason to think that cattlemen in the Oregon Country profited from such advice or from their dire experience. Few of them were as foresighted as a Yakima rancher, F. M. Thorp, who in 1862 accumulated stacks of hay, which still stood intact five years later, because he had not been required to feed his cattle during the intervening years.[44]

For the next decade stockmen of the Oregon Country were not embarrassed in any single year by comparable losses of livestock, and, accordingly, it was easy for them to settle into the slovenly ways of former years. It is true that in eastern Oregon, southern Idaho, and parts of eastern Washington cattlemen experienced adverse weather during the winter of 1864-65, and it is equally true that in January and February, 1865, many cattle were dying in northeastern Oregon, the Owyhee country, Ada County, Idaho, the Boise Basin, and on the Spokane prairie.[45] But these

[43] *Washington Statesman*, March 29, 1864; Medicus, writing from "Steptoeville, April 10, 1862," in *ibid.*, April 19, 1862. Steptoeville was the first name of what became the city of Walla Walla.

[44] *Oregon Farmer* (Oct. 1, 1862), p. 28; J. Ross Browne, in the 40th Cong., 2nd sess., H. Ex. Doc. 202 (Serial 1342), p. 553.

[45] *Oregon Statesman*, Jan. 23, Feb. 20, 1865; *Walla Walla Statesman*, Jan. 6, March 31, April 7, 1865; *Washington Standard*, Feb. 11, 1865, quoting the Boise *Statesman*; Captain Frederick Seidenstricker, writing on Feb. 13, 1865, from Fort Boise to the Adjutant General, District of Oregon, in *The War of the Rebellion* ... Series I, L, Pt. 1, 400.

losses were slight in comparison with those of 1861-62. Nevertheless, a rise in the price of oxen and other cattle in the Walla Walla Valley was reported in March, 1865, presumably, as an editor in Walla Walla believed, because so many cattle had "died during the winter in the valleys east of the mountains." During the next winter, severe weather, attended by some loss of livestock, was reported in the Grande Ronde and Powder River valleys in northeastern Oregon, as well as in the Bitter Root Valley in western Montana; but, with these exceptions, there was apparently little loss of livestock in Transcascadia.[46] During the next five years, the newspapers of the Oregon Country contain only sporadic references to losses of cattle from inclement weather, but one does find a significant number of editorials and more than a few letters from correspondents, telling of cattle growing fat by eating nutritious grass on ranges blest with salubrious weather during mildish winters. Such, for example, was the condition of cattle in the Walla Walla Valley in mid-February, 1867, and such also, as another example, was the condition during the winter of 1870-71 of cattle in the "Kitatash Valley, Yakima Co., W. T.," from which F. M. Thorp, on April 15, 1871, wrote to a newspaper in Seattle, saying, "The winter just past has been very mild, and at the present time our hills and valleys are covered with the finest new bunch grass."

No such idyllic utterances, however, described the winter of 1871-72. So severe was this winter that the *Weekly Mountaineer* for January 6, 1872, was obliged to say that, thus far, it had "proved to be the most severe winter . . . in eastern Washington since the never-to-be-forgotten winter of 1861-62." A recent snow, he said, had "caused a very big scare" in his region—one that would not soon be forgotten. Elsewhere there was also reason for a "big scare," for killing weather was experienced in the Yakima and Kittitas valleys, in the Palouse country, in southeastern Washington, in the Snake River Valley in Idaho, and, eastward of the Oregon Country, on the ranges of Colorado.[47]

[46] *Walla Walla Statesman*, March 3, 1865, Jan. 5, 12, 1866; Portland *Pacific Christian Advocate*, Jan. 20, 1866; Owen, *Journal and Letters*, II, 19.
[47] *Walla Walla Statesman*, Feb. 15, 1867, Jan. 22, 1869; *Weekly Mountaineer*, March 15, 1870, Jan. 6, 1872; *Pacific Christian Advocate*, Feb. 4, 25, 1871; *Seattle*

By early February, 1872, cattle which had been driven eastward across the Cascades in the preceding autumn were dying rapidly in Klickitat County, Washington; and a month later, in the Snake River Valley in Idaho, cattle were dying from lack of shelter. In Whitman County, Washington, the spell of cold weather was said to be "one of the worst on record," although it was not so prolonged as that of 1861-62; and, wonderful to relate, in some districts there was adequate feed for the cattle. Speaking generally, the losses were less than those of the winter of 1861-62, but, in the aggregate, they were so large that not a few persons, on viewing the disaster, appeared to be conscience-stricken.[48]

The lesson taught by the winter of 1871-72, as the editor of the *Willamette Farmer* believed, was to "cut hay and put up sheds" —a lesson which, of course, should have been learned from earlier devastating winters. But the feeling that he was pleading a lost cause seemed to possess his mind, for he expressed the belief that, given a few winters of mild weather, stockmen would forget whatever this winter had taught them.[49]

The winter of 1872-73 appears to have been mild throughout the entire Oregon Country. Nevertheless, when the Salem Farmers' Club, on April 17, 1873, debated in the Marion County courthouse the question whether it paid better "to feed and house livestock in winter" than to let the animals "run on pasture," the consensus favored feeding.[50] Whether such a verdict could then have been obtained in most districts east of the Cascades is

Intelligencer, May 1, 1871. On the severity of this winter in Colorado, see the *Daily Central City Register*, Feb. 18, 1872, and J. Max Clark, "The Losses of Stock in Colorado the Past Winter," *National Live-Stock Journal*, III (July, 1872), 231-32.

[48] *Weekly Mountaineer*, Jan. 13, Feb. 3, 24, 1872; *Walla Walla Union*, Feb. 17, March 16, 1872; Lewiston *Idaho Signal*, March 9, 1872; *Walla Walla Statesman*, April 20, 1872; *Willamette Farmer*, Jan. 6, 20, Feb. 3, 17, March 9, 1872. Nevertheless, a letter dated at Goose Lake on March 20, 1872, says that the winter in that country had been a "pleasant one." *Pacific Christian Advocate*, April 11, 1872. On this winter see also Northern Pacific Railroad, *Settlers' Guide to Washington Territory, and to the Lands of the Northern Pacific Railroad on the Pacific Slope* (New York, [1878]), p. 17; Mrs. W. E. Baskett, "The History of the Early Whitman County Pioneers," in the *Colfax Commoner*, July 16, 1920.

[49] *Willamette Farmer*, Feb. 3, 1872.

[50] *Walla Walla Union*, Jan. 25, March 1, 15, 1873; La Grande *Mountain Sentinel*, March 1, 1873; *Pacific Christian Advocate*, Feb. 27, April 3, 1873; *Willamette Farmer*, May 3, 1873.

questionable. The next winter struck the Pacific Northwest with uneven force. In some districts, such as Wasco County, Oregon, and the panhandle of Idaho, livestock fared well; but elsewhere late winter storms were damaging. From about the end of February until well into April, considerable losses of cattle were being reported in Umatilla County, south-central and northeastern Oregon, and southern Idaho.[51] The effects of this winter generally were perhaps exaggerated by "D.B.R.," who remarked in a letter from Canyon City, Oregon, on April 18, 1874, that the winter "just past" would "no doubt long be remembered throughout the North Pacific slope as one of severity." Although the destruction of stock, "proportionately," was not so great as that of 1861-62, it had, he said, been greater in some localities. The total loss, amounting perhaps to 10 per cent of the cattle and sheep in the Oregon Country, he attributed to lack of "proper provision of forage and shelter."[52]

The losses of the winter of 1874-75, which had broken with fury over the Oregon Country by the middle of January, 1875, were undoubtedly heavy. As this winter progressed, letters from widely separated communities appeared in some newspapers, and the contents of these letters, whether precise or imprecise, were quickly disseminated throughout the Pacific Northwest in the exchange columns of other newspapers. At the outset, such correspondents appeared to waver between the desire to be truthful and the wish to avoid seeming pessimistic. It is possible, of course, that events marched so rapidly that an accurate description of one day became an inaccurate description of the next day. But presently certain facts became so obvious that no pretense of optimism could conceal them. In some localities, where the snow was deep, cattle were dying for want of feed and shelter; elsewhere, because streams and other watering places were frozen over, cattle were dying of thirst. The Snake River

[51] *Sacramento Daily Union*, Jan. 11, Feb. 6, 11, March 17-18, 24, 30, 31, April 6, 1874, quoting various newspapers of the Oregon Country; *Yreka Union*, Feb. 7, March 7, 31, 1874; *Walla Walla Union*, Dec. 20, 27, 1873; Jan. 10, 24, March 14, April 4, 1874; *Walla Walla Statesman*, Feb. 14, April 18, 1874; Lewiston *Idaho Signal*, Feb. 28, March 14, 21, April 4, 1874; *Willamette Farmer*, Feb. 21, 28, March 7, 21, April 25, 1874; Winnemucca *Silver State*, Sept. 17, 1874.
[52] *Willamette Farmer*, May 1, 1873 (supplement).

Valley, previously reckoned a winter paradise for cattle, had fallen into the deadly clutch of winter. Everywhere in this valley, from Fort Hall in the east to the mouth of the Snake River in the west, cattle were suffering.[53] Early in February, 1875, Joseph Freeman, on returning to Walla Walla from an inspection of his herd on the north side of this river, "below the mouth of the Palouse," reported that "the water . . . [was] frozen up and the cattle . . . [were] suffering terribly from thirst. He did not find more than a dozen dead cattle, but thinks that if the water remains frozen up as at present for two or three weeks there would hardly be a cow left to tell the tale of bovine suffering." His fears were realized, and stockmen in Whitman County, Washington, who had depended on the Snake River Valley for a winter range, suffered heavy losses of livestock. No surviving cow told a tale of "bovine suffering" in the Snake River Valley, but a Whitman County pioneer recalled in later years his experiences of that frightful winter:

Most of the settlers had driven their cattle to the Snake river valley for the reason that [there] the three previous winters had been mild and the cattle wintered there without hay. Snow seldom fell along the Snake. But in 1874 and 1875, the snow was as deep on Snake river as it was elsewhere. Thousands of cattle milled up and down the river and died in droves in the deep canyons. . . . I attempted to gather up my cattle, but the deepness of the snow and the bitter cold made it impossible for me to move them from the Snake river to my homestead near Colfax. When winter started, I had 150 head. When spring came, 15 were alive.[54]

Everywhere along the Snake River dead cattle were so numerous that they challenged scavengers to become proficient in gathering a grim harvest. We learn of their proficiency from the *Weekly Mountaineer* of March 27, 1875, which reported that some persons were

[53] On this winter throughout the Pacific Northwest generally, including Montana, see not only the *Walla Walla Union*, Jan. 30, Feb. 6-27, March 13-20, 1875, the Virginia City *Montanian*, March 4, 1875, and the *Pacific Christian Advocate*, March 4, 25, 1875, but also the *Morning Oregonian*, Jan. 27-30, Feb. 1-27, March 8-23, April 1-24, 1875, the Olympia *North-Western Farmer*, Feb. 27, 1875, the Seattle *Weekly Intelligencer*, May 6, 1875, quoting the *Walla Walla Statesman*, and the *Willamette Farmer*, Feb. 5 through April 9, 1875.
[54] *Walla Walla Union*, Feb. 13, 1875; J. B. Holt, in the Spokane *Sunday Spokesman-Review*, Part IV, May 1, 1932.

making good wages skinning dead cattle. They have a quicker process than is generally employed. They tie the head of the dead animal to a stake driven in the ground, cut the skin around the neck and rip the hide open down the legs and belly, then hitch a span of horses to the skin at the neck and in a minute pull it clear off quicker and easier than any other way. Two men with a span of horses make $20 a day in this way.[55]

Estimates of the losses of cattle made for various localities during this winter varied from 10 to 50 per cent. What seemed to be perfectly clear, however, was that losses tended to be slight where cattle were properly cared for, and heavy where they were left to scrounge for themselves. As in past years, many cattlemen, trusting their luck, had made little or no provision for feeding and sheltering their stock. Naturally, editorial advice in this trying time was as abundant as it was cheap and unwanted. The *Walla Walla Union* took as the text for a sermon the disreputable practice of keeping larger herds than could be properly cared for, and the *Idaho Tri-Weekly Statesman,* the *Willamette Farmer,* and other newspapers appealed to stockmen to adhere to the principles of humanitarianism and to be more regardful of their own interests.[56]

But evidence that such admonitions availed much is far to seek. The return of mild weather lulled many stockmen into the feeling of security from which they had been momentarily shaken. Surely, many of them seemed to think, there must be some way to justify the old practice of neglect. In Wasco County some stockmen thought that they had the answer to the problem. As "Mr. Luckey, of Ochoco," told an editor at The Dalles, these men, observing that the loss of livestock in their section had been heavy where the grass was "grazed down," were either gathering, or talking of gathering, "their cattle and driving them further back to secure new range, which he [Mr. Luckey] thinks will be done from year to year until sheep will entirely take the place of cattle in that country." Of similar mind was "Mr. Baker," a stockman who, as the editor of the Union *Mountain Sentinel* learned, was planning to drive his herd to a range on the Snake River,

[55] *Weekly Mountaineer,* March 27, 1885.
[56] *Walla Walla Union,* Feb. 13, 20, 1875, quoting the *Pendleton Tribune; Idaho Tri-Weekly Statesman,* Jan. 26, 1875; *Willamette Farmer,* May 14, 1875.

near "the old Brownlee ferry," where other cattle had safely passed the winter of 1874-75, and where Mr. Baker did not "expect to require any hay" for his cattle. The editor of the *Mountain Sentinel* approved of Mr. Baker's idea, saying, "We have a vast extent of country capable of grazing millions of head of cattle and horses, and raising them to maturity without the trouble and expense necessarily incurred in any of the Western States, and our cattle command as high prices as do theirs."[57] Presumably these men were not troubled by the thought that they were deferring the solution of a problem which could not be ignored indefinitely if the business of grazing livestock on open ranges were to continue. In truth, it seems that the memory of most cattlemen was short, and that the train of their thought at times did not lead them to common sense.

Be that as it may, the winters during the second half of the 1870's were, in the aggregate, perhaps not so troublesome in the Oregon Country as those of the first half of this decade. The winter of 1875-76 inflicted on stockmen some losses both on the Snake River and in the country of the Salmon River in Idaho, and it brought severe weather to the Lake country of southern Oregon, where the loss of livestock was "pretty heavy."[58] In the Yakima Valley, however, that winter, at least as late as mid-February, had been "the pleasant exception of the past five years," and to that time it also had been mild in the Kittitas Valley.[59] The next two winters were of like character, that of 1876-77 being delightfully "spring-like" everywhere in Oregon, and presumably also in Washington and Idaho, and that of 1877-78 being generally mild throughout the Oregon Country. But the winter of 1878-79, at least in some parts of the Pacific Northwest, was severe enough to cause a considerable loss of livestock.[60] In retrospect it was perhaps regarded as a winter of transition.

[57] *Weekly Mountaineer*, May 29, 1875; *Mountain Sentinel*, Nov. 20, 1875.
[58] *Sacramento Daily Union*, Feb. 19, 23, 1876, quoting newspapers of Idaho; *Morning Oregonian*, March 23-25, May 17, 1876; *Weekly Mountaineer*, April 1, 8, 1876; *Pacific Christian Advocate*, March 30, April 6, 1876.
[59] Letter from Yakima, dated Feb. 16, 1876, in the *Weekly Mountaineer*, Feb. 26, 1876; report of F. D. Schnebly on the mild winter in the Kittitas Valley, *ibid.*, April 16, 1876, quoting the *Walla Walla Union*.
[60] *Willamette Farmer*, Feb. 2, 9, March 16, 1877; *Weekly Mountaineer*, March

The winter of 1879-80 was presumably even more severe than that of 1871-72. It caused losses of livestock in Montana, Nevada, Utah, and northern California, as well as in Oregon, Washington, and Idaho. But it was not uniformly destructive in the Oregon Country. In eastern Washington it was somewhat damaging to livestock, although in most parts of that country the losses were perhaps no greater than those of ordinary winters. In southern Idaho cattle on the ranges suffered much from want of feed and shelter, but there were no reports of heavy losses. Indeed, as late as March 6, 1880, the *Idaho Tri-Weekly Statesman* confessed that Idaho, comparatively speaking, had been fortunate. Although many cattle in Idaho were then thin, most of them were expected to be in good condition by the middle of April "for their march across the Rocky Mountains in search of pastures green or to fill the stalls in the markets of our Eastern cities."[61]

Oregon, however, was less fortunate than Washington and Idaho during this winter. On February 22, 1880, a correspondent at Fort Harney reported that it was then estimated that "one fourth of the cattle in the Harney Basin" would not survive; and a few days later J. C. Abbott, "a prominent cattleman of Grant County, Oregon," remarked in Winnemucca, Nevada, that the winter of 1879-80 had been "the most severe on stock ever experienced in southeastern Oregon and northern Nevada. In Harney Valley and on the north side of Stein mountain, fully twenty-five per cent of the cattle running at large . . . [had] perished of cold and hunger."[62] Even more discouraging was a letter which

17, 1877; *Idaho Weekly Statesman*, Jan. 19, 1878; *Willamette Farmer*, March 15, April 26, 1878; *Lewiston Teller*, Jan. 10, 31, Feb. 7-28, March 21, 1879; *Idaho Tri-Weekly Statesman*, Jan. 30, 1879; *Pacific Christian Advocate*, April 3, 1879. Of the losses of livestock in eastern Washington, the *Walla Walla Union* of March 1, 1879, said: "Parties interested inform us that the loss of stock in this country will hardly reach ten per cent. This although a severe loss is not near as great as it was supposed to be. From the section of country north of Snake river, the lower Palouse and Crab Creek countries, the reports indicate a greater percentage of loss."

[61] *Tenth Federal Census, 1880*, Vol. III, *Agriculture* (Washington, D.C., 1883), pp. 1025, 1036, 1066, 1072, 1080; *Yakima Record*, March 20, 1880; *Spokan Times*, April 1, 1880; *Dayton News*, Feb. 21, 1880; Oxford *Idaho Enterprise*, Feb. 5, 1880; *Idaho Tri-Weekly Statesman*, March 6, 1880.

[62] Canyon City *Grant County News*, Feb. 28, 1880; *Sacramento Daily Record-Union*, March 20, 1880, quoting the *Silver State*; Virginia City, Nev., *Daily Territorial Enterprise*, March 26, 1880; *Weekly Mountaineer*, April 8, 1880.

Frank Sweetser wrote to his wife from Silvies Valley on April 17, 1880, saying, "I arrived here all safe tonight at 7 o'clock. I am about discouraged, the first sight that greeted me on entering the valley was 14 head of dead cattle under one pine tree, this was three miles from the house and from there to the 'shanty' I counted 73 dead cattle. . . . I see a few head of cattle on the meadows, but they are very few, and poor as crows. . . ."[63]

If the loss in southeastern Oregon was serious, that in Lake County (which then included present-day Klamath County) was more so. The agent at the Klamath Indian Reservation, Linus M. Nickerson, wrote on August 9, 1880, that a "winter of hitherto unknown severity, of unusual length, and of great depth of snow, destroyed fully 75 per cent of the Indian cattle and over 40 per cent of their horses." Such loss, he said, "was severely felt, but it was borne with a creditable spirit of resignation. . . .The loss of stockmen outside of and contiguous to this reservation has been quite as great as within it." The winter was perhaps equally severe at the Warm Springs Indian Reservation in north-central Oregon, as it also was nearby, in the neighborhood of Prineville, situated in what was then Wasco County.[64]

East of the Klamath Reservation, in Lake County, the losses were distressingly large. Early in February, 1880, cattle in this country were suffering severely, and some had died; near the end of that month large numbers of them were reported to be dying. Early in March more snow was falling, more cattle were dying, and feed was giving out. A few weeks later a correspondent, writing from Alkali in Lake County, estimated that the losses would "range from 10 to 40 per cent in different localities," the greatest loss being in the Langell Valley. Early in May, 1880, a private letter from Lake County revealed that the Applegate brothers had lost six hundred head, J. D. Carr twelve hundred head, Langell brothers 60 per cent, and Fulkerson and Campbell their whole band. Interestingly enough, the writer of this letter said that the cattle and horses that were not fed came through

[63] Original letter in the possession of a daughter of Frank W. Sweetser, Mrs. K. M. C. Neill, Grants Pass, Oregon.
[64] Commissioner of Indian Affairs, *Report* (1880), pp. 139, 271; Lakeview, Ore., *State Line Herald*, March 20, 1880.

the winter better than those that were fed.[65] More accurate, perhaps, was a later report published in the *Jacksonville Times* and quoted by the *Morning Oregonian* of June 22, 1880, as follows:

> Arthur Langell, of Lost River, estimates the average loss of stock at 40 per cent in that region, his firm losing about 300 head, and other large stock-raisers in proportion. Jesse D. Carr is the heaviest loser, his fine stock perishing by thousands. Some parties lost nearly their entire bands after feeding them the greater portion of the season. Lake County has suffered a heavy blow, and it will be some time before she will fully recover from it.

Even more to the point is a report, published several months later, which affirms that "Langell Bros. branded 323 calves in 1879 and only 73 in 1880, while Jesse D. Carr branded 800 in 1879 and 53 a year later." There is little wonder that the winter of 1879-80 caused "a great deal of discouragement among stock men" in Lake County, Oregon.[66]

The winter of 1880-81, as severe perhaps as that of 1861-62, caused widespread discouragement not only in the Oregon Country, but also on the ranges of the Great Plains east of the Rockies. This was winter at its deadliest worst in the American West. Nearly everywhere there was complaint of crusted snow. Early in the winter the Chinook wind had breathed "softly on the snow" in the Oregon Country, but only long enough to melt the surface, which soon froze hard again. "The unfortunate sheep and cattle," as one perceptive observer wrote, "tried in vain to scratch through the icy crust, and died from starvation within a few inches of their food." Such was the case on the Yakima Indian Reservation and in the Kittitas Valley, as well as in the Spokane country, the Big Bend of the Columbia River, and the Walla Walla country, and also, no doubt, in many other parts of the Pacific Northwest,[67] and of the country as far east as

---

[65] *Morning Oregonian*, Feb. 3, 24, 1880; *Oregon Sentinel*, Feb. 18, March 24, April 7, 1880; *Weekly Mountaineer*, March 18, 1880; *State Line Herald*, April 10, 17, May 19, 1880.

[66] *Morning Oregonian*, Jan. 12, 1881, Sept. 22, Oct. 7, 1880.

[67] *Yakima Record*, Jan. 22, 1881; *Northwest Tribune*, Feb. 4, 1881, quoting the Dayton, Wash., *Columbia Chronicle*; *Lewiston Teller*, Jan. 21, 1881; Nash, *Two Years in Oregon*, p. 171; *Willamette Farmer*, Feb. 11, March 4, 1881; *Morning Oregonian*, March 24, April 13, 1881; Olympia *Puget Sound Weekly Courier*,

Nebraska.[68] By January 26, 1881, stockmen in the Tygh Valley, Wasco County, Oregon, were "praying for a Chinook wind to take off the snow," and the sooner it came the better pleased they would be.[69]

But the Chinook did not come again, and cattle went down, frequently in heaps, never to rise again. Feed which had been stored up by some stockmen gave out, and, in most instances, could not be replaced, even at exorbitant prices. In desperation some cattlemen, sickened by the suffering of their cattle, offered to sell their herds at buyers' prices; but there were no buyers. Before the end of January, 1881, an editor in Walla Walla was ready to face the blunt truth. "There is," he wrote, "no use denying or trying to conceal the fact that large numbers of cattle, horses and sheep have perished and will perish in Eastern Washington and Oregon this winter for lack of feed and shelter." As the winter proceeded, the extent of the disaster became appalling. Correspondents writing from numerous stock-raising districts, and travelers passing through various parts of the country, reported ghastly tales of dead or dying cattle; and these reports were printed and reprinted in newspapers throughout the Oregon Country, and sometimes in newspapers south and east of the Oregon Country, where the severity of that winter was also felt.[70] Cattle which had been driven eastward from Oregon and Washington during the preceding summer perished in large numbers, some in Montana and others along the Platte River in Nebraska.[71] But it was cold comfort that the editor of the *Morning Oregonian* gave to stockmen in the Pacific Northwest when, on

April 22, 1881; report of James H. Wilbur, Aug. 15, 1881, in Commissioner of Indian Affairs, *Report* (1881), p. 173.

[68] Of the suffering of cattle in western Nebraska, see the account in the *National Live-Stock Journal*, XII (February, 1881), 45, 63.

[69] *Willamette Farmer*, Feb. 11, 1881, quoting a letter written in the Tygh Valley on Jan. 26, 1881.

[70] *Yakima Record*, Jan. 22, 1881; Idaho City *Idaho Semi-Weekly World*, March 11, 1881; *Willamette Farmer*, Feb. 11, March 4, April 1, 1881; *Morning Oregonian*, March 24, 1881, quoting the *Yakima Record*; *Sacramento Daily Record-Union*, March 2, April 4, 26, 1881.

[71] In the Colorado Springs *Weekly Gazette* of March 26, 1881, the secretary of the Board of Cattle Inspection Commissioners of Colorado says: "The cattle dead on the Platte are, in great measure, Oregon and Texas through cattle," of which about one-half were owned in Wyoming.

March 21, 1881, he remarked that the stockmen of "Oregon and Washington are not alone in the losses they have met during the past winter. The usefulness of the great plains, as a stock range, is about exhausted."[72]

The disaster in the Oregon Country during this winter would have been even greater had there not been very large drives of cattle eastward from the Pacific Northwest during the summer of 1880.[73] Nevertheless, the passing of winter disclosed scenes like those of 1862, recollections of which were still vivid in the minds of older settlers in Transcascadia. By February, 1881, coyotes in eastern Washington were busy "feeding on dead stock," and before and after that time cattle skinners were doing a thriving business. Far and wide putrefying carcasses defiled the air of springtime. In Yakima City a public meeting was called to devise means of disposing of dead cattle; and in Pataha City an editor wrote that the "stench from the dead cattle over the hills ... [was] terrific. If something is not done to get rid of it, it may breed an epidemic."[74] Again and again the familiar refrain of "the lesson learned" was heard in the land: it was chanted by editors and correspondents, perhaps with the momentary approval of most stockmen. But the hope of making much by doing little was as tough as it was enduring, and for years to come some stockmen, oblivious to the fact that increasing settlement of the country was constricting the area for grazing, would continue to anticipate getting rich "by owning cattle ranging on Government land and receiving no other care or attention than the application of the branding iron to the calves."[75]

The determination of cattlemen of the Oregon Country to stick to their guns, notwithstanding their losses, was affirmed by the editor of the *Walla Walla Statesman* late in May, 1881. He did

[72] Quoted in Harvey W. Scott, *History of the Oregon Country*, compiled by Leslie M. Scott (Cambridge, Mass., 1924), III, 104.

[73] J. Orin Oliphant, "The Eastward Movement of Cattle from the Oregon Country," *AH*, XX (January, 1946), 19-43.

[74] *Willamette Farmer*, Feb. 15, 1881; *Lewiston Teller*, Jan. 28, 1881; *Sacramento Daily Record-Union*, April 4, 26, 1881; *Northwest Tribune*, Feb. 4, 1881, quoting the *Columbia Chronicle*; *Walla Walla Union*, March 19, 1881. Pendleton, Oregon, was confronted with a similar problem. *Morning Oregonian*, March 29, 1881.

[75] Colfax *Palouse Gazette*, Jan. 28, 1881, quoting the *Walla Walla Union*.

not minimize their losses. When the "full account" of the recent disaster was rendered after the roundups were completed "in the Snake and Columbia river basin up to the British line," he perceived that the disaster had been greater than that of 1861-62, and reported that "Messrs. Phelps & Wadleigh lose about 17,000 head out of 24,000. G. J. Germane, 4,400 out of 6,000. Austin, 2,500 out of 3,200. Kennedy & Neice, 4,000 out of 5,000, and others in proportion. Of herds of 1,000 and 2,000 head on the Columbia, 50 to 100 or 200 head only have been found." But, he continued, despite such heavy losses, stockmen "do not feel inclined to give up the business, but will stick to it another twenty years, in which interval more large fortunes can be made. Cattle raising, like mining and other speculative business, has bad spots in it occasionally, but when well stuck to always pays in the end."[76]

To men of such mind who came through that winter with at least a few head of cattle and with their credit unimpaired, the damage was not irreparable. Cattle prices in the Pacific Northwest had started upward; the years of depression were passing by. Eastward drives of cattle since 1876 and winter storms had wiped out an embarrassing surplus, and had given the ranges of the Oregon Country an opportunity to recover from years of overgrazing. Accordingly, cattlemen in this country looked forward with their usual confidence to the years ahead.

But with one exception, that of 1888-89, winters in the Oregon Country during the 1880's could not rightly be called mild. During most of those years, however, cattle fared reasonably well, despite the fact that many ranges for cattle were shrinking because of the advance of both farmers and sheepmen. There was considerable suffering, and some loss of cattle, during the winter of 1881-82, and apparently more suffering and somewhat greater losses during the winter of 1882-83; but there was no widespread disaster in either of those winters. Most of the losses of cattle during 1882-83 occurred in February, 1883, and by March most parts of the Oregon Country could report that the worry of stockmen about their cattle had been greater than their losses war-

[76] Quoted by the *National Live-Stock Journal*, XII (July, 1881), 312.

ranted.[77] In that month the *Yakima Signal* could say that, near the mouth of the Yakima River, the loss of cattle was not more than 3 per cent. On the Indian reservation the damage had been greater. "Perhaps," the *Signal* concluded, "much of the loss was occasioned by the frozen condition of the watering places." A few weeks earlier this newspaper had affirmed that stockmen of the Yakima Valley had profited by the experience of two years earlier, but early in March the *Yakima Record* had endorsed an editorial in which the *Portland News* had expressed astonishment at the improvidence of stockmen in not making adequate provision for the care of their livestock in winter, and considerable bewilderment at their having so lightly regarded the disaster of 1880-81. "The *News* is right," this newspaper affirmed, "and the *Record* for years has endeavored to induce our farmers to adopt a more provident policy. However, it is possible [that] experience is the best teacher. The losses of two or three winters may teach them prudence."[78]

Perhaps a considerable number of cattlemen had learned to be prudent, but even so the losses of cattle in the Oregon Country were not slight through the remaining years of the 1880's. During the next three winters, such losses were rather light; but the effects of the winter of 1886-87 on the ranges of the American West were not soon forgotten. Its damage was devastating on the northern Great Plains, especially in Montana; but in the Oregon Country the damage, although severe in some parts of eastern Oregon and southern Idaho, was not generally upsetting. Perhaps the Grangeville, Idaho, *Free Press* accurately expressed

[77] *Idaho Avalanche*, Feb. 11, 25, 1882; *Idaho Weekly Statesman*, Feb. 11, March 25, 1882; *Pataha City Spirit*, March 11, 1882; *Idaho Semi-Weekly World*, April 14, 1882. On the Great Plains this winter was relatively mild. Denver *Rocky Mountain News*, March 11, 1882, and *Omaha Daily Republican*, May 5, 1882; Portland *West Shore*, VIII (March, 1883), 65; *Idaho Semi-Weekly World*, March 6, 1883.

[78] *Yakima Signal*, Feb. 17, March 17, 1883; *Yakima Record*, March 10, 1883. In an editorial on March 24, 1883, the *Morning Oregonian* remarked that the considerable loss of cattle in Oregon during the preceding winter had been localized. "With us," it said, "in the worst winter known, the severe weather was confined to a belt about thirty miles on either side of the Columbia river. So that while in this comparatively small area there was a considerable loss of stock, yet from a point thirty miles south of The Dalles to the Nevada line and beyond, stock came through the winter in splendid condition."

the difference between the experiences of stockmen in Montana and those in the Oregon Country when it said, in the summer of 1887, that "in Montana stockmen are congratulating themselves that they only lost fifty per cent of their stock last winter, while here our cattlemen are kicking and cursing because a few of them lost ten per cent."[79] During the next two winters, losses in the Oregon Country were not noticeably high. In 1887-88 they probably averaged less than those of a "usual" winter, and in 1888-89 the winter was truly mild—in striking contrast to the winter that would see the 1880's merge into the 1890's.[80]

The winter of 1889-90 in the Pacific Northwest was one of the four worst winters recorded there before 1900. Neither the winter of 1861-62 nor that of 1880-81 had been more severe or more devastating in its effects. Stockmen, in general, were ill-prepared for it. The preceding three or four summers had been unusually dry, and the exceedingly dry summer of 1889 had caused a scarcity of hay and of feed on the ranges everywhere in the Oregon Country. As early as August, stockmen in northern Idaho were beginning to "feel scared" about feed for their animals because of dry weather and "recent fires in the mountains." Everywhere in the Pacific Northwest, it seems, cattle entered that winter in poor condition because of the depleted ranges. The winter which struck those cattle was, as the Governor of Idaho reported in 1890, the "most severe ever experienced since the settlement of this country." Consequently, the losses of livestock were extraordinarily large, as we learn not only from the newspapers of the Oregon Country, but also from the federal census of 1890 and from the Report of the Commissioner of Indian Affairs in that

[79] Osgood, *Day of the Cattleman*, pp. 218-22; W. Turrentine Jackson, "British Interests in the Range Cattle Business," in Maurice Frink *et al.*, *When Grass Was King* (Boulder, Colo., 1956), pp. 257-60; *National Live-Stock Journal*, January through May, 1887; *Willamette Farmer*, Feb. 18, April 6, 27, 1887; Harold E. Briggs, *Frontiers of the Northwest* (New York, 1940), pp. 240-44; *Northwest Tribune*, April 7, 1887, quoting the *Helena Independent*; *Idaho Semi-Weekly World*, March 1, 1887; *Lewiston Teller*, Feb. 17, 24, March 10, 1887; *Morning Oregonian*, Oct. 20, 1887, quoting an "Ochoco paper"; *Northwestern Live-Stock Journal*, July 22, 1887, quoting the Grangeville, Ida., *Free Press*.

[80] *Morning Oregonian*, Jan. 14—Feb. 12, 1888; *Walla Walla Union*, Jan. 14, Feb. 11, 1888; *Idaho Weekly Statesman*, Jan. 12, 1888; *Palouse Gazette*, Jan. 27, Feb. 10, 1888; *Walla Walla Union*, March 9, 1889; *Oregon Statesman*, Feb. 15, 1889; *Morning Oregonian*, Feb. 21, 1889.

year.[81] If fewer cattle perished in that winter in the Pacific Northwest than in 1880-81, the reason was that fewer cattle were there in the later than in the earlier winter. As the *Weekly Oregonian* had remarked on August 27, 1889, "owing to the influx of settlers," the ranges were "growing smaller," and "the palmy days of the cattlemen" had become "a thing of the past."

Notwithstanding the fact that some of the cattlemen had provided some feed for their cattle, the losses nearly everywhere were appalling. During January and February, 1890, when the snow was deep and the temperature low, there was a common tale of woe. It came from every direction—from the Big Bend of the Columbia River to Lake County in south-central Oregon, from the Yakima Valley to the Snake River plains, from the Palouse country southward through the Walla Walla Valley and northeastern Oregon to the Owyhee and Malheur countries. It was a gruesome tale of cattle dying from lack of feed, water, and shelter.[82] The diary of Benedict Gubser[83] recites a dismal story of the suffering of cattle in the Okanogan Valley; but similar stories came from other parts of the Oregon Country. A letter of March 12, 1890, from the Jordan Valley in the Owyhee country, for example, tells us that it is "an awful sight to see horses and cattle actually starving to death," and a few days earlier a report from the Spokane country had noted that a considerable number of hides, "taken from animals which perished during the late severe storm for want of food, are coming into the market."[84]

Early in March, according to one estimate, half of the pre-

[81] *Weekly Oregonian*, Aug. 16-23, 1889; *Lewiston Teller*, Aug. 9, 1889; *Northwest Tribune*, April 25, 1890; *East Oregon Herald*, Dec. 26, 1889; Secretary of the Interior, *Report* (1890), p. 544; *Eleventh Federal Census 1890: Agriculture* (Washington, D.C., 1895), p. 39; Commissioner of Indian Affairs, *Report* (1890), pp. 80, 220, 222; *Weekly Oregonian*, Jan. 31, Feb. 14-28, March 28, 1890; "Winter on the Stock Ranges," *West Shore* XVI (Feb. 8, 1890), 166-67.

[82] *Spokane Spokesman*, March 16, 1890; *Cheney Enterprise*, Jan. 30, 1890, quoting the Davenport, Wash., *Lincoln County Times*; *Morning Oregonian*, Feb. 24–April 9, 1890; *East Oregon Herald*, Jan. 23–April 3, 1890; *Weekly Oregonian*, April 4—May 31, 1890; *Idaho Weekly Statesman*, March 1, 1890; *Idaho Avalanche*, March 22, 1890; *Palouse Gazette*, Feb. 28, March 28, 1890; Commissioner of Indian Affairs, *Report* (1890), p. 204.

[83] Excerpts from this diary were published in *Glimpses of Pioneer Life* (Okanogan, Wash., 1924), pp. 104-6.

[84] *Idaho Avalanche*, March 15, 1890; *Sprague Herald*, Feb. 27, 1890. An editor in Boise remarked, somewhat dryly, that "stockmen hereabouts may derive some

sumed twenty thousand head of cattle in the Yakima Valley had perished, and at about the same time livestock on the open spaces of the Big Bend country were dying in large numbers. Some of the Big Bend losses were of "immigrant stocks" which had recently been driven in from Oregon, and one "resident" stockman openly hinted what no doubt many others were thinking— namely, that it served the intruders right. Farther eastward, on the hills of the Palouse country, the people were experiencing "two winters in one season." A few weeks earlier, as the *Palouse Gazette* of February 28, 1890, affirmed,

When the warm breath of the Chinook passed over the country, . . . even the wisest of the weather prophets and "old settlers" confidently predicted the rout of the storm king. But stern fate willed it otherwise and the second winter, which folded the country in its cold embrace, has been even more severe than the first, though the depth of snow is not so great. . . . Reports from the large cattle ranches west of Colfax are anything but pleasant. The mortality among cattle, sheep and horses is said to be very great, some placing it as high as fifty per cent in some bands. . . .

In southeastern Oregon, in March, 1890, it was estimated that Jesse D. Carr, "the cattle king of Southern Oregon," had lost "$80,000 worth of cattle during the past winter."[85]

More than ever before, cattlemen in the Oregon Country during the winter of 1889-90 were troubled in spirit because of the suffering of their livestock; more than ever before, newspaper editors and others were asserting that, at long last, the lesson had been learned—namely, that livestock must receive adequate care during winters.[86] Sound business sense required such care, and civilized human beings were demanding it. Presently the Governor of Idaho was assuring the Secretary of the Interior

comfort from the fact that the loss has been so great in all parts of the country from Texas to Montana, that the scarcity will tend to enhance the price." *Idaho Weekly Statesman*, March 29, 1890.

[85] *Yakima Herald*, March 6, 1890, quoted in *An Illustrated History of Klickitat, Yakima and Kittitas Counties* . . . (Chicago, 1904), p. 181; *Spokane Spokesman*, March 9, 13, 1890, quoting the *Wilbur Register*; *East Oregon Herald*, March 20, 1890.

[86] In eastern Washington the Ritzville *Adams County Times*, for example, affirmed that the winter of 1889-90 provided "a pretty severe lesson to stock growers in the state of Washington" by demonstrating "the folly and actual wickedness of relying upon the ranges to carry stock through the winter season." Quoted in the *Palouse Gazette*, March 25, 1890.

that Idaho cattlemen were "guarding against future heavy losses by providing winter feed."[87] No doubt many of them did so, and no doubt many stockmen in both Oregon and Washington also did so. Nevertheless, the loss of livestock during severe winters in the Oregon Country was not a thing of the past. Because of the heavy losses during the winter of 1892-93, the *Morning Oregonian* demanded that the law against cruelty to animals be invoked to put a stop to the "barbarous custom" of making no provision for winter feeding of livestock.[88] Presumably nothing of the sort was done, for in the winter of 1898-99 there was considerable loss of livestock in eastern Oregon; and, as late as February, 1907, stockmen in Harney County, who were well provided with feed, were not disturbed by the reports of "fearful loss of stock" in Idaho, Wyoming, and Montana.[89] Such losses might raise the price of cattle in Oregon.

The notion that severe winters in the Oregon Country are exceptional has been cherished by the inhabitants of this region. Winters of extreme, prolonged, and widespread severity have been exceptional, as this chapter has revealed, but winters devoid of some "killing" weather have been infrequent. As late as 1924-25, there was exceptionally severe weather throughout the Pacific Northwest during the week of Christmas. The thermometer in Burns, Oregon, registered "45 below," and the loss of livestock on feeding grounds in Harney County was heavy. At the same time, in Spokane and elsewhere in eastern Washington the temperature was well below zero; in Oregon City the falls of the Willamette River were frozen; and in White Salmon people were walking on ice across the Columbia River. But more than a year later, near the end of the balmy winter of 1925-26—a winter like that of 1876-77 or 1888-89—an editorial writer for the Spokane *Spokesman-Review* argued that, since only three severe winters —those of 1846-47, 1861-62, and 1889-90—stood out in "a record

[87] 51st Cong., 2nd sess., H. Ex. Doc. 1, XIII, 544. See also Governor George L. Shoup's letter to the "Farmers and Stock Growers of Idaho," in which he urged upon them "the importance of cultivating a large area of hay land." *Idaho Weekly Statesman* (*Extra Sheet*, May 10, 1890).

[88] *Morning Oregonian*, March 8, 1893, quoted in Scott, *History of the Oregon Country*, III, 107-8.

[89] Burns *Times-Herald*, March 29, May 17, 1899, Feb. 2, 1907.

of 80 years as exceptional," the proof was clear that the winters
of the Inland Empire are "mild—not so mild as this winter, but
moderate and exhilarating."[90] Somewhat closer to the truth is
a pronouncement made more than fifty years earlier, when an
editor in Oregon, recalling twenty-five years of experience in the
Pacific Northwest, said forthrightly that delightful winters in
this country are exceptional—not usual.[91]

[90] *Morning Oregonian,* Dec. 27, 1924; *Spokesman-Review,* March 5, 1926.
[91] *Willamette Farmer,* Jan. 22, 1875.

CHAPTER IX

Lo, the Poor Indian

LESS dangerous to stockmen than the problem of severe winters, but nevertheless at times highly exasperating, was the abiding problem of the Indians. Even after the wars of the 1850's had brought a semblance of peace to the Oregon Country, Indians continued to get in the way of both stockmen and settlers in some parts of this region. To these newcomers the Indians, at worst, were a menace; at best, they were a nuisance. During the 1860's and 1870's, there came from the intermontane area of the Pacific Northwest numerous complaints of damages done by marauding Indians, and during the Bannock War of 1878 there was some loss of life and considerable losses of livestock by both settlers and stockmen.[1] Neither before this war nor for some time after it did all the Indians in this region live upon established reservations,[2] and some of those who did so occasionally wandered therefrom and either disturbed or stole cattle belonging to white men. As late as August, 1880, an editor in the Yakima Valley could say that "Indians in and about White Bluffs are again at their old trade of killing settlers' and stockmen's cattle." He was willing to "prophesy" that, "should one be caught

---

[1] See, for example, the Silver City *Owyhee Avalanche*, Oct. 5, Nov. 23, 1867; the *Sacramento Daily Union*, Sept. 21, 1867; the Commissioner of Indian Affairs, *Report* (1870), p. 532; and George Francis Brimlow, *The Bannock Indian War of 1878* (Caldwell, Ida., 1938), *passim*.

[2] Herman J. Deutsch, "Indian and White in the Inland Empire: The Contest for the Land, 1880-1912," *PNQ*, XLVII (April, 1956), 45-46.

in the act, ... a 'good' Indian would be immediately found."[3]

The belief that good Indians were dead Indians was, as we have noted, generally held by stockmen of the Oregon Country. Although now and again a stockman would employ an Indian he trusted to care for his cattle;[4] most stockmen, like other frontiersmen in the Pacific Northwest, looked upon Indians as untrustworthy, degraded, and incapable of becoming civilized. Consequently, the rank and file of the white men who were then taking possession of the Oregon Country looked forward, more or less hopefully, to the day when the Indians would be put where they belonged—either underground or in restricted areas not needed by white men for developing the country.

Because this was their prevailing view of red men, we can understand why some stockmen in the Oregon Country—men who thought that their interests were being adversely affected— came to resent the way in which the federal government operated the reservations which it had set apart from the public domain for the exclusive use of its wards, the "noble" red men. Accordingly, as the years went by and the ranges became more and more restricted, for stockmen in the Oregon Country the Indian problem became increasingly the problem of the Indian reservations. "The poor Indian" faced troubled times on lands "given" to him by the federal government.

In the Oregon Country during much of the 1870's and 1880's, there were four Indian reservations in eastern Oregon, four in Idaho, and, for a short time after 1881, four in eastern Washington. Some were of considerable size; but, whether large or small, they were all, with the possible exception of two in southern Idaho, encroached upon by stockmen of Transcascadia. Naturally, these encroachments were more frequent and more flagrant in areas where the grazing interest was large and where it continued to be important than in other parts of the Pacific Northwest. Consequently, this chapter, which treats of such encroach-

[3] Salem *Willamette Farmer*, July 9, 1871; Colfax *Northwest Tribune*, June 30, 1880; *Yakima Record*, Aug. 14, 1880.
[4] See, for example, a report (Aug. 14, 1883) of John Smith, agent at the Warm Springs Reservation, in Commissioner of Indian Affairs, *Report* (1883), p. 136. On May 15, 1880, the *Yakima Record* reported that Chief Moses was looking after the interests of Phelps and Wadleigh in the Okanogan country.

ments, is principally concerned with the reservations in eastern Oregon; with the Yakima[5] Reservation in eastern Washington, a large area lying within the great angle formed by the Columbia River where it turns westward to the Pacific; and with the Lapwai, or Nez Percé, Reservation resting astride the Clearwater River in the southern part of the panhandle of Idaho. The other reservations in eastern Washington and northern Idaho, as well as those in southern Idaho, perhaps in part because they lay on the fringes of the great intermontane cattle country, are only incidentally important for the present study.

By the early 1870's, the four reservations in eastern Oregon had been established. Southernmost of these was the Klamath Reservation, spread out on either side of the Klamath River and in 1880 embracing 1,056,000 acres. Northward of this reservation was the smaller Warm Springs Reservation, stretching westward from the Deschutes River and having in 1880 an area of 464,000 acres. Southeastward of this reservation was the huge Malheur Reservation, whose area in 1880 was 1,778,560 acres. North of the Malheur was the Umatilla Reservation, with an area in 1880 of 268,800 acres. Thus, in eastern Oregon in 1880 there were in Indian reservations 3,567,360 acres, an area which by 1890 had been reduced to 1,788,800 acres, not by a process of whittling away, but by the blotting out of the Malheur Reservation.

In 1880 the three Indian reservations in eastern Washington had a total area of 6,592,240 acres, of which 800,000 acres were in the Yakima Reservation. The remaining land reserved for Indians in eastern Washington was in the Colville and Columbia reservations, situated north of the Big Bend of the Columbia River and north of the Spokane River. In 1890 the Yakima Reservation still consisted of 800,000 acres, but in the northeastern part of the newly formed state of Washington the area in reservations had been so much curtailed that, notwithstanding the creation of the Spokane Reservation in 1881, the total area reserved for Indians in eastern Washington in 1890 amounted to only 3,977,820 acres.

Between 1880 and 1890, the area of Indian reservations in

[5] Except where it appears in direct quotations, the older word *Yakama* has been replaced in this chapter by the newer word *Yakima*.

Idaho was also reduced, but not so much as the area in eastern Oregon and eastern Washington. The two reservations in the panhandle, the Coeur d'Alene and the Lapwai, had an area of 1,482,651 acres in 1880, and 1,345,151 acres in 1890. In 1880 the two reservations in southern Idaho, Lemhi and Fort Hall, had an area of 1,266,330 acres, which by 1890 had been reduced to 928,270 acres.[6]

All these reservations had some good grazing land, and in greater or less measure the Indians living there acquired cattle and other livestock with the passing years. As early as 1872, the Commissioner of Indian Affairs reported that the Klamath Reservation, although of little value for agricultural purposes, was "a good grazing country"; and fourteen years later the agent for this reservation wrote that on "the low lands, plains, and hills abounds the celebrated Oregon 'bunch grass,' affording luxuriant pasturage, sufficient to support ten times the number of cattle owned by the agency and the Indians." The Warm Springs Reservation was also valuable for grazing. In 1886 the agent estimated that here Indians were grazing fifty-five hundred head of horses, eleven hundred head of cattle, and eighteen hundred head of sheep. The larger Malheur Reservation contained an abundance of choice grazing land, and the problem thereby raised will be treated at length in subsequent paragraphs of this chapter. The Umatilla Reservation, though relatively small, was so extraordinarily rich in grazing land that, as early as August 15, 1870, Lieutenant W. H. Boyle could write from the Umatilla Agency that the amount of grass on this reservation was "without limit." "The horses and cattle," he observed, "are always in

---

[6] Commissioner of Indian Affairs, *Report* (1874), pp. 132-33; *ibid.* (1880), pp. 229-30, 235-36; *ibid.* (1890), pp. 436, 443-44. One reason, perhaps, for the lack of reports of encroachments on the Fort Hall Reservation is that there "accommodations" were made whereby, under some color of legality, the cattle of white men were allowed to graze on Indian lands. In the tenth federal census, for example, it was reported that twenty-five hundred head of cattle were grazing on this reservation, for which privilege a fee of thirty cents a head was paid; and in 1889 it was also reported that, pursuant to an agreement with the Indians, stockmen were annually wintering some twenty-five thousand head of horses and cattle on the Fort Hall Reservation. Clarence W. Gordon, "Report on Cattle, Sheep, and Swine, Supplementary to Enumeration of Live Stock on Farms in 1880," *Tenth Federal Census, 1880*, Vol. III, *Agriculture* (Washington, D.C., 1883), p. 1095; Portland *Weekly Oregonian*, Oct. 18, 1889.

splendid condition, and scarcely need any care in winter, as grazing is good all the year, rendering it a very popular as well as profitable business to raise stock." Eight years later the Commissioner of Indian Affairs reported that this reservation contained "some of the finest grazing and agricultural land" in the state of Oregon.[7]

Of the pastoral wealth of the other Indian reservations in the Pacific Northwest, we need here notice only that of the Yakima Reservation in Washington and the Lapwai Reservation in Idaho. The former was by nature "well adapted for farming and grazing," and as early as September 2, 1874, "Father" James H. Wilbur, agent for the Yakimas, told the Commissioner of Indian Affairs that the Indians under his charge had about thirteen thousand horses and about twelve hundred head of cattle. Perhaps even richer in grasslands was the Lapwai Reservation, on which the Nez Percés, in the summer of 1886, were said to have "large herds of horses and cattle, and enough land for ten times their number." So valuable indeed was this reservation for grazing that George W. Norris, agent for the Nez Percés, could write, as late as August 15, 1887, that its "advantages for stock raising are unsurpassed."[8]

Upon the choice grazing lands of these reservations some of the cattlemen of the Pacific Northwest cast greedy eyes, and the longer they looked the less disposed they were to put temptation behind them. From the later 1860's through the decades of the 1870's and 1880's, the Indian Office in Washington, D.C., received from one or another of these reservations complaint after complaint that cattlemen were encroaching on Indian grazing lands, to the increasing exasperation of the Indians. Such complaints, however, should not have surprised any informed person, least of all the Commissioner of Indian Affairs. As we have seen, this was the period during which the range- and ranch-cattle business in the Pacific Northwest reached the peak of its development, and it was also the period during which, in many districts

[7] Commissioner of Indian Affairs, *Report* (1872), p. 665; *ibid.* (1870), p. 56; *ibid.* (1878), p. xxxvii; *ibid.* (1886), pp. 430, 441.

[8] *Ibid.* (1871), p. 275; *ibid.* (1874), p. 339; *ibid.* (1886), p. 112; *ibid.* (1887), p. 71.

of that region, it was being hard pressed because of the increase of sheep breeding, and, more especially, because large areas of arable lands were being brought under cultivation, particularly in eastern Washington, north-central and northeastern Oregon, and northern Idaho. In southeastern Oregon, with less abundant land suitable for farming than in eastern Washington and the untimbered parts of the panhandle of Idaho, the range- and ranch-cattle business, though squeezed, cramped, and in places retreating, persisted, as we shall see, to 1890 and beyond. Naturally, as competition for the grasslands and sage lands became keener, the pressure of cattlemen upon the Indian reservations increased.

As early as July, 1867, the agent for the Umatilla Reservation reported that the Indians, fearful of losing their reservation, were causing him no end of "trouble and vexation." "The reservation," he wrote, "is completely surrounded by white settlements. . . . So anxious are the white people in the vicinity to possess this land, that threats to remove the Indians by violence are not infrequently heard." Five years later the new agent for the Umatillas reported that he had been compelled to order the white men to remove their stock from this reservation, and that court action had been required in one or two instances to enforce this order.[9] Although for the time being he appeared to be content with his accomplishment, he was compelled to say, in September, 1874, that he could not prevent altogether the stock of settlers living near this reservation from trespassing on the Indians' grazing land. Four years later, because of the increasing pressure of the whites, the Commissioner of Indian Affairs recommended that the Indians be removed from Umatilla to Yakima, and that the lands of the Umatilla Reservation be sold.[10]

[9] *Ibid.*, (1867), p. 83; *ibid.* (1872), p. 362. "C. J. Matlock, of Lane Co., was fined $1,800 by the United States Court, for driving 1800 head of sheep on the Umatilla Reservation, in violation of provisions in the Indian Treaty." Portland *Pacific Christian Advocate*, Feb. 8, 1872.

[10] Commissioner of Indian Affairs, *Report* (1874), p. 322; *ibid.* (1878), p. xxxvii. On Aug. 27, 1878, the agent at Umatilla told the Commissioner of Indian Affairs that he believed that ten thousand head of cattle and three thousand head of horses, belonging to white settlers off the reservation, were grazing on the Indians' land. "Much of the stock belonging to the whites in this vicinity," he wrote, "range off and on the reservation at pleasure." Commissioner of Indian

This recommendation, however, was not adopted, and the problem of encroachments persisted. As late as the summer of 1887, it was still acute. Writing on August 15, the agent advised the Commissioner that the Indians on the Umatilla Reservation had approved an act of Congress (March 3, 1885) to give them lands in severalty, and he added in English not above reproach:

The Indians seem to be satisfied with all the arrangements with few exceptions, and these only form a few Indians led on by surrounding whites and cattle-men who are, of course, opposed to the whole arrangement, as, when the business is completed, it will seriously interfere with their usual trespassing for grazing purposes on the reservation, as when every Indian owns his own lands and knows exactly his rights, he will know how to maintain them.

Only by "very hard work" could the agent for these Indians, as late as the summer of 1890, keep outside stock off the Umatilla Reservation.[11]

On the Klamath Reservation trespassing began at an early date, but there the encroachments of cattlemen appear to have caused no serious trouble until near the end of the 1870's. As late as July 7, 1879, the agent could write that there was "a friendly feeling existing between the Indians and most of the whites in the vicinity of the reservation." Yet even as he wrote these words trouble was no doubt brewing, for in December, 1879, he asked for instructions for dealing with stockmen who deliberately allowed large bands of stock to run on the reservation. Some five years later the problem had assumed serious proportions, for in September, 1884, the agent complained that several white settlers in this neighborhood were "continually allowing their cattle to trespass upon this part of the reservation, especially during the winter, [and were] causing the Indians a great deal of trouble." One of them, he said, had been sued for trespassing.[12]

Affairs, Incoming Letters, Oregon, C375 (1878) (MSS in the National Archives, Washington, D.C.). All letters cited hereafter in this chapter are from the records of the Office of Indian Affairs in the National Archives.

[11] Commissioner of Indian Affairs, *Report* (1887), p. 191; *ibid.* (1890), p. 209. "Cattle and sheep illegally on the Umatilla reservation are now being driven therefrom under instructions from the government." Portland *Morning Oregonian*, May 10, 1889. See also the Colfax *Palouse Gazette*, Nov. 12, 1889.

[12] Commissioner of Indian Affairs, *Report* (1879), p. 127; L. M. Nickerson to the Commissioner of Indian Affairs, Dec. 15, 1879, Incoming Letters, Oregon,

By the later years of the 1880's, the situation at Klamath was becoming dangerous, and in the summer of 1888 a cavalry company was sent to eject trespassing cattle from this reservation; but the agent, reporting in mid-August of that year that at least ten thousand head of trespassing cattle had been removed by these troops, advised the Commissioner of Indian Affairs that without the continuing aid of the military forces he could not hope to keep off this reservation "the large bands of cattle hovering around its borders."[13] In the summer of 1889 the same thing was happening again, and on July 24, 1889, the Commissioner advised the agent by telegram to notify the owners to remove their trespassing cattle, and, if they neglected to do so, to request the district attorney for the United States to bring action against them. On August 10, 1889, the agent, obviously discouraged, reported as follows:

Large herds of cattle have been constantly depredating on the rightful domain of the Indians. This has been going on for the last twenty years. I have kept the Indian office informed as to these depredations and have followed their instructions; and yet I have found it impossible with eight police to guard 250 miles of an out-boundary line against the swarms of cattle that hover on all sides and sweep over the boundaries of the reservation upon its rich pasture lands. The Indians are exasperated, and unless more vigorous measures are instituted against these trespassers serious trouble will be the result.[14]

Somewhat less serious, if we may trust the reports of the agent, was the problem of trespassing on the Warm Springs Reservation. On February 19, 1878, the agent could write that there was so much good grazing country adjacent to this reservation on the north, south, and east that stockmen were not tempted to intrude

---

N498 (1879); *Leases of Lands in the Indian Territory*, 48th Cong., 2nd sess., S. Ex. Doc. 17, p. 216.

[13] A. B. Upshaw to Joseph Emery, July 25, 1888, Department of Indian Affairs, Land Division, Letter Book 176, p. 99; Commissioner of Indian Affairs, *Report* (1888), p. 209. A letter dated at Summer Lake, Oregon, on July 12, 1888, and signed Justice, gives the view on this subject of at least one stockman. "The Klamath Indian reservation is to be patrolled by three companies of cavalry to keep off the cattle and horses belonging to settlers; this will make short range for a good many stockmen, but, then, we must protect the noble red man or else he would not receive JUSTICE." Burns *East Oregon Herald*, July 25, 1888.

[14] Land Division, Letter Book 187, p. 299; Commissioner of Indian Affairs, *Report* (1889), p. 273.

on Indian lands. But by mutual consent the stock of both Indians and settlers was permitted "to cross and re-cross at pleasure" the north line of the reservation, near which white settlements had been made. Occasionally, while driving across the
reservation, stockmen would lose a few head of cattle. These cattle the agent expected to be removed from the reservation as
soon as practicable.[15]

Ten years later, however, there was a different story to tell. On
August 27, 1888, the agent wrote:

The unsettled boundaries of the north and west lines of this reservation
should be settled at once, for, as at present, it is a constant source of turmoil
and trouble. Stockmen, with their stock, constantly infringe upon the rights
of the Indians under the plea that they don't know where the line is, and
then our trouble and chagrin commences [sic], for we can not show it to
them with any degree of satisfaction either to them or ourselves.[16]

But it was on the Malheur Reservation that stockmen made the
most flagrant and persistent encroachments. We know more
about trespassing on this than on other reservations in the Pacific
Northwest, thanks to the fact that, during the years of the most
flagrant trespassing—that is, from 1877 to 1882—the agent at
Malheur, W. V. Rinehart, was an uncommon man for such a
position. Besides being interested in the well-being of the Indians in his charge, and persistent in efforts to help them, he was
more than ordinarily articulate. His frequent and illuminating
letters and reports to the Commissioner of Indian Affairs provide
abundant material for a significant chapter on the relations of
white men and Indians in the Oregon Country.[17]

As early as December 18, 1877, Rinehart reported that the Indians were increasingly discontented because stockmen were

---

[15] Incoming Letters, Oregon, S300 (1878).

[16] Commissioner of Indian Affairs, *Report* (1888), p. 217.

[17] Rinehart, according to his own testimony, took charge of the Malheur Reservation on July 1, 1876, but received from his predecessor no records of this
agency. W. V. Rinehart to the Commissioner of Indian Affairs, June 4, 1878, Malheur Agency Letter Book, Dec. 17, 1877–Sept. 30, 1878, p. 180. Fortunately, two
of Rinehart's letter books, the one just cited and another one covering the period
between June 14, 1880, and July 18, 1882, have been preserved and are now
deposited in the National Archives. During his later years at Malheur, while the
reservation was in process of liquidation, Rinehart ceased to be agent and, as
custodian for the federal government, was designated farmer-in-charge.

grazing cattle on the Malheur Reservation, and that the stockmen were indifferent to warnings that they were violating a law.
Some of them, indeed, had been so bold as to take residence on
the reservation and to "make no secret of their intention to
occupy and use the land." On February 27, 1878, Rinehart reported at length on the encroachments, naming the trespassers
and listing the numbers of their trespassing stock. In general, he
found these stockmen defiant, asking how the government would
enforce payment for grazing on the reserve; and some of them,
he averred, were even suggesting that the government, if it
wanted to save the grass on the reservation, should put a fence
around it.[18] "It is simply the old story over," Rinehart declared.
"Scarcely any Indian Reservation has escaped similar trouble.
While it is to be deplored that such measures become necessary,
it can not be denied that prompt and rigorous enforcement of
the law is the only remedy for such troubles." By August 1,
1878, an order had been issued from Camp Harney to the intruders to remove their stock, but Rinehart observed that none of
them had done so.[19]

In the meantime, the Bannock War, which broke out in June,
1878, had completely altered the situation. When this war began,
as the Commissioner of Indian Affairs explained in 1880, the 600
Indians confined on the Malheur Reservation left the reservation, some of them to raid and fight. When this war was over,

[18] Incoming Letters, Oregon R 7/78. The contention that the federal government should fence the Indian reservations was quickly disposed of by Judge
Matthew P. Deady in the cases on trespass that were tried in the United States
District Court, Portland, Oregon, in June, 1880. See note 22, above. His decision,
as summarized by W. V. Rinehart in a letter to the Commissioner of Indian Affairs, July 7, 1882, held that the mere setting apart of a reservation was in itself a
governmental *notice* of the establishment of such reservation, and that settlers, if
they elected to live near such reservation, must take proper precautions to keep
their livestock from trespassing. Malheur Agency Letter Book, June 14, 1880–July
18, 1882, pp. 230-31. Nevertheless, as late as Aug. 20, 1888, the agent for the Nez
Percé Indians could write that settlers living near the Lapwai Reservation "strenuously insisted" on their right to let their cattle graze upon the Nez Percé grasslands "because, as they say, the Indians do not fence their reservation." Commissioner of Indian Affairs, *Report* (1888), p. 85.
[19] Incoming Letters, Oregon, R153 (1878); Commissioner of Indian Affairs,
Report (1878), p. 118. The contempt that stockmen in the Pacific Northwest felt
for such an order was well expressed in an editorial in the Silver City *Idaho
Avalanche,* March 23, 1878. Here, it was presumed, "some wiseacres at Washington" doubted whether a white man is "as good as an Indian."

"those who had taken part in the hostilities, together with 100 other Pi-Utes who belonged at Malheur, were removed with their women and children to the Yakama [sic] agency. There then remained 230 Indians, under Chiefs Ochoco, Winnemucca, and Weiser, who properly belonged to Malheur"; but these Indians did not return there. In the light of these changed conditions, the Commissioner recommended that the Malheur agency be discontinued and that the lands included in the reserve be sold, the proceeds of such sale to "be invested for the benefit of the Indians."[20]

Despite this proposed change of policy, Rinehart was still charged with the difficult task of enforcing the law against trespassing. On March 29, April 21, and May 20, 1879, he reported that, since the removal of the Indians to Yakima, stockmen had penetrated deeper into the Malheur Reservation, notwithstanding his published notice that they must withdraw; and on August 15 he further reported that stories had appeared in newspapers of the Pacific Northwest predicting that the Malheur Reservation would be broken up. Encouraged by such rumors, stockmen and settlers had begun to lay hold of its choicest lands in defiance of the military order of the preceding year. Despairing of the assistance of troops to remove these trespassers, Rinehart turned hopefully to the Department of Justice, from which he expected a "speedy and effectual remedy."[21] Not without reason did he suppose that the federal courts would give him effective aid, for on July 12, 1880, he could write that some of the trespassers had been convicted in the federal district court in Portland and that fines totaling $2,046 had been assessed against them.[22] But, in

[20] Commissioner of Indian Affairs, *Report* (1880), p. xlvi. On Oct. 4, 1879, the Canyon City *Grant County News,* observing that warrants had been sent to "quite a number of our citizens to go to Portland to answer the charge of letting stock graze on or near the Malheur Reservation," remarked that these men would be "assessed all the way from $300 to $5,000 damages. It would cost the citizens less than that," it continued, "to kill all the Reservation Indians." On Aug. 14, 1880, the editor remarked that "the worst curse in Eastern Oregon is the Malheur Reservation."

[21] Incoming Letters, Oregon, R253, R305, R371 (1879); Commissioner of Indian Affairs, *Report* (1879), p. 130.

[22] Rinehart to Commissioner of Indian Affairs, July 12, 1880, Malheur Agency Letter Book, June 14, 1880—July 18, 1882, p. 2. In his fifth statistical report, dated

the main, the problem was still unsolved; trespassing continued, and convictions of trespassers were not easy to get.

It was plainly demonstrated in the trial of the cases reported [Rinehart told the Commissioner] that juries are averse to the punishment of settlers for grazing their stock upon Indian land—especially when the Indians are themselves absent from and not occupying their reservation. In the case of J. S. Miller the testimony showed that 600 head had trespassed and by a compromise verdict only 300 head were brought in their finding.

I have no information of any movement among the stock-men to take their cattle off the reservation; and it may become necessary to invoke the aid of the Courts again before they can be induced to observe the law.[23]

Rinehart might have added, had he known then what he was to learn later, that the opposition of juries in Oregon to punishing stockmen for grazing their animals on a reservation not occupied by Indians was by no means odd. For the district attorney for the United States in Portland, Rufus Mallory, took no action against trespassing cattlemen, despite the fact that Rinehart reported to him more than once the names of offenders; and presently the two men became involved in a sharp controversy. Mallory argued that grazing cattle and cutting hay on an unoccupied Indian reservation were nothing more than "technical" violations of the law, inasmuch as such practices did no harm to any Indian. "The grass that grows there is wild," he explained to the Commissioner of Indian Affairs on August 6, 1881, "and if not cut will fall down and rot. It will do no good to the Indians nor to any one else, and under these circumstances I do not see how any one is harmed if the people in that country cut and preserve this grass by making hay of it which may save the lives of many

---

Oct. 14, 1880, Rinehart wrote: "The encroachments of stock-men upon the grazing lands of the reservation continue and gradually increase. Of thirty-two stock-owners, representing about 18,000 cattle and 600 horses, now upon the reservation, six have been made to pay penalties, to wit:

John S. Miller, trial by jury, verdict for	$300.00
J. D. Walker, judgment by default for	312.00
J. Shepherd, judgment by default for	294.00
Hall Bros., judgment by confession	240.00
Peter Stinger, judgment by confession	100.00
Todhunter & Devine, judgment by confession	800.00

"Two cases failed for want of testimony; and the other parties have not been proceeded against by the U.S. Dist. Attorney." *Ibid.*, p. 74.
  [23] *Ibid.*, pp. 2-3.

hundred dollars worth of livestock when winter comes."[24] In like vein, on July 23, 1881, he had written to Rinehart, saying, "The grass was growing and if not fed down would fall down and rot. Yet technically the cattle upon the ground were trespassing and there was ground for suits to be commenced. I did not care to commence them and as I now remember I did not until I was instructed to do so by the Department at Washington." But Mallory distinguished carefully between the practice of grazing government-owned lands that "technically" were in the possession of Indians and that of occupying such lands. He was in favor of removing persons who had actually "settled" upon the reservation.[25]

To this argument Rinehart replied quickly and vigorously. "As a matter of fact," he wrote Mallory on August 4, 1881,

these "technical violations" as you are pleased to term them have done and are now doing immeasurably more damage than the graver violations of those persons erecting cabins, corrals and other improvements. Bunch-grass once trodden out, and it is never again reproduced [sic]. The hills and ridges upon which it grows are utterly worthless when it is once destroyed. Bunch-grass upon these hills more than eight miles from water is entirely worthless, because not accessible [sic] for grazing. As proof that bunch-grass range can be eaten out and destroyed, I need only refer you to the John Day Valley, the hills about The Dalles and in Umatilla County. No better range than these localities once afforded has even been known in this country; and today, even the number of cattle now upon the reservation could not find subsistence upon the whole of that vast region.

. . . The truth is, let this reservation be over-run for five years more as it has been for three years past, and the grazing lands, which were valuable then will not sell for ten cents an acre.[26]

Though he kept up a good fight to the end, Rinehart knew that he was losing a campaign. After the Commissioner of Indian

[24] Incoming Letters, Oregon, 14642 (1881). On this subject Mallory undoubtedly spoke the mind of the far West. Seven years later, the agent for the Nez Percés, George W. Norris, writing on Aug. 20, 1888, on the subject of cattlemen's encroachments on the Lapwai Reservation, observed: "It is urged by some [cattlemen] that the Indians have more pasturage than they can make use of; that it would be utterly lost unless occupied by them; that no harm is done by their cattle taking the benefit of what the Indians suffer to waste." Commissioner of Indian Affairs, *Report* (1888), p. 85.
[25] Incoming Letters, Oregon, 14648, Incl. No. 1, 14642 (1881).
[26] *Ibid.*, 14684 (1881).

Affairs had issued his report in 1880, it was certain that sooner or later the Malheur Reservation would be broken up; yet Rinehart considered it his duty to take thought of the ultimate disposal of those lands. Accordingly, he wrote to the Commissioner on June 10, 1881, saying that the trespassers were bold and unscrupulous men who not only were enjoying "the benefit of fresh range for their stock and first choice of locations, near streams, timber and other natural advantages," but who were excluding "a much better class of people, who would gladly participate in these benefits but for the prohibitions of the law."[27]

Naturally, the pressure of public opinion in Oregon and elsewhere in the Pacific Northwest—pressure exerted through the press, through members of the Congress, and through the legislature of Oregon—was brought to bear on the President to obtain an executive order to restore this reservation to the public domain.[28] Meanwhile, Rinehart, standing by in Oregon, was a target for vilification and could do no more than report to the Commissioner of Indian Affairs on the continuing encroachments and on the trend of local public opinion in respect to the ultimate disposal of the Malheur Reservation.[29] He endured a goodly share of abuse, a part of which he reported to the Commissioner in Washington. One illustration of how he was belabored must suffice.

On July 16, 1880, soon after his being convicted of trespassing

[27] Malheur Agency Letter Book, June 14, 1880–July 18, 1882, pp. 149-50; Incoming Letters, Oregon, 10962 (1881).

[28] For an excellent illustration of one type of pressure brought to bear on the federal government, see a long memorial adopted by the Oregon Legislature in October, 1880, a few months after several Oregon cattlemen had been convicted of trespassing on the Malheur Reservation. Legislature of Oregon, *Session Laws* (1880), pp. 180-82. For some observations on encouragement alleged to have been given trespassers on the Malheur Reservation by the "Oregon delegation in Congress," see W. V. Rinehart's letter to the Commissioner of Indian Affairs, April 17, 1882, in the Malheur Agency Letter Book, June 14, 1880–July 18, 1882, pp. 192-97.

[29] As might have been expected, encroachments on the Malheur Reservation became worse after 1880. The list of intruders submitted by Rinehart to the Commissioner of Indian Affairs on April 17, 1882, was little less than a roster of prominent stockmen of southeastern Oregon. It included the important firms of Todhunter and Devine, French and Glenn, and Overfelt and Sweetser. Malheur Agency Letter Book, June 14, 1880–July 18, 1882, pp. 192-97. See also Rinehart's letter to the Commissioner, July 7, 1882, *ibid.*, pp. 230-32.

on the Malheur Reservation, J. S. Miller wrote a letter to Rinehart, apologizing in a left-handed way for a short letter written earlier "in the heat of passion." He now announced that he was moving his cattle off the "sacred soil" of Malheur, but he wished Rinehart to know that cattle and horses are not smart enough "to understand that it is wrong to cross imaginary lines, or air lines or small streams," and for that reason he wished to know what sort of terms he could make with the "Noble Red Man" so that he would not be further molested. He thought that he might pay the Indians as much as one hundred dollars a year for grazing privileges, even though they had murdered his relatives and stolen his property, for after all he was only a white man—only an American citizen—good for nothing but "to pay taxes & vote." "Oh," he groaned, "what a magnanimous Government we live under. Oppression is the order of the day, as against the Taxpayer."[30] Nor was Rinehart yet done with Miller, even though he presently sold his band of cattle for thirty-nine thousand dollars; for Rinehart believed that Miller and other cattlemen had instigated an editorial published in the Canyon City *Grant County News* on August 4, 1880, in which "Carl Schurtz" was upbraided, the management of the Malheur Reservation condemned, and the people of Grant County, Oregon, alleged to have been "grossly and sorrowfully abused."[31]

While events were thus running their course in eastern Oregon, the Commissioner of Indian Affairs in Washington, D.C., although he had recommended that the Malheur Reservation be discontinued, was firmly resolved, as late as the autumn of 1881, that its lands should be disposed of for the benefit of the Indians. Accordingly, he disapproved a memorial in which the Oregon Legislature prayed that these lands be restored to the public domain, and he recommended that the Department of the In-

[30] Rinehart to the Commissioner, July 24, 1880, with a copy of Miller's letter enclosed, Incoming Letters, Oregon, R750 (1880); Malheur Agency Letter Book, June 14, 1880—July 18, 1882, pp. 13-16.
[31] Rinehart to the Commissioner, Aug. 20, 1880, enclosing an editorial from the *Grant County News*. Incoming Letters, Oregon, R875 (1880); Malheur Agency Letter Book, June 14, 1880—July 18, 1882, pp. 44-45. For an interesting letter written by J. S. Miller in "Douglas County, Jan. 22, 1881," see the *Willamette Farmer*, Feb. 4, 1881.

terior withhold its approval of any plan to dispose of them that did not "contemplate and provide substantial return to the Indians."[32] But presently he would learn that he had spoken out of turn. The spirit that informed the pressure exerted upon the White House for the restoration of these lands to the public domain is perhaps accurately illustrated by an editorial that appeared in the spring of 1882 in the widely known Boise newspaper, the *Idaho Weekly Statesman*, which said:

Some of our Oregon exchanges say that an order has been made requiring all cattle to be driven off the Malheur Indian reservation. Ever since the Bannock War, in 1878, there has not been an Indian or an agent on this reservation, and there is not to-day an Indian within a hundred miles of the reservation. There is no more probability of the Piute Indians going back to the Malheur Reservation to live than there is of their going to Alaska. The Piute Indians joined the Bannocks in the Bannock war on account of the maladministration of the agent on that reservation. Since then the Christian Indian Ring in New York have used this reservation as a good hiding place for stealing. . . . The order to drive the cattle off this reservation is just as sensible as it would be to order the cattle all driven off the public lands of the Government. Is the Christian Indian Ring and their Christian agent afraid the cattle will eat up all the grass? . . . The cattle that happen to roam over the Malheur reservation do no more harm than the wild goats on our mountain peaks. . . . We hope the Government has not made so silly an order; but we are prepared to believe any crookedness that may be published about the Malheur reservation.[33]

In his annual report for 1882, the Commissioner of Indian Affairs, after observing that an executive order of September 13, 1882, had restored the greater part of the Malheur Reservation to the public domain, explained his own surrender in words that must have seared his tongue. He repeated the statement on this subject in his report for 1881, and affirmed once again that ever since it had been decided to abandon this reservation his office had been determined that these lands should be disposed of for

[32] Commissioner of Indian Affairs, *Report* (1881), p. lxvi. For the memorial referred to by the Commissioner, see note 28, above.
[33] " 'Lo'—The Malheur Reservation," Boise *Idaho Weekly Statesman*, March 18, 1882. The "silly order" was no doubt the order of the Commissioner of Indian Affairs, dated Dec. 13, 1881, which W. V. Rinehart mentioned in his letter to the Commissioner, April 17, 1882. Malheur Agency Letter Book, June 14, 1880—July 18, 1882, p. 193.

the benefit of the Indians for whom this reserve had been set apart. But he confessed that

in response to most urgent and persistent appeals on the part of the people of Oregon for the restoration of these lands to the public domain, in order that they might become subject to settlement under the homestead and preemption laws, this office was led to so far modify former recommendations as to reduce the quantity to be retained and sold for the benefit of the Indians to considerably less than one-quarter of the whole reservation, and to recommend the reduction of the reservation accordingly. It was upon this recommendation, concurred in by the department, that the order for the reduction was made.

This concession, however, was only a beginning. On May 21, 1883, another executive order restored to the public domain the entire Malheur Reservation except 320 acres, and still another order, dated March 2, 1889, restored this parcel.[34]

Before the Malheur affair had been finally disposed of, other trouble for the Indian Office had begun in Washington Territory. Here, for many years, it had been the practice of both cattlemen and sheepmen to pay a small fee for the privilege of grazing their livestock on the Yakima Indian Reservation, and by this arrangement both the stockmen and the Indians had profited. In fact, the money thus obtained had been spent on improvements for the benefit of the Yakima Indians. But trouble appears to have begun with the expiration on July 1, 1885, of an agreement that Snipes and Allen had made with these Indians to pasture one thousand head of cattle on their reservation. These men were accused of pasturing more cattle than their agreement with the Indians authorized, and on September 22, 1885, they were ordered to remove their cattle from the reservation.[35]

[34] Commissioner of Indian Affairs, *Report* (1882), p. lxxii; *ibid.* (1883), p. 282; *ibid.* (1889), p. 479. An interesting sidelight is thrown on the whole affair by an editorial, "The Malheur Reservation," in the *Idaho Weekly Statesman*, July 14, 1883, which says: "On the 21st of May last the president issued an order restoring to the public domain the Malheur reservation except 320 acres, on which the old military post of Camp Harney stands . . . and settlers may choose homes from any part, except the section on which the post stands, and that will probably be open to settlement as soon as Uncle Sam removes his buildings, and he will probably be saved that trouble, as the settlers are in a fair way to remove them for him. We are reliably informed that the choice portions of the reservation are already located."

[35] Commissioner of Indian Affairs, *Report* (1878), p. 141; Charles H. Dickson

That the problem of trespassing cattle and sheep at Yakima became more acute as the months went by, there is little reason to doubt. On May 7, 1888, the Commissioner of Indian Affairs referred to Thomas Priestly, agent for the Yakimas, a complaint that settlers living near the Yakima Reservation had sent to C. S. Voorhees, the congressional delegate from Washington Territory. These settlers objected strenuously to the practice of letting the Indians on the reservation round up the trespassing cattle and charge the owners a dollar a head. They alleged that the Indians took advantage of this opportunity to steal cattle from the white men. After investigating this matter, the Acting Commissioner informed Voorhees that the complaint was without foundation. In fact, he presented evidence showing that the ranges outside the reservation were virtually depleted, and that cattlemen had turned their stock loose with the expectation that they would "go to graze on the Indian lands." Furthermore, he was convinced that the Indians had not injured any stock belonging to white men. But tranquillity had not yet come to the Yakima Reservation. Having received further complaints in February and March, 1889, of trespassing cattle on this reservation, the Acting Commissioner directed the agent for the Yakimas, on June 6, 1889, to remove all such cattle and to warn the owners that legal action would be taken against them if they did not prevent a recurrence of such trespasses. Yet this warning was of little avail, for two years later the Yakima agent was again harping on this subject, saying,

Another source of complaint is the stock on the reservation belonging to the whites. As these questions must be settled by the courts and the Indians seem to have lost all confidence in the courts doing anything to assist them, it is very difficult for the agent to prosecute a case successfully, depending as

---

to the Commissioner of Indian Affairs, June 28, 1886, Incoming Letters, Oregon, 17598 (1886); Timothy A. Byrnes to Snipes and Allen, Sept. 22, 1885, Incoming Letters, Oregon, L1484 (1886). Later the grazing privilege of Snipes and Allen appears to have been renewed, for the Indian Office, in a telegram dated June 22, 1887, thus instructed the agent at Yakima: "You may receive the one thousand dollars tendered by Snipes and Allen for pasturage to July first next, and pay same into depository to credit of the Indians." Land Division, Letter Book 161, p. 28. See also Letter Book 160, pp. 338-40.

he does and must altogether upon the Indians for witnesses, as the Indians say, "White man's court no good for Indian."[36]

In the meantime, similar happenings were disturbing the tranquillity of the Nez Percés. From the early 1870's to the middle 1880's, we get an occasional glimpse of trespassing stock on the Lapwai Reservation, but it was not until the closing years of the 1880's that the agents' annual reports began to reveal a special concern about the encroachments of stockmen. Failing ranges outside this reservation, no doubt, account for the remarks with which the agent for the Nez Percés began his annual report on August 20, 1888.

This reservation is bounded on the north, west, south, and east by a wide and almost boundless extent of rich, productive agricultural land, nearly all of which, except upon the east, has been taken up by settlers, that bordering on the reservation being in the possession of those whose principal pursuit is stock raising. Their flocks and herds naturally seek pasturage upon the reservation, where grass and water is both good and abundant. . . . White settlers and speculators are thus profiting while the Indians are losing the benefit derivable from the use of their rich agricultural lands.

. . . It is impracticable with a force of but five policemen to protect from encroachment a reservation the exterior lines of which measure about 150 miles, and properly attend to other police duties, while the public sentiment of the country surrounding it ignores such treaty obligations of the Government as interfere with the appropriation of Indian rights by white settlers.

The following summer, in compliance with a Government order, "most of the stockmen" in the neighborhood of the Lapwai Reservation were reported to be removing their cattle from the lands of the Indians; but in his annual report for 1890 the agent for the Nez Percés confessed that the "stock question" was one of the "most perplexing questions" that confronted him. With his limited police force he had been unable to clear the reservation of intruding cattle, and he was at a loss to know what to do about the matter.[37]

[36] Commissioner of Indian Affairs to Thomas Priestly, May 7, 1888, Land Division, Letter Book 173, p. 237; Acting Commissioner of Indian Affairs to C. S. Voorhees, June 25, 1888, *ibid.*, Letter Book 175, pp. 142-43; Acting Commissioner of Indian Affairs to Thomas Priestly, June 6, 1889, *ibid.*, Letter Book 185, pp. 313-14; Commissioner of Indian Affairs, *Report* (1891), I, 462.

[37] Lewiston *Idaho Signal*, June 29, 1872; Charles E. Montieth to the Commissioner of Indian Affairs, Dec. 7, 1885, Incoming Letters, Oregon, 30044

Besides such large-scale encroachments as those just described, stockmen resorted to other illegal practices—less obvious and perhaps on occasion even ingenious—to gain access to Indian grasslands. One such practice was that of driving herds across reservations and allowing the stock to proceed so leisurely that they grew fat as they traveled. The government acknowledged the right of stockmen to move their herds, free of charge, at normal driving pace on established trails and roads across Indian reservations, but stockmen who abused this privilege by allowing their stock to range and feed on a reservation were liable to a penalty of a dollar a head on their stock, such penalty to be "recoverable by process at law."[38] Another practice, reported by the agent for the Nez Percés, was that of men who profited by their presence on the Lapwai Reservation as keepers of taverns or of mail stations to pasture herds on that reservation. In 1889 all such persons were ordered to be removed. Still another devious practice, more widespread perhaps than the evidence in hand would indicate, involved a stockman's making an agreement with an Indian to look after the stockman's cattle that grazed on the reservation. On September 18, 1890, the agent for the Yakimas reported such an arrangement that Pleas Bounds, a stockman of North Yakima, had made with Tom McKay, a half-breed Indian, whereby Bounds was unlawfully pasturing from fifteen hundred to two thousand head of cattle on the Yakima Reservation. As the agent explained,

These cattle, of course, are branded with McKay's brand, and, ostensibly, Bounds holds McKay's notes for the cattle, and as fast as Bounds and a partner need the cattle for their butchering business at Roslyn and Tacoma, they are gathered up by McKay and shipped to them. The scheme is such that Bounds avoids paying taxes on the cattle to the county authorities of Yakima, and the Indians are likewise deprived of a large revenue under the "grazing tax."[39]

(1885); Commissioner of Indian Affairs, *Report* (1888), p. 85; *Lewiston Teller*, June 27, 1889; Commissioner of Indian Affairs, *Report* (1890), pp. 81-82.

[38] Acting Commissioner of Indian Affairs to B. P. Moore, May 6, 1887, Land Division, Letter Book 159, pp. 351-52. See also the Commissioner of Indian Affairs to Thomas Priestly, March 14, 1887, *ibid.*, Letter Book 157, pp. 194-95.

[39] Commissioner of Indian Affairs to George W. Gordon, Nov. 12, 1889, *ibid.*, Letter Book 191, pp. 223-24; Commissioner of Indian Affairs, *Report* (1890), p. 233. In this report the agent affirmed that the principal employment of his Indian

A similar arrangement, but one that was sought openly, had been refused two years earlier to a man who wished to pasture cattle on the Colville Reservation.[40]

The height of ingenuity was approached, if not actually attained, by certain white men who conceived the idea of marrying their way into the Indian grasslands. At least some "squaw men" professed to believe that through their wives—dark-haired and dusky-hued maidens—they had acquired, by what might be called *klootchman* dowry right, a share in the natural resources of an Indian reservation. In 1889 the Indian Office was alerted to the fact that white men, married to Colville Indian women and living outside the Colville Reservation, had been driving their cattle upon that reservation under the pretense of having sold the cattle to their wives; and the Indian Office was also informed that some Indians of Chief Tonasket's band had sold land claims to Indian women, "the wives of white men," whose husbands were using these lands for pasturing cattle. Both these practices the Indian Office condemned: the first on the ground that no squaw man had any rights in an Indian reservation and could remain there only "upon sufferance during good behavior," and the second on the ground that no Indian on a reservation could transfer any land claim to another Indian. Accordingly, all the cattle that had been put upon the Colville Reservation by either of the foregoing arrangements were ordered to be removed.[41]

Thus far our story has shown a harassed Indian Office and suffering agents struggling to keep law-breaking frontiersmen from laying hold of what was not their own. But there is another side to the story. It is time to inquire whether the Congress had imposed on the Indian Office a policy that could not be carried out by that office, even when it was served by honest and capable agents.

---

police had been to "prevent illegal pasturage by stockmen, who use fair means and sometimes foul to herd their cattle, horses, sheep, etc., on the rich pasture lands on some portions of the reserve."

[40] Acting Commissioner of Indian Affairs to R. D. Gwydir, Aug. 3, 1888, Land Division, Letter Book 176, p. 232.

[41] Acting Commissioner of Indian Affairs to Hal J. Cole, Nov. 6, 1889, *ibid.*, Letter Book 191, pp. 89-90. Devices such as those described herein were, of course, not confined to the Pacific Northwest, as we are told by the Commissioner of Indian Affairs in his *Report* (1878), pp. xliv-xlvi.

An Indian reservation, let it be remembered, was a government-owned refuge, either surrounded by or contiguous to other government-owned land that was destined, sooner or later, to be occupied by white men—men who had been disciplined in the school of acquisitiveness, men who were disdainful of the rights of Indians, men who were not altogether respectful of the rights of their own government. Ordinarily such men were not much given to making subtle distinctions. In general, they considered the difference between government-owned land which they could freely use and government-owned land which they could not use because some Indians were not yet exterminated to be a lawyer's distinction—that is, one without a difference. What impressed them most of all was their knowledge that cattle which lived out their lives with half-empty bellies made poor beef. Accordingly, to formulate a policy for reservations that would be adequate to the exigencies of so difficult a situation, and to administer that policy successfully, required all agencies concerned to exhibit courage and hard-boiled realism—characteristics which, perhaps more often than not, such agencies did not possess. The problem, moreover, was one admitting of no dilatoriness, if justice were to prevail; it would not wait while Indians, who could not vote, were learning humility, and while cattlemen, who could vote, were acquiring perspective. How the problem was dealt with we shall now endeavor to understand.

Speaking generally, the Indian reservations in eastern Oregon, as in various other places in the Pacific Northwest, were larger than they should have been. This is a fact, however brutal it may appear to be. To say that the Indians who were put upon such reservations got little enough for what they gave up is a truism that is not now, as in our national history it never was, important. In the long run, the white men, by virtue of their superior power, would determine what was appropriate for the Indians. Accordingly, the Indians retained only so much of their lands as the white men were willing for them to keep. The frontiersmen of America were, of course, not without ideals. Having exposed themselves to the rigorous life of the American West, they were desirous of making full use of what the Lord had provided for them, and of employing their talents to help build up the country;[42] but their idealism, by some odd quirk of human nature, was understood no better by philanthropists who observed it from our eastern cities than by the Indians who studied it at close range in the American West. The government of the United States, knowing that a conflict of ideals obtained, was asking for trouble when it set aside for the Indians more land than they could immediately use, in a country open to white men whose land hunger was insatiable. And trouble it got. With Indian reservations ill-defined and ill-guarded, it is little wonder that now and again an efficient cattleman, fearful lest a single blade of grass outside a reservation should go to waste, put his cattle where they could conceivably wander across indistinct lines to grasslands on reservations. Such an act he might do, either innocently because he knew not where the lines should be or, under severe provocation, maliciously because he believed that he could not be prevented from doing so.

The problem of protecting the grasslands of the Indian reservations was further bedeviled by the fact that neither the Indian Office nor honest stockmen could count much on the cooperation of the cattle. There is no denying the sharpness of the point to J. S. Miller's insinuation that it would have been difficult for cattle on the ranges of Oregon (whose I.Q.'s were perhaps not noticeably higher than those of longhorns from Texas) to master the United States Statutes at Large and to abide by them; and thrifty cattlemen of the Oregon Country, imbued with the spirit of free enterprise, would naturally object to spending time and money on a project to teach their cattle to make distinctions which agents for the Indians sometimes could not make.[43] The

[42] The attitude of the people of the Pacific Northwest on this subject is clearly revealed, between 1874 and 1889, in memorials to the Congress from the legislatures of Oregon, Washington, and Idaho; and as early as 1886 the Governor of Washington Territory was recommending the allotment of lands in severalty to the Indians and the opening to settlement of what remained of the Indian reservations. J. Orin Oliphant, "Encroachments of Cattlemen on Indian Reservations in the Pacific Northwest, 1870-1890," AH, XXIV (January, 1950), 53-54, notes 66 and 67.

[43] As late as July 7, 1882, six years after he had taken charge of the Malheur Reservation, W. V. Rinehart was obliged to tell the Commissioner that he had "never claimed to know," and did not then know, "where the reservation line passes, in the vicinity of the Little Malheur." Malheur Agency Letter Book, June 14, 1880–July 18,1882, p. 229.

government, they thought, should long before have learned to use common sense. Had the government in the beginning made the reservations smaller, and had it at once carefully staked off their respective boundaries, the problem of policing should not have been an impossible one. By thus minimizing temptation, the trespassing of cattle on Indian reservations in the Pacific Northwest should not have become a problem of great consequence, and the embarrassing truth about the intellectual and ethical shortcomings of Oregon cattle might never have leaked out.

The neglect of the government to establish precise boundaries for the Indian reservations, besides causing much discord between Indians and cattlemen in the Oregon Country, opened the way to considerable "chiseling" by stockmen; for encroachments on reservations, once begun, were not easily stopped. Such neglect—neglect that caused trouble elsewhere than in the Pacific Northwest—was, it appears, due to the niggardliness of the Congress. In 1883 the Commissioner of Indian Affairs, deeply discouraged, gave vent to his feelings on this subject when he wrote as follows:

It would seem that the experience of the last few years had demonstrated the utter futility of endeavoring to procure adequate appropriations for the survey of Indian reservations. Year after year proper estimates are prepared and submitted to Congress with the most urgent recommendations. . . . There are thousands of miles of reservation boundaries that have never been defined and marked by official survey. . . . The settlers, miners, or herders, as the case may be, approaching from all directions, and gradually circumscribing the Indians to the vicinity of their agencies, are finally confronted by the Indians or their agent with the warning that they are encroaching upon the reservation. This, in all likelihood, is disputed, and in the absence of proper marks indicating the boundaries of the reservation the dispute continues, engendering the bitterest feeling which too often ends in unfortunate strife.[44]

We have already noted the embarrassment produced at the Warm Springs Reservation by the want of clearly marked boundary lines.[45] Nor was this an isolated instance in the Pacific North-

[44] Commissioner of Indian Affairs, *Report* (1883), p. xvii.
[45] As late as the autumn of 1889, the boundaries of the Warm Springs Reservation had not been completely surveyed. The northern boundary, as surveyed in

west. As late as the autumn of 1886, official word came from the Yakima Reservation that unsettled boundaries had given rise to no end of disputing. "There is," wrote the special agent, Charles H. Dickson on November 9, 1886, "but one portion of the reservation that is well defined, that portion of the northern and eastern line bounded by the Yakama [sic] and Ahtannum [sic] Rivers. The other boundaries are in dispute, giving rise to endless trouble to agent and the Indians. As the country adjacent to this reservation is rapidly settling up the trouble will constantly increase."[46] As late as 1890 the boundary of the Yakima Reservation was still a subject of concern, for on September 18 the agent for the Yakimas reported that "Surveyor Swartz, of the surveyor-general's office of this State, is now in the field surveying the boundary of this reservation, a work very much needed on account of the constant disputes arising between stockmen of Klickitat County and my Indians, as to the boundary lines, a portion of which has never been surveyed, and many of the landmarks of the surveyed part have been obliterated."[47]

Meanwhile, on the Klamath Reservation the boundary question was of even greater concern to the Indian Office. Since the survey of 1871, there had been a boundary dispute here, one which, in July, 1886, all but caused bloodshed, for white men had built barbed-wire fences on land that the Indians claimed as their own. In this case action followed rather quickly the recommendation of the Commissioner of Indian Affairs, who, in October, 1886, advised a resurvey of this reservation in accordance with the provisions of the treaty of October 14, 1864. In his report for 1887, the Commissioner announced that, after investigation, it had been decided to leave the boundary as it had been surveyed in 1871 and not to disturb the settlements made on the disputed land, "although," as he naïvely observed, "the claim of the Indians seemed to be well substantiated." "When the line is

1887, was accepted by the Department of the Interior on July 19, 1889, but in October, 1889, the western boundary was still uncertain. Ibid. (1889), p. 83. See also Salem Oregon Statesman, Jan. 17, 1890.

[46] Commissioner of Indian Affairs, Report (1886), p. 246. See also the report of William Parsons, dated at Salem, Oregon, Sept. 11, 1886. Incoming Letters, Oregon, L25228 (1886).

[47] Commissioner of Indian Affairs, Report (1890), p. 233.

re-marked," he continued, "the military will be requested to protect the reservation from encroachments of cattlemen, concerning which the Indians have made complaints." But he did not
rest his case here; he was even willing to entertain the thought
that the Indians of the Klamath Reservation might be entitled
to some compensation for the land they had lost by the "loca-
tion" of the boundary.[48]

What was true of the boundaries of reservations in both Washington and Oregon was also more or less true in Idaho. There,
in 1868 and again in 1869, the Surveyor-General most urgently
advised that the boundaries of the Indian reservations be surveyed. "If these *reservation lines* are not to be considered a myth
by the settler," he wrote in 1869, "they should be surveyed and
permanently marked as soon as possible. The truth is, the whole
Indian policy is a farce." Still later, Indian agents urged that the
boundaries of these reservations be established. As early as 1872,
the agent at the Fort Hall Reservation was urging that its southern and eastern boundaries be surveyed, and as late as the summer of 1883 the agent at the Colville Indian Agency was complaining that white settlers were "trespassing upon the timber of
the Coeur d'Alene Reservation in consequence of the undefined
boundaries of the reserve."[49] Some months later the agent at the
Lemhi Reservation let go this blast: "In regard to the reservation
being surveyed, that has been suggested and urged so often as
to become rather monotonous. I am, however, hopeful that it will
be done some time during the present century." Whether this
sarcasm helped the cause or hindered it, the fact is that the agent
for this reservation could report in August, 1887, that in "the
month of June this reservation was surveyed, which has been a
long-felt want."[50] Thus it appears that the problem of the boundaries of reservations was a general one in the Pacific Northwest,
and a cause of considerable apprehension to more than one Indian agent.

Occasionally even settlers could, in a pinch, lament the un-

[48] *Ibid.* (1886), p. 215; *ibid.* (1887), p. lxxviii.
[49] U.S. General Land Office, *Report* (1868), p. 390; *ibid.* (1869), p. 346;
Commissioner of Indian Affairs, *Report* (1883), p. 142.
[50] *Ibid.* (1884), p. 65; *ibid.* (1887), p. 70.

wisdom of the government's tolerating indefinite boundary lines
of reservations, especially if such lament would bolster their contention that Indian reservations were undesirable because they
deprived white men of "a large amount of grazing land." A case
in point is the action taken by a meeting of settlers in Yakima
City on September 17, 1878. Gathered for the purpose of expressing opposition to a proposed reservation for Chief Moses
and his band of Indians, the settlers adopted resolutions affirming, *inter alia,* that such reservation would be marked by "no
well defined lines," with the result that there would be unending
conflict between "whites and Indians in regard to stock trespassing on each other's lands."[51]

From the subject of congressional neglect in respect to reservation boundaries, we now pass on to the subject of congressional
neglect in respect to another, and perhaps more important, matter. Through all the years covered by this chapter the Congress
withheld its sanction of a practice which, according to the testimony of competent persons, would have gone far toward solving
the problem of encroachments by stockmen on Indian reservations. From reservation after reservation in the Oregon Country,
beginning in 1878 and continuing at least to 1890—the final limit
of this study—came word not only that the Indians were eager
to lease their surplus lands for grazing purposes, but also that
there were stockmen who were equally eager to enter into such
leases. On December 3, 1878, the Commissioner of Indian Affairs learned from the agent that the Klamath Indians wished to
rent a part of their reservation to stockmen, a desire of which the
agent approved, provided that "the right kind of white man"
would enter into a lease with them for a seven-year period and
pay for his grazing privilege five hundred dollars a year.[52]

In May, 1878, the agent for the Malheur Reservation received
two requests from cattlemen to lease a part of this reservation.
The first offer was from Todhunter and Devine, a large firm
which desired to lease for fifteen years, at the rate of two hundred dollars a year, an area of about five hundred square miles
on which some three thousand head of cattle were then tres-

[51] Incoming Letters, Oregon, W2064 (1878).
[52] *Ibid.,* R866 (1878).

passing. Rinehart thought the price ridiculously low, but, in order to avoid further trouble, he recommended the leasing to cattle-men of the part of the reservation that they desired, provided that they paid "a reasonable price for its use." Two days after reporting this offer, Rinehart informed the Commissioner of Indian Affairs that another and better offer to lease the same tract had been made by J. W. Scott, of Camp Harney, who was willing to pay for the privilege fifteen hundred dollars annually for a term of five years. Rinehart strongly advised the acceptance of this offer, in part no doubt because he thought that it might stop a movement then under way to have a large area which embraced that of the proposed lease separated from the reservation and restored to the public domain.[53] During the next two years, other requests to lease parts of the reservation for grazing cattle and sheep were received by the Commissioner of Indian Affairs from the Malheur, the Umatilla, the Klamath, the Yakima, and other reservations in the Pacific Northwest.[54]

The subject of leases, however, remained in unstable equili-brium. Although the Commissioner of Indian Affairs clearly saw the advantage of leasing Indian grazing lands to dependable persons, he was stopped by law from approving even informal agreements by means of which cattlemen might exploit reserva-tions to their own and the Indians' profit. Nevertheless, as the Commissioner confessed in 1884, a few agreements, not approved by the department, had been entered into by some Indian tribes on their own responsibility. He urged that the Congress, for the benefit of the Indians, put this "vexed question" of leasing upon a proper basis.[55] If there had been any doubt as to the legality of leasing lands of the reservations, it was set at rest for the time being at least by the Attorney General of the United States, in an opinion handed down on July 21, 1885. This opinion, as sum-marized on May 31, 1887, by the Commissioner of Indian Affairs in a letter to an Oregonian who had expressed a desire to lease a part of the Siletz Reservation, held that "Indian nations and

[53] Malheur Agency Letter Book, Dec. 17, 1877–Sept. 30, 1878, pp. 150-52.
[54] Incoming Letters, Oregon, R451 (1879), F163 (1880), 11187 (1884), 11190 (1884), L23228 (1886); Land Division, Letter Book 160, pp. 363-64; *Leases of Land in the Indian Territory*, pp. 200-202, 216-19, 219-20.
[55] Commissioner of Indian Affairs, *Report* (1884), p. xiv.

tribes are precluded by the force and effect of the Statute (Section 2116, Revised Statutes) from alienating or leasing any part of the reservation, or imparting any interest or claim thereto, without the consent of the Government of the United States."[56]

From 1885 forward, the Commissioner of Indian Affairs, year after year, urged that legislation be enacted to authorize the leasing of Indian lands "under proper restrictions"; but in 1889 he rather grimly remarked that, "so far, Congress has not seen fit to enact the necessary legislation."[57] Nevertheless, while the Congress was procrastinating, cattlemen were acting. As the Commissioner had observed in 1888, cattle owners, since grazing lands were in demand and no law prohibited the use of Indian lands for such purpose, would continue to get from Indians grazing privileges which the department could not legally approve.[58] Here, indeed, was the nub of the matter. Every agreement by which cattlemen grazed their herds upon Indian reservations was extralegal, if not downright illegal; hence neither party to such an agreement could be punished for not fulfilling the obligation of a contract ostensibly embodied therein.

That grazing leases, if properly drawn, could have been used to prevent cattlemen from trespassing on Indian reservations is abundantly proved by an agreement entered into on November 1, 1884, between Linus M. Nickerson, agent for the Klamath Indians, and Matt Obenchain, a large-scale cattleman of Klamath County, Oregon, whereby Obenchain, in consideration of the sum of three hundred dollars per annum, payable semiannually, was to be allowed to graze as many as five hundred head of cattle on a part of the Klamath Reservation for five years. Obenchain specifically bound himself to see to it that, during the time of the agreement, the cattle of all other white men were kept

[56] J. D. C. Atkins to John Bones, May 31, 1887, Land Division, Letter Book 160, pp. 363-64.

[57] Commissioner of Indian Affairs, *Report* (1889), p. 30.

[58] *Ibid.* (1888), p. xxxxix-xl. In October, 1889, the Commissioner of Indian Affairs wrote as follows: "In order to overcome in a measure this difficulty, and to enable the Indians to receive some benefit from the spontaneous products of their lands, the Department has authorized several tribes to take a limited number of cattle to herd and graze upon the reservations at a stipulated price to be paid by the owners of the cattle to the United States Indian agent for the benefit of the tribe." *Ibid.* (1889), pp. 30-31.

off the tract that he had leased. But the Commissioner of Indian Affairs disallowed this agreement on the grounds that leases of lands that were a part of an Indian reservation could not lawfully be made, and that grazing privileges could be granted only by the "proper authority of the tribe."[59] Even without so specific an obligation as Obenchain was willing to take, it may be presumed that every cattleman who leased reservation grazing lands would protect the right he was paying for by seeing to it that no other white man's cattle grazed on that land.

Again and again agents for Indian reservations in the Pacific Northwest affirmed that authorization "to receive cattle for pasturage" on reservations would be beneficial to the Indians whose lands would be so used. But never was such affirmation more forcefully made than by an agent for the Nez Percés, who, on August 20, 1888, wrote to the Commissioner of Indian Affairs, saying that such authority would enable him to give employment to his Indians as herders and to convert to their use "a source of revenue that would . . . do much towards settling them upon their allotments and otherwise materially improve their condition with less direct aid from Congress."[60]

In 1886 the agent for the Yakimas gave a rather unusual, perhaps even unique, reason for wishing to lease a part of the reservation for which he was responsible. He advised that the borders of the Yakima Reservation be leased for the grazing of sheep in order to provide, besides an income for the Indians, an effective "fence" for keeping white men's cattle off, and Indians' cattle on, the reservation. This proposal, he believed, would have the desired effect, for, as he said, where "sheep pasture usually cattle or horses will not."[61] But binding leases of parts of Indian reservations could no more be made for this purpose than for any other

[59] *Leases of Land in the Indian Territory*, pp. 217-19.
[60] Commissioner of Indian Affairs, *Report* (1888), p. 85.
[61] Charles H. Dickson to the Commissioner of Indian Affairs, June 28, 1886, Incoming Letters, Oregon, 17598 (1886). On Sept. 28, 1886, the Commissioner submitted this request to the Secretary of the Interior. Land Division, Letter Book 152, pp. 275-76. Recently an able student has maintained that the widespread belief that sheep "tainted" the grass so that cattle would not eat it had no basis in fact. Edward Norris Wentworth, *America's Sheep Trails* (Ames, Iowa, 1948), p. 523.

purpose. As late as 1890 the Congress had not granted general authority to lease lands on Indian reservations.[62]

Thus we have seen that the failure of the Commissioner of Indian Affairs to protect the Indian reservations in the Pacific Northwest from the encroachments of cattlemen was caused as much by defects of governmental policy as by the ruthlessness of cattlemen. The problem of such encroachments was general, not regional, in the American West. Cattlemen in Oregon, Washington, and Idaho were presumably no better and no worse than cattlemen elsewhere in the open-range country of the American trans-Mississippi West. Taught by long experience, the Congress should have known well the traits of the frontier mind and have acted pursuant to such knowledge. By putting temptation in the way of western cattlemen, and then by neglecting to adopt measures to offset such temptation, the Congress imposed upon the Commissioner of Indian Affairs a problem which that officer could not solve.

[62] Commissioner of Indian Affairs, *Report* (1890), p. lxxi.

CHAPTER X

Through Changing Times

THE continuing encroachments of cattlemen upon Indian reservations in the Pacific Northwest—encroachments which were especially noticeable during the 1880's—disclosed a significant indication of rapidly changing conditions in that country. The ranges were rapidly contracting; incoming settlers, pursuant to law, were acquiring, as had settlers on earlier American frontiers, tracts of land, some of which were arable; and these settlers, also pursuant to law, were enclosing such parts of their acquired lands as they wished to cultivate. In other words, stockmen and settlers then occupying the Oregon Country were repeating a process which had transformed economic life on American frontiers from earliest times. Through the years of advancing settlements, either custom or local law had given an "implied license" to stockmen on American frontiers to graze their cattle or other livestock upon all unenclosed lands, whether publicly owned or privately owned. Unenclosed America had been "a public common on which . . . horses, cattle, hogs and sheep could run and graze." But the progress of settlement wrought significant and enduring changes in pastoral America. In districts where agricultural pursuits became more important than stock raising, occupational conflicts arose, especially in areas where, owing to a scarcity of timber, the cost of fencing was excessive. Here the farmers insisted that this long-standing custom be replaced by "a principle of law derived from England"—namely, "that every man must restrain his stock within his own grounds, and if he does not do so, and they get upon the unenclosed grounds of his neighbor, it is a trespass for which their owner is responsible."[1]

In 1890, the Supreme Court of the United States declared that this principle had not prevailed during the settlement of the United States because it would have been "ill-adapted to the nature and condition of the country at that time." Nevertheless, in the case here under review, this court took "judicial notice" of the fact that the settlement of the public lands had led to the formation of states in any one of which the legislature, in case of need, would enact a law providing for the modification by popular vote of "this custom of nearly a hundred years." Such law would permit "certain counties, or parts of the state, or the whole of the state, by a vote of the people within such sub-division, to determine whether cattle shall longer be permitted to run at large and the owners of the soil compelled to rely upon their fences for protection, or whether the cattle owner shall keep them confined, and in that manner protect his neighbor without the necessity on the part of the latter of relying upon fences."[2]

Such legislation invariably came in the train of "herd-law" or "no-fence" movements. Agitation for such a law, as we have seen, was under way in California in the early 1860's, and the matter had not yet been fully settled on a statewide basis at the beginning of the 1870's.[3] By this time, moreover, the subject of a herd law had become one of considerable concern in Illinois, Iowa, Kansas, and Nebraska.[4] The idea of such a law, being highly

[1] Buford v. Houtz, 133 U.S. 326 (1890), and the state cases and state laws therein cited.

[2] Ibid., pp. 326-29.

[3] The Statutes of California, Passed at the Fifteenth Session of the Legislature, 1863-64 (Sacramento, 1864), pp. 170-71; Sacramento Daily Union, Feb. 27, March 3, April 11, 1864, March 25, Oct. 3, 1871; Yreka Weekly Union, March 15, April 5, 1871.

[4] Public Laws . . . of Illinois, 1871-72 (Springfield, 1872), pp. 116-17; Public Laws . . . of Iowa, 1874 (Des Moines, 1874), pp. 91-92; Laws of . . . Kansas, 1870 (Topeka, 1870), pp. 236-38; Laws of . . . Nebraska, 1871 (Des Moines, 1871), pp. 120-22; on a proposed herd law in Nevada, "That 'No-Fence' Law," Cheyenne Northwestern Live Stock Journal, Jan. 21, 1887. See also Paul W. Gates, "Cattle Kings in the Prairies," MVHR (December, 1948), 409, and Paul C. Henlein, Cattle Kingdom in the Ohio Valley, 1783-1860 (Lexington, Ky., 1959), p. 59.

contagious, soon spread to the Oregon Country. As early as May, 1872, the editor of the *Willamette Farmer* was arguing that, in the Willamette Valley, the time had come when it would cost less "to fence the pastures than to fence the grain fields." When "the country was new," he readily conceded, "it would have been a hardship to fence the stock from all the public pasturage," just as now it would be a hardship to require the fencing of the public pastures in eastern Oregon. But, he concluded, "would it not be a measure of protection to the grain growing regions of the Willamette Valley?"[5]

A few days before this question was raised in the Willamette Valley, an editor east of the Cascades was commenting on the growing scarcity of fencing material for use in the Walla Walla Valley, and was recommending that farmers in this valley make experiments "in hedging," or in growing timber from which fences could be made. "It is evident," he wrote, "that our people can not depend on the Blue Mountains to furnish fencing material much longer, as the supply within available distance is nearly exhausted."[6] As if to emphasize his point, he reported a few weeks later that these mountains were "filled with rail-makers," and that the people of the Walla Walla Valley not only seemed to have "a general desire to get more land into cultivation," but also appeared to feel "the necessity of fencing up lands for pastures." In midsummer of 1873, in an editorial entitled "Fence or No Fence," he said that Californians were discussing the question "whether the farmers shall fence in their crops and turn out their cattle, or fence in their cattle and turn out their crops," and remarked that some were arguing that farmers in the Walla Walla Valley should have the benefit of a no-fence law. But the time for such a law in the Walla Walla Valley, he thought, was not yet. He suggested, however, that this subject be discussed by the "County Grange."[7]

Presently this subject did evoke general concern in some of the pastoral districts of the Oregon Country. Late in June of 1875, an editor in northwestern Washington called attention to a "lively

[5] Salem *Willamette Farmer,* May 11, 1872.
[6] *Walla Walla Union,* April 27, 1872.
[7] *Ibid.,* May 25, 1872, July 5, 1873.

discussion" in the Walla Walla Valley between the friends and opponents of a no-fence law in that region. "It is," he said, "the
interest of a large class of agriculturists who may be called poor,
against another class of rich stock-owners who count their flocks
and herds by the hundreds." Although he confessed that this
matter was none of his business, he seemed to think that it was
his duty to remark that, in his opinion, "justice would seem to be
on the 'no-fence' side of the question." During July of that year,
the editor of the *Walla Walla Statesman* was offering the columns
of his newspaper for a "full and free discussion" of this subject,
and on August 7, after what he called a full discussion had taken
place, he felt justified in saying that "a large majority" of the
settlers in the Walla Walla Valley were opposed to a no-fence
law.[8]

He was right for the time being, but the sands were running
fast. Before the end of 1875, a narrow-gauge railroad was carrying agricultural products from the heart of the Walla Walla Valley
to Wallula for shipment down the Columbia River. Nor was this
all. Settlers were continuing to move into eastern Washington
south of the Snake River, and on November 11, 1875, a new
county called Columbia was carved from Walla Walla County.
Meanwhile, north of the Snake River, the settlement of the Palouse country, as we have noticed in an earlier chapter, was
continuing, and well before the end of the 1870's settlers in the
eastern part of Whitman County were sending wheat and other
agricultural products to ports on the Snake River in such quantities that the Oregon Steam Navigation Company was hard put to
it to provide enough boats to carry such products down the Snake
and Columbia rivers.[9] By this time some of the men concerned
about the growing agricultural interest in eastern Washington,
north as well as south of the Snake River, were showing some
inclination to measure their strength against that of the cattlemen
in that area.

Between 1875 and 1879, however, the discussion of a no-fence
law appears to have been spasmodic in southeastern Washing-

[8] Whatcom *Bellingham Bay Mail*, June 26, 1875; *Walla Walla Statesman*,
July 10, 17, Aug. 7, 1875.
[9] *Spokan Times*, Sept. 25, 1879, quoting the *Walla Walla Watchman*.

ton.[10] In 1877 this subject received some attention in both Walla Walla and Columbia counties, and north of the Snake River the changing situation was revealed in mid-April, 1878, when the Portland *Morning Oregonian* observed, somewhat tersely, that farmers were "running logs for fence rails down the Palouse river."[11] Less than a year later the *Walla Walla Union* came out strongly in favor of a herd law, affirming that, since grain raising had become the chief occupation in Walla Walla County, there was no longer any justice in enforcing a fence law there. This view the *Union* would continue to maintain.[12]

Meanwhile, in Whitman County, the Colfax *Palouse Gazette,* having invited a discussion of this important subject, was being deluged with communications from its readers. Whether they wrote from Leitchville, Union Flat, Pleasant Flat, Spring Flat, Little Almota, Steptoe, Hangman Creek, or elsewhere, the writers' views indicated that they were influenced not only by their nearness to timber or to navigable water, but also by their experience of herd or no-fence laws in other states or territories. "Observer," writing from Leitchville on March 29, 1879, was certain that a herd law would double the production of the county within two years. In Illinois, he said, such a law had worked very well. But later, other Leitchville correspondents opposed this view. Letters from Pleasant Flat were favorable to such a law, but A. J. Wimer, for example, writing from Union Flat on March 3, 1879, said that such a law would favor only large-scale farmers, and would encourage the removal of livestock from Whitman County. But when R. H. Hibbs, writing from Spring Flat on April 22 to affirm that a herd law would accelerate cultivation in Whitman County and that, having seen "something of the herd law in California," he knew whereof he spoke, he was answered on May 6, 1879, by J. M. Baker, of Cottonwood, who said that such a law

[10] See a letter signed S. M. W. and dated at "Dayton, W. T., June 7, 1875," in the *Walla Walla Union,* June 12, 1875.

[11] *Dayton News,* March 3, 1877; *Walla Walla Union,* March 3, 1877; Salt Lake City *Deseret News,* July 4, 1877; Portland *Morning Oregonian,* April 19, 1878. In 1877 the question of "fence or no fence" was being discussed in Tooele County, Utah.

[12] The *Dayton News,* however, reported on June 21, 1879, that "Union Grange No. 12, Pataha Prairie, voted its opposition to a Herd Law on June 14, 1879."

would "limit the poor man to one team and a cow," and that he would either have "to stake them out or pay to get them herded."[13] Elsewhere in Whitman County there was opposition to a herd law, and one man, George W. Wolf of Clinton, maintained that such a law had ruined both Kansas and Nebraska: "The herd law," he wrote, "makes a fat thing for lawyers, brother lawing brother, father against son, a perfect hell on earth." Opposition came also from Little Almota when J. F. Thayer, writing on April 8, condemned the idea of such a law. Without actually predicting that a herd law would "raise hell" anywhere, he insisted that it had produced "commotion" in Cerro Gordo County, Iowa. "The farmers of Little Almota," he wrote, "are twenty-five miles from the mountains, but, as far as I know, are willing to fence their crops and have peace and friendship in our community." Contributions from other places in Whitman County added little or nothing to the elucidation of either side of the controversy.

Emotion apart, the "economics" of this controversy for people south of the Snake River was clearly expressed when the editor of the *Dayton News*, on June 21, 1879, said that "Those who live tolerably near to timber are opposed to a Herd Law, while those living ten to twenty miles from timber are in favor of the law." North of the Palouse hills, in the neighborhood of Hangman Creek, J. Roberts wrote with equal clarity on April 17, 1879, saying that the people in this district would oppose a herd law because they had plenty of timber for fencing, because they were "too far from navigation to make grain raising a permanent business at a profit," and because they believed that a herd law was not beneficial to any "new country where pasture is so abundant as it is in this Territory north of Snake river."[14]

In the autumn of 1879 the discussion of a herd law was transferred from the newspapers of eastern Washington to the legislative halls in Olympia, where there would be lobbying as well as oratory about this matter. That the issue under discussion was

---

[13] Colfax *Palouse Gazette*, March 7, April 4, 11, 18, 25, May 9, 23, 1879. Mr. Baker believed that the greater part of the Palouse country was "too hilly" to be farmed.

[14] *Ibid.*, April 25, May 2, 23, 1879. The *Palouse Gazette* on May 30, 1879, announced that it favored a herd law for the agricultural parts of Whitman County.

important to interests other than that of farming in eastern Washington is revealed in a letter from H. Thielsen, the chief engineer of the newly formed Oregon Railway and Navigation Company, to Henry Villard. Thielsen said that, in order to promote the interests of the farmers—and of the company—in southeastern Washington, he had taken steps to urge the legislature of Washington to pass a no-fence law.[15] But such "steps," whatever their character may have been, did not accomplish the desired end. The territorial legislature did enact a law, approved on November 5, 1879, prohibiting hogs from running at large in the counties of Columbia, Whitman, Stevens, Walla Walla, Yakima, and Lewis, but the house of representatives, on November 9, 1879, refused by a vote of sixteen to fourteen to pass H.B. 111—a bill for an act to repeal the fence laws of Walla Walla, Columbia, Whitman, Spokane, and Stevens counties. As the Olympia correspondent for the *Morning Oregonian* wrote on November 8, the harmony which previously had marked the career of the legislative delegation from eastern Washington "was most signally departed from when the, to them, vital question of 'fence or no fence' came up to be debated in the house this afternoon. Probably no bill, which has been introduced this session, affects so large a moneyed interest, and certainly no debate has taken place that will be as closely followed and commented upon by as great a number of your territorial readers."[16]

On the subject of fence or no fence it turned out that the delegation from Walla Walla County was divided, but that from the other counties directly involved, all the representatives were opposed to such a law. Of the delegation from Walla Walla, only Representative John A. Taylor favored this bill, and he spoke "long and earnestly" in its behalf. The law which it would repeal, he affirmed, "was a law for the rich as against the poor." He was certain that it would "cost the struggling wheat farmer more to fence and keep out the cattle belonging to capitalists from abroad than his wheat netted him." But his colleagues thought other-

---

[15] Henry Villard Papers, letter dated Oct. 1, 1879, in Box 57, Folder 414 (MSS in the Widener Library, Harvard University).

[16] *Laws of Washington, 1879* (Olympia, 1879), p. 217; *Morning Oregonian*, Nov. 11, 1879.

wise. D. J. Storms of Walla Walla said that he had previously made only one speech, "and that was to a lady," but that he would attempt another one in order to defeat this bill; and J. M. Dunbar, also of Walla Walla, had no hesitancy in saying that the passage of this bill would be the "most disastrous thing" that could happen to "his section" of the country. "It was," he affirmed, "the town speculators, railroad and steamboat men who talked no fence where he lived." T. C. Frary, of Columbia County, remarked bluntly that in his county "there were two interests to protect, the stock men as well as the wheat raisers, and he did not propose to slaughter one for the benefit of the other"; and his colleague from Columbia County, D. C. Guernsey, said that, "should the house see fit to pass this law [,] he wished Columbia County stricken out of the list of counties named."

The representatives from both Whitman and Stevens counties spoke against this bill. James A. Perkins said that the people of Whitman County were "bitterly opposed" to this measure, a statement which he no doubt wished to be understood as meaning that a considerable number of his constituents were opposed to it. His colleague from Stevens County, D. F. Percival, assured the house that the people of his section were "bitterly opposed" to such a measure. "The cattle interest," he said, "was the largest interest of his county, and such a law would virtually wipe it out of existence."[17]

But the advocates of a no-fence law were not left with empty hands. Their representatives took back from Olympia to the "cow counties" of eastern Washington a renewal of the debate on the subject of fence or no fence, for on November 13, 1879, the territorial legislative assembly had passed an act "to ascertain the wishes of the people in certain counties in regard to the fence law." The part of the territory affected by this law consisted not only of Walla Walla, Columbia, Whitman, and Stevens counties, but also Klickitat and Yakima counties, and the newly created Spokane County, which had been carved from Stevens County on October 30, 1879. In other words, the whole of eastern Washington would be "polled" on this question at the next general

17 *Ibid.; Palouse Gazette*, Nov. 28, 1879, quoting the special letter from Olympia, Nov. 8, 1879, in the *Morning Oregonian*, Nov. 11, 1879.

election held for choosing a delegate from the territory to the Congress; and in each county in this vast area the vote thus taken in November, 1880, would be "returned to the county auditor," who would pass on this information to "each member elected to the legislative assembly as a guide for legislation in regard to fence laws in their respective counties."[18] By passing this law, the legislative assembly tossed an apple of discord into the "cow counties" of eastern Washington, and there "large stock raisers" and "poor farmers" began forthwith to gird themselves for an impending struggle.

The *Walla Walla Union* displayed no remarkable insight when it predicted that the taking of such an "opinion poll" would make the "fence question" prominent in territorial politics in 1880. This newspaper, proud of the fact that it had been the first one in Washington Territory to advocate a no-fence law, began the campaign with an emotional editorial in which, as in an apocalyptic vision, it foretold how the contending forces would stand up to be counted on the day of judgment in November, 1880. "Then," it said,

all who favor the conversion of the hundreds of thousands of acres of bunch grass lands, now occupied by a few thousand cattle and sheep belonging to men who do not own one acre in a thousand that they use, into fields of waving grain, dotted with farm houses inhabited by happy, prosperous men, women and children, beautified with orchards, while here and there a schoolhouse gives evidence of the intelligence of the community, will be found advocating a "no fence law." On the other side will be found all those whose interests are in the rearing of cattle and sheep, and a few pioneer farmers, who having complied with the laws of the land at great expense by fencing their acres, now fear to compete with the new comer who would not have to fence, if the law was changed.[19]

Here was a sentiment not unwelcome to an increasing number of settlers in the eastern part of Whitman County. The newspaper which represented their views, the Colfax *Palouse Gazette*, remarked on November 21, 1879, that "the weight of argument" was on the side of a herd law. "Large stock-raisers are pitted against poor farmers upon the proposition." In nearby Colton,

[18] *Laws of Washington, 1879*, pp. 234-35.
[19] Quoted by the *Morning Oregonian*, Nov. 19, 1879, and by the *Spokan Times*, July 4, 1879.

on January 7, 1880, a correspondent of the *Gazette* endorsed this view: "With a railroad and a herd law this section of the county would be one immense wheatfield."[20]

The issue of poor farmers against large stock raisers proved to be exciting elsewhere in the Pacific Northwest in 1880. In January it was arousing interest in Umatilla County, Oregon, and presently it evoked from a newspaper in the territorial capital, west of the Cascades, words of sympathy for the poor men who, in a region where timber was scarce, were required to fence their crops in order to protect them from cattle and horses belonging to men who not only did not own the land upon which their livestock grazed, but who were "virtually trespassers upon the public domain." Such being the state of affairs on the ranges of the Oregon Country, the editor of this newspaper anticipated "an immense vote in favor of 'no fence.' "[21]

In the great debate now getting under way, men untrained in argumentation and little versed in the niceties of rhetoric and of grammar turned their attention away from herding or plowing to contribute their bits to a growing literature on the subject of fence or no fence. Some of them wrote in dignified language, presenting their arguments and unburdening their prejudices in an orderly manner; others gave way to incoherent outbursts which did little to conceal the wrath that was choking them. Editorials, reports of debates conducted by literary societies, letters pro and con to the editors of newspapers, resolutions of political conventions[22]—all this was made public in the columns of newspapers in eastern Washington; and presumably those who read such writings were comforted by the utterances that sup-

[20] *Palouse Gazette,* Nov. 21, 1879, Jan. 16, 1880.

[21] *Morning Oregonian,* Jan. 21, 29, 1880; *Palouse Gazette,* Feb. 6, 1880, quoting the Olympia *Courier.* In an article entitled "Up the Columbia," which the *Willamette Farmer* published on Aug. 20, 1880, S. A. Clarke described the diversity of the fences which he saw in Washington Territory south of the Snake River, saying, "Fencing is an expensive item, where timber is so scarce and lumber is so high priced." In this region, he remarked, the "old fashioned worm fence is never seen at all."

[22] Both the Democratic and the Republican conventions in Whitman County instructed their representatives in the legislature to vote against a no-fence law. Colfax *Northwest Tribune,* Sept. 1, 8, 1880; *Palouse Gazette,* Sept. 3, 1880. The Democratic Convention in Yakima County also opposed a no-fence law. *Yakima Record,* Sept. 11, 1880.

ported their own views on this subject. Moreover, the arguments and the prejudices thus expressed by residents of Whitman County were bolstered by arguments and prejudices solicited from persons living in states in which no-fence laws had been, or still were, in operation.[23] But among these contributors to the argument there was no consensus.

South of the Snake River, the controversy centered in Walla Walla, the largest community in eastern Washington; north of the Snake, it centered in Colfax, the "metropolis" of the rapidly settling Palouse country. In Walla Walla the *Union,* still preening itself as the protagonist of no-fence legislation in Washington, remained the champion of "the poor farmer"; in Colfax the *Palouse Gazette,* a newspaper founded in 1877, took upon itself the defense of the farmers' interest in the Palouse country. Some of the other newspapers in eastern Washington espoused, more or less cautiously, the cause of the cattlemen. In mid-August, for example, the *Yakima Record,* a defender of cattlemen's interests, cautiously "sprang" the issue in Yakima County. In Spokane County the Cheney *Northwest Tribune* opposed a no-fence law, and in Columbia County the Pomeroy *Washington Independent* and the *Dayton Weekly News* did likewise. For editors of newspapers in areas of heavy controversy about this issue, the choice of side was a ticklish one, and naturally they took care not to bite the hands that were feeding them. Some of them, as we shall see, guessed badly. In this controversy, however, their principal role consisted in opening their columns to those who wished to argue the question.

The debate on this issue in the "cow counties" of eastern Washington in 1880 deserves serious attention not only because it marks a crisis in the economic transition of the Inland Empire, but also because it provides adequate material for a "case study" illustrating an occupational conflict that took place on every frontier of the American West. For this purpose it is as significant as another controversy in eastern Washington in 1880—the struggle

[23] The controversy about the issue of "fence or no fence" can be followed in the *Palouse Gazette* and in the *Walla Walla Union* during the spring, summer, and autumn of 1880.

between Cheney and Spokane Falls for possession of the seat of government of Spokane County. Here, too, we may find materials for an interesting case study of another type of persistent conflict that attended political organization on successive frontiers of the emerging American West.

Perhaps the main theme of those who agitated for a no-fence law was the alleged injustice of requiring the poor settler, situated a long way from timber, to construct a fence to protect his crop from the cattle of wealthy, and perhaps absentee, stockmen who exploited free pastures but did nothing to "build up" the country in which they were prospering. This argument for a no-fence law, either expressly stated or broadly insinuated, was widely pervasive, and on at least one occasion it appeared in an effusion of doggerel, as follows:

> The man who comes to make a home
> In this far Western land
> For capital brings honest heart,
> And brawny, willing hands,
> But little more has he in store. . . .
>
> Should laws be made the rich to aid
> Which makes the poor man poorer?
> That law is blest above the rest,
> Where work men's rights are surer.
>
> Those men who borrow arguments
> From stock kings and repeat them,
> Should be fenced in; green things are scarce—
> Some passing cow might eat them.[24]

This argument was supplemented by affirmations that the new settler, who ordinarily was poor, would sooner derive benefits from the production of grain if he were saved the cost of building fences; that the wheat such settlers would raise would produce from the land a greater revenue than stock raising; and that the production of crops which "could not walk to market" would hasten the building of railroads into eastern Washington. Moreover, some supporters of the no-fence law affirmed that such laws had proved to be beneficial elsewhere—in Kansas, California, and

[24] Contributed by Irene to the Dayton *Columbia Chronicle*, May 15, 1880.

other states—and that the problem of herding cattle for poor settlers, if the fencing of crops were discontinued, could be solved by cooperation in employing a herder for such livestock. Interestingly enough, a man in the Yakima Valley, where the cattle interest was still strong, said that he had observed the working of a no-fence law in "three different states," and that in each one of them the law had been

the best means of fencing up the farm lands that could have been devised, for it enabled the poor man to make crops which he could not do if he were compelled to fence first. But if he could raise a crop or two without a fence he would then be able to fence, and you may rest assured that he would fence as soon as he could. After the country is fenced, the "no fence" law is not wanted, and is a "dead letter."[25]

The arguments of those who favored the status quo varied from *ad crumenam* to *ad hominem*. They affirmed not only that a no-fence law would drive most of the livestock from the county adopting it, and thus increase the price of beef as well as the taxes on other property, but that such a law, besides destroying every industry except wheat raising, which was less profitable than stock raising, would encourage large land holdings and tenant farming, and thus injure the poor man who could not afford to herd his cattle. Moreover, despite some evidence to the contrary adduced by their opponents, they affirmed that a no-fence law, wherever it had been tried in other states or territories, had been ruinous.[26] Finally, among those who opposed such new-fangled legislation, especially among the old settlers, there was a pervasive feeling that men who were not willing to fence their cultivated tracts would be neither good neighbors nor desirable citizens.

As the debate progressed, not a few of the contributions to it shed more heat than light on the issue. But most of the partici-

[25] *Yakima Record*, Sept. 4, 1880.
[26] Perhaps unknown to the "debaters" in eastern Washington in 1880 was the fact that, in Dakota Territory, the *Bismarck Tribune* of April 23, 1880, remarked that, whereas the "herd law" of Dakota had been of value to the settlers when the country was new, now more cultivated fields and a restricted range were making enclosures necessary for domestic animals. In 1882, Dakota passed a law making the owners of cattle responsible for damages that animals did to crops whether such crops were fenced or not fenced. Harold E. Briggs, *Frontiers of the Northwest* (New York, 1940), p. 496.

pants, despite much incoherence, invective, and vituperation, let it be known how they would vote on this issue in the election in November, 1880; and that, presumably, was something worth knowing. But for some who were slow of comprehension, neither vituperation nor logic sufficed, and to such persons it was necessary to give assurance that the passage of a no-fence law would not require them to demolish fences that they had built. A high point of the controversy was undoubtedly reached when a waggish person—unknown and perhaps not fully appreciated at the time—rose high enough above the sound and fury to produce "a very interesting and able article in favor of every man fencing his grain to keep it from straying into his neighbor's cattle and harming them."[27]

One of the most interesting aspects of this controversy—and perhaps the most regrettable one—was the deepening of the gulf between the "old settlers" and the "new settlers." Some settlers who had moved north of the Snake River before Whitman County had been organized, and who had borne the burden of pioneering in the heat of the day, had adjusted themselves to the difficult requirement of fencing fields. Now they were both hurt and alarmed at the radicalism of newcomers who urged the enactment of a law depriving these farmer-stockmen of the bunch grass they had "so nobly earned." M. H. Leitch of Leitchville, who had come to Whitman County from Idaho in 1871, suspected that the no-fence agitation was the work of subversive persons who wanted Kearneyism. He also may have suspected, without saying so, that such persons, besides being "soft" on the idea of free enterprise, were "pinkish" enough to entertain the notion that a Chinaman or an Indian had rights that a white man should respect. Things indeed were getting into a bad way, and Mr. Leitch wanted nothing to do with them. "I am satisfied," he wrote, "to raise grain and stock, and to fence my land. I always find peace and plenty by so doing."[28] Why, he was thinking, should conditions be made more favorable for the later settlers than for the early settlers?

[27] Quoted from the *Palouse Gazette* by the *Walla Walla Union* of April 3, 1880.
[28] *Palouse Gazette*, April 16, 1880.

Equally aroused by the agitators for a no-fence law was "Farmer's Wife," who had come to Union Flat in 1869. "We landed here," she wrote,

on a wave of adversity; our labor was our capital; we did not howl for a no fence law; we went to work to build up the country. There are a great many of the old settlers who have done the same. . . . Let [the immigrants] come and go to work as the first settlers did, and build up homes and fences, then they will be able to appreciate them. Any man with common sense should know that the herd law offers no inducement to people of energy and enterprise. On the contrary, it will fill the country with worthless tramps, who are too numerous at present for the good of all concerned.

Her advice to the old settlers, in the event of their being deprived of their bunch grass, was to gather up their herds and flocks, shake the dust of Whitman County "from off" their feet, and go to Idaho, where the people had enough sense to keep the bunch grass "free to all."[29] Such advice would have been entirely acceptable to Mr. Leitch, of Leitchville.

Presently, discussion of the big issue gave way to action. Weeks in advance of the election, a careful observer had predicted its outcome. "From what we can learn," wrote the editor of the Pomeroy *Washington Independent* on September 30, 1880, "it is safe to say that the people will vote for a fence law. We are of opinion that this should be done. It would work hardship on farmers, to herd the few cattle and milch cows they now keep for use in their families. The farmers make no money on grain, and shut them away from the revenue derived from the little bands of stock raised, and they will become bankrupt." When the vote was cast in November of that year, the advocates of a no-fence law were everywhere badly beaten. In four important counties the result was as follows: Whitman County, 290 for and 954 against; Walla Walla County, 343 for and 1,218 against; Columbia County, 260 for and 948 against; Yakima County, 39 for and 456 against.[30] The results in the other counties concerned have not come to light, but the outcome is not in doubt. On this

---

[29] *Ibid.,* May 21, 1880.

[30] Pomeroy *Washington Independent,* Sept. 30, 1880; *Palouse Gazette,* Nov. 12, 1880; *Yakima Record,* Nov. 13, 1880; *Walla Walla Union,* Nov. 13, 1880; *Columbia Chronicle,* Nov. 13, 1880.

subject the voice of the people in eastern Washington in November, 1880, had been loud and clear: a no-fence or herd law was not wanted in the "cow counties" of this territory, and the legislative assembly was so advised. In eastern Washington the day of the cattlemen on the open ranges had not yet ended. Once again, after the returns were in, the editor of the *Washington Independent* spoke out on this subject, saying on November 26, 1880, "The herd law did not get enough votes for it to be incorporated in our Statutes. Our opinion is the people did right in killing it at the polls."

The old settlers of eastern Washington could now relax. The spirit of free enterprise, at least for the time being, had been saved, and it would not be necessary for "Farmer's Wife" and Mr. Leitch, of Leitchville, to shake the dust "from off" their feet and move into the free territory of Idaho. The bunch grass in Whitman County was still free.

But the decision in 1880 on this issue was not final. Thereafter events moved rapidly in eastern Washington, and as early as January 21, 1882, the editor of the *Walla Walla Union* reported, not without personal interest, that many men who had opposed no-fence legislation in 1880 were now in favor of such a law. "It makes us feel good to hear such expressions," this editor confessed, and he ventured the opinion that presently a majority would "call for a herd law." In May there was some agitation in favor of such a law in the recently organized Garfield County,[31] and early in the autumn of 1883 the *Kittitas Localizer*, observing that a gradual change of opinion had taken place in respect to a no-fence law, predicted that several districts of eastern Washington would, when settled, be compelled to "adopt the herd law no matter how distasteful it may be."[32] At about the same time, petitions requesting the territorial legislative assembly to enact a no-herd law were receiving numerous signatures in Walla Walla County, and the *Waitsburg Times* remarked on September 28, 1883, that "no principle of right" would require one man "to fence his grain against another man's stock," but that every prin-

[31] *Washington Independent,* May 4, 1882; *Pataha City Spirit,* May 13, 1882.
[32] Quoted in the *Walla Walla Union,* Sept. 22, 1883.

ciple of right would require "every man to keep his stock off every other man's grain." Across the line in Oregon, in October of that year, the *Umatilla Examiner* was arguing for a no-fence law for its district,[33] and the *Willamette Farmer,* being cognizant of the problem of fencing in the treeless districts of eastern Washington, announced that it would watch with interest whatever action the legislative assembly of Washington might take in its forth-coming session on the subject of no fence. This question, the *Farmer* remarked, "will come up for decision in our own State east of the Cascades." The decision the legislative assembly of Washington Territory made was embodied in a measure, ap-proved on November 27, 1883, to "Provide for a Herd Law."[34]

In this law the legislature resorted to an expedient used in numerous western states. It made the owners of livestock running at large liable for the trespass of such animals upon cultivated fields, but restricted the application of this law to those counties in which the qualified voters, at the next general election, should express by a majority vote their desire for such a law. A vote to determine this question, however, could be taken only after a petition requesting such a vote had been signed by legal voters of a county to the number equal to one-fourth of the votes cast at the latest general election in such county, and had been pre-sented to the county commissioners at least sixty days before the next general election. By enacting this law the legislative assem-bly had done what the editor of the *Waitsburg Times* had said a "just legislature" would "certainly not refuse" to do—that is, "to submit . . . to an intelligent people" the question of having or not having a herd law. "All we ask," he said, "is that the matter [of a herd law] be so shaped as to let the people decide by ballot which they prefer: to fence their wheat or fence their stock."[35]

This victory of the "poor farmer" over the "affluent stockman" appears, however, to have been a moral rather than a practical one. As yet, no evidence has appeared to show that this act was anywhere put into effect. There is no evidence to prove that, in

[33] Quoted in the *Walla Walla Union,* Oct. 13, 1883.
[34] *Willamette Farmer,* Oct. 12, 1883; *Laws of Washington, 1883* (Olympia, 1883), pp. 55-56.
[35] *Waitsburg Times,* Sept. 28, 1883.

any one of the three counties of Spokane, Whitman, and Walla Walla, a vote pursuant to the provisions of this law was held in the general elections of 1884 or 1886. This fact is significant, for the herd-law controversy centered in these three counties. Furthermore, as we have seen, the Supreme Court of Washington declared in 1887 that no law in Washington Territory required cattle to be fenced or herded.[36]

Why the herd law was not used by those who eagerly sought it, we do not know. Perhaps the requirement of a petition signed by one-fourth of the voters was a considerable deterrent, but it is more likely that by this time the problem of expensive fencing in the untimbered parts of the Oregon Country was being solved by the use of barbed wire. As early as June 12, 1875, Purdin and Wood, "sole agents for Glidden's patent barbed wire fence," were advertising in the Winnemucca, Nevada, *Silver State* that such a fence, "proof against horses and cattle," was the "cheapest and most durable fence made," and, consequently, "just the thing for farmers in this country." Fences that were both good and cheap for farmers in northern Nevada would have been both good and cheap for farmers in Idaho, eastern Oregon, and eastern Washington. Significantly, the *Morning Oregonian* reported on January 1, 1883, that barbed wire was extensively used for fencing in the neighborhood of Waitsburg, Washington. Accordingly, it may be that the "poor farmer's" perception of the advantages accruing to him by having relatively inexpensive barbed-wire fences enclosing cultivated fields in which, after harvest, his own livestock would find rich grazing persuaded him to believe that justice did not move and have its being in a no-fence law. Perhaps also the opportunity to acquire such fences persuaded him to believe that there might be a grain of truth in the affirmation of old settlers that a herd law offered little or no inducement to "people of energy and enterprise."

Unlike Washington, both Idaho and Oregon appear to have escaped a serious controversy on the subject of fence or no fence. Here, as in Washington, the conventional laws pertaining to fences had been enacted, but it appears that neither Idaho nor Oregon

[36] Chapter VII, note 45, above.

authorized a vote in any county on the question of fencing crops or of herding cattle. In 1885 the legislature of Oregon authorized the voters in any county to vote "for or against swine running at large" in the same manner as the legislative assembly of Washington had authorized the voters in any county to vote on the question of fence or no fence. The legislature of Idaho, as we shall see, enacted certain laws imposing restrictions on the grazing of sheep on open ranges, but apparently it enacted no such law pertaining to cattle.

If the struggle between cattlemen and farmers for the grasslands of the Oregon Country was both spirited and amusing, the struggle there between cattlemen and sheepmen presently became bitter and ominous. Nor was this all. Sheepmen also incurred the enmity of some farmers, who wished their cattle to graze upon lands adjacent to their farms. Consequently, such farmers were exasperated by the "encroachments" of sheepmen, whose "woolies," it was generally believed, ruined the ranges and drove cattle and horses away. Thus it fell out that pioneer sheepmen with their "intruding" flocks were not welcomed by men whose cattle or horses were grazing on the open ranges of the Oregon Country.

Yet sheep were not tardy comers to some of the ranges of Transcascadia. In the early 1840's Dr. Marcus Whitman, as we have seen in an earlier chapter, had at Waiilatpu a small flock of sheep which he prized.[37] After the close of the Indian wars of the 1850's, sheep in considerable numbers were driven to the ranges east of the Cascades from both east and west. Other flocks, no doubt, came up from California to ranges in the Pacific Northwest. As early as the spring of 1872, the raising of sheep was rapidly becoming "one of the leading industries" of the Walla Walla Valley, and by midsummer of that year the editor of the *Walla Walla Union* was discussing "the sheep question." It was a troublesome question, he confessed, not only because the large bands of sheep herded on the prairies were "eating out the pasturage" and "poisoning and scenting the grass" so that stock of

[37] Chapter I, note 30, above. Dr. Whitman's pride in his flock of sheep is revealed in his letter to "Father" Prentiss on April 8, 1845. OPA, *Transactions* (1893), p. 70.

other kinds would not eat it, but also because sheep were becoming numerous as well as remunerative. He further remarked that

Last winter the Legislature passed a law making the owner responsible for any damage done by his sheep on the inclosed land of another. This, however, does not seem to meet the wants of those who have cattle and horses and do not own sheep. They say, and truly too, that a band of sheep turned on the common or outside range where their stock has been used to run is equivalent to depriving them of any outside range at all. And this feature of the case looks hard, for in some neighborhoods where there had been for years large bands of cattle and horses, owned by the settlers, a band or two of sheep has been driven in and the farmers have had to sell their stock because the sheep had run it out of their neighborhood, or else they had to sell their farms and take their stock to some place where sheep did not, as yet, molest them.[38]

Here then, bluntly stated, was a problem that would trouble the rangelands of the Oregon Country through many years. It was the problem of two conflicting interests on unpoliced lands open without cost to each of these interests. This problem, moreover, would be intensified when cattlemen and sheepmen would be forced to contend for ranges which were being contracted by the advance of farmers into the choicest lands of the Oregon Country east of the Cascades.

In this rich grazing country, the "sheep business" expanded rapidly. By 1875 it had become more lucrative than the cattle business in the Walla Walla Valley, and in nearby Umatilla County, Oregon, it had also become important. There, as one writer affirmed in 1876, the cattlemen were "hurling bitter anathemas at the sheepmen," for, as he said, "Cattle will not feed where sheep have been; consequently the cattle men have good cause to be alarmed at the aggressive movements of the rapidly increasing flocks of sheep around them." Nearly a year later, in the neighborhood of Bridge Creek in Wasco County, Oregon, cattlemen met and prescribed "certain boundaries to that 'cattle district,' within which they request[ed] sheep raisers not to enter, as the two classes of stock do not thrive well on the same range." This was no isolated expression of disapproval at the "intrusion"

[38] *Walla Walla Union*, April 27, July 13, 1872. The Dalles *Mountaineer* of April 1, 1871, reported an unsuccessful attempt to keep a sheep raiser out of Whitman County.

of sheep. In that same year, many of the "old settlers" opposed the bringing of sheep to the grasslands of northern Idaho; two years later, a large band of sheep being moved northward from the Snake River to a summer range on the Spokane prairie prepared the way for subsequent protest in that area; and the people in the Wallowa Valley, in northeastern Oregon, were at that time becoming "mad" because sheep were ruining the range for their cattle.[39]

But, despite objections, the sheep continued to come. As the 1870's gave way to the 1880's, sheep raising was becoming an important vested interest on numerous ranges east of the Cascades. By October, 1879, sheep had become a nuisance to cattlemen whose herds were grazing near Oxford, Idaho, and a few weeks later a report from northeastern Oregon asserted that about fifty thousand head of cattle would be removed from a large range in Grant County, and that this range would be restocked with sheep. Also, according to the preliminary report of the Federal Public Lands Commission, created by an act of March 3, 1879, testimony gathered by the commission throughout the Oregon Country revealed a remarkably uniform opinion in respect to the effect of sheep raising and cattle raising on open ranges: cattle and sheep would not graze on the same ground.[40]

Thus, the grazing of sheep on the open ranges of the Oregon Country was generating occupational strife before 1880. It was doing even more: it was beginning to revolutionize the economy of Transcascadia. As John Minto, a man of moderation who knew much about the breeding of sheep in Oregon, remarked for the benefit of the tenth federal census, "At nearly all points of the vast grazing country east of the Cascades cattle are giving way to sheep." This was his way of saying that sheep raising was becoming an important interest in Transcascadia. How important it was we learn from the findings of this same census. On July 1, 1880, there were 1,368,162 sheep in Oregon. Of this number 724,987 were in the three large counties then embracing north-

[39] *Willamette Farmer*, Sept. 3, 1875; J.J.B., "Umatilla County," in the *Morning Oregonian*, May 19, 1876; *Walla Walla Union*, Feb. 17, 1877; *Lewiston Teller*, June 9, 1877; *Spokan Times*, July 4, 1879; *Morning Oregonian*, July 22, 1879.
[40] Oxford *Idaho Enterprise*, Oct. 9, 1879; Canyon City *Grant County News*, Nov. 29, 1879; 46th Cong., 2nd sess., H. Ex. Doc. 46 (Serial 1923), pp. 467, 676.

central and northeastern Oregon—that is, Wasco, Umatilla, and Union. In the three larger counties then embracing south-central and southeastern Oregon—that is, Lake, Grant, and Baker—there were only 130,743 sheep. On that same date there were 388,364 sheep in Washington Territory, and of this number nearly 320,000 were in the counties east of the Cascades. In the counties of Klickitat and Yakima there were 74,046, in the counties of Whitman and Spokane there were 61,089, and in the two counties south of the Snake River—Walla Walla and Columbia—there were 184,192. In like manner, the number of sheep in Idaho had been increasing. Some bands of sheep had entered this territory before 1870, and during the 1870's the number increased greatly. On July 1, 1880, there were 117,326 sheep in Idaho, and of this number more than half were in the counties south of the Snake River.[41]

Still they came, and still they multiplied. With the passing years, as tension mounted and passion deepened, events moved toward a crisis on the ranges of Transcascadia. An Englishman who had learned much about Oregon in the late 1870's described, in a book published in 1882, the "loathing and contempt" of cattlemen of eastern Oregon for the "encroaching sheep" which killed the young grass and pushed the cattlemen farther into the wilderness. He confessed to having listened to "many a growl" from cattlemen at the advance of the "woolly tide," and to having heard absurd threats of resistance, "even to the length of breeding coyotes or prairie-wolves for the special benefit of the mutton." The prairie wolves, he said, did not molest cattle, but played havoc with flocks.[42]

Such being the case, cattlemen in Transcascadia during the 1880's were confronted by the twofold problem of retreating as gracefully as they could from the arable grasslands which the farmers were taking, and of holding, if they could, the nonarable ranges from which the "pestilence" of sheep threatened to drive them. Here, indeed, was a difficult problem, but it was one not

[41] *Tenth Federal Census, 1880,* Vol. III, *Agriculture* (Washington, D.C., 1883), pp. 1085, 1088, 1094, 1101; *Eleventh Federal Census, 1890,* Vol. XV, *Wealth and Industry* (Washington, D.C., 1895), p. 129.
[42] Wallis Nash, *Two Years in Oregon* (New York, 1882), pp. 120, 232.

peculiar to the Oregon Country; it was, sooner or later, a problem of cattlemen everywhere on the open ranges of the far-flung American West.[43]

Cattlemen of the Oregon Country sought in various ways to adjust their operations to a changing era. The first impulse of most of them, no doubt, was to move to new pastures, and many did so. The evidence seems conclusive that, by 1888, cattlemen were fleeing eastward from both Oregon and Washington. In June, 1888, when the Burns *East Oregon Herald* was quoting the *Ochoco Review* as saying that hundreds of cattle would be removed from Crook County, Oregon, to ranges on the Snake River, the *Lewiston Teller* was remarking that a party with four hundred head of cattle, having abandoned the "eaten out" range in Kittitas County, Washington, was passing through Lewiston, Idaho, on the way to Camas Prairie in Idaho. Moreover, earlier in the same month, the editor of the *East Oregon Herald* had expressed the hope that "the stockmen from adjoining counties . . . [would] keep out of Harney Valley. . . . If . . . [they did not, he continued,] large owners of stock in this section will be compelled to drive."[44]

Somewhat less than a year later, B. F. Morris, a "prominent" stockman of Lewiston, Idaho, told the editor of a stockmen's journal in Montana that the "heavy immigration" into northern Idaho, eastern Washington, and eastern Oregon had "about closed the stock interest" in the Pacific Northwest. Some of the stockmen, he said, are "moving their herds into Montana and Dakota, some are reducing their herds and [are] raising better grades, while others have closed out and joined the van of home seekers, raising wheat and other cereals."[45]

Other cattlemen, however, believing that the raising of sheep would be "the wave of the future" in the Oregon Country, turned

[43] It was emphatically a problem on some of the ranges east of the Rockies. Late in the spring of 1880, the *Colorado Mountaineer* affirmed that cattlemen in Colorado were proving that the fencing of large tracts of land was "a very satisfactory manner of deciding the vexed question of sheep *vs.* cattle." Quoted in the Chicago *National Live-Stock Journal*, XI (May, 1880), 217.

[44] Burns *East Oregon Herald*, June 6, 20, 1888; *Lewiston Teller*, June 21, 1888. In both 1885 and 1886 stockmen in the area of Prineville, in order to escape intruding sheep, were preparing to drive their horses to the Malheur country. Prineville *Ochoco Review*, Sept. 19, 1885, Aug. 7, 1886.

[45] Miles City, Mont., *Stock Growers Journal*, May 4, 1889.

their coats, swallowed their pride, and moved "downward" from the "high" status of cattleman to the "lower" status of sheepman. A few wavered, hoping that something might turn up to arrest the ominous tide of change. Everywhere cattlemen were protesting against the "invasion" of "their" ranges, and to a greater or less extent they were forming, sometimes with the aid of farmers who were part-time cattlemen, organizations for self-help. From 1877, when cattlemen staked out in Wasco County the boundaries of a "cattle district" which sheep were expected not to cross, the idea of forming voluntary associations to keep sheep away from cattlemen's ranges gained momentum. In January, 1884, John Fleming, a sheepman in Idaho, wrote from American Falls to the Secretary of the Interior, saying that cattlemen, armed with rifles, were patrolling what they called "their range" and threatening to shoot if he did not keep his band of five thousand sheep away from this range. In midsummer of 1885, citizens of the northeastern part of Whitman County and of the southeastern part of Spokane County met to devise some means of keeping sheepmen from ruining their range by bringing flocks of sheep into that area. In April, 1886, the Whitman County Wool Growers' Association took up a collection for "Mr. Cox, to aid in prosecuting the party who fired his herder's tent some time ago." In the spring of 1887, cattlemen on "the North Powder" River in northeastern Oregon were telling sheepmen that "their room" was preferred to "their company." Two years later even more drastic action was being contemplated in central Washington. In the spring of 1889, a meeting of settlers on Lake Chelan warned sheepmen to keep their flocks away "under penalty of having their bands exterminated," and before the end of that year cattlemen in the Big Bend of the Columbia were determined to stop the summer grazing on their ranges of sheep from Oregon "by fencing in the springs and water courses." They would take such action because they wanted the "open pasture ranges for the increase of their own stock."[46]

To understand the problems of adjustment confronting cattle-

[46] *Morning Oregonian*, Feb. 12, 1877; 48th Cong., 1st sess., S. Ex. Doc. 127, p. 26; *Palouse Gazette*, June 26, 1885, April 23, 1886; Cheney *Northwest Tribune*, June 26, 1885, Dec. 13, 1886; Boise *Idaho Weekly Statesman*, May 21, 1887.

men in the Oregon Country, we must examine, at least in outline, the nature and the scope of the transformation which was threatening their enterprise. We begin by reminding ourselves that the year 1883, which saw the so-called completion of the Northern Pacific Railroad, gave the ranges of the Oregon Country access by rail to tidewater on both the Atlantic and Pacific seaboards. Thereafter the transforming process proceeded rapidly. During the next seven years, an enduring pattern of railway transportation emerged in eastern Washington, northern Idaho, northeastern Oregon, and southern Idaho, and by 1887, as we already have learned, eastern Washington had been directly connected by rail with Puget Sound. Before the end of 1889, Washington had 1,548 miles of railroad, and a year later the new state of Idaho had 940 miles of railroad. By that year all parts of the Oregon Country, south-central and southeastern Oregon excepted, had relatively easy access to railway transportation. Now, throughout most of the vast Oregon Country, products not able to "walk to market" could be raised in great abundance.[47]

Thanks in large part to this rising system of transportation, the development of the Oregon Country was prodigious. People now came to the Inland Empire to stay. The Northern Pacific Railroad reported in 1887 that there had been "a steady movement of people from the East to the Pacific Slope," and in that year "crops of all kinds" had been the largest in the history of Washington Territory. Two years later the Governor of Washington Territory, which now was standing on the threshold of statehood, reported that in his territory "no considerable portion" of arable land remained available for homesteading, and that the Northern Pacific Railroad had sold there during 1889 to 2,279 purchasers 416,321 acres of its granted lands "at an average price of $3.68 an acre."[48]

[47] Northern Pacific Railroad, *Report of the Board of Directors . . . September 15, 1887* (New York, 1887), p. 14; *ibid.,* 1889, p. 11; N.W. Durham, *History of the City of Spokane and Spokane Country, from Its Earliest Settlement to the Present Time* (Spokane, Wash., 1912), I, 616-17, 640-41; John Fahey, *Inland Empire: D.C. Corbin and Spokane* (Seattle, Wash., 1965), pp. 108-22; 51st Cong., 1st sess., H. Ex. Doc. 1, XIII, 525; 51st Cong., 2nd sess., H. Ex. Doc. 1, XI, xcii. Cf. Chapter VI, notes 41-45, above.
[48] Northern Pacific Railroad, *Report of the Board of Directors, 1887,* p. 48; 51st Cong., 1st sess., H. Ex. Doc. 1, XIII, 510-11.

The extent of the influx of people during the 1880's is shown by the federal census of 1890. The population of Washington increased during the preceding decade from 75,111 to 349,390, and east of the Cascades the increase had been from 35,206 to 120,454. Similar, but less rapid, growth took place elsewhere in the Oregon Country during that decade. The population of Oregon grew from 174,768 in 1880 to 313,767 in 1890, and east of the Cascades the increase was from 39,100 to 73,162. In Idaho the population increased from 32,610 to 84,385. Such growth, of course, hastened the political organization of this region. In Washington during the 1880's nine new counties were created, eight of which were east of the Cascades; in Oregon nine new counties were organized, eight of which were east of the Cascades; and in Idaho five new counties were created.[49]

Equally significant were the economic changes in the Oregon Country during the 1880's. The farming area increased by 2,305,-996 acres in eastern Washington, by 2,354,225 acres in eastern Oregon, and by 974,458 acres in Idaho. In both Washington and Oregon there was a noteworthy increase in the area devoted to the raising of wheat—in Washington from 81,554 acres in 1880 to 372,658 acres in 1890; in Oregon from 445,077 acres in 1880 to 553,052 acres in 1890. In Oregon during the 1880's considerable wheat was raised in the Willamette Valley and elsewhere west of the Cascades, but in Washington very little wheat was raised west of the Cascades. East of the Cascades, however, there were noteworthy increases in the production of wheat in the counties of Columbia, Garfield, Walla Walla, Whitman, Spokane, and Lincoln, all of which comprised an area noted for its grazing a few years earlier. Also during the 1880's there was a noteworthy enlargement of the area of wheat farms in north-central and northeastern Oregon, especially in the counties of Sherman, Gilliam, Morrow, Umatilla, and Union. As late as 1890, however, wheat raising had made little progress in south-central and southeastern Oregon—the region comprising the counties of Lake, Harney, and Malheur, bounded on the north by Crook County

[49] *Report on the Population of the United States at the Eleventh Census* (Washington, D.C., 1895), Pt. 1, pp. 15, 36, 39, 44.

and the now greatly contracted counties of Grant and Baker, and on the south by the line separating Oregon from California and Nevada. Here and in Wallowa County, in the far northeastern corner of Oregon, there was, at the end of the 1880's, still a considerable interest in the grazing of cattle on open ranges. In Idaho, during the 1880's, wheat raising was a relatively unimportant interest when compared with those of mining and the raising of livestock.[50]

High on the list of the growing economic interests in the Oregon Country during the later 1880's was that of raising sheep. Not only was the increasing production of wool important; the large and increasing movement of sheep eastward, by rail and by trail, from the Pacific Northwest to the ranges of Montana, Nebraska, and Dakota was an important part of the export trade of the Oregon Country in livestock during those years. As late as 1888, according to the leading newspaper of Idaho, "Ada and nearly all the southern counties of Idaho suffer severely on account of the large herds that are driven through Idaho to Montana, Wyoming and Nebraska. If a licence could be imposed [on the owners of such sheep] it might be some remuneration for the damage the sheep do, for they consume the grass all the way through the territory [on a route] several miles in width."[51]

Perhaps because of the eastward movement in the late 1880's and of heavy losses in Transcascadia during the winter of 1889-90, sheep in eastern Washington were fewer in 1890 than in 1880. Whatever the cause, the number decreased from 319,689 in 1880 to 231,253 in 1890. The three leading "sheep counties" in that area in 1890 were, respectively, Kittitas, Klickitat, and Garfield. In Walla Walla and Whitman counties, which by 1890 had become the leading wheat-producing counties of this newly admitted state, the decline in the number of sheep had been startling— from more than 128,000 in 1880 to less than 38,000 in 1890. In eastern Oregon, however, there was a recorded increase of sheep from 855,730 in 1880 to 1,431,577 in 1890, the leading "sheep

[50] *Report on the Statistics of Agriculture in the United States at the Eleventh Census: 1890* (Washington, D.C., 1895), pp. 204, 224-25, 233, 381, 389; *Tenth Federal Census, 1880,* Vol. III, *Agriculture,* pp. 145, 164, 172-73, 236, 244.
[51] *Idaho Weekly Statesman,* Feb. 11, 1888.

counties" of Oregon in 1890 being in the northern tier of counties of eastern Oregon—Crook, Grant, Morrow, Wasco, and Umatilla. The country comprising these counties had once been famous for its cattle ranges. Elsewhere in eastern Oregon the breeding of sheep had also been making progress. By 1890 there had been a substantial advance in both south-central and southeastern Oregon, Lake County leading the way with 108,410 sheep, and Malheur and Harney following with, respectively, 57,974 and 56,699.[52]

Meanwhile, east of Oregon in the Snake River Valley, the raising of sheep had made so much progress that, early in the autumn of 1886, the *Willamette Farmer* could say that the "sheep interests in Southern Idaho" had increased so rapidly in recent years that it was interfering "seriously" with ranges previously occupied "exclusively by horses and cattle." In Idaho as a whole the number of sheep increased more than threefold during the 1880's—from 117,326 in 1880 to 357,712 in 1890—Owyhee County, with 55,801 sheep, being the leading "sheep county" in the newly admitted state of Idaho. And, as if to emphasize the remarkable change taking place in the pastoral interests of Idaho, the Governor remarked in his report to the Secretary of the Interior in 1889 that, owing to the low prices for cattle during the preceding two years, many stockmen in Idaho had sold their cattle and invested the proceeds in sheep. "Sheep-raising," he emphasized, "is rapidly on the increase, and returns handsome profits to all engaged in raising them."[53]

As early as the beginning of the 1880's, thoughtful editors of important newspapers in the Oregon Country perceived that the old, haphazard "ranch system" of raising cattle east of the Cascades would soon be replaced by a better way of raising cattle for beef—a system that would combine both farming and the raising of cattle. This change, as the *Morning Oregonian* unctuously and erroneously averred on January 10, 1880, "all will welcome." More than two years later the *Oregon and Washington Farmer* remarked that presently the stockman would be re-

[52] *Tenth Federal Census, 1880*, Vol. III, *Agriculture*, p. 1094; *Eleventh Federal Census, 1890: Agriculture*, pp. 271-72.

[53] *Willamette Farmer*, Sept. 3, 1886; *Tenth Federal Census, 1880*, Vol. III, *Agriculture*, p. 1101; *Eleventh Federal Census, 1890: Agriculture*, p. 243.

placed by the farmer who would be a stockman "on a moderate
scale." The passing months gave credence to such views. In May,
1883, the *Willamette Farmer,* using information gathered by the
Walla Walla Union, affirmed that much of the range in the Walla
Walla country had been taken up for the purpose of cultivation,
and that, because on the remaining grazing lands in that area
water had become "very unhandy," a great deal of livestock had
been driven "to Whitman and other counties north of the Snake
River for better grazing." In the same month the *Morning Oregonian,* asserting that the "famous ranges of eastern Oregon"
were being rapidly cut up into farms, and that "Wasco" had
become almost entirely a farming region, predicted, notwithstanding, that there would be a steady increase in the production
of beef cattle in Oregon. But this increase, it insisted, would
come "from the farm and not from the range."[54] Some two years
later this same newspaper summed up its predictions for the
cattle-breeding industry east of the Cascades by saying that there
"will be no great roving bands, no gigantic round-ups, no big
annual drives; but there will be more and better cattle to market
each fall, and they will yield a larger aggregate profit than formerly."[55] Other evidence that was gathered and published by the
Federal Bureau of Animal Industry tells us that, by the mid-
1880's, thousands of settlers in California, Oregon and Washington were "crowding into the edges of the range."[56] By the beginning of 1890, the Seattle *Weekly Post-Intelligencer,* looking
back nostalgically upon the days "when Eastern Washington was
a wild and boundless range," affirmed that the "palmy day of the
stock-owner" there was ended; and at the same time the Portland
West Shore solemnly announced that in both Oregon and Washington the range-cattle industry was outward bound.[57]

Before 1890 neither Washington nor Oregon had made much

[54] Portland *Oregon and Washington Farmer* (July, 1882), p. 15; *Willamette
Farmer,* May 11, 1883; *Morning Oregonian,* May 29, 1883.

[55] *Morning Oregonian,* June 10, 1885, quoted in Harvey W. Scott, *History of
the Oregon Country,* compiled by Leslie M. Scott (Cambridge, Mass., 1924), III,
105.

[56] U.S. Bureau of Animal Industry, *Third Annual Report* (1886), p. 105.

[57] Seattle *Weekly Post-Intelligencer,* Jan. 1, 1890; Portland *West Shore* (Hol-
iday Number), XV (1890), p. 278.

use of its police power to settle conflicts of interests on public ranges left unpoliced by the federal government. Idaho, however, perhaps because of the extraordinary importance of the cattle-raising industry to that territory, took legal action at an early date to protect the ranges of its settlers from encroachments by sheep. Its famous "two-mile" law, dating from the middle 1870's, prohibited the grazing of sheep within two miles of a dwelling. Although challenged as unconstitutional, this law was twice upheld by the Supreme Court of Idaho, and the decision of this court was confirmed in 1907 by the Supreme Court of the United States.[58] Another Idaho law of still larger import—applied in 1883 to five counties of that territory and made a general law in 1887—forbade the grazing of sheep upon "any range usually occupied by any cattle grower, either as a spring, summer, or winter range for his cattle"; and the right to use any range in Idaho was to be determined "by the priority in the usual and customary use of the range, either as a cattle or sheep range." This law the Supreme Court of Idaho also upheld, and its decision was confirmed in 1918 by the Supreme Court of the United States in an opinion illumined by the scholarship and the wisdom of Mr. Justice Louis D. Brandeis.[59] Thus Idaho had made a distinctive contribution toward defining the extent to which states or territories, within their respective jurisdictions, could apply their police power to regulate the use of public lands of the United States.

But in northeastern Oregon, a region of increasing conflict of interests, and also to some extent in central Washington, the tendency to settle controversies about the use of ranges by in-

---

[58] *Laws of Oregon, 1882*, pp. 36-37; *Laws of Oregon, 1885*, pp. 47-48; *Laws of Washington, 1887-88*, p. 204; *Laws of Idaho, 1879* (Boise, 1879), pp. 54-55; *Laws of Idaho, 1882-83* (Boise, 1883), pp. 126-27; *Revised Statutes of Idaho Territory . . . in Force June 1, 1887* (Boise, 1887), p. 183; Bacon v. Walker, 204 U.S. 311 (1907). See in the *Idaho Weekly Statesman*, June 26, 1886, an editorial, "Sheep vs. Cattle and Horses," in which a policy of understanding and accommodation in the use of the ranges of Idaho is urged upon cattlemen and sheepmen. Idaho, it was here argued, was large enough for both these interests.

[59] *Laws of Idaho, 1882-83*, pp. 126-27; *Revised Statutes of Idaho Territory . . . 1887*, p. 740; State v. Omaechevarria, 27 Idaho 802 (1915). In Omaechevarria v. State of Idaho, 246 U.S. 343 (1918), Mr. Justice Brandeis reviewed the legislation of Idaho restricting the use of ranges.

timidation or violence became strong near the end of the 1880's. In the spring of 1887, cattlemen on the North Powder River threatened to kill sheep by mixing saltpeter with salt, and in the autumn of that year saltpeter was scattered on the Wenas range in the Yakima Valley, presumably "for the purpose of killing sheep that graze[d] there against the wishes of the cattle rangers." Two years later there came from the John Day country reports not only that cattlemen had poisoned sheep, but also that horsemen had joined cattlemen in swearing that no sheep would be allowed to "summer on the range."[60]

By this time, just as the period of our study is ending, the controversy between cattlemen and sheepmen in northeastern and central Oregon was hastening to a crisis.[61] Herds and flocks continued to graze, and summer range had progressively become inadequate. By the middle 1890's, cattlemen in Grant County were shooting sheep driven in from Crook County, and by 1901 war was impending in eastern Oregon, where sheep were being driven into "territory reserved by agreement for cattle." A time of reckoning had come. In permitting the unregulated use of its grazing lands, the federal government had long been sowing the wind; now, on the shrinking ranges in Grant County and elsewhere in "darkest Oregon," stockmen were beginning to reap the whirlwind. The wars of the Oregon ranges, at their height in 1904 and 1905, were virtually ended by January, 1906, when the federal government began the practice of leasing grazing lands within its forest reserves.[62] Henceforth there would be regulation of grazing on these summer ranges.

But a new deal for the public lands in Oregon, predicted by the *Morning Oregonian* on December 15, 1904, as "not far distant," was not brought to Oregon until, nearly thirty years later, the Taylor Grazing Act was approved by the President of the

[60] *Willamette Farmer,* May 13, 1887; *Morning Oregonian,* Oct. 3, 1887; *Palouse Gazette,* April 12, 1889.
[61] On the scarcity of summer ranges, see, *inter alia,* A. H., a staff writer of the *Oregonian,* in "The Range War," *Morning Oregonian,* Sept. 9, 1902, and "Forage Utilization on Summer Cattle Ranges in Eastern Oregon" (U.S. Department of Agriculture, Circular No. 796) (September, 1948), p. 1. See also "Crimes of the Cattlemen," *Morning Oregonian,* April 28, 1905.
[62] *Morning Oregonian,* Dec. 12, 15, 1904, June 18, 1905.

United States on June 28, 1934. Besides providing for the "orderly use, improvement, and development" of the public grazing lands, this act sought to "stop injury" to these lands by "preventing overgrazing and soil deterioration," and "to stabilize the livestock industry dependent upon the public range. . . ."[63]

We have permitted an unresolved conflict between cattlemen and sheepmen to lure us across our deadline for a peep into the twentieth century. Here we must stop. The story of the trials and tribulations of those who bred cattle for beef in the Oregon Country after 1890 belongs to a period beyond the scope of this study.

---

[63] For a discussion of the Taylor Grazing Act, see E. Louise Peffer, *The Closing of the Public Domain: Disposal and Reservation Policies, 1900-1950* (Stanford, Calif., 1951), chap. xii. See also *Morning Oregonian*, Nov. 22, 1906; Roy Marvin Robbins, *Our Landed Heritage: The Public Domain, 1776-1936* (Princeton, N.J., 1942), p. 345; Samuel T. Dana, *Forest and Range Policy: Its Development in the United States* (New York, 1956), p. 145.

Bibliographical Essay

THE sources for the study of the early history of cattle breeding in the Oregon Country are numerous and diverse. There is no one body of documents, printed or unprinted, which will serve as a broad foundation for such a study. Accordingly, a student of this subject must examine not only the surviving records made by explorers, fur traders, missionaries, travelers, and early settlers in this region, but also the records of various branches and agencies of the federal government as well as those of the appropriate territorial, state, and county governments. Nor may he stop here. He must pay attention to both the official reports and the promotional books and pamphlets of the railroads that operated in the Pacific Northwest during the 1880's, and, from 1846 forward, he also must examine the files of an increasing number of newspapers and the files of a few magazines published west of the Rockies, as well as the files of not a few newspapers and magazines published east of these mountains.

Moreover, the collections of such materials are widely scattered. Some of them are in libraries as far east as Massachusetts, Connecticut, New York, and the District of Columbia, and others are in libraries as far west as California, Oregon, Washington, and British Columbia. Throughout the entire Pacific Northwest, in libraries of colleges, universities, and historical societies, there are collections of materials important for this study. Unhappily, some valuable material relating to this subject is still in private possession, and therefore is not generally accessible for study.

GUIDES AND OTHER AIDS

The best guide to books and pamphlets dealing with the subject of this book is Charles W. Smith's *Pacific Northwest Americana: A Check List of Books and Pamphlets Relating to the History of the Pacific Northwest*

(2nd ed.; New York, 1921). This work, revised and extended by Isabel Mayhew, was brought out in a third edition (Portland, Ore., 1950) as a project of the Bibliography Committee of the Pacific Northwest Library Association. Also important for one category of books bearing upon this subject are Henry R. Wagner's *The Plains and the Rockies* ... (rev. ed.; San Francisco, Calif., 1937) and the second volume of Edward Godfrey Cox's *A Reference Guide to the Literature of Travel* (Seattle, Wash., 1935-38). Books and pamphlets touching this subject that have appeared since the publication of the foregoing guides are listed in the *Cumulative Book Index*, a continuation of *The United States Catalogue* (4th ed.; New York, 1928).

Records of the federal government that have a bearing on this subject may be found with the aid of Isadore Gilbert Mudge's *Guide to Reference Books* (6th ed.; Chicago, 1936) and its supplements. Also important for finding material of this sort is Katharine B. Judson's *Subject Index to the History of the Pacific Northwest and of Alaska as Found in the United States Government Documents, Congressional Series, in the American State Papers, and in Other Documents* (Olympia, Wash., 1913). State and territorial documents of Oregon and Washington for the period of this study are listed in Eleanor Ruth Rockwood's *Oregon State Documents: A Check List, 1843-1925* (Portland, Ore., [1947]) and in J. M. Hitt's *A Reference List of Public Documents, 1854-1918, Found in the Files of the [Washington] State Library* (Olympia, Wash., 1920). Two compilations made by Grace E. McDonald—a *Check-List of Session Laws* (New York, 1936) and a *Check-List of Statutes of States of the United States of America, Including Revisions, Compilations, Digests, Codes and Indexes* (Providence, R.I., 1937)—will serve as useful guides to the laws of Oregon, Washington, and Idaho.

Manuscripts of importance for this subject may be found in the archives of the Hudson's Bay Company and in the letters and papers of the societies which supported missionaries in the Oregon Country. The archives of the Hudson's Bay Company are in London. The letters and papers of the American Board of Commissioners for Foreign Missions for the period of this study are in the Houghton Library of Harvard University; those of the American Home Missionary Society are in the library of the Chicago Theological Seminary; and some of the letters and papers of the Missionary Society of the Methodist Episcopal Church are preserved on microfilm in the library of Willamette University. Still another collection containing important letters written by early missionaries in the Oregon Country is described in a compilation by Mary C. Withington entitled *A Catalogue of Manuscripts in the Collection of Western Americana Founded by William Robertson Coe, Yale University* (New Haven, Conn., 1952).

West of the Rocky Mountains collections of manuscripts of varying importance for this study are in the Huntington Library in San Marino, the Bancroft Library of the University of California in Berkeley, the library of the University of Oregon, Eugene, the library of Willamette University, and the collections of the Oregon Historical Society, Portland, of the University of Washington, Seattle, of the Washington State University, Pullman, of Whitman College, Walla Walla, Washington, of the Provincial Library in Victoria, British Columbia, and of other libraries in this region. Collections of letters and diaries of missionaries supported in the Oregon Country by the American Board are described by Clifford M. Drury in the "Sources and Acknowledgments" of his *First White Women Over the Rockies . . .* (Glendale, Calif., 1963), I, 13-15. Moreover, in his *Henry Harmon Spalding, Pioneer of Old Oregon* (Caldwell, Ida., 1936), Dr. Drury has listed the "Spalding Correspondence" that he had consulted, and to his subsequent *Marcus Whitman, M.D., Pioneer and Martyr* (Caldwell, Ida., 1937) he appended an "Index to the Letters of Dr. and Mrs. Marcus Whitman." For the years which they cover, the following guides are helpful: *A Union List of Manuscripts in Libraries of the Pacific Northwest* (Seattle, Wash., 1931), compiled by Charles W. Smith, and the *Guide to the Manuscript Collections of the Oregon Historical Society* (Portland, Ore., 1940), compiled by the Oregon Historical Records Survey.

Materials in manuscript of more than ordinary value for the subject of this study are available in the National Archives, Washington, D.C. As a general introduction to this material, one should consult the *Guide to the Records in the National Archives* (Washington, D.C., 1948). The titles of some archival materials that originated in the Pacific Northwest, and that are now available on microfilm, may be found in the *List of National Archives Microfilm Publications, 1961* (Washington, D.C., 1961). Material of particular interest to students of cattle breeding in the far West is described, in broad terms, by Peter Kahn in "Records in the National Archives Relating to the Range Cattle Industry, 1865-1895," *Agricultural History,* XX (July, 1946), 187-90. On this subject one should also consult James R. Masterson's "The Records of the Washington Superintendency of Indian Affairs, 1853-1874," *Pacific Northwest Quarterly,* XXXVII (January, 1946), 31-57.

Perhaps even more important than manuscripts for the study of this subject are periodical publications of one sort or another. An excellent guide to serial or periodical publications not ordinarily catalogued as newspapers is Edna Titus Brown's *Union List of Serials in Libraries of the United States and Canada* (3rd ed.; New York, 1965), 5 vols. Here, among many other things, will be found titles of publications that will give one an introduction to a category of historical literature not much exploited by students of the livestock industry—namely, published reports of missionary societies that supported ministers in the Oregon Country and periodical publications that such societies maintained. In such reports and periodicals, letters of missionaries containing information about economic developments in Oregon were frequently published, in whole or in part. Examples of such periodicals that have particular value for this subject are the *Missionary Herald* (Boston), the *Christian Advocate and Journal* (New York), and the *Home Missionary* (New York).

Important as serial or periodical publications of a religious character may be to students of this study, there are three such publications of general character that stand above all others in the category of periodical literature. The oldest of these, the *Transactions* of the Oregon Pioneer Association, dates from 1873. The other two are the *Oregon Historical Quarterly,* dating from 1900, and the *Pacific Northwest Quarterly,* successor to the *Washington Historical Quarterly,* dating from 1906. The *Transactions* are especially valuable for this study because they contain the journals of numerous early overland immigrants to Oregon. The two quarterlies are important not only because of documents and articles which they contain, but also because of their notices or reviews of current books. The materials in the older of these quarterlies became relatively easy to find when the Oregon Historical Society, in 1941, brought out the *Oregon Historical Quarterly Index: Volumes I to XL, 1900-1939,* and then, in 1967, published a sequential volume covering the years 1940-60 (volumes XLI-LXI) of this quarterly. The *Washington Historical Quarterly* published two decennial indexes (X [October, 1919], No. 4; XX [October, 1929], No. 4), and its successor, in 1938, published Jesse S. Douglas' "Guide to *The Washington Historical Quarterly* and *The Pacific Northwest Quarterly,* 1906-1938," *Pacific Northwest Quarterly,* XXIX, 339-416. Twenty-six years later Earl Connette brought out his *Pacific Northwest Quarterly Index, 1906-1962* (Hamden, Conn., 1964).

Still another bibliographical aid to this study, one of wider scope than any mentioned in the preceding paragraph, is Oscar O. Winther's *A Classified Bibliography of the Periodical Literature of the Trans-Mississippi West* (Bloomington, Ind., 1961). This work is highly useful to students of all aspects of the history of the Pacific Northwest.

No category of material is more important for studying the early history of cattle breeding in the Pacific Northwest than that of newspapers published within the bounds of the Oregon Country. A valuable guide to the holdings of newspapers by important libraries is Winifred Gregory's *American Newspapers, 1821-1936: A Union List of Files Available in the United States and Canada* (New York, 1931). A useful guide to one important collection in the state of Washington is the compilation by Roman Mostar and J. Ronald Todd entitled *A Check List of Pacific Northwest Newspapers Held by the University of Washington Library* (Seattle, Wash., 1950). But there are other important collections of such newspapers, one of which is in the Library of Congress. On the Pacific Coast the collections of the Oregon Historical Society, of the Historical Society of Montana (Helena), of the University of Oregon, and of the Bancroft Library may be mentioned, without prejudice to other such collections. For the purpose of identifying some of the older newspapers of the Oregon Country that are not mentioned in Gregory's *Union List,* some students may wish to consult for the territory of Washington Edmond S. Meany's *Newspapers of Washington Territory* (reprinted from the *Washington Historical Quarterly*, Seattle, 1923), and the additions thereto by J. Orin Oliphant and by Douglas C. McMurtrie (*Washington Historical Quarterly*, XVIII [January, 1927], 33-54; XXVI [January, 1935], 34-64, 128-63). A similar work for the newspapers of Oregon to 1870 is Flora Belle Ludington's "The Newspapers of Oregon, 1846-1870," *Oregon Historical Quarterly*, XXVI (September, 1925), 229-62.

NEWSPAPERS OF PARTICULAR IMPORTANCE

Naturally, some newspapers published in the Pacific Northwest, or on its fringes, are more useful than others to students of cattle breeding in the Oregon Country. For this entire region perhaps the Portland *Oregonian*, weekly and daily, is the most valuable for most of the years of this study. Happily, the Portland Public Library and the Oregon Historical Society have typed copies of an index to this newspaper from 1850 to 1909. But there were other newspapers published in the Pacific Northwest, which, because of their strategic situations or because of the alertness of their editors, were able to record information of great value to students of the history of early cattle breeding in this region. To these we now turn.

Among such newspapers published in Oregon west of the Cascades were the Oregon City *Oregon Spectator*, the Salem *Willamette Farmer*, and the Jacksonville *Oregon Sentinel;* and in Oregon east of the Cascades there were published two such newspapers, The Dalles *Weekly Mountaineer* and its successor, the *Times-Mountaineer*, and, farther east, the Canyon City *Grant County News.* For only one of these newspapers has an index been published. In 1941, under the joint sponsorship of the city of Portland and the Oregon Historical Society, there was brought out a two-volume mimeographed work entitled the *Oregon Spectator Index, 1846-1854.*

Elsewhere in the Oregon Country other newspapers of much significance for this subject were published. In western Washington there were the Olympia *Columbian* and its successor, the *Pioneer and Democrat*, the Olympia *Washington Standard*, and the Seattle *Weekly Post-Intelligencer* and its predecessors. East of the Cascades, in the Yakima Valley, there were the *Yakima Record* and the *Yakima Signal;* in the Palouse country there was the Colfax *Palouse Gazette;* in the Spokane country there were the Cheney *Northwest Tribune* and the Spokane Falls *Spokan Times;* and in Washington Territory south of the Snake River there were the *Walla Walla Statesman* and the *Walla Walla Union.* In northern Idaho there was the *Lewiston Teller*, and in southern Idaho there were the Silver City *Owyhee Avalanche* (later the *Idaho Avalanche*) and the Boise City *Weekly Statesman* and *Tri-Weekly Statesman.*

Some newspapers that were not published in Oregon, Washington, or Idaho have more than passing value for students of this subject. Not least among them is the *British Colonist*, published in Victoria. This newspaper contains, among other things, valuable information on the cattle trade on Puget Sound between 1858 and the late 1860's. In the territories and states east and south of the Oregon Country appeared still other newspapers of value for this study. Among these were the *Weekly Missoulian* and the Helena *Montana Live Stock Journal*, the Cheyenne *Weekly Leader* and *Northwestern Live Stock Journal*, the Winnemucca (Nevada) *Silver State*, the *Salt Lake Tribune*, and the *Sacramento Daily Union* and its successor, the *Sacramento Daily Record-Union*. The two last-named journals are peculiarly important, the *Silver State* for its excellent reporting for more than a decade of the movement of cattle from eastern Oregon and southern Idaho through Winnemucca, and the Sacramento daily for its valuable summaries of news gathered principally from newspapers in the Pacific Northwest and for the letters that it published from its correspondents in Oregon.

Three newspapers that were much concerned with the interests of stockmen everywhere in the American West were published in Chicago within the period of this study. These journals, named the *Breeders' Gazette*, the *Weekly Drovers' Journal*, and the *National Live-Stock Journal*, contain considerable useful information on the range-cattle industry in the Oregon Country.

Finally, mention must be made of one periodical which was *sui generis* in its time, but which today would probably be called a news magazine. It was founded in Baltimore in 1811 by Hezekiah Niles, who called it *Niles' Weekly Register*. Later it became *Niles' National Register*. Throughout its career, this periodical was greatly interested in the developing American West, and for the 1830's and 1840's it contains information which no serious student of the history of the Oregon Country would think of neglecting.

BOOKS AND PAMPHLETS ON THE EARLY DAYS

Interesting glimpses of Spaniards and their cattle on the Northwest Coast in the early 1790's may be found in these works: George Vancouver, *A Voyage of Discovery to the North Pacific Ocean, and Round the World* ... (London, 1801), 6 vols.; Edmond S. Meany (ed.), *A New Vancouver Journal on the Discovery of Puget Sound, by a Member of the Chatham's Crew* (Seattle, Wash., 1915); John Boit's *A New Log of the Columbia*, ed. by Edmond S. Meany (Seattle, Wash., 1921); and Archibald Menzies' *Journal of Vancouver's Voyage, April to October, 1792*, ed. by C. F. Newcombe (Victoria, B.C., 1923).

On the keeping of livestock by the Astorians and the North Westers, the earliest fur traders in the valley of the Columbia, one should consult Gabriel Franchère, *Narrative of a Voyage to the Northwest Coast of America ... 1811-1814* (New York, 1854), trans. from the French edition (Montreal, 1820) by J. V. Huntington; Alexander Ross, *Adventures of the First Settlers on the Columbia River* (London, 1849) and *Fur Hunters of the*

Far West (London, 1855), both of which works were subsequently reprinted in the *Lakeside Classics;* Peter Corney, *Voyages in the Northern Pacific . . .* (Honolulu, 1896); Elliott Coues (ed.), *New Light on the Early History of the Greater Northwest; The Manuscript Journals of Alexander Henry . . . and of David Thompson . . . 1799-1814* (New York, 1897), 3 vols.; and Hiram Martin Chittenden, *The American Fur Trade of the Far West . . .* (New York, 1902), 3 vols.

The beginning of serious efforts in agricultural activity and in the breeding of livestock in the valley of the Columbia River dates from the first visit to this region of Governor George Simpson in 1824-25, some three years after the Hudson's Bay Company had absorbed the North West Company. Of this visit Simpson has given his own account in *Fur Trade and Empire: George Simpson's Journal . . . 1824-25 . . .* (Cambridge, Mass., 1931), to which the editor, Professor Frederick Merk, contributed a delightful and highly informing introduction. The development in subsequent years, under the supervision of Dr. John McLoughlin, of the breeding of cattle and other livestock at posts of the Hudson's Bay Company in the Pacific Northwest can be traced in the three volumes of *The Letters of John McLoughlin from Fort Vancouver to the Governor and Committee, 1825-1846,* ed. by E. E. Rich and illumined by the splendid introductions of W. Kaye Lamb (Hudson's Bay Record Society, *Publications,* IV, VI, VII, 1941-44). Another significant but smaller collection of McLoughlin's letters, edited by Burt Brown Barker, is entitled *Letters of Dr. John McLoughlin Written at Vancouver, 1829-1833* (Portland, Ore., 1948). Further interesting information on this subject and on the organization and activities of the Puget's Sound Agricultural Company, which was formed in 1839 as a subsidiary of the Hudson's Bay Company to carry on agricultural operations and the breeding of cattle and sheep in the Oregon Country, may be found in Edmund H. Oliver (ed.), *The Canadian Northwest . . .* (Ottawa, 1914-15), 2 vols., and more especially in the fourteen volumes of papers which the British and American Joint Commission for the Final Settlement of the Claims of the Hudson's Bay Company and Puget's Sound Agricultural Company assembled and published, in part in Montreal and in part in Washington, D.C., between 1865 and 1869. For the purposes of this study the most useful of these volumes are *Evidence on the Part of the Puget's Sound Agricultural Company* (Montreal, 1868), *Evidence for the United States in the Matter of the Claim of the Puget's Sound Agricultural Company* (Washington, D.C., 1867), *Evidence on the Part of the Hudson's Bay Company* (Montreal, 1868), and *Evidence for the United States in the Matter of the Claim of the Hudson's Bay Company* (Washington, D.C., 1867). In the secondary writings dealing with the Puget's Sound Agricultural Company, there is nothing superior to chaps. x and xiii of John S. Galbraith's *The Hudson's Bay Company as an Imperial Factor, 1821-1869* (Berkeley and Los Angeles, 1957).

Because the early missionaries in Oregon, both Protestant and Catholic,

helped to bring cattle into the Pacific Northwest and encouraged Indians
to acquire cattle and other livestock, such published reports of their activities as are available are of considerable value to students of this subject.
Of the contributions of the Methodist missionaries to agriculture and cattle
breeding in Oregon, one can learn much from such published writings as
the diary of Jason Lee (*Oregon Historical Quarterly*, XVII [June, September, December, 1911], 117-46, 240-66, 397-430), the diary of George Gary
(*ibid.*, XXIV [March, June, September, December, 1923], 68-105, 153-
85, 269-333, 386-433), and the Oregon Mission Record Book (*ibid.*, XXIII
[September, 1922], 230-66). An associate of Jason Lee in the overland
journey in 1834, Philip L. Edwards, who was later a member of a party
headed by Ewing Young to procure cattle in California and drive them to
Oregon, has told some of his experiences in this venture of driving cattle
in *California in 1837* . . . (Sacramento, 1890). Additional information of
importance on the contributions of Methodist missionaries to the early history of cattle in the Oregon Country may be found in Charles Wilkes,
Narrative of the United States Exploring Expedition, 1838-42 (Philadelphia, 1845), Vol. IV, and in Edmond S. Meany (ed.), *Diary of Wilkes in
the Northwest*, reprinted in 1926 from the *Washington Historical Quarterly*, 1925-26. In his book entitled *Jason Lee, Prophet of the New Oregon*
(New York, 1932), Cornelius J. Brosnan tells of Lee's contribution to the
introduction of cattle into Oregon and appends to his book a useful bibliography.

Among the publications revealing the contributions of missionaries of the
American Board of Commissioners for Foreign Missions to the beginnings
of cattle breeding in the Oregon Country, the writings of Clifford M. Drury
hold high place. Besides the biographies of Dr. Marcus Whitman and
Henry H. Spalding, already mentioned, Dr. Drury has written a biograph-
ical work entitled *Elkanah and Mary Walker* . . . (Caldwell, Ida., 1940),
and he has edited not only a volume entitled *The Diaries and Letters of
Henry H. Spalding and Asa Bowen Smith Relating to the Nez Percé Mission, 1838-1842* (Glendale, Calif., 1958), but also three volumes of letters
and diaries entitled *First White Women Over the Rockies* . . . *1836-38*
(Glendale, Calif., 1963-66). Also important for this subject is an earlier
compilation by the late T. C. Elliott entitled *The Coming of the White
Women, 1836, as Told in the Letters and Journals of Narcissa Whitman*
(Portland, Ore., 1937).

The efforts of Catholic missionaries to introduce cattle among Indians in
the Oregon Country are described, in part, by Father Pierre Jean de Smet
in his *Oregon Missions and Travels Over the Rocky Mountains in 1845-46*
(New York, 1847), a work which was reprinted in 1906 in *Early Western
Travels*, Vol. XXIX, and in his *Life, Letters and Travels* . . . *1801-1873*,
ed. by H. M. Chittenden and A. T. Richardson (New York, 1905), 4 vols.

Other sources which have a bearing on the beginnings of the cattle industry in the Oregon Country are the *Correspondence and Journals of*

Captain Nathaniel J. Wyeth, 1831-6 . . . ed. by F. G. Young (*Sources of the History of Oregon*, I) (Eugene, Ore., 1899), *The Journals and Letters of Major John Owen, Pioneer of the Northwest, 1850-1871* . . . ed. by Seymour Dunbar and Paul C. Phillips (New York, 1927), 2 vols., and Granville Stuart's *Forty Years on the Frontier as Seen in the Journals and Reminiscences of Granville Stuart, Gold-Miner, Trader, Merchant, Rancher and Politician*, ed. by Paul C. Phillips (Cleveland, 1925), 2 vols.

LITERATURE OF TRAVEL

The writings of numerous persons who traveled in Oregon in the 1830's and 1840's, and who published accounts of their observations, laid the foundation of what may be called a literature of travel in the Oregon Country. For the purposes of this study, the best of such books are as follows:

Samuel Parker, *Journal of an Exploring Tour Beyond the Rocky Mountains* . . . *in the Years 1835, '36, and '37* (Ithaca, N.Y., 1838); John K. Townsend, *Sporting Excursions in the Rocky Mountains, Including a Journey to the Columbia River* . . . (London, 1840), 2 vols.; Thomas J. Farnham, *Travels in the Great Western Prairies, the Anahuac and Rocky Mountains, and in the Oregon Territory*, a work which appeared in several editions in the early 1840's, and which, more than a half-century later, was reprinted in 1906 in *Early Western Travels*, Vol. XXVIII; Joel Palmer, *Journal of Travels over the Rocky Mountains to the Mouth of the Columbia River* . . . *During the Years 1845 and 1846* . . . , a work published in Cincinnati in 1847 and reprinted in 1906 in *Early Western Travels*, Vol. XXX; Sir George Simpson, *Narrative of a Journey Round the World, During the Years 1841 and 1842* (London, 1847), 2 vols.; John C. Fremont, *Narrative of the Exploring Expedition to the Rocky Mountains in the Year 1842, and to Oregon and North California in the Years 1843-44* (Syracuse, N.Y., 1847); Paul Kane, *Wanderings of an Artist Among the Indians of North America and Canada to Vancouver's Island and Oregon* . . . , a work which was published in London in 1859 and reprinted in Toronto, 1925, in *Masterpieces of Canadian Authors;* and Joseph Williams, *Narrative of a Tour from the State of Indiana to the Oregon Territory in the Years 1841-42* (New York, 1921).

Two other travelers of a later period, both Englishmen, gave to their readers somewhat more than passing notices of cattle breeding in Oregon during the late 1870's. One of these men, Henry N. Moseley, brought out in London in 1878 a book entitled *Oregon: Its Resources, Climate, People and Productions;* and, at about the same time, Wallis Nash published two books which touch this subject—namely, *Oregon: There and Back in 1877* (London, 1878) and *Two Years in Oregon* (New York, 1882).

GOVERNMENT DOCUMENTS

Publications by one or another branch, bureau, or agency of the federal government impinge upon the subject of this study, at one point or another, from the 1830's through the 1880's. Here there is space for listing only a few specific documents of such character and for calling attention to the most important series of government documents relating to this study. From William Slacum, "Slacum's Report on Oregon, 1836-7," *Oregon Historical Quarterly*, XIII, 175-224, reprinted from the 25th Cong., 2nd sess., S. Ex. Doc. 2, Vol. I, one passes to Lieutenant Neil M. Howison's "Report on Oregon, 1846," *Oregon Historical Quarterly*, XIV (March, 1913), 1-60, reprinted from H. Misc. Doc. 29 of the 30th Cong., 1st sess. During the last half of the 1850's, the U.S. Department of War published in twelve volumes the *Reports of Explorations and Surveys to Ascertain the Most Practicable and Economical Route for a Railroad from the Mississippi River to the Pacific Ocean* (Washington, 1855-60), volumes I and XII of which contain information important for this study. Other significant information on cattle in the Pacific Northwest, during the early 1860's, may be found in *The War of the Rebellion: Compilation of Official Records of the Union and Confederate Armies, Series I* (Washington, D.C., 1897), L, Pt. 1.

From 1850 through 1890 the statistical tables in the decennial reports of the U.S. Census Bureau are significant for this study. The tenth federal census (1880), however, is one of unusual importance to students of cattle breeding in the American West, for it contains Clarence W. Gordon's valuable but somewhat neglected "Report on Cattle, Sheep, and Swine, Supplementary to Enumeration of Live Stock on Farms in 1880," in its third volume entitled *Report on the Productions of Agriculture . . .* (Washington, D.C., 1883), 951-1116. For the range-cattle industry in the Oregon Country, this report is much more valuable than a later similar and better-known work by Joseph Nimmo, Jr., entitled *Report in Regard to the Range and Ranch Cattle Business of the United States, May 16, 1885* (Washington, D.C., 1885).

Federal documents consisting of annual reports of departments, bureaus, and agencies of the federal government that have value for this study are as follows: Bureau of Animal Industry, *Reports, 1884-1890;* Commissioner of Agriculture, *Reports, 1862-1888;* Commissioner of Patents, *Reports, 1850-1854;* Secretary of the Interior, *Reports, 1860-1890;* Commissioner of Indian Affairs, *Reports, 1845-1890;* Secretary of the Treasury, *Reports . . . on the Commerce and Navigation of the United States, 1856-1890;* Secretary of War, *Reports, 1855-1860, 1867;* Commissioner of the General Land Office, *Reports, 1857-1890;* and the annual reports to the Secretary of the Interior of the governors of Idaho Territory (1878-90), Washington Territory (1878-89), and Wyoming Territory (1878-85).

Other government documents having a bearing on such subjects as Indian wars, mineral resources, ranges, rivers, the Hudson's Bay Company, the Puget's Sound Agricultural Company, and the illegal use of the public domain by cattlemen throw more or less light on the subject of the range-cattle industry in the Oregon Country. On one important aspect of the

Indian war of the 1850's and on the construction in the Pacific Northwest of a celebrated military road, one may consult John Mullan's *Preliminary Topographic Memoir of Colonel George Wright's Campaign Against the Hostile Northern Indians in Oregon and Washington Territories*, 35th Cong., 2nd sess., S. Ex. Doc. 32, and his *Report on the Construction of a Military Road from Fort Walla Walla to Fort Benton* (Washington, D.C., 1863). On mines and mining two useful books are J. Ross Browne's *Report on the Mineral Resources of the States and Territories West of the Rocky Mountains* (Washington, D.C., 1868) and Rossiter W. Raymond's *Statistics of Mines and Mining in the States and Territories West of the Rocky Mountains* (Washington, D.C., 1873). For some understanding of the problems of cattlemen on the ranges, including that of the growth of poisonous plants, one may turn to David Griffiths' *Range Conditions and Problems in Eastern Washington, Eastern Oregon, Northeastern California, and Northwestern Nevada* (Washington, D.C., 1903), and to Farmers' Bulletin No. 2106, *16 Plants Poisonous to Livestock in the Western States*, a pamphlet which the U.S. Department of Agriculture published in 1958. Governor Isaac I. Stevens' report to the Department of State on June 21, 1854, *Relative to the Property of the Hudson's Bay and Puget's Sound Company in Washington Territory*, was published by the 33rd Cong., 2nd sess., as S. Ex. Doc. 37; and Lieutenant Thomas W. Symons' *Report of an Examination of the Upper Columbia River and the Territory in Its Vicinity, in September and October, 1881* . . . , was published by the 47th Cong., 1st sess., as S. Ex. Doc. 186.

Problems arising from the misuse by cattlemen of the public lands in the American West are dealt with in the *Preliminary Report of the Public Land Commission Created by the Act of March 3, 1879*, 46th Cong., 2nd sess., H. Ex. Doc. 46, in the *Unauthorized Fencing of the Public Lands* (1884), 48th Cong., 1st sess., S. Ex. Doc. 127, and in the *Unlawful Occupancy of the Public Lands* (1884), 48th Cong., 1st sess., H. Rep. 1325.

CATTLEMEN AND CATTLE IN TRANSCASCADIA

The story of the opening of the vast country east of the Cascades, and of the exploitation of grasslands and sagelands by stockmen from the late 1850's through the late 1880's can be traced in outline by piecing together information about this subject that appears in numerous writings.

For the era of placer mining one may consult Arthur L. Throckmorton, *Oregon Argonauts: Merchant Adventurers on the Western Frontier* (Portland, Ore., 1961); William J. Trimble, *The Mining Advance into the Inland Empire* . . . (Madison, Wis., 1914); R. C. Lundin-Brown, *British Columbia: An Essay* (New Westminster, B.C., 1863); F. W. Howay, *British Columbia: The Making of a Province* (Toronto, 1928); Walter N. Sage, *Sir James Douglas and British Columbia* (Toronto, 1930); and William E. Lass, *A History of Steamboating on the Upper Missouri River* (Lincoln, Neb., 1962).

For a description of the intermontane province called in this study

Transcascadia, a province which became a celebrated cattle country, one may turn either to an article entitled "Physiographic Divisions of the Columbia Intermontane Province," *Annals of the Association of American Geographers,* XXXV (1935), 53-75, by Otis W. Freeman, J. D. Forrester, and R. L. Lupher, or to a book entitled *The Pacific Northwest: An Overall Appreciation* (2nd ed.; New York, 1954), ed. by Otis W. Freeman and Howard H. Martin. From one or the other of these descriptions, one may proceed to an examination of the occupation of this country, district by district, by stockmen and settlers.

On the movement into the northern part of Transcascadia, one might consult B. F. Manring, *The Conquest of the Coeur d'Alenes, Spokanes, and Palouses* (Spokane, Wash., 1912); Frank T. Gilbert, *Historic Sketches of Walla Walla, Whitman, Columbia and Garfield Counties, Washington Territory, and Umatilla County, Oregon* (Portland, Ore., 1882); *An Illustrated History of the Big Bend Country . . .* (Spokane, Wash., 1904); A. J. Splawn, *Ka-mi-akin, the Last Hero of the Yakimas* (2nd ed.; Portland, Ore., 1944); and Mrs. W. E. Baskett, "The History of the Early Whitman County Pioneers," *Colfax Commoner,* July 16, 1920.

For the occupation of various areas in the southern part of Transcascadia, one may examine George Francis Brimlow, *Harney County, Oregon, and Its Range Land* (Portland, Ore., 1951); Jacob R. Gregg, *Pioneer Days in Malheur County . . .* (Los Angeles, 1950); George Francis Brimlow, *The Bannock Indian War of 1878* (Caldwell, Ida., 1938); *An Illustrated History of Central Oregon . . .* (Spokane, Wash., 1905); Robert E. Strahorn, *The Resources and Attractions of Idaho Territory . . .* (Boise City, Ida., 1881); and C. Marc Miller, *An Appraisal of the Snake-Piute Tract, State of Oregon, January, 1879: Case Number 17 Before the Indian Claims Commission* (prepared for the Lands Division, U.S. Department of Justice; Seattle, Wash., July, 1958). A recent but unpublished study of cattle breeding in southeastern Oregon during the early years of the occupation of this region has been made by Margaret Justine Lo Piccolo in a dissertation entitled "Some Aspects of the Range Cattle Industry of Harney County, Oregon, 1870-1890" (M.A. thesis, University of Oregon, 1962). Two works of general character that are useful for studying the cattle industry in the Oregon Country from the late 1860's through the 1880's and beyond are Harvey W. Scott's *History of the Oregon Country,* compiled in six volumes from his writings in the *Oregonian* by Leslie M. Scott (Cambridge, Mass., 1924), and Lewis A. McArthur's *Oregon Geographic Names* (3rd ed.; Portland, Ore., 1965).

Because not much has been written by or about them, the "cattle kings" of the Oregon Country are not very well known to a later generation. In *Ka-mi-akin, the Last Hero of the Yakimas* (2nd ed.; Portland, Ore., 1944), A. J. Splawn has written of cattle days as he knew them in the Inland Empire, and in *"Uncle Dan" Drumheller Tells Thrills of Western Trails in 1854* (Spokane, Wash., 1925), a misnamed book, there is another account by a stockman of some of his experiences on the ranges of the Pacific Northwest. In *Early Klickitat Valley Days* (Goldendale, Wash., 1938), Robert Ballou gave some account of Benjamin Snipes, of the firm of Snipes and Allen, and nineteen years later Roscoe Sheller brought out a dramatized biography entitled *Ben Snipes: Northwest Cattle King* (Portland, Ore., 1957). Perhaps the greatest of all the cattle kings who had interests in the Pacific Northwest was Henry Miller, of the California firm of Miller and Lux. A popular life of this man, written by Edward F. Treadwell, was published in New York in 1931 under the title of *The Cattle King, A Dramatized Biography.* In the *Oregonian* for April 7, 1946, Kenneth W. Fitzgerald told the story of John Edwards, a pioneer cattle-and-sheep king of Crook County, Oregon. More than a decade earlier Anne Shannon Monroe published in the *Sunday Oregonian* of April 14 and 21, 1935, a highly dramatized article entitled "Pete French: Oregon's Cattle King Who 'Had to Be Killed.' " But a fuller and better account of Peter French appeared recently in Giles French's *Cattle Country of Peter French* (Portland, Ore., 1964). Charles S. Walgamott's *Reminiscences of Early Days: A Series of Historical Sketches and Happenings in the Early Days of Snake River Valley* were published in two volumes in Twin Falls, Idaho, in 1926-27, and *The Cattle Drives of David Shirk from Texas to the Idaho Mines, 1871 and 1873,* ed. by Martin F. Schmitt, appeared in Portland, Oregon, in 1956.

Useful information on the movement of cattle from the Pacific Northwest to markets east of the Rockies, in the later 1870's and early 1880's, may be found in William Adolph Baillie-Grohman, *Camps in the Rockies . . . with an Account of the Cattle Ranches of the West* (London, 1882); Charles J. Steedman, *Bucking the Sage Brush, or the Oregon Trail in the Seventies* (New York, 1904); John Clay, *My Life on the Range* (Chicago, 1924); John K. Rollinson, *Wyoming Cattle Trails: History of the Migration of Oregon-Raised Herds to Mid-Western Markets* (Caldwell, Ida., 1948); Maurice Frink *et al., When Grass Was King* (Boulder, Colo., 1956); Agnes Wright Spring, *Seventy Years: A Panoramic History of the Wyoming Stock Growers' Association* (1943); and Charles Lindsay, *The Big Horn Basin* (Lincoln, Neb., 1932). A very valuable account of one of the earliest drives of cattle eastward from Oregon is William Emsley Jackson's "Diary of a Cattle Drive from La Grande, Oregon, to Cheyenne, Wyoming, in 1876," *Agricultural History,* XXIII (October, 1949), 260-73.

Some of the effects upon the activities of stockmen in the Pacific Northwest of the coming of railroads into this region is disclosed in Henry Villard, *The Early History of Transportation in Oregon* (Eugene, Ore., 1944); Nelson Trottman, *History of the Union Pacific: A Financial and Economic Survey* (New York, 1923); James B. Hedges, *Henry Villard and the Railways of the Northwest* (New Haven, Conn., 1930); E. V. Smalley, *History of the Northern Pacific Railroad* (New York, 1883); N. W. Durham, *History of the City of Spokane, and Spokane Country, Washington, from Its Earliest Settlement to the Present Time* [frequently cited as

Spokane and the Inland Empire] (Spokane, Wash., 1912), 3 vols.; and John Fahey, *Inland Empire: D. C. Corbin and Spokane* (Seattle, Wash., 1965).

Policies of the federal government of interest to graziers on the public domain may be studied in Benjamin H. Hibbard, *History of the Public Land Policies* (New York, 1924); Roy M. Robbins, *Our Landed Heritage: The Public Domain, 1776-1936* (Princeton, N.J., 1942); Will C. Barnes, *Winter Grazing Grounds and Forest Ranges* (Chicago, 1913); Samuel T. Dana, *Forest and Range Policy: Its Development in the United States* (New York, 1956); and E. Louise Peffer, *The Closing of the Public Domain: Disposal and Reservation Policies, 1900-1950* (Stanford, Calif., 1951). Also important for references touching the public lands and other matters of concern in this study is the bibliography appended to Ernest Staples Osgood's *The Day of the Cattleman* (Minneapolis, 1929), pp. 259-68.

Index

Abbott, J. C.: on severe winter (1879-80) in Grant County, Ore., 276

Agriculture: beginnings on Northwest Coast, 3, 4; by Spaniards, 3, 4; by American ship captains, 5; in Palouse country, 322

American Board of Commissioners for Foreign Missions: missionaries of drive cattle to Oregon, 12, 13, 17, 18; cattle at stations of Oregon missions of—Waiilaptu, 17; Lapwai, 17; Kamiah, 18; Tshimakain, 18

American cattle: overland to Oregon, 30-32 *passim*; supplant Spanish cattle, 30, 31; early distribution of in Oregon, 32-33

Applegate, E. L.: reports settlements in north-central Oregon, 86; surveyor of Oregon, 86

Applegate, I. D., 93, 94

Applegate, Jesse: testifies on cattle movement from western Oregon to Puget Sound, 55, 56; on severe winter (1847-48) in Willamette Valley, 264

Associations: voluntary, 186

Astorians: cultivate crops, 6; keep livestock, 6

Baillie-Grohman, William A.: asserts superiority of Oregon cattle, 166

Bannock Indian War: effect on Malheur Indian Reservation, 297

Barbed-wire fences, 336. *See also* Fences

Barlow Road, 116

Beef-canning enterprise: on lower Columbia River, 112; failure of, 113, 114

Big Bend country (southern): defined, 101, 105; cattlemen enter, 105

Blackleg: ravages of, 253, 254; vaccine for, 254

Bodega y Quadra, Don Juan Francisco de, 3

Boit, John: reports on Spanish cattle, 4

Boyle, W. H., 291

Brand books: published in Whitman County, Wash., 228

Brandeis, Louis D., 348

Brands and marks: purpose of, 213; laws concerning, 213n, 223-26 *passim*; publicizing of, 227, 228; running brand forbidden in Idaho, 234; road brand required on cattle passing through Idaho, 234

Browne, J. Ross: on Oregon winters, 256

Bull, Walter A., 126

Burnett, Peter H.: advises cattle be driven to Oregon, 30

California: early Oregon trade to, 41; Oregon cattle driven to, 42, 43; decline in Oregon trade to, 43; cattle from to northern mines, 68

Carr, Jesse D.: buys cattle in Klickitat County, Wash., 147; heavy winter loss of cattle (1879-80), 278; (1889-90), 285

Cattle: on Northwest Coast, 3; first breeding in Pacific Northwest, 6; for "gold spike" party, 131n; thoroughbred bulls, 195; losses from hazards of ranges, 241

Cattle drives: from California to Oregon, 21, 22; to California, 41-43 *passim*; to northern mines, 45, 46; to Montana mines, 58, 60, 69; westward through passes in Cascade Mountains, 61-65 *passim*, 69, 74; from southeastern Oregon to Transcascadia, 93, 94; to The Dalles, 129, 129n, 130; to Nevada, 134, 135; from Oregon Country to California, 134-47 *passim*; from Umpqua to California, 135; to Winnemucca, Nev., 137-46 *passim*; Idaho cattle to Winnemucca, 141n, 146; on earlier American frontiers, 148; eastward from Ohio Valley, 149; from Walla Walla to Wyoming, 151; to Montana (1879-83) via Mullan Road and via southern Idaho, 178

Cattle drives eastward (1875-83): beginning, 152, 153; peak of, 169; end of, 177, 178; significance of, 180-83
—in 1876: general driving begins, 153, 156, 157
—in 1877, 157-60; account of drive from eastern Washington to Black Eagle Rock, Ida., 100
—in 1878, 162-65
—in 1879: numerous buyers, 167-69
—in 1880: estimates of number driven, 170, 171; enormous purchases by Lang and Ryan, 171, 172; E. O. Grimes tells of smaller drive, 172, 173
—in 1881: relatively small drive, 173, 174
—in 1882: relatively large, but one of cattle, horses, and sheep, 175, 176; last important drives from Oregon Country, 177
—in 1883: eastward driving of cattle relatively slight, 177, 178

Cattle driving: persisted in Oregon Country after need for it was gone, 179

Cattle drovers: Lang and Ryan, 152, 154; others, 157, 159, 164, 167, 172, 177

"Cattle kings": in Columbia Basin, 187, 188; in Winnemucca province, 187, 189; activities of 196

Cattle markets: California, 40-43 *passim*, 134-46 *passim*; mines of British Columbia, 63-67 *passim*; mines of Idaho and Montana, 70-73 *passim*; Puget Sound, 118-29 *passim*; western Oregon, 123, 129, 130; beyond the Rockies, 153-78

Cattlemen: small-scale, 187; gaining access to Indian grasslands, 307, 308

Cattlemen vs. farmers, 320-37 *passim*

Cattlemen vs. sheepmen, 337-42, 348-49; retreat of some cattlemen from, 340, 341n; threats of cattlemen, 342; some cattlemen become sheepmen, 342; hastening crisis on ranges of Transcascadia, 349; wars on Oregon ranges, 349; leasing summer ranges in forest reserves, 349; Taylor Grazing Act, 349, 350

Cattle neglected in winter: in Oregon Country, 255, 256, 268; tradition of all-year grazing, 256; editors warn of danger, 257, 258n, 259; on earlier frontiers, 259

Cattle trade: on Puget Sound, 45-58 *passim*; from western Oregon to Puget Sound, 46, 54-56 *passim*; to northern mines via The Dalles and Okanogan Valley, 46-67 *passim*; temporarily interrupted, 51-53; change in national trade, 165, 166; choice (after 1883) of shipments by rail from Transcascadia, 179

Chase, Salmon P., 52

Chinook wind: defined, 255; "stockmen's god," 257

Clarke, S. A.: describes fences in southeastern Washington, 328n

Columbia River: route for eastward movement of cattle, 46, 61, 72, 73; route for movement of cattle westward, 128-31 *passim*

Colville Indian Reservation: problem of white men's cattle on, 308

Colville Valley: cattlemen in, 105

Corney, Peter: observes cattle at Fort George, 6

for mines, 59, 60n, 69; gateway to Palouse and Spokane countries, 103, 104, 104n

Walla Walla Valley: attracts stockmen and settlers, 81; cattle in, 82

Waller, Alvin F. (sometimes Alvan F.): observes Indians in trade for cattle, 34

Warm Springs Indian Reservation: boundaries "unsettled," 296, 311n

Warre, Henry J.: British agent in Oregon, 15; report on livestock, 28

Whatcom trails, 45, 46

White Bluffs: landing on Columbia River, 60, 72

White sage: winter forage for cattle, 80, 80n

Whitman, Marcus: on cattle of Hudson's Bay Company, 10, 11; kills no cattle before 1841, 17n; reports acquisition of cattle by Indians, 33, 34

Whitman, Mrs. Marcus: on cattle at Vancouver, 11; observes cattle and other livestock at Fort Walla Walla, 12; notes trade of Indians for cattle, 35

Whitman massacre, 18

Wilbur, James H.: reports winter losses of livestock, 267; agent for Yakima Indians, 292

Wilkes, Charles, 20

Wilkes Exploring Expedition, 15, 22

Willamette Cattle Company: formed, 20; imports cattle from California, 21

Willamette Valley: cattle from to northern mines, 73, 74; eastward movement from, 77, 78; nursery for range cattle of Transcascadia, 78

Winemucca, Nev.: cattle-shipping point, 137; capital of pastoral province, 138; growing importance of, 138, 141, 142; shipments from to California, 142-46 passim; shipments eastward from, 142-46 passim; decline of, 146

Winnemucca province: defined, 77

Winter losses of cattle: in Arkansas, 259; on the Great Plains, 260; extent of in Oregon Country, 261; causes of, 262

—in 1846-47: west of Cascades, 262, 263; east of Cascades, 263, 263n, 264

—in 1852-53: in western Oregon, 264, 264n, 265; east of Cascades, 265, north of Columbia, 265

—in 1858-59: in western Oregon, 266; in western Washington, 266

—in 1861-62: in Oregon, 267; extent of, 268; in Walla Walla Valley, 269

—in 1871-72: east of Cascades, 270, 271

—in 1873-74: in Transcascadia, 272

—in 1874-75: in Transcascadia, 272-74; editors aroused, 274; cattle-skinners profit, 274; extent of losses, 274

—in 1879-80: in Winnemucca province, 276, 277; on Klamath Indian Reservation, 277; on Warm Springs Indian Reservation, 277; in Lake County, Oregon, 277, 278

—in 1880-81: throughout Transcascadia, 278-79; in Montana and along Platte River, 279-80; compared with 1861-62, 280; extent of in Columbia Basin, 281; stockmen to persevere, 281

—in 1886-87: extensive throughout American West, 282; relatively small in Oregon Country, 283

—in 1889-90: in Transcascadia, 283-85 passim; consequences, 285, 286

Winters in Oregon Country: 1872-73, 271; late 1870's, 275; 1878-79, 275; 1888-89, 283; as a whole, 287. See also Severe winters in Oregon Country

Work, John: on farming at Fort Colvile, 15; McLoughlin writes to, 24

Wright, George: punitive expedition against northern Indians, 37

Wyeth, Nathaniel J.: founds Fort Hall, 13; founds Fort William, 20; imports cattle from Sandwich Islands, 20

Yakima country: cattlemen enter, 83-86 passim

Yakima Indian Reservation: trespassing cattle on, 305; boundaries disputed, 312; survey of, 312

Young, Ewing, 21

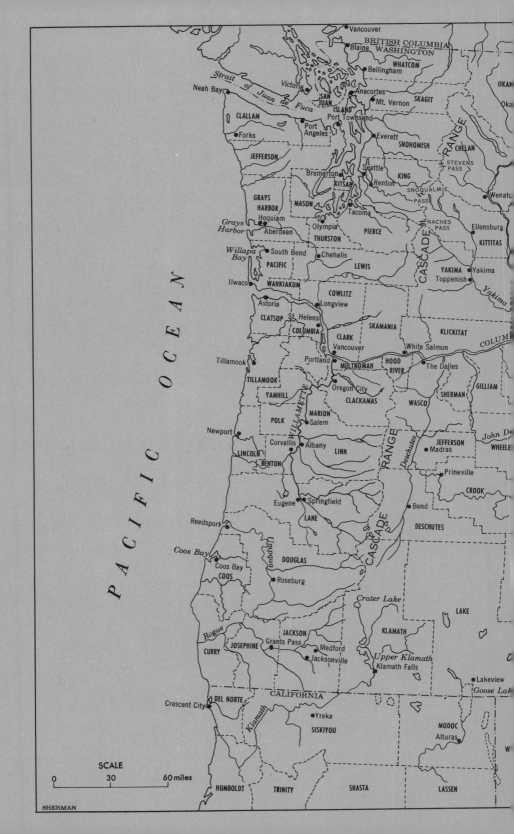

SHERMAN

SCALE

0   30   60 miles